THE

SOLDIER'S STORY

OF HIS CAPTIVITY AT

ANDERSONVILLE, BELLE ISLE,

AND OTHER REBEL PRISONS.

H. W. Smith.

Warren Lee Goss

Presented to

By

THE

SOLDIER'S STORY

OF HIS CAPTIVITY AT

ANDERSONVILLE, BELLE ISLE,

AND OTHER REBEL PRISONS.

BY

WARREN LEE GOSS,

OF THE SECOND MASSACHUSETTS REGIMENT OF HEAVY ARTILLERY.

WITH AN APPENDIX,

CONTAINING

THE NAMES OF THE UNION SOLDIERS WHO DIED AT ANDERSONVILLE,

WITH THE NUMBERS OF THEIR GRAVES, THEIR RANK, THE COMPANIES
AND REGIMENTS TO WHICH THEY BELONGED, THE DATES
OF THEIR DECEASE, AND THE DISEASES
OF WHICH THEY DIED.

AND ALSO,

MANY CERTIFICATES TO THE TRUTHFULNESS OF THE BOOK.

EMBELLISHED WITH

A Beautiful Presentation Page and Four Full Page Illustrations,

BY THOMAS NAST, THE CELEBRATED AMERICAN ARTIST;

A STEEL PORTRAIT OF THE AUTHOR; SEVERAL MAPS DRAWN FROM
ACTUAL MEASUREMENTS,

AND MANY ACCURATE ILLUSTRATIONS OF PRISON LIFE,
TAKEN FROM REBEL PHOTOGRAPHS NOW
IN THE POSSESSION OF THE
PUBLISHERS

SOLD ONLY BY SUBSCRIPTION.

BOSTON:

LEE & SHEPARD, PUBLISHERS.

STEREOTYPED AT THE
BOSTON STEREOTYPE FOUNDRY,
No. 4 Spring Lane.

For classroom or special event printing please
contact DSI via email Info@Digitalscanning.com.

THE SOLDIER'S STORY

By Warren Lee Goss
Originally Published in 1866 by Lee & Shephard

©2001 DSI digital reproduction
First DSI Printing: January 2001

Published by **DIGITAL SCANNING, INC.**
Scituate, MA 02066
www.digitalscanning.com

Trade Paperback ISBN: 1-58218-227-2
Hardcover ISBN: 1-58218-228-0
eBook ISBN: 1-58218-226-4

Digital Scanning and Publishing is a leader in the electronic republication of historical books and documents. We publish our titles as eBooks, as well as traditional hardcover and trade paper editions. DSI is committed to bringing many traditional and little known books back to life, retaining the look and feel of the original work.

DIGITAL SCANNING
& PUBLISHING

PREFACE.

If the cause for which so many sacrifices were made — which so many died in prison to perpetuate — was worth suffering for, are not the scenes through which they passed worthy of commemoration and remembrance in the hearts of their fellow-countrymen? Justice to the living who suffered, impartial history, and the martyred dead, demand a full, unexaggerated record by a survivor of these horrors. For this purpose this book, through agonizing memories, at last has been finished. With the author it has been rather a work of solemn duty than of pleasure. He simply states facts, and depicts those scenes of prison life best fitted to convey to the minds of general readers some of its

characteristic phases, just as prisoners saw it,—
giving to history material for its verdict, and
the reader a full understanding of the subject.

In almost every household throughout the
land there are saddened memories of these
dreadful prisons; but as terrible as has been the
past, thousands of the same patriotic men are
ready to spring to arms again for the preservation of national life and honor. On his crutch,
the author makes his bow to the public, hoping
that in THE SOLDIER'S STORY they may find
instruction and profit.

CONTENTS.

———◦◦❀◦◦———

CHAPTER I.

CHAPTER II.

CHAPTER III.

CHAPTER IV.

CHAPTER V.

CHAPTER VI.

CHAPTER VII.

CHAPTER VIII.

CHAPTER IX.

CHAPTER X.

CHAPTER XI.

CHAPTER XII.

CHAPTER XIII.

CHAPTER XIV.

APPENDIX.

LIST OF ILLUSTRATIONS

INTRODUCTION.

THE world's ear is full of cries from the land of rebel barbarism, where starvation walked at the side of every captive, and suffering, despair, and death sat at every prison door. In these prisons thousands of patriotic hearts ceased to beat during the war that has recently closed. Torn with hunger and hapless despair, they sadly and mournfully died during the long and bitter imprisonments to which rebel cruelty subjected them. Thousands of hearts have bled at the mere recital of the horrors of Libby, Andersonville, Florence, Danville, and Salisbury. And far lands, looking across the ocean, have shuddered at the spectacle of rebel barbarity, developed before their eyes, wondering how in a Christian country such things could be. It is, perhaps, an old story now; but, as no detailed account of any one of great experience has ever been presented to the public by the sufferer himself, the writer of this narrative proposes to tell what he has seen, and felt, and known, of the slaveholders' mercy while yet the touch of their fierce cruelty is upon him.

During the progress of the war, it has been my misfortune to have been twice a prisoner, once in 1862, and again in 1864, — the first period of captivity four months, the second nine months, — making in all over year of the most unparalleled misery which man ever survived. My experience in these prisons was of a kind which few endure and live. Mr. Richardson, the correspondent, who has done so much to enlighten the public mind on this subject, by his own acknowledgment, a great part of his time enjoyed the comparative luxury of a hospital. Sergeant Kellogg, who has written a very true account of his imprisonment at Andersonville, was a sergeant of a hundred men, and drew extra rations; and a good portion of his time was also spent in hospitals of the prisons. Very hard fare was his, it is true, but a luxury to what the great mass of prisoners enjoyed. My imprisonment was without mitigation of this kind, except the last three weeks of my last confinement.

I propose to relate the tale of horrors experienced in these prisons without exaggeration. All language which my poor pen can command is powerless to convey even a faint impression of what men suffered there. Very few went through those imprisonments without becoming idiotic — mere wrecks of humanity, unfit to convey their impressions by reason of weakness of mind, and unwilling, even if they had the power, because of the soul-harrowing, frightful memories which were thus recalled. Therefore it is that the most terrible sufferings have never been delineated, or even attempted. Though it may be presumption in me to attempt it, yet I will try to make the world acquainted with some of the details of prison life and experience. I know how hard it is to realize that men can live through some of the cruelties which I shall relate; but "truth is stranger than fiction," and no truth is stranger than "man's inhumanity to man," as developed in rebel prisons.

THE SOLDIER'S STORY.

———oo؛؋؛oo———

CHAPTER I.

Enlistment in the Engineer Corps. — A Prophecy of Dining in Rich-
mond fulfilled different from Expectations. — Battle at Savage's
Station. — Terrible Conflict. — The Army of the Potomac saved.
— An Incident. — Heroism in a Wounded Soldier. — A Retreat. —
Wounded taken Prisoners. — First Treatment as a Prisoner. —
Rebel Prediction of the Capture of Washington. — Confidence in
McClellan. — Stonewall Jackson. — False Promises. — Taken to
Richmond. — A Sad Scene. — A Rebel Officer's Wit. — A Retort.
— Search and Confiscation of Personal Effects. — Description of
Prison. — Life in Libby Prison. — Horrors of such Life. — Va-
rious Incidents. — Change of Quarters. — Hope for the Better
disappointed.

A T an early date in the war, I was a member of the
United States engineer corps of the regular
army, at that time consisting of one company, and
two others partially formed, all under Captain Duane,
for some time chief engineer of the army of the
Potomac. I performed the usual duties of an engineer
at Yorktown, at Williamsburg, and on the Chicka-
hominy, until, being in the first stages of a fever, I
was sent to Savage's Station, where I was taken prisoner. About two weeks previous to my being captured,

2   (17)

I had written to my friends, that, in course of a week
or more, I expected to dine in Richmond. Though it
proved to be a *prophecy,* circumstances, in interpreting
the language, seemed to have taken me more at my
word than at my wish; for it would have been more
congenial with the wishes of the prophet to have
entered the "city of his hopes" in a very different
style than that which fate ordained.

On the 27th of June I arrived at Savage's Station,
the sound of battle on every side telling how desperate
was the nature of the contest. On the 28th and 29th,
the Williamsburg road, which passed the camp near
Savage's Station, was crowded with baggage wagons,
ammunition, pontoon trains, and all the indescribable
material of a vast army. The hospital camp at Savage's
Station consisted of three hundred hospital tents and
several negro shanties full of sick and wounded soldiers
from the battle-fields.

"There is an open plain of several hundred acres
opposite Savage's Station. It was along this plain
the Williamsburg road passes, by which our troops
were mainly to effect their retreat," or change of base.
"Beyond the level plain was a dense pine forest." It
was here, on the edge of the road, that, on the afternoon of the 29th, General Sumner was stationed with
twenty thousand men, who were to hold in check the
enemy until our troops had escaped beyond the White
Oak Swamp. "Here these men awaited, in one dark
mass, for hours, the approach of the trebly outnumber-

ing foe, while regiments, divisions, and trains filed by them. The fate of the army was in their hands, and they proved worthy of the trust."

About five o'clock in the afternoon, dense clouds of dust rising in the wood beyond heralded the approach of the enemy. "As they drew near, from their whole mass of artillery in front they opened a terrific fire, to which our guns responded," until through the dense smoke was seen only the flash of artillery, like lightning from the tempest cloud. Sometimes the roar of the conflict would almost cease, but only to be renewed with more terrible vigor. "For an hour not a musket was discharged, but the reverberating thunder of the cannon shook the hills; then the whole majestic mass of rebels," with their peculiar yell, in marked contrast with the three distinct cheers of our men, "sprang forward upon the plain, presenting a crested billow of glittering bayonets, which, it would seem, no mortal power could withstand. Every musket in the Union lines was brought into deliberate aim. For a moment, there was a pause, until it was certain that every bullet would fulfil its mission, and then a flash, followed by a storm of lead, which covered the ground with dead and dying." The three distinct cheers of our men responded to the hyena-like yell of the rebels. Beaten back by this storm of lead, the rebel host wavered, broke, and retreated to the railroad. Troops coming up behind pressed them forward again to our lines. "Again there leaped from ten thousand guns the fiery blast, and yell

answered yell; for a moment a pause, to be proceeded by the instantaneous discharge of ten thousand
guns." And then, as if stung to frenzy, the rage of
the conflict was redoubled — the clash of arms interrupted by the occasional arrival of reënforcements in
the field on the rebel side, who, as they came up,
cheered their companions with loud shouts.

The battle raged incessantly until half past eight or
nine o'clock, when cheer after cheer went up from our
men, to which was heard no answering rebel yell, telling
that the army of the Potomac was saved. The rebels
brought into the field fifty thousand men, and were
beaten back by the gallant, devoted men under Sumner.

During the action, and afterwards, I was rendering
to the wounded such assistance as it was in my power
to contribute. At one time, while aiding a young surgeon (whose name I did not learn) who was ampu-
tating a limb, as I turned aside to obtain water for
his use, the surgeon and patient were both killed and
terribly mutilated by the explosion of a shell.

On the battle-field one sometimes hears sentiments
from the rough soldier which would do credit to the
most refined and chivalrous. At Savage's Station a
young soldier belonging, I think, to the fifteenth
Massachusetts regiment, was brought in wounded, had
his wound dressed, and lay with closed eyes, apparently
thinking. Presently he began to talk with me and
others. "I have been thinking," said he, "how proud
I shall be some day of these scars" (placing his hand

upon the dressing of the terrible sabre wound he had received across the face). "How proud my mother will be of them!" Suddenly the terrible discharge of artillery brought him to his feet. "Where is my rifle?" inquired he. "Surely," said one, "you will not go into the fight wounded as you are!" He turned his large, intelligent eye upon the speaker, and, with an expression on his face I never can forget, in those low, suppressed tones which men sometimes use when keeping down or repressing excitement, said, while he buckled on his war harness, "Look yonder! On the hill-side is the flag of my brigade, and I never could forgive myself if I neglected this chance to render service to my country." He went, and my heart went with him. I saw him reach and mingle with his comrades in time to take part in the conflict.

It was no wonder we were victorious, no wonder that the rebel hosts were driven back, and that there came no answering yell to the cheers of victory from the Union army; for our army was made up of patriotic material — men who perilled life for their good government — the material to wring victory from defeat! Hence, too, it was, that our army, though retreating and outnumbered, whipped the enemy in almost every battle during the seven days' fighting which terminated at Malvern Hill. After the battle of Savage's Station, says the Rev. Mr. Marks, "General Sumner called for reënforcements to drive the enemy into the Chicka-hominy, thus showing how complete was our victory."

When this conflict was over, worn and exhausted with sickness and my exertions, yet content in the conviction that the victory was ours, I wrapped myself in my blanket and slept soundly, but awoke in the morning to find myself a prisoner. Our force had retreated during the night, leaving the whole hospital camp at Savage's Station prisoners in the hands of the enemy. The first intimation was on finding a rebel guard around the camp. During the three or four days we remained here, the treatment experienced in the main was good, although no attention was given us, such as providing rations and medicines Even our ice, of which there was a meagre quantity for the wounded, was taken by the rebel authorities, and sent to Richmond for the use of the Confederate sick and wounded. The enemy whom we came in contact with from the battle-fields, as a general thing, treated us kindly, or rather let us alone.

As an instance of coolness manifested by our wounded at this time, I recollect one soldier desperately wounded in the leg, who had taken up his abode under a large tree near the station. He was as merry as a cricket, cracked jokes, whistled, and sang, and whittled like a veritable Yankee, as he doubtless was. A Union surgeon gave him some ice one day to put on his wound to prevent mortification, for the heat was intense. The poor fellow eyed the ice, and commenced eating it, and at last had eaten all except a small piece, when he began to look first at his leg and then at the ice, as if doubtful whether to finish eating the ice or to use it to cool his leg. He hesitated but a moment, and then said to himself, "G—d, I guess I'll eat it all and let it 'strike out.'"

Several correspondents of the Richmond press visited us at Savage's Station. "Our army," said one of them to me, casually, while taking notes, "will be in Washington in a few days." I could not refrain from answering the boast,, by saying, "Undoubtedly, but they will go there as I shall go to Richmond soon." And such was my confidence in McClellan at that time, that I fully believed him to be manœuvring to bag the whole rebel army. The correspondent, after recommending me to keep a civil tongue in my head, turned sneeringly away.

About the same time, a seedy-looking officer rode up, whom I accosted with the question of how we were to be sent into Richmond. "In ambulances," said he. "That," said a rebel guard, as the officer rode away, "is Jackson, our general." True enough, as I ascertained afterwards, it was Stonewall Jackson, who proved himself, in the few words of conversation I held with him, to be as big a liar as the rest of the rebels I had met; for he must have known that the rebel army were greatly deficient in the article for the use of their wounded.

On the 5th July, we were packed into filthy cattle cars, the sick and wounded crowded together, and sent into Richmond. About twenty of our wounded are said to have died during the passage of little over one hour. Arriving at the depot in Richmond, me were

formed in order around the canal, preparatory to marching to prison. We were a hard-looking crowd, made
greatly so through suffering. The heat of the day was
such as to make the thinnest garment intolerable. Many
cast away their shirts and coats, and others their pantaloons and shoes. "So many wounded and sick men in
the streets of the rebel capital, pale, bleeding, and in
some cases nearly naked, starting on their march for the
prison" — an imprisonment which, with the great majority, ended only with death — was calculated to excite
pity in the hardest heart.

Many were hopping on rude crutches; others, with
amputated arms and shattered shoulders, moved as far
as possible from their staggering companions, and were
constantly pressed back into the surging mass by the
bayonets of the brutal guard. Several blind men were
guided by the arms of the wounded, who leaned upon
them for support. Others, confused and uncertain,
groped and staggered every step like the palsied.
"Here," says Rev. Mr. Marks, who was a witness of
the scene, "one, wounded in the leg, had thrown away
his torn and bloody pants, and was limping along with
nothing but his crimson bandages; another, wounded in
the chest and arm, had thrown off his blood-stiffened
shirt, and, with the upper portion of the body bare,
moved along in the crowd, leaning upon a less injured
companion."

Such was the crowd that left the depot and slowly
moved around the canal. One would think such a

"Many were hopping on rude crutches; others, with amputated arms and shattered shoulders, moved as far as possible from their staggering companions, and were constantly pressed back into the surging mass by the bayonets of the brutal guard." — Page 24.

spectacle was calculated to excite pity, but in this case it excited scoffs and derision. Even the children took the tone of their elders, and one little fellow, about six years of age, perched exultantly upon a gate, condensed in the single sentence of, "We've got you, you d—d Yankees you!" a whole volume of rebel hate and triumph. If we did not then believe ourselves to be that description of a Yankee, we had occasion to change our opinion when we arrived at our destination. On our way an officer rode up to us, tinselled with gold lace in a most extraordinary manner, — doubtless some officer of the home guard, — and sneering, asked if that was "Falstaff's army of recruits!" "No," replied one of the boys at my side, who understood the insult, "we are not; but here they come;" pointing to a detachment of dilapidated rebels coming around a corner with the shuffling, unmilitary gait which is peculiar to the Johnnies. The officer rode away without any more attempts at wit.

In the mean time, the sidewalks were lined with citizens who came to see the "Yanks," as they would to the exhibition of some strange animal. A very few exhibited any pity. A few women — mostly Irish or German — gave us food at the risk of their lives. While we halted before the prison, on Cary Street, the shades of night had come over the city. Many of the sick and wounded had fallen upon the pavements and sidewalks from sheer exhaustion. After remaining two hours before prison No. 2, on Cary Street, we were ordered in, and there went through with the ceremony of being searched. Everything the chivalry took a fancy to was confiscated as contraband. Not even my jackknife and comb escaped, and I found myself, after the search, destitute of every thing but my blanket and the clothes on my back.

The prison was one of the large tobacco warehouses, three stories high; the rooms were large, poorly ventilated, and disgustingly filthy. The dust and tobacco juice of years had gathered in hillocks and ridges over the floor. These apartments were indescribably foul. They had been filled with prisoners who had but just been removed to make room for us, and had left behind them all the offal of mortal maladies, weakness, and wounds. There had been no sweeping or cleaning, but into these rooms we were forced, compelled to drink in the suffocating air, the first breath of which caused one to shudder.

The room in which I, with about two hundred of my companions, was placed, was too filthy for description. Here, for five days, almost suffocating from want of air, and crowded for room, I remained, having rations issued to me only twice during the five days, and those poor in quality, and insufficient in quantity for a sick man. So with all the sick and wounded. No medical attention was given, and the horror of our situation seemed more than could be borne. To such a degree were we crowded, that we were obliged to arrange ourselves in tiers, like pins on paper, when we slept

HERO.

This dog is a Russian Bloodhound, and was used during the war at Libby Prison and Castle Thunder, Richmond, Virginia, to guard Union prisoners and recapture those who escaped. Weight, 198 pounds; height, three feet and two inches; length, from tip to tip, seven feet one and a half inches. Taken from a photograph in possession of the publishers. Page 27.

at night. And even with this precaution we were crowded for sleeping-room. Constant interference of some one's feet with another's head or shins caused such continued wrangling as to make night and day more like an abode of fiends than one of human beings.

At last I was taken from this place, and sent to Libby Prison, which has often been described; and yet from the description given, no adequate idea of the sufferings endured can be formed. The filth and heat were greater than even the place I had left. With some five hundred others I was crowded into the garret, next the roof, of the prison. The hot sun, beating down upon the roof, made the filthy garret, crowded with men clamoring for standing-room, suffocating in a degree which one cannot well understand who never experienced it. During the day, in the corners of our garret the dead remained among the living, and from these through all the rooms came the pestilent breath of a charnel-house. The vermin swarmed in every crack and crevice; the floors had not been cleaned for years. To consign men to such quarters was like signing their death warrant. Two men were shot by the rebel guard while trying to get breath at the windows.

The third day of my confinement in this abode of torture, I noticed a young soldier dying: his long, fair hair was matted in the indescribable liquid filth and dirt which clotted and ran over the floor of the prison. He was covered with vermin; the flies had gathered on his wasted hands, on his face, and in the sunken sockets of his eyes. But even in this condition hunger had not left him. The scene seemed to fascinate me, and in spite of the repulsiveness of the picture, I continued to look upon it, though it was much against my will. I saw him try to get to his mouth a dirty piece of bread, which he held in his hand: the effort was in vain; the hand fell nerveless by his side; a convulsive shudder, and he was dead. After he had been dead half an hour, his hand still clasped over the poor dirty piece of bread, a Zouave who had one leg amputated, observing the bread, dragged himself through the filth and dirt, and unclasping the dead man's fingers, took the bread from the rigid hand, and ate it like a famished wolf.

Men lay on the filthy floor unable to help themselves, gasping for breath, while their more healthy companions trod upon and stumbled over them. The common expression used was, "I shall die unless I get fresh air." Every breath they breathed was loaded with the poison of fever and the effluvia of the dead. When rations were issued, two thirds of the very sick got nothing, for the manner of issuing was without order, and the distribution was by a general scramble among those who were the best able to wrangle for it. I was fortunate in getting rations the first day in Libby, but the second and third I got none. Meanwhile, my fever grew worse and worse; oppressed for breath, crowded for room, unable to get into the prison yard to perform the common functions of nature, to which was added the want of medicines and even common food, made my situation so horribly intolerable that I could only hope for relief in death. All this was made worse by the constant wrangling for room, for air, and food. I succeeded in obtaining some pieces of board, by which means I raised myself from the dirty floor and the liquid filth around me.

I had been in Libby about a week, when an officer passed through the rooms, announcing that those who were able to walk could be accommodated with quarters in a healthy location on Belle Island. None of us had heard of Belle Island as a prison at that time, and we were eager to better our condition. Worse it did not seem possible it could be, and we believed there would be some truth even with rebels in dealing with men in our situation. The chance of benefiting myself was irresistible, and so I managed to crawl and stumble down stairs into the streets. The breathing of fresh air once more was refreshing; but, trying to get into line, I stumbled, and fell fainting to the ground. I was carried by some kind people into an Irishwoman's shop, where I was treated to raspberry wine and baker's bread. She asked me if I thought our army would come into Richmond. I answered her (believing it true), that I thought our army would have Richmond in a week or two. "I hope they will," said she; "for this is a devilish place, and I wish I was in New York." I got into line after being persuaded by the bayonet of the guard, and, being too weak to stand, fell down on the pavement. A rebel guard, addressing me, said, "I guess you'd better not go down there, old hoss; Belle Isle's a right smart hard place, and I *reckon* you won't any more'n live to get down thar any way." About the time we commenced our line of march for Belle Isle, it began to rain in torrents, drenching me through. I should never have reached the prison camp alive, had it not been for the kind assistance tendered me by the rebel soldier who had previously addressed me as "old hoss."

We arrived at one of the long bridges which cross the James River between Belle Isle and Richmond; after which I have a confused recollection of falling, succeeded by a blank. I knew no more, until I found myself lying on the damp ground, with no shelter from the driving rain, and hundreds of others around me in the same situation. I have only a confused recollection of what occurred for four or five days after my arrival, when I inquired where I was. I was addressed as "old crazy" by my companions, and told to keep still. I afterwards learned that I had been delirious most of the time for four or five days, during which I had received no medical attention or care except the cold-water cure of nature. This came in such copious quantities as to remind one of what is related of Charles Lamb, who, on being questioned concerning the cold-water cure, replied that he never knew where it had been tried on an extensive principle since the deluge, when he believed it killed more than it cured

It was three weeks before I got a shelter, though there were quite a number of tents on the Island; and the shelter which I became possessed of consisted of an old striped bedtick ripped open, and set upon sticks, in poor imitation of an A tent.

CHAPTER II.

Belle Island. — Sickness and Insensibility. — Want of Medical
Treatment. — Description of Belle Isle Prison. — Strict Regulations evaded. — Trading with the Rebels. — Insufficiency of Food.
— High Prices of Commissary Stores. — Depreciated and Counterfeit Currency. — Comparative Virtue and Intelligence of Rebels
of different States. — Extreme Suffering from Hunger. — Effects
on the Character. — Philosophy on the Subject. — A Goose Question. — Exchange on the Brain. — Increased Mortality. — A Gleam
of Hope. — Exchange and Disappointment. — Escape and its Punishment. — A Rebel Admission that Richmond might have been
captured by McClellan. — More Prisoners and Suffering. — Exchange. — Sight of the Old Flag.

BELLE ISLAND is situated on a bend of the James
River, about half a mile west of Richmond. The
river at this point is very swift of current, and full of
fantastic groups of rocks and little islands, covered with
luxuriant foliage, among which the water dashes in
sparkling foam. Three bridges span the river between
the island and the city. The island contains some
forty or fifty superficial acres, rises at the lower extremity, towards Richmond, in a gentle, sandy plain,
and upon this was situated the prison camp, consisting
of about four acres of the lowest land on the James
River — almost on a level with the river, and conse

quently unhealthy. Beyond the prison grounds to the westward the island rises into a precipitous bluff, there crowned by strong earthworks, which commanded the river above. The prison grounds were surrounded by a low board railing, around which guards were stationed at intervals of fifteen paces.

The guard regulations on the island were very strict. The rules established were, that there should be no conversation between the prisoners and the guard, and that no prisoner was to come within three feet of the railing or fence which enclosed the prison. But, in spite of rules and regulations, the irresistible Yankee spirit of trade and dicker perverted even the virtuous grayback guardians of the prison. Trading over the line on the sly was one of the professions, and all became more or less expert at the business. As the guard had orders to shoot or bayonet any one infringing these rules, the business was sometimes risky, especially when a new guard was put on who knew not the ways of those who were before them, when some contrary Secesh was on duty who did not care to learn, or some confiding individual of the grayback species who had been cheated in a sharp trading speculation.

The common way in opening negotiations for trade with a new or ugly guard was to hold up, at a safe distance, some article of a tempting nature, — a jackknife, watch, or a pair of boots, — making signs that they were to be purchased cheap, until the virtuous Secesh broke the ice by inquiring the price. A lookout being

established to give warning of the approach of the offi
cers of the guard, trade would commence, and spread
from guard to guard, and sometimes beyond the guard
all along the line. In this manner a whole guard
would be seduced from virtue, and put to silence by
the fascination of high-top Yankee boots and pinchbeck
watches. The commodities of trade on the Yankee
side were articles of clothing which could ill be afforded,
bone rings of prison manufacture, watches, chains, and
jackknives; the last-named being temptations against
which the most obdurate of Johnnies was not proof.
Even a commissioned officer would condescend to
chaffer and trade for a pair of boots or a jackknife.
In return, we were the recipients of hoe-cake, wood
to cook with, apples, and sometimes potatoes and
tobacco. Occasionally officers from Richmond came
into the prison, and traded for clothing, and were not
too honest sometimes to walk off without paying for
their purchases.

I had been steadily getting up from the fever which
had prostrated me, the turning-point of which occurred
during my first week's experience at "Belle Isle," when
I gradually regained strength, though the food was so
insufficient and poor as to reduce the inmates of the
prison to an almost starving condition. I found by
personal experience and observation that, when hungry,
men will adopt very ungenteel habits to satisfy their
cravings, such as picking up bones rejected by others,
and gnawing them like dogs, struggling for stray

potato peelings, in fact, anything of an eatable nature.

I saw one day an Irish acquaintance who had possessed himself of a bacon bone with some meat on it, but more maggots than meat. "What are you doing, Jim?" I interrogated. "Quarrelling with the maggots," said Pat, with a comic leer, "to see who will have the bone." Whereupon he brushed the maggots off, contemptuously, and went in for a meal.

Our rations at this time consisted of one half loaf to each man per day, and beans, cooked in water in which bacon had been boiled for the guard, — usually containing about twenty per cent. of maggots, — owing to scarcity of salt; thirty per cent. of beans, and the remainder in water. There may have been a very small percentage of salt, but the fact was not ascertainable by the sense of taste. Only through faith — which could give no great flavor to the palate — could one see its existence in the soup — for such was the name with which this compound was dignified. It was issued sometimes twice a week, and sometimes not at all. The bread was of a very good quality, but so spongy that our poor daily half loaf could be enclosed in the half shut hand. The insufficiency of food was aggravated by neglect of the prison authorities to issue regularly; sometimes we got no rations from Saturday morning until Monday night. The excuse usually given was, that the bakers in the city were on a drunk, or that there were no blank requisitions, which excuses didn't seem to fill our stomachs, and though they had to be taken in place of rations, we found them a poor substitute. No "back rations" were ever issued.

The buildings of the commissary department were just outside the prison limits, near the water's edge, on the south side. Here non-commissioned officers of the prison, having charge of the issue of rations, were called out, when the bread was counted out to them and brought in in blankets. The fact that these blankets were infested with vermin did not detract from the tremendous cravings of appetite. At the commissary's, molasses, pies, and sugar were kept for sale at exorbitant rates — molasses, one dollar per pint, sugar, one dollar and fifty cents per pound, onions, twenty-five cents apiece, and every thing else proportionally high. Butter and milk could rarely be had at any price. Though not acknowledging any superiority, at that time, of the value of greenbacks over their shinplaster currency, they much preferred the former, in payment, to their own. It was quite noticeable that they showed a good deal of hesitation in taking their own scrip. Their fractional currency consisted of bills issued by cities, towns, and private individuals. Petersburg money, or the fractional currency of any other town, would not pass current. On the sly, even at that date, rebel officers would buy up greenbacks at the rate of three dollars for one. Fellows in our condition developed some talents, which under other circumstances, and among decent people, would have been considered dangerous. Two dollar greenbacks were altered into twenties, ones into tens, &c. Broken down banks of northern States were passed by us, and received with grasping eagerness, and even rebel shinplasters were changed into higher denominations than they were ever intended to represent. Counterfeited brass was also worked up into heavy gold chains by ingenious Yankees. In fact, every means, however desperate, was resorted to, all for the purpose of obtaining food. Except in some very rare cases, we did not swindle the rebel guard, which would have been for our disadvantage. But woe to the unsuspecting citizen, who, in his greed of gain, seduced the virtuous (?) graybacks to enable him to trade over their post with the Yanks.

As soon as I obtained sufficient strength to walk round, I entered into competition with others, and after trading away my shoes and coat for food, set up as a kind of commission merchant, for dealing in boots and any other article of clothing of trading value. By this means, with perseverance I managed occasionally to obtain an extra johnny-cake, a potato, or an onion. I might have been seen at any time during the day passing slowly around the guard line, trying to strike up a trade for something to eat. In passing thus around the camp, I had a chance to become acquainted with the disposition of the guard belonging to different States. I found the Alabama and Georgia men to be the most intelligent, while the rank and file belonging to Virginia regiments were the most ignorant and vindictive. A common question proposed to me was, "What do you'uns come down to fight we'uns for?" It was of no use to state facts, however impartial, or to argue, for it would only bring a repetition of the same question. They seemed to be oblivious of the fact that the quarrel was commenced by themselves, and any instructions volunteered by a Yank would be argued by the angry thrust of the bayonet, which was too powerful an argument to be met; consequently the Johnny considered himself a victor in all argument, since where he failed in reason, he parried with the less sentimental but more powerful argument of force, which has always seemed to me to be the distinctive method adopted by the two sections. It makes, in the end, however, but little difference, as they have been soundly beaten with their own favorite arguments of force, which they applied indiscriminately to the heads of our legislators before the war, and during its progress to prisoners of war and non-combatants.

During the last of July our sufferings were intense. All other thoughts and feelings had become concentrated in that of hunger. Even home was associated only with the various descriptions of good food. John H—, a sergeant of the eighteenth Massachusetts, used to answer my questions of how he was, with the invariable expression, "Hungry as h—ll," which may have been correct, as far as torment of that description exists in the place mentioned. There were three stages

of hunger in my experience; first, the common hungry
craving one experiences after missing his dinner and
supper; second, this passed away, and was succeeded
by headache and a gnawing at the stomach; then
came weakness, trembling of the limbs, which, if not
relieved by food, was followed by death. Ordinarily we
received just enough food to keep us hungry, which
may seem a doubtful expression to the general reader;
but those who have been similarly circumstanced, who
read this, will recognize it as a truth. Men became,
under such surroundings, indifferent to almost everything, except their own miseries, and found an excuse
in their sufferings for any violations of the ordinary
usages of humanity. An incident occurred illustrative
of this which came to my notice while I was trading
around the camp.

Near the dead line, on the west side of the camp,
were one or two wild-cherry trees, which formed the
only shade in the prison limits, and these not much, as,
from time to time, their branches had been cut off for
fuel, in spite of the vigilance of the guard, and the
necessity of shade for the prisoners. Here, one afternoon, I found a German dying. No one was there to
care for him and soothe his dying moments; the parched,
filthy ground was his death-bed; over his wasted hands
and sunken face the flies were gathering, while the
disgusting sores of his flesh swarmed with maggots
and other vermin. Moved by such a spectacle, I sat
down by his side to brush the flies from his pallid face,

and moisten the parched lips with water from my canteen. Quite a number thereupon gathered around. One, professing sympathy with so pitiable an object, suggested that he would feel better to have his boots off, and forthwith pulling them off, coolly walked away with them, and sold them. I afterwards met and recognized him, and expressed very freely my opinion that he had been guilty of a detestable act, unworthy of anything human. He confessed that it was rather rough, but excused himself by saying he was hungry, and thought it not so bad to steal from a dying man as from one likely to live; and he thought the boots would do him more good than a dead man. There was some show of reason in this, and so much effrontery that I made no reply.

Different minds are no doubt affected in a different degree by prison life, which in its best phase is simply inhuman, unnatural. But whatever the mental constitution, it must be influenced to a certain degree by terrible sufferings, and deflected, as it were, from it habitual angle. It is the calm, phlegmatic man of philosophical balance, who is best calculated to endure, to look at the best side of every misfortune, and who brings to his aid the reflection that every moment is complete in itself, and adopts for his motto in all his sufferings "Sufficient unto the moment is the evil thereof." One who is naturally ill-tempered, under the aggravations of imprisonment becomes an insupportable monster. But if bad qualities are so forcibly developed

in some, the good also in others expands in the same
ratio. The generous carry liberality into improvi-
dence, while the charitable become self-sacrificing in
their bounty. Suffering develops real character; dis-
guise throws off its mask under bodily and mental
anguish, unreservedly, and indeed unawares, and shows
the true character. Suffering is the crucible of human
metal, and pure indeed must be the gold which is not
tarnished or turned to dross by the heat of unmitigated
afflictions. Under the tortures of imprisonment, that
goodness must indeed be real which never forgets itself,
but stands firmly upon its pedestal to the last.

I was mixed up in some "right smart tall grass," as
the expression goes among the "rebs," on account of
the stealing of a Secesh goose. As the circumstances
are illustrative of the risks men were willing to run in
order to obtain food, although trivial I will relate them.
A squad of geese belonging to the Secesh officers were
often on parade just outside of prison limits, headed by
a gander who seemed to take some pride in the dis-
cipline and organization of his fellows — their drill and
marching being fully equal, if not superior to that of
their owners — the Secesh. The mouths of the prisoners often watered at the bare thought of a boiled
goose. One evening, about sundown, while the attention of the sentinel was occupied with trade, the unsuspecting geese were enticed under the guard railing with
corn, a dash was made, and a goose and gander were
captured. Their necks were wrung in a hurry. The

cackling was drowned by some unusual noise furnished for the purpose, and although the guard mistrusted "something was up," they did not find out the secret until next morning, when it was ascertained and particularly noticed that "goosy, goosy gander, no more did wander," and was missed from his accustomed haunts. Meanwhile, the goose had been eaten, without salt or sauce, and relished immensely. I was suspected of being concerned; but although many inquiries and threats were made, the inquirers were no wiser nor sounder on the "goose question" than before. Our conscience did not trouble us, for had it not been written, "Rebel property shall be confiscated."

The 1st of August developed a fearful epidemic in prison, known as Exchange on the Brain. The symptoms among those infected were, they were continually rushing around camp, with the very latest news about exchange, to the great neglect of their personal cleanliness, and their skirmishing duties (a term usually applied to the act of hunting for vermin, a partial hunt being termed driving in the pickets). The victims of this epidemic were willing to bet on being exchanged "to-morrow;" their hopes were raised high during the day, followed by a corresponding depression, on the morrow, at being disappointed. With an anxious, haggard look, inquiring of every one who would listen, "What about exchange?" and, thus inquiring, would before noon obtain information (?) which would raise their expectations to a high pitch, to be followed by despondency and discouragement, and sometimes death. The best philosophy was neither to believe nor doubt, but to wait patiently and hope much in a general manner, without setting the heart upon any particular time for its fulfilment.

The contemplation of misery teaches the necessity of hope; cut off from comforts and tender sympathies, from the daily intercourse with friends, from the habitual avocations of life, — shut out from social pleasures, doomed to mental and physical sufferings, to the lethargy of the heart, — he is lost, indeed, who loses hope. But while preserving hope, we should not build expectations on frail foundations and in disappointments lose it. While some of the prisoners endeavored by all sorts of ingenious stratagems to divert their minds from ennui and the monotony and misery of captivity, others gave up to sorrow, and pined away in the midst of morbid reflections and dismal forebodings. Some would lie for hours reading and re-reading old letters, which had perhaps been their companions in peril; and now, as they re-peruse them, were brought back slumbering recollections of home. In the species of existence which the prisoner leads, the memories of the past, the kindly sympathies expressed in tender messages of the dear ones far away in the sphere of real life, the affectionate tokens which he carries with him warm from the heart of unforgotten friends, — all these seem but the echoes of familiar voices borne from another world. They discourse to him pleasantly of departed joys, and past happy hours. There is a piteous consolation in it, like the mournful solace of the remembrance of friends who plant a dear grave with flowers.

Prisoners gather together in groups, as evening comes on, to talk of home, and while away the tedium of the hour by recalling the pleasure which once was theirs; the pleasures of the table were uppermost in their thoughts; the eager attention given when some favorite dish was described in its minutest details, attested the interest taken in everything eatable. Upon lying down at night, the talk was of what we had eaten in times past, and what we would have when we could get it. Suffering as we were from hunger, the sum total of all joy seemed to be condensed in the one act of eating. Some of the prisoners employed their moments in making finger rings of bone, handkerchief slides, napkin rings, watch seals, &c., many of which were very fine, and were bought up by the 'Sesesh' guard to be sent home as specimens of "Yankee fixings," as they termed them.

Our fare daily grew worse, and new prisoners coming in, the prison was crowded in such a manner that, it seemed impossible to get around. Deaths increased in prison to such a degree that a load of bread for the living was usually accompanied by a load of coffins for the dead. The coffins were of rough pine boards, the only decent thing provided for the prisoners. Rumors of exchange, which flooded the camp, were listened to only by a credulous few, the thoughts of the majority being cast in that rigid mould of philosophy which teaches us not so much to fly from the evils that beset us, as to grapple with them and trample them under foot — a system of ethics which, however admirable, it is not easy to follow.

Suddenly a gleam of hope burst upon the wretched camp of prisoners, and the horizon of prison life is made bright by the certainty of exchange. Officers came into the prison and made the announcement, and we all were excited with the joyful prospect of exchange. On this occasion of exchange, the rebels prided themselves on the performance of what they termed a "Yankee trick," in order to get all the men who were not sick separated from those who were not able to travel, and by this means they saved themselves much trouble. All the men who could not march seven miles were ordered to pass outside of prison bounds with their blankets and canteens, haversacks, and such rations as they might have on hand, intimating that such were to be sent by some mode of conveyance to City Point to be exchanged. There was a general rush to go out with those who were thus designated. Many good stout men, who might easily have marched twice the distance required, desirous of getting home, scrambled for a place among cripples and invalids. After lying all night, waiting with the highest expectations, we awoke in the morning to find that those who remained in camp had been marched out for exchange; and we were sent back, after being kept in a broiling sun a large portion of the day. In common with the rest, I was disheartened, and men wept like children at this bitter disappointment. I had not, however, the reflection of regret, which many had, who could have marched the required distance.

About half the camp had been exchanged, which in one respect was beneficial to those remaining. We had more room and better quarters. Though our accommodations were better, and for the first time during my imprisonment I had the pleasure of living under a tent, the food became daily worse, less in quantity, and poorer in quality. To make our wretchedness greater, the rations intended for us were sold at the commissary's; and in this manner, for a time, about a third of the men each day were cheated out of their food. The law would not allow the Confederate commissary to take greenbacks; so he employed Yankee prisoners to sell for him, and they became engaged in the transactions of cheating and stealing from their more miserable companions. Such men were generally despised by their comrades for the crouching, cringing subserviency with which they identified themselves with the rebels, upholding and subscribing to their sentiments.

The nights and mornings now became cold, and men who had disposed of their clothes during the warmest weather, sadly felt the need of them. Suffering from cold nights and during rainy weather, was severe, and told terribly on the health of those who, unfortunately, had given way to hunger, and sold their clothing for food. It is hard, however, to determine whether they would have suffered more to have been deprived of the food thus obtained or from the deprivation of garments. Death was almost certain to him who got no food except that furnished by the prison authorities.

Thus affairs became so desperate that, though surrounded by a vigilant guard, and on three sides with water, men were continually trying to make their escape. An Irishman, trying to escape, swam the river, evaded the bullets by diving and good fortune, and reached unhurt the opposite shore. There he was caught and brought into the guard quarters near the prison, and a double guard was established for his safe keeping. To punish him for his attempt at escape, he was "bucked," when he let loose such a piece of his mind, and such a rating with the unruly member, telling his tormentors more truth than they cared to hear, that they gagged him to keep him still. Thus they kept him in a burning sun, until he bled at the mouth and fainted. As soon as he recovered, the gag being removed, nothing daunted, he again gave them a "bit of his mind." They tried to make him clean their rusty guns, but he would not; and they resorted again to the torture. What finally became of him I do not know; but I heard the rumor, of which I have but a little doubt, that he died during the night from cruelty experienced at the hands of his relentless enemies.

On the 1st of September, the guard, which had consisted chiefly of Alabama and Georgia regiments, were sent away, and were relieved by citizens from Richmond, many of them boys not over thirteen years of age, who could hardly carry a musket. One of these citizen soldiers one day ran a bayonet through a New York boy, from the effects of which he died in a few hours. A soldier of the Hawkins Zouaves sprang at the guard, and, reaching over the railing, seized him by the throat, lifted him from the ground, shook him until the "rebel brave" was black in the face, then hurled him from him like a dog. The officer of the guard, coming up at the time, was saluted with a brick, which knocked him down. When inquiries were instituted, no information was to be got inside the prison. No one knew who threw the brick, or choked the guard! I ever found our foreign soldiers in prison among the most inveterate haters of rebels, and unyielding as iron. During the last of August and first of September, no less than eight men were killed by the rebel guard.

Captain Montgomery at that time was in command of the rebel post at Belle Island. In conversation with him one day, he remarked that, after the battle of Fair Oaks, our forces might have taken Richmond; that there was a panic among their troops, through apprehension of our following up the advantage gained during the last day's fight; and that the James River bridges had been got ready to be destroyed by fire. He seemed very inquisitive about public sentiment at the North, and as to how long the North would fight.

Some two thousand prisoners were added to our

number from Salisbury during September. They had been much better fed than ourselves, and were much dirtier, having been deprived of the advantages of water, which we had from the river, and from little shallow wells from five to eight feet deep, which we dug all over the prison grounds. Several officers accompanied them, among whom was Colonel Corcoran, who, with other commissioned officers, was sent over to Richmond. After this arrival of prisoners, we were again crowded for room; and the hopes of another exchange had almost died out, when our camp was flooded with rumors of release by parole. Day after day passed. Hunger-stricken and pinched with cold, these walking spectres wandered around camp, gathering in groups to talk of home and exchange.

About this time I got a Richmond paper, which argued that dirty people required less food than people who were clean, instancing the Yankee prisoners of Belle Isle as an illustration of the truth of the assumption. Another paragraph announced that prisoners at Belle Isle would be exchanged on the coming Tuesday. Tuesday came, but no parole or exchange! We waited patiently, in hopes that something might turn up to relieve us; but no relief came. It was so hard to wait, even a few days, for relief from our condition, that the uncertainty to which everything in rebeldom seemed condemned was excruciating mental torment, added to the physical misery endured. This jumbling together of so much of hopeless mortality, this endless crash of

4

matter and ceaseless shock of tortured humanity, is a curse to the mind. Some were on the "tip-toe" of expectation; others, in their gloomy despondency, were resigned to the desperate idea of making a winter of it in this dreadful place, when a bow of promise appeared upon the dark background of adversity that overshadowed the prison, and a bright day of deliverance dawned upon us.

The dark night of misery passed away, and I was called out to write in paroling the prisoners. With eager, trembling hand, I wrote first my own parole, and then worked all night. There were some funny descriptions accompanying the paroles — for instance, red hair, blue eyes, and dark complexion. Before morning the blanks of liberty were made out, and as morning dawned, we all hurried out of prison, — a motley crowd, ragged, dirty, and famine-stricken.

The sick took fresh courage, and under Freedom's inspiration the lame walked, and rejoiced that their term of captivity was ended; that once again they were to be under the protecting folds of Liberty's starry banner. Again we entered Richmond; and, as we passed through its streets, skeletons in form, from which almost all semblance of humanity had fled under the torture of imprisonment, we excited pity among even the virulent women of the capital. They filled our canteens with water, and their kind faces showed that they were not dead to all pity. This revulsion of feeling in our favor since first passing through the rebel capital, was caused, perhaps, by their own sufferings — the lose of some father or brother. Be it as it may, I know that while the expressions of hate were few, the kindly expressions were many in our behalf. Perhaps military restrictions were removed, which before had checked expression, and the rebel authorities were willing we should have some kindly remembrances upon our departure from such scenes. The shops of the city had mostly been closed, and one of the guard told me that every house in Richmond was either a prison or a hospital. Though this may have been exaggeration, it was no doubt a fact that all the dwellings of Richmond had their spare rooms occupied by Confederate sick and wounded. In this city the infantry guards were relieved, and a cavalry escort furnished, who showed their confidence in our desire to reach our lines by letting us straggle as we had a mind to.

During the day we marched without food, and finally, late in the afternoon, a feeble cheer went up from the advance, which told that the old flag on our transports was in sight. Need I say how wildly our hearts beat at sight of that dear old flag which we had followed in battle, and which had floated among the peaceful scenes of home! The feeling was too deep to be expressed in words or cheers. Tears of joy started to eyes unused to weep at misery; the voice that attempted expression was lost in choking sobs. Men sat quietly down, tears coursing their dirt-furrowed cheeks, contented to look up and see the "old flag" floating over them. I sat in this manner, having without knowing it, a quiet, joyful cry, when a com rade came along, inquiring, "What are you blubbering about, old fellow?" I looked up, and saw he hadn't much to brag about, and replied, that I was crying because folks were such fools as to live under a flag with three stripes, when they might have one with thirteen over them.

We hoisted anchor, left those scenes, and came, at last, a sick, maimed, emaciated company, to Annapolis. There kind hands cared for us, kind welcomes cheered us, and we knew we were at home at last — at home with the arms of a great nation around us, with the great love of noble loyal hearts. When I left Belle Island I had no hair or hat on my head, and my clothing con- sisted only of a pair of pantaloons and a shirt. Neither hat, shoes, or jacket had I.

CHAPTER III.

THREE months followed in the parole camp, where I regained strength; and the hardships through which I had passed seemed rather a distorted dream than a dreadful reality. Does the mind lose the sharp impressions of hardships, that it is inclined to look upon the pleasures rather than upon the dangers and disagreeable incidents of the past? I will not tire the reader with details of incidents which in a few months ended in my discharge for disability, resulting from injuries received in the line of duty.

Once more I returned to my home, where its comforts and kind friends contributed to my restoration to health. Possessed naturally of a strong constitution, I recovered with almost marvellous quickness from disabilities which an able board of medical men had pronounced incurable. With returning health came the desire to be again with my companions in the field. The clash of arms, the excitement of battle, the hurried military parades and displays, awoke all the pleasurable recollections, and there are many in the soldier's life. Hardships suffered were remembered only to revive my hatred of the enemy who had caused them.

I secretly longed again to be in arms, and finally joined company H, second Massachusetts heavy artillery, upon its original formation at Readville. It is not my purpose to give the common experiences of the field, and therefore I omit the months that followed.

April, 1864, found at Plymouth, N. C., two companies, H and G, of the second Massachusetts heavy artillery, garrisoning the forts and redoubts on the hostile borders of a rebellious State. Plymouth is situated on the Roanoke River, at the head of the Albemarle Sound. This post was commanded by Brigadier-General Wessels, whose brigade consisted, besides the two companies mentioned, of the following regiments: sixteenth Connecticut, one hundred and first Pennsylvania, eighty-fifth New York, a New York independent battery, twenty men of the twelfth New York cavalry, a few negro recruits, and two companies of loyal North Carolinians. Upon our arrival (which was in February, 1864), we found the place in what a wag of our company termed a dilapidated condition. It was the mere remnant of what had once been quite a thriving village. The rebel forces and our own had had each a turn at attempting to burn it, and thus the best built portion of the town had been consumed. At the time mentioned, the town consisted of a few tumble-down houses that had escaped the flames, two or three brick stores and houses, and the rest a medley of negro shanties, made of staves split from pitch-pine logs, in which the surrounding country abounded, and a number of rude frame buildings, made for government use, from material sawed at the steam mill which government possessed by confiscation.

The place was a general rendezvous for fugitive negroes, who came into our lines by families, while escaping from conscription or persecution, and for rebel deserters, who had become lean, hungry, ragged, and dissatisfied with fighting against the Union. Schools had been established for the young and middle-aged colored population, under the able tuition of Mrs. and Miss Freeman, of Milford, Mass. The whole place had a Rip Van Winkle look, as though it had composed itself into a long sleep to awake after the era of revolution and rebellion had passed. The forts protecting this place were five in number. Extending along a line of two miles were Fort Williams, covering the centre of the town, Battery Worth, commanding the river above, Compher and Coneby redoubts, commanding the approaches of the left; while on the right, standing out half a mile, unconnected with those described, was Fort Wessels. Still farther to the right was Fort Gray, standing alone, one mile and a half up the river, on what is known as "War Neck," having no communication with the works described except by a foot-bridge consisting of single logs laid across a swamp, or by a boat on the river. A little tug-boat, called the Dolly, was continually plying between Fort Gray and the town. A line of rifle-pits connected Fort Williams, Coneby and Compher redoubts, with Battery Worth.

On the morning of April 17, 1864, the consolidated morning report to the adjutant-general gave eighteen hundred men armed and equipped for duty. These men were to guard and defend a line of nearly three miles, where the difficulty of communication, and consequent concentration of men at the point of attack, was very great. The theory that a long line is a weak line was here exemplified. One strong bastioned work, with a good water battery connected by parallels, with strong abatis work, would, with the same number of men, have made the place much stronger, if not impregnable. On the afternoon of the 17th, while on my way to Fort Wessels, I met two drummer boys belonging to Fort Gray on their way to the commanding general, with the information that the rebels were approaching in strong force within two miles of Fort Gray. This alarm sent me back to Fort Williams, where I arrived just as the enemy opened fire from the edge of the surrounding woods. That evening a battery opened on Fort Gray, followed by two charges of the rebel infantry, in which the rebels were repulsed with heavy losses. Thereafter, at that point of our line, they contented themselves by skirmishing, and an occasional shot from their artillery.

On the afternoon of the 18th, our pickets, after disputing every step of the way, were driven in, and the rebel artillery, from their whole line in front, opened fire upon Fort Williams and the town. We returned the fire. The gunboats Miami and Smithfield did terrible execution. The battle was raging fiercely, when, in obedience to orders, I passed down through the town to the river. The shot and shell shrieked through the town, crushing through the walls and roofs of the houses and shanties. On the side of the houses towards the river were amusing groups of negro men, women, and children, who had gathered in the rear of their frail shanties, as if vainly hoping they might prove a protection against the iron messengers of death. They made a preposterous noise, in which were mingled religious exclamations, prayer and supplication, with shrieks and lamentations.

I passed safely through the town, and getting up steam on board the "Dolly," was fortunate enough to get her, with rations, to Fort Gray, much in want of supplies. A rebel battery, commanding the river, had made it difficult and dangerous to make the attempt.

I was fortunate in escaping the attention of the rebel battery, and arrived with the dead from Fort Gray. That night Sergeant Evans and myself buried the dead we had brought down. The rebels had been repulsed all along the line, with the exception of Fort Wessels, which, with a garrison of eighty men, had twice repulsed the rebels, and had taken thirty prisoners, but at last had surrendered to overwhelming numbers, not, however, until a rebel battery had been planted less than a hundred yards from them.

After the fight I visited my old quarters, but found them knocked to pieces by shell and shot. I extricated from the ruins two blankets, in which I rolled myself, to sleep. This was about two o'clock in the morning. In about an hour I was aroused by hearing a heavy firing in the direction of Fort Gray. Rumors came that a rebel ram was coming down the river. Without firing a shot, — throwing from her smoke-stack huge volumes of pitch-pine smoke, — she passed within a few rods of Battery Worth, commanded by Lieutenant Hoppin, who was ordered, some five minutes before she hove in sight, to fire on the first thing coming down the river, as it would be the rebel ram. At this battery was mounted a rifled gun, carrying a chilled end shot, weighing two hundred pounds, — enough, one would think, to blow the ram into the swamp on the opposite side of the river. Yet not a shot was fired from this gun until after she had passed below her, and sunk the Smithfield, whose crew were killed, captured, or drowned, while the Miami ran away. Captain Flusher, commanding the gunboats, had lashed the Miami and the Smithfield together with heavy chains, hoping in this way to detain the ram and sink her. While endeavoring to throw a shell down the smoke-stack of the ram he was killed.

From the time the rebel ram passed our batteries, the loss of Plymouth was a foregone conclusion. During the night the rebels had thrown a pontoon bridge across the river on our left, and early the same morning they carried, by assault, our redoubts on this flank, which gave them the town in our rear, and soon had sharpshooters in every house, picking off our gunners. Such was our situation on the morning of the 20th. There was no fighting at Fort Gray; Fort Williams alone returned a feeble fire upon the artillery planted upon all sides of them. The outworks soon surrendered, and Fort Williams sustained the conflict alone. Though summoned to surrender, and threatened with "no quarters" if we did not comply, we fought them single-handed until afternoon, when again being summoned, and our situation such that it was useless to contend longer against overwhelming numbers, the commanding General reluctantly surrendered, and I was again a prisoner of war.

It is a pleasure to know that most of the men and officers of the second behaved with gallantry, as also did the other regiments in the field. The conduct of one woman here deserves to be mentioned, — Margaret

Leonard, — the wife of a private of Company H, second Massachusetts heavy artillery. During the battle, she was engaged making coffee for the men in a building exposed to a heavy fire. At one time a solid shot passed through the building, taking with it one of her dresses, which hung on a nail by the wall Another carried away the front legs of her cooking-stove. Yet when the fight was over, on the evening of the 19th, she had coffee for the men, and supper for the officers. She was in Fort Williams during the remainder of the fight, and subsequently went through with a long and severe imprisonment at Andersonville, Macon, and Castle Thunder, Richmond.

During the fight, we had armed and equipped for action eighteen hundred men. The rebels acknowledged, in the Petersburg papers of the 27th, the loss of seventeen hundred men, in killed and wounded, before the defences of Plymouth; thus paying very dear for their bargain, on their own showing. When we surrendered, our ammunition was gone, and our rations nearly exhausted. In the face of these facts, and with a full knowledge of them, a rebel captain boasted that had the Confederates possessed the forts, the whole Yankee nation couldn't have taken them. He probably had forgotten Vicksburg and Port Hudson. The forces at Plymouth surrendered only to overwhelming numbers.

We were marched out between two lines of rebel infantry. As we passed along, the Secesh did us the honor to swap hats with us, by taking them from our heads and substituting their own in their place. I lost my tall dress hat, which had caught the eye of a reb, on account of the ostrich plume which embellished it. I would have preferred keeping it, as it had two very ornamental bullet holes in the top, made by some complimentary rebel sharpshooters during the action. Here let me record the fact, that many of the pretended Union men and women of the town were suddenly developed into exultant Secesh, and shouted their defiance as we passed through the place after our capture, — the same who, a few days before, were glad to draw government rations, and accept of like favors.

We were marched into the open field in front of Plymouth, where we were strongly guarded for the night. Here, also, had been driven from the town, like so many cattle, the whole population of Plymouth, except those known as Secesh. Little children at the breast, — white, yellow, and black, — old women and young, were all huddled together in an open field, preparatory to — they knew not what. There were about twenty negro soldiers at Plymouth, who fled to the swamps when the capture of the place became certain; these soldiers were hunted down and killed, while those who surrendered in good faith were drawn up in line, and shot down also like dogs. Every negro found with United States equipments, or uniforms, was (we were told by the rebel guard) shot without mercy.

The Buffaloes, as the North Carolina companies were called, escaped in some cases by swimming the river before the final surrender. On those who were not thus fortunate, fell all the concentrated rage and hatred of the rebels. Many of these Buffaloes had assumed the garb and name of our dead artillerists, and in this manner, in some instances, escaped detection and death. On our way from Plymouth to Tarboro' I saw several of our North Carolina men selected out as deserters, and, without even the ceremony of a drum-head court-martial, strung up to the limb of trees by the road-side. We were closely guarded, but not, as a general thing, badly treated.

On the afternoon of the 21st we were rationed with our captured "hard-tack" and pork, formed into line, and sadly turning our faces from Plymouth, where we had left our unburied dead, were marched into the interior. On the first day we marched about fifteen miles, and on the next, without any issue of rations, to Hamilton, where we were turned into a grove while our captors awaited orders respecting our destination. At Hamilton the citizen Secesh of the surrounding country flocked to see the captured Yankees. They were mostly women, who were curious specimens of the feminine gender, — straight-skirted, without crinoline, and invariably addressing us as "you'uns Yanks." One of the unvarying inquiries among the women was, "Has you'uns Yanks got any snuff?" It was rumored that we were to be exchanged for "Hoke's Brigade." This rumor was doubtless for the purpose of keeping us quiet and cheerful, in order that we might be easy to manage.

On the 24th we left Hamilton for Tarboro', which place we reached about noon, and where we received rations of raw meal, beans, and bacon. During the day I traded my overcoat for a two-quart tin pail, which my previous prison experience told me would be as useful as anything I could possess. It came in early demand, for that night we cooked mush. Many wry faces were made at this fare, without salt; yet, for many weeks and months after, we were glad when we got enough even of that. Here, also, the people from the town and surrounding country flocked to see the captured Yanks, bringing with them articles to trade, the women more anxious for snuff than even at Hamilton. Some of them were quite well dressed; but the majority were uncrinolined, and had a withered look of premature age, noticeable among the middle-aged and young women at the South; induced, I have no doubt, by the disgusting habit so prevalent there of "dipping," as it is called. This is performed by dipping the chewed end of a stick in snuff, and rubbing it among their teeth and gums. This habit may be accounted for from the fact that they have no useful pursuits to occupy their minds.

Most of the men taken at Plymouth were well-dressed and good-looking, and I overheard one of the young rebel ladies (?) say that she thought some of the Yanks were red "pootey," and enthusiastically declared she would like to have one to keep. Whether she meant to have one as a plaything and pet, or to keep as negroes are

kept, I know not. But the keeping, I think, by power
of attraction, would have been difficult, so destitute of
charms of person and conversation were most of the Secesh damsels there congregated. One of the sixteenth
Connecticut regiment, having a brass chain in imitation
of gold dollars linked together, traded it off as genuine,
realizing a hatful of Confederate scrip. The women
traded with us for biscuits of hoe-cake and corn, at
exorbitant prices, all anxious to get greenbacks in return, and generally seeming to shun their own currency,
especially the bills of their beloved Confederacy. They
were willing to converse, if they were allowed to do
all the talking; but were very indignant at some of
our boys, who persisted in calling their would-be nation
the Corn-fed-racy. All this dicker and talk and chaff
was carried on over the guard line. I traded off my
boots for shoes at this place, and got ten dollars "to
boot" in greenbacks, — all the money I had during an
imprisonment of ten months. Silver brought a big
premium. The common expression in exchange was,
"ten cents in silver, or ten dollars in Confederate
scrip;" and at that rate the silver was eagerly seized
upon.

We marched through the streets of Tarboro', which
were thronged with boys, negroes, old men, and ill-
dressed women and children. Some of the youngsters
wore rejected Confederate forage caps, of C. S. A.
make, much too big for them; yet they seemed to consider them a military covering, which, on that occasion,

did them honor. Passing the post-office, one of our men asked, jokingly, for a letter. The savage reply was, that they had nothing but bullets for Yankees. Arriving at the depot, we were crammed into filthy box-cars, while heavy guards were stationed on top and at the entrance of the cars. Thus packed, sixty and seventy to a car, we started, at a slow rate, forward to our destination, the engine throwing out dense volumes of pitch-pine smoke, making our journey rather uncomfortable. At noon we halted, to cook by the wayside, and again my little pail came into requisition; for, after using it myself, it was lent to several other parties, who cooked their mush in it. A great many were without cooking utensils; and having drawn nothing but raw rations, were forced to go hungry, borrow, or eat their Indian meal raw. Hunger will soon reduce one even to that expedient, in order to satisfy its demands.

We observed, while off the train, at different points along the route, that the track was much worn, occasionally replaced by rails of English manufacture. The guard, doubtless acting under instructions, kept alive the hopes of speedy exchange by relating fictitious conversations, which they pretended to have overheard among the officers. This was well calculated to deceive the majority, but it did not deceive me. I was on the lookout for a convenient chance to escape, and was soon favored with what appeared to be an *"opening."* There was a hole in the side of the car in which I was located, through which a man might possibly squeeze;

5

and a companion and myself determined, if we could get possession of the place occupied by two of our company, to try and escape during the night, while the train was in motion, by jumping from the car. With this idea we communicated our intentions to them, thinking they would be generous enough to afford an opportunity for our escape, if they did not wish to escape themselves. But upon our making them confidants of our intentions, they raised an outcry against us, and threatened to inform the guards if we did not desist. "We shall be shot by the guards if you escape," said they. One of these men repented of his folly after arriving in prison, and bitterly lamented that he had not then availed himself of the chances of that night. The general impression among our men at that time was, if they kept quiet, and did not trouble the rebels, their treatment, when we arrived in prison, would be much improved. Although I informed them of the manner in which prisoners were treated, they could not be brought to believe it was so bad after all.

So liable are men to deceive themselves with false hopes and expectations, that when the rebel guard informed them that their destination was Andersonville, a beautifully laid out camp, with luxuriant shade trees filled with birds, and a running stream, in which fish sported, they swallowed the whole story undoubtingly. So great was their confidence, that the rebels might safely have dispensed with a guard for a majority of the prisoners. Yet the vigilance of the guard was increased instead of relaxed, as we neared our destination, so that escape became impossible.

All along the route, at every stopping place, men, women, and children flocked to see us as to a show. Even in the night, the "Southern heart" was encouraged by a sight of the captured Yankees. They came with "pitch-pine torches" to catch glimpses of the detested Yanks. One talkative boy at a station one evening seemed very curious to see the Yanks, whom he had been informed had horns; but we told him we had "hauled in our horns" considerably since our capture, which accounted for their not being visible. The little fellow said they used no lights in that part of the country, except pitch-pine; they were rather smoky, he acknowledged, but they would put up with that willingly, "rather than not lick the Yankees." We had some talk with an intelligent Lieutenant at the same place, who acknowledged the worthlessness of their money, but said they were going to fight it out upon the resources of the country. The Confederacy, he said, had a year's provisions on hand, and would fight as long as their means lasted. "Well, then," said I, "you might as well give up your cause, for when your resources fail you are conquered, while the resources of the North are, if anything, more plentiful than before the war. Every man you bring into the field is taken from the producing powers of the country." At that instant the officer of the guard came up, and forbid further conversation with the "Yanks." Of course all conversations were carried on by us from the cars, where we were caged.

On our arrival at Wilmington, we were halted at the depot, and again were rationed with bacon and hard-tack, three of the latter to a man. During our half hour's stop at this place we set fire to a high stack of cotton bales near us, which slowly burned, but did not attract attention of our guard at the time. Feeling bound to do all the injury we could in an enemy's country, we were much gratified to learn, when we arrived at Charleston, South Carolina, that "a large amount of cotton had been destroyed, supposed to have been fired by malicious Yankee prisoners, who passed through the place en route for Andersonville." We crossed the river at Wilmington, on board of a ferry-boat, halted at Florence, South Carolina, the next day, and received rations of Indian meal. That night we arrived in Charleston, and were locked up in the work-house yard. Next morning received rations of three hard-tack per man, and a slice of bacon.

During the day we remained in the yard, bartering and trading with all who came to see us. I gave a man three dollars to get me some drawing paper. He returned, after a few hours, with two pages of an old ledger, one side of which had been written upon. I was rather angry at such a return, when he said, "You needn't flare up, old fellow, 'tis the best we uns have." I subsequently was informed that it was the best I could have got had I gone for it myself. I wrote a

letter, and put on it a Confederate postage stamp, to
mail it for home. I was promised it should be sent, but
it never was received. We got bread at this place for
one dollar per loaf, United States greenbacks, but the
desire to speculate on our necessities raised it to three
dollars per loaf before we left the jail yard. The day
was passed in talking and joking with such as came and
felt disposed to talk with the Yanks.

In the afternoon we were taken out of prison and
passed through the streets of Charleston, which we saw
for the first time by daylight. Women and children
crowded the streets, and showed us much sympathy in
various ways, by acts as well as words, the women furnishing the prisoners with tobacco, cigars, and food, for
which they would accept no recompense whatever;
these, however, were mostly Irish or German. But
through the whole of Charleston not a disrespectful or
unkind word was uttered in our hearing. Sympathy
with the Union cause, or possibly the constant firing
down the harbor, had a beneficial effect upon the inhab-
itants, and in their conduct towards us. We halted on
our march through the town at a German cigar manu-
factory, where a fine-looking, keen-eyed young German presented us with cigars and food, and a very
pretty young lady made a present of a bouquet to a good
looking young fellow of our number. Having some
paper with me, while seated on the pavement waiting
for orders I drew several hasty sketches, and presented
them to the people, thus leaving my card. Knowing

a few words of German, I made known my wish to escape. Quite a pleasant conversation was carried on between the prisoners and the occupants of the sidewalks and houses.

On our way to the depot, we were taken through a part of the town where the shell and shot of our guns had done comparatively little injury, yet on every side was evidence of the terrific effects of our guns. At one place was a building destitute of a corner; another had a round hole punctured through the brick walls, where the shot and shell had travelled. I guessed at the object in thus taking us through that part of the town which had suffered least, as having reference to our probable exchange at no very distant day. They wished us to get a favorable opinion of the damage done to the town by our shot and shell from the islands and marshes. We were so kindly treated at Charleston that we left the city with regret, and were again packed on board of box-cars, preparatory to leaving for Andersonville. The captain, commanding our guard while in the city, was the son of the Irish patriot (?) Mitchel. Before the cars started, an old German woman came around inquiring for me; and I have no doubt I missed a good chance of escape in being forbidden by the guard to talk with citizens.

The next day we arrived at Macon, Georgia, where we halted for a time. Macon had quite a prim, New England look, unlike any southern village I had before seen. It reminded me of Augusta, Maine.

VIEW OF OFFICERS' STOCKADE,

With Rebel Hospitals and Barracks, and Camps in the distance.

"The guard answered our interrogations as to where we were going to put up, by ironically pointing out some comfortable-looking barracks as our habitations." Page 71.

The weather was rainy, drizzly, and suffocating on the last of our journey, and a gloom pervaded our thoughts and feelings. During the whole day, through anxiety, as we neared our destination, scarcely a word was spoken. We arrived at Andersonville about four o'clock P. M., May 1, 1864. It was raining severely when the train reached the place. Even then we did not imagine to what kind of quarters we were to be consigned. Th guard answered our interrogations as to where we were going to put up, by ironically pointing out some comfortable looking barracks as our habitations.

Suddenly the whole scene changed! A ferocious, round-shouldered little man, mounted upon a bay mare, surrounded by the guard who were to take the place of those who had accompanied us on the cars, came raving, swearing, and tearing round in a most extravagant manner. So ridiculous appeared to us his gestures, person, and looks, that we burst into a roar of laughter; whereupon he turned upon us, bristling with rage, exclaiming, "By Got! you tam Yankees; you won't laugh ven you gets into the pull pen." It was a gratuitous prophecy, afterwards understood in all its horrors; and the threats of Captain Wirz had too much significance in them to be laughed at. The recollection, even now, of the light manner we received so gross a monster, causes a shudder when I think what action our laugh might have prompted him to. I was selected out on account of my sergeant's uniform.

when, asking me if I could write, I was furnished with paper, and told to take the names, regiment, and company of my car load of companions. When it was done, the names of some thirty more were given me, making in all ninety men, which was called "Detachment 21–30." The other prisoners were similarly divided, and placed under non-commissioned officers.

The new guard belonging to the station relieved the old one, and we were marched a short distance, where a curious-looking structure, fifteen feet high, loomed up before us. Sentries were stationed on the top of little platforms, scaffolded up near and at the height of the enclosure. This was the "Stockade," which was to become our future quarters. It was composed of the trunks of pine trees, which were set vertically into a trench, so close as to touch together, forming a close fence. In this manner about fifteen acres were fenced in. As we halted before the headquarters of the prison, waiting, like so many drowning rats, crouching in the rain, the guard, in answer to our questions as to what kind of a place it was inside the stockade, replied, we would find out when we got in there. They said prisoners tried to escape sometimes, but the dogs always caught them. Never, to their knowledge, had a man escaped, except one, and he was drowned while trying to swim a pond to get clear of the dogs. This was a crusher to the idea I had formed that the stockade might prove a good place for an escape.

As we waited, the great gates of the prison swung

VIEW OF THE BLOODHOUNDS.

And the Hut in which they were kept. There was not only a large pack kept here, but several other packs kept in the vicinity, for the purpose of recapturing escaped prisoners.

"They said prisoners tried to escape sometimes, but the dogs always caught them." Page 72.

VIEW OF THE MAIN GATE.

"As we waited, the great gates of the prison swung on their ponderous oaken hinges, and we were ushered into what seemed to us Hades itself." Page 72.

on their ponderous oaken hinges, and we were ushered
into what seemed to us Hades itself. Strange, skeleton
men, in tattered, faded blue, — and not much of blue
either, so obscured with dirt were their habiliments, —
gathered and crowded around us; their faces were so
begrimed with pitch-pine smoke and dirt, that for a
while we could not discern whether they were negroes
or white men. They gathered and crowded around us
to ask the news, and inquire from whence we came;
and in return we received the information that they had
mostly come from Belle Island, whence they were sent
the 1st of March. The air of the prison seemed putrid;
offal and filth covered the ground; and the hearts,
buoyed with expectation of good quarters, sank within
them when they knew that no shelter was furnished
beyond what could be constructed of blankets or garments. All my former experience of prison life had
not prepared me for such unmitigated misery as met me
everywhere. Our poor fellows, who had so confidingly
believed in the humanity of rebels, were now depressed
by despondency and gloomy forebodings, destined to be
more than fulfilled. Of those of our company who that
day entered these prison gates, not one third passed beyond them again, except to their pitiful, hastily-made,
almost begrudged graves.

CHAPTER IV.

THE prison at Andersonville was situated on two hill-
sides, and through the centre ran a sluggish brook,
branch, as it was commonly termed. There were no
signs of vegetation in the pen — it had all been trampled out. Our squads were ordered to take their positions near the hill-side, on the borders, and partially in a
murky slough or swamp. This was between the brook,
or branch, on the north side, and was used by the prisoners as a "sink," until it had become pestilent with

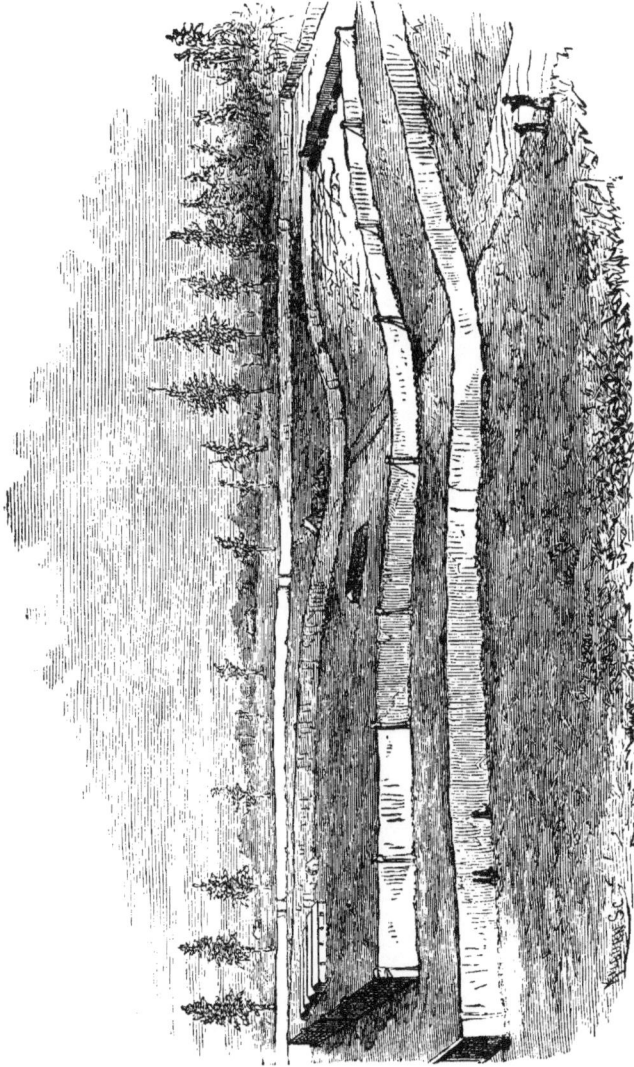

VIEW OF THE STOCKADE. — as the Rebels left it.

"The prison at Andersonville was situated on two hill-sides, and through the centre ran a sluggish brook, branch, as it was commonly called. There were no signs of vegetation in the pen; it had all been trampled out." Page 74.

dreadful stench. Sadly thinking of home, and its dreadful contrast here, that night we lay down in the rain and dirt, on the filthy hill-side, to endeavor to get rest. But when sleep visited us, it was with an accompaniment of horrid dreams and fancies, more than realized in the horrors of the future, and familiar now, more or less, to the whole civilized world. With burdened hearts we realized how hard was our position. The first morning after our arrival about twenty pounds of bacon and a bushel of Indian meal was given me to distribute among ninety men. We had no wood to cook with, when two of my comrades, with myself, succeeded in buying six or seven small pieces for two dollars, and soon got some johnny-cake made. At our coming into the stockade there were about ten thousand prisoners, increased to about twelve thousand by our arrival. The next day three others with myself formed a mess together; and taking two of our blankets, constructed a temporary shelter from sun and rain, and thus settled down, experiencing the common life of hunger and privations of prisoners. We soon became conversant with the ways and means of the prison. There is a certain flexibility of character in men that adapts itself with readiness to their circumstances. This adaptability to inevitable, unalterable fate, against which it is useless to strive, or where it is death to repine, softens much of the sufferings otherwise unendurable in such a life. In no position is this adaptability more fruitful of good results to its possessor than in prison. It en

ables the luckless prisoner to extract whatever of com
fort there may be in the barren species of existence
which surrounds him, and mitigates the mental torments
and pains endured by those who are suddenly thrown
upon their own resources, amid the acutest sufferings
which squalid misery can inflict. While some pass their
time in useless repinings, others set themselves resolutely
at work, like Robinson Crusoe, to develop the resources
of their surroundings into all the comforts they can
force them to yield.

Originally the interior of the prison had been densely
wooded with pitch-pine, in which that country abounds;
but at the time of our arrival it had been, with the exception of two trees, entirely cut to supply the want
of fuel demanded by the prisoners. The camp at that
time was dependent upon the roots and stumps of the
trees which had been cut down for fuel. A limited
number of those who were among the first arrivals
had constructed rude shelters of the branches of trees,
thatched with pitch-pines to shed the rain. The common shelter was, however, constructed with blankets,
old shirts, &c., while a great number had no shelter at
all, or burrowed for the want of one in the ground. An
aristocratic shelter, which few could indulge in, was
made of two blankets pinned together with wooden pegs,
stretched upon a ridgepole running across two uprights
stuck into the ground, in imitation of an A tent; or two
poles were tied together, with both the ends stuck into
the ground, forming a semicircle. Over three of these

VIEW OF THE HUTS
Occupied by a few of the more fortunate Prisoners.

"The common shelter was, however, constructed with blankets, old shirts, &c.; while a great number had no shelter at all, or burrowed, for the want of one, in the ground." Page 76.

VIEW OF THE BAKERY,
Which was one story high, and contained two rooms, one of which communicated with two ovens; these two ovens, fourteen feet in length by seven feet in width, supplied the prisoners with all the bread they obtained.

a blanket was stretched. A hole was then dug two or three feet deep under the space sheltered by the blankets. These, as a rebel surgeon one day remarked, were little better than graves. When there was a sudden shower, as was often the case, these holes would as suddenly fill with water, situated as most of them were on the side hill. All over camp men might be seen crawling out of holes like half-drowned kittens, wet, disconsolate, and crestfallen. Those who could summon the philosophy to laugh at the ludicrous view of their troubles, would find but little comfort in such uncomfortable circumstances. These shelters were, at best, but poor protection against rain or a tropical sun; but, as poor as they were, many who had blankets could not, though surrounded by woods on the exterior of the prison, get the necessary poles or branches to construct them. Under such circumstances the unlucky prisoner burrowed in the earth, or laid exposed to the fury of rain and sun, and often chilly nights and mornings.

The organization in camp for the issue of rations was as follows: The men were divided into squads of ninety, over which one of their own sergeants was placed. Over three nineties was also a chief sergeant, who drew rations for the whole. Every twenty-four hours these sergeants issued rations, which they drew at the gate from the prison authorities. The sergeants of nineties issued to sergeants of thirty or ten to suit convenience, and facilitate the distribution of rations.

The rations were brought into camp by mule teams, driven by negroes, or, more commonly, by prisoners paroled and detailed for the purpose. A sergeant of ninety men was entitled to an extra ration for his trouble. I resigned, however, my position as sergeant of ninety before I had held it twenty-four hours, as I had foreseen that the position required a great deal of work, and I did not believe in taking an extra ration, which would not have benefited me. It was a task, however, which many among a multitude of hungry mouths were ready to take upon themselves, and but very few qualified to fill in an honorable, impartial manner. When men are cut down to very low rations, they are not always discriminating in attaching blame to the proper source, which made the place all the more difficult to fill with credit. This I early foresaw, and, therefore, left the position to some one anxious to fill it.

During the first month of our imprisonment the rations were better than at any subsequent period, except wood, of which by chance we got none. Yet even at this time the rations were miserably inadequate to anything like a healthy organization. Our rations per day, during the first month, were a little over a pint of Indian meal, partly of cob ground with the meal, which was made into mush, and which we called by the appropriate name of chicken feed. Once in two days we got about a teaspoonful of salt. At first, bacon was issued in small quantities of fifteen to twenty

47 ft. 9 in.

Trough unfinished.

Mounds of earth
use unknown

83 ft 1 in.

Office.

oven
13 ft. 7 in.

Pan Rack

oven

Kneading trough

18 ft.

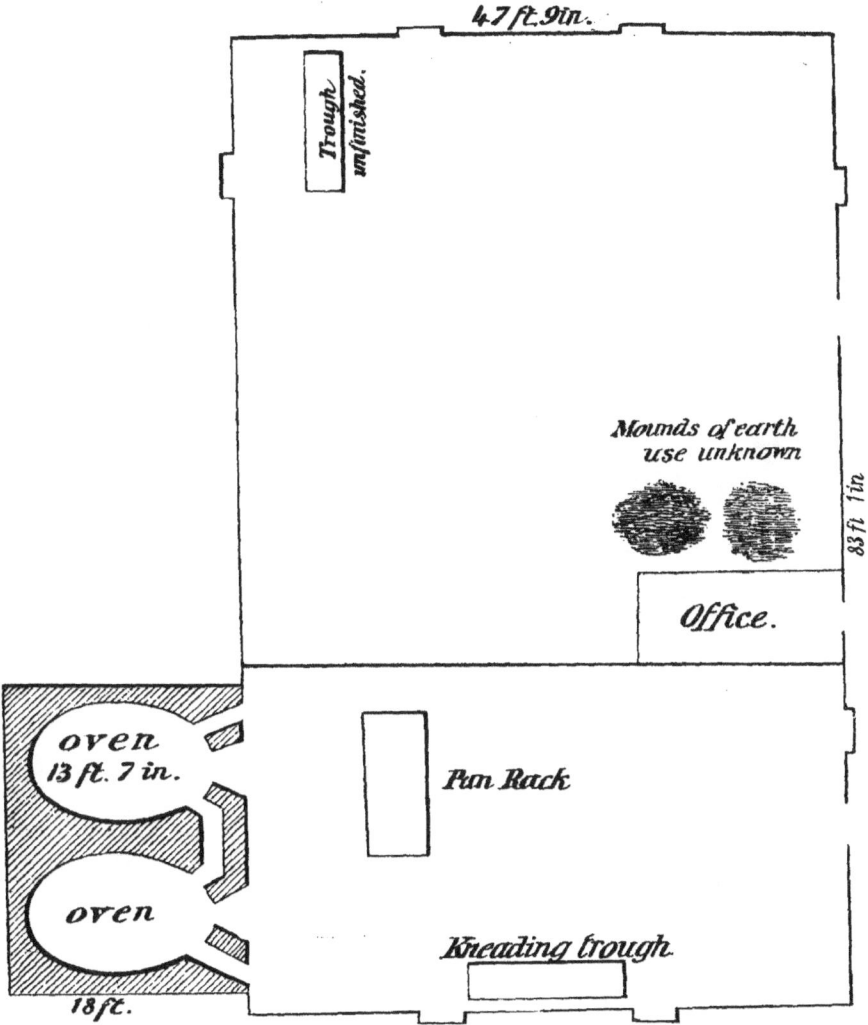

PLAN OF PRISON BAKERY
ANDERSONYILLE
Ga.

pounds to ninety men, but, after the first of July, this was dropped almost entirely from prison rations. Sometimes, instead of Indian meal, we got rice or beans; but each bean had had an occupant in the shape of a grub or worm. Our modes of cooking were entirely primitive. The meal was stirred into water, making a thick dough; then a little meal was sprinkled on the bottom of a plate or half of a canteen, to keep the dough from sticking. The dough was then placed in a plate or canteen, which was set up at an angle of forty-five degrees, to be cooked before a fire. When the front of the cake was "done brown," the plate was fixed upon a split stick, and held over the coals until it was baked or burned upon the bottom. Our meal was sometimes sifted through a split half of a canteen, in which holes had been punched with a sixpenny nail. But even this coarse sieve left us so little of meal for food, it was gradually abandoned as impracticable. In sheer necessity of hunger, we sacrificed quality to quantity.

It was an amusing scene, sometimes, when three or four would group together to concoct a johnny-cake. One split wood with a wedge or a jackknife, another stirred up the meal, while a third got the fire ready. The process of baking brought out the amusing features of the group. One, on his hands and knees, acted as a pair of bellows, blowing up the fire; another held, extended on a split stick, the johnny-cake, varying its position to suit the blaze or coals; while a third split sticks, and fed the fire. In this manner, at certain hours of the day, could be seen groups of men all over the stockade, with anxiety painted on their features, in pitch-pine smoke; the fireman, on his hands and knees, blowing until red in the face, tears running down, making white furrows on his smoke-begrimed features; sweating, puffing, blowing, coughing, crying, and choking with smoke, especially when, as was often the case, an unlucky gust of wind blew the smoke down the fireman's throat.

I remember, at this time, the history of one day's exertion in trying to get some food ready for my hungry stomach, which is so illustrative of the difficulty generally experienced, that I will relate it. I opened the programme one morning by getting ready to cook "mush." The wood consisted of some roots which I had "extracted" from the ground the day previous, and consequently was not very dry; so, when I was stirring the meal the fire would go out, and while I was blowing the fire the tin pail would tip over. I worked three or four hours in this way without success, when I abandoned the task on account of a rain coming up, putting the wood in my pockets and hat to keep it dry. In the afternoon it cleared away, when a comrade and myself, impelled to the same purpose by a common hunger, went to work jointly for our mush. But after nearly blowing the breath out of our bodies, and getting the fire fairly under way, the wood gave out, or, more properly,

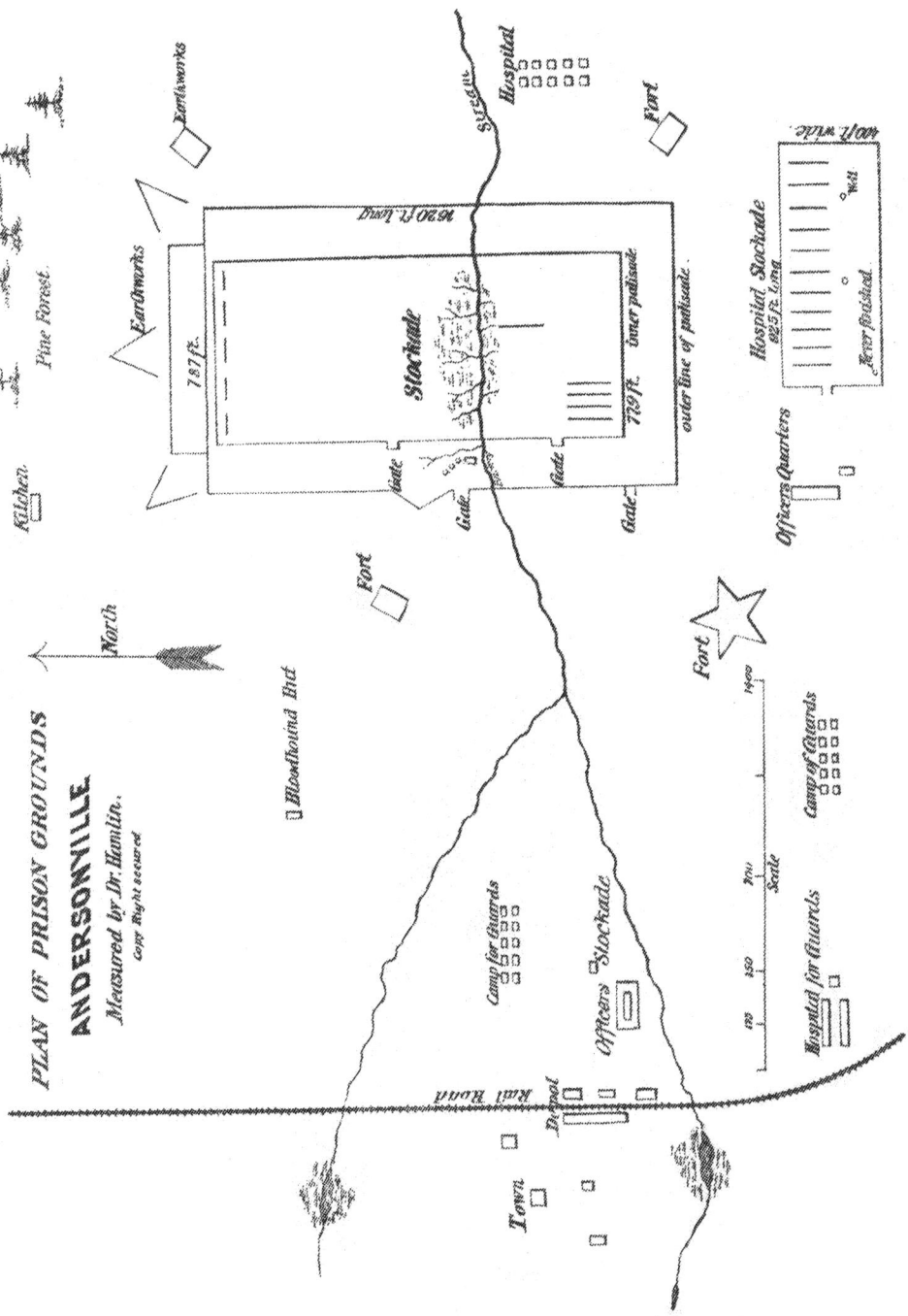

PLAN OF PRISON GROUNDS

ANDERSONVILLE

Measured by Dr. Hamlin.
Copyright secured

North

Grave Yard

Kitchen.

Pine Forest.

Earthworks

Earthworks

787 ft.

1620 ft. Long

Stockade

inner palisade

719 ft.

outer line of palisade.

Gate

Gate

Gate

Stream

Hospital

Fort

Fort

Bloodhound Hut

Fort

Officers Quarters

Hospital Stockade
1275 ft. long

Fence Prostrated.

Well

400 ft. wide.

Rail Road

Depot

Town

Officers Stockade

Camp for Guards

Camp of Guards

Hospital for Guards

Scale

100   200   300   400

50   150

was burned out. And, while we were in pursuit of more to finish our "scald" (for, with our most sanguine hopes, we did not expect anything more than merely to scald the meal), some one passing along stumbled, and upset the ingredients of our mush, and We arrived on the spot just in season to save the pail from the hands of ruthless "flankers" — another term for thieves used among us. Ruefully we looked at the composition on the ground, and then at each other's faces, and went to bed that night sadder and hungrier than We got up, without breakfast, dinner, or supper.

The next morning, in sheer desperation through hunger, to which we had not got so thoroughly accustomed as we subsequently did, we sold some article of clothing for a johnny-cake about the size of the top of my hat, and ate it with comic voracity; and I confess, with all my hunger, I could not but laugh, the whole group was so exceedingly comical and ludicrous. One of our number, never too fat, in about a month after our capture had become a picturesque combination of skin and bones, pitch-pine smoke, and dingy blue, surmounted by an old hat, through a hole in the top of which his hair projected like an Indian plume. As he eagerly, but critically, broke piece after piece for mouthfuls, and, as he termed the process of eating, demolished it, his critical eye detected a substance foreign to johnny-cake, which, upon nearer examination, proved to be an overgrown louse, which had tragically met his fate in Indian meal. The reader will

query, Did this spoil your appetite? I assure such
"not a bit;" for we ate it down to the crumbs, and
hungrily looked into each other's face as though some
one was to blame that there was no more.

Cooking our bacon was generally performed by fix-
ing it upon a sharp stick, and holding it over a fire;
by those who were lucky enough to possess the implements, or utensils, by frying over a fire; but in a great
majority of cases was eaten raw, which was also the
popular way of eating fresh meat, when we got it, as
it was considered a cure and preventive for scurvy.
But the custom, I believe, to be more owing to the
scarcity of wood, than from any sanitary provision or
forethought of ours. What was prompted by necessity
we made a virtue of, by seeing some good in every
extreme into which we were forced by circumstances.
I, for one, was always too hungry to wait for it to be
cooked, especially when I had to build a fire and find
wood.

A favorite dish was prepared, by taking a pint of
Indian meal, mixing it in water, and the dough thus
made was formed into dumplings about the size of a
hen's egg. These were boiled with bits of bacon, about
as big as marbles, until they floated upon the top of the
soup. Thus made, the dumplings were taken out, cut
open, and the soup poured on, giving us a dish which
was a great luxury, although under other circumstances we would not have insulted our palates with
such a concoction. Sometimes we made coffee of

burned bits of bread, by boiling them in a tin cup, which was greedily drank, without sweetening or milk. This was our introduction into the living death of Andersonville, which, in spite of its comic side, had not one gleam of comfort to illuminate the misery of bondage. Sad as was the introduction during our first month's imprisonment, it afterwards became inexpressibly worse.

About this time, I became acquainted with a soldier who had been in the Confederate prison at Cahawba. He had then been a prisoner a year, and was worn down to a mere shadow, by his restless spirit and want of nourishing food. He was pointed out to me repeatedly as one who had escaped several times, and had been recaptured by bloodhounds. He introduced himself one day in a very characteristic manner. Coming along, he observed us eating, saying, "How are ye?" sat down, and looking first at one of our party and then at another, to see how far it would do to go, he gradually helped himself to johnny-cake and molasses, which we happened to have as a luxury. With great coolness he gave a relishing smack to his lips, as he used up the last of the molasses on the last piece of johnny-cake, and said, "Those 'lasses are good." He was a Kentuckian, and naturally a good deal of a fellow. Nature, at least, had stocked him well with shrewdness, impudence, and daring, — qualities not to be despised in such a place. Through him I became initiated into all the mysteries of tunnelling, and other modes of egress from prison. I commenced my first tunnel with him, and was conversant with all his plans.

One day this man said to me, that about all the way he knew of getting out the prison was to "die." They carry the dead out, but it is hard work for the living to get a sight. I did not exactly understand Billy, for I knew he had too much of the game character to give up in despondency; and as for dying, I had no idea he thought seriously of such a thing as long as there was a kick in him. You can imagine my surprise, to see two comrades seriously lugging poor Billy out on a stretcher one morning, with his toes tied together, — which was all the ceremony we had in prison in laying out the dead. I took a last look at poor Billy as he lay upon the stretcher, and said, "Poor fellow! I little thought he would go in this way." "He makes a very natural corpse," said one of the boys; and sure enough, he looked the same almost as in life, only his face was a little dirtier if anything. The next day I was startled to hear, that after Billy was laid in the dead-house, he took to his legs as lively as ever, and walked away. He never was heard of in my prison experiences again, and probably escaped to Sherman's army, which was then at Marietta.

Tunnelling was performed in much the manner woodchucks dig their holes. First, a hole was sunk about five feet in the ground, then were commenced parallels, the hole sufficiently large to admit one. The labor was performed during the night, and the dirt

"He was shot through the lungs, and laid near the dead line writhing in torments during most of the forenoon." — Page 85.

carried off in haversacks and bags, and scattered around
camp. The mouth of the tunnel was covered up during
the day to prevent discovery, which was more liable
to happen than otherwise, from the fact that great
inducements of extra rations were offered to spies. I
was engaged in digging, during the first month, on no
less than four, which were all discovered before being
finished.

One of the great instruments of death in the prison
was the dead line. This line consisted of a row of
stakes driven into the ground, with narrow board strips
nailed down upon the top, at the distance of about
fifteen feet from the stockade, on the interior side.
This line was closely guarded by sentinels, stationed
above on the stockade, and any person who approached
it, as many unconsciously did, and as in the crowd was
often unavoidable, was shot dead, with no warning whatever to admonish him that death was near. An instance
of this kind came to my notice the second day I was in
prison. A poor one-legged cripple placed one hand on
the dead line to support him while he got his crutch,
which had fallen from his feeble grasp to the ground.
In this position he was shot through the lungs, and laid
near the dead line writhing in torments during most of
the forenoon, until at last death came to his relief. None
dared approach him to relieve his sufferings through
fear of the same fate. The guard loaded his musket
after he had performed this dastardly act, and grinning
with satisfaction, viewed the body of the dying, mur-

dered man, for nearly an hour, with apparent pleasure, occasionally raising the gun to threaten any one who, from curiosity or pity, dared to approach the poor fellow. In a similar manner men were continually shot upon the smallest pretext, and that it was nothing but a pretext was apparent from the fact that one man approaching the dead line could have in no manner harmed the cumbersome stockade, even had he been inclined so to do, and a hundred men could not, with their united strength, have forced it. Frequently the guard fired indiscriminately into a crowd. On one occasion I saw a man wounded and another killed; one was lying under his blanket asleep, the other standing some distance from the dead line.

A key to this murderous, inhuman practice was to be found in a standing order at rebel headquarters, that "any sentinel killing a Federal soldier, approaching the dead line, shall receive a furlough of sixty days; while for wounding one he shall receive a furlough for thirty days." This order not only offered a permium for murder, but encouraged the guard in other outrages, against which we had no defence whatever. Men innocent of any intention to infringe the prison regulations were not safe when lying in the quiet of their blankets at night. Four or five instances happened within range of my observation at Andersonville, and there were dozens of cases which I heard of, succeeding the report of guns in the stockade. Scarcely a night or day passed but the sharp crack of a rifle told of the murder of another defenceless victim. Men becoming tired of life committed suicide in this manner, They had but to get under the dead line, or lean upon it, and their fate was sealed in death.

An incident of this kind came to my knowledge in July. A New York soldier had tried once or twice to escape, by which means he had lost his cooking utensils and his blanket, and was obliged to endure the rain and heat without protection, and to borrow, beg, or steal cooking implements, eat his food raw, or starve. Lying in the rain often at night, followed by the tropical heat of day, was torture which goaded him to desperation. He announced his determination to die, and getting over the dead line, was shot through the heart. One cannot be a constant witness to such scenes without being affected by them. I doubt not he saved himself by such a course much trouble and pain, anticipating by only a few weeks a death he must eventually have suffered.

Under the tortures of imprisonment, where its continuation is certain, is a man blamable in hastening or anticipating death by a few weeks or days, thus saving himself from the lingering tortures of death by exposure and starvation? God in his mercy only can answer it, and will at the final judgment day, when the prison victim and his unrelenting foe shall be arraigned before Him who noteth even the fall of a sparrow!

There being no sanitary regulations in camp, and no proper medical provisions, sickness and death were inevitable accompaniments of our imprisonment. Thousands of prisoners were so affected with scurvy, caused by want of vegetables, or of nutritious food, that their limbs were ready to drop from their bodies. I have often seen maggots scooped out by the handful from the sores of those thus afflicted. Upon the first attack of scurvy, an enervating weakness creeps over the body, which is followed by a disinclination to exercise; the legs become swollen and weak, and often the cords contract, drawing the leg out of shape; the color of the skin becomes black and blue, and retains pressure from the fingers as putty will. This is frequently followed by dropsical symptoms, swelling of the feet and legs. If the patient was subject to trouble with the throat, the scurvy would attack that part; if afflicted with or pre-disposed to any disease, there it would seize and develop, or aggravate it in the system.

In cases of this character, persons ignorant of their condition would often be trying to do something for a disease which in reality should have been treated as scurvy, and could have been prevented or cured by proper food. A common form of scurvy was in the mouth: this was the most horrible in its final results of any that afflicted the prisoners. The teeth would become loosened, the gums rot away, and swallowing the saliva thus tainted with the poison of scurvy, would produce scurvy in the bowels, which often took the form of chronic diarrhœa. Sometimes bloating of the bowels would take place, followed by terrible suffering

VIEW OF THE PALISADE AND DEAD LINE

"He announced his determination to die, and getting over the dead line. was shot through the heart." Page 87.

and death. Often scurvy sores would gangrene, and maggots would crawl from the flesh, and pass from the bowels, and, under the tortures of a slow death, the body would become, in part, putrid before death. In this manner died Corporal Gibson, an old, esteemed, and pious man of my company. Two or three others also died in much the same manner. Corporal Gibson especially had his reason and senses clear, after most of his body was in a putrid condition. In other cases, persons wasted to mere skeletons by starvation and disease, unable to help themselves, died by inches the most terrible of deaths, with not a particle of medicine, or a hand lifted by those in charge of the prison for their relief.

There was a portion of the camp, forming a kind of a swamp, on the north side of the branch, as it was termed by the rebels, which ran through the centre of the camp. This swamp was used as a sink by the prisoners, and was putrid with the corruption of human offal. The stench polluted and pervaded the whole atmosphere of the prison. When the prisoner was fortunate enough to get a breath of air outside the prison, it seemed like a new development of creation, so different was it from the poisonous vapors inhaled from this cesspool with which the prison air was reeking. During the day the sun drank up the most noxious of these vapors, but in the night the terrible miasma and stench pervaded the atmosphere almost to suffocation.

In the month of July, it became apparent that, unless something was done to abate the nuisance, the whole camp would be swept away by some terrible disease engendered by it. Impelled by apprehensions for the safety of themselves and the troops stationed around the camp, on guard, the rebel authorities of the prison furnished the necessary implements to the prisoners, who filled about half an acre of the worst of the sink with earth excavated from the hill-side. The space thus filled in was occupied, almost to the very verge of the sink, by the prisoners, gathered here for the conveniences of the place, and for obtaining water. Men, reduced by starvation and disease, would drag themselves to this locality, to lie down and die uncared for, almost unnoticed. I have counted fifteen dead bodies in one morning near this sink, where they had died during the night. I have seen forty or fifty men in a dying condition, who, with their little remaining strength, had dragged themselves to this place for its conveniences, and, unable to get back again, were exposed in the sun, often without food, until death relieved them of the burden of life. Frequently, on passing them, some were found reduced to idiocy, and many, unable to articulate, would stretch forth their wasted hands in piteous supplication for food or water, or point to their lips, their glazed eyes presenting that staring fixedness which immediately precedes death. On some the flesh would be dropping from their bones with scurvy; in others little of humanity remained in

VIEW OF THE INTERIOR OF THE PRISON,

With the quagmire, and crowds of huts and men beyond. Taken from rebel photographs.
"The space thus filled in was occupied, almost to the very verge of the sink, by the prisoners,
gathered here for the conveniences of the place, and for obtaining water." Page 90.

their wasted forms but skin drawn over bones. Nothing
ever before seen in a civilized country could give one
an adequate idea of the physical condition to which
disease, starvation, and exposure reduced these men.
It was only strange that men should retain life so long
as to be reduced to the skeleton condition of the great
mass who died in prison.

In June prisoners from Sherman's and Grant's armies
came in great numbers. After the battles of Spottsyl-
vania and of the Wilderness, over two thousand prisoners came in at one time. Most of those who came
through Richmond had their blankets taken from them,
and in many instances were left with only shirt, hat,
and pantaloons. These lay in groups, often wet through
with rain at night, and exposed to the heat of a tropical
sun daily. With such night and day were alike to be
dreaded. The terrible rains of June were prolific of
disease and death. It rained almost incessantly twenty-
one days during the month. Those of the prisoners
who were not by nature possessed of unyielding courage
and iron constitutions broke down under the terrible
inflictions of hunger, exposure, and mental torments.
The scenes that met the eye on every side were not
calculated to give hopeful tendencies to the mind distressed by physical and mental torture. Men died at
so rapid a rate that one often found himself wondering
and speculating when and how his turn would come;
for that it must come, and that soon, seemed inevitable
under the circumstances. No words can express the

terrible sufferings which hunger and exposure inflicted upon the luckless inmates of Andersonville Prison. During one week there were said to have died thirteen hundred and eighty men. Death lost all its sanctity by reason of its frequent occurrence, and because of the inability of suffering men, liable at any moment to experience a like fate, to help others. To show funeral honors to the dead, or soothe the last moments of the dying, was impracticable, if not impossible. Those whose natures had not raised them superior to fate lost their good humor and gayety, and pined away in hopeless repinings; — dreaming of home, and giving way to melancholy forebodings, which could be productive of no good result. Others, of an opposite mould of character, whom nothing could daunt, still retained something of their natural gayety and humor amid all the wretchedness by which they were surrounded. To such trials were but so many incentives to surmount and overcome difficulties. If the prisoner gave way to languor and weakness, and failed to take necessary exercise, — if he did not dispose his mind to take cheerful views of his condition, and look upon the bright side of that which seemed to be but darkness and misery, — he might as well give up hope of life at once.

In prison one must adapt himself to the circumstances which threaten to crowd him out of existence, or die. He must look upon filth, dirt, innumerable vermin, and even death, with complacency, and not distress himself about that which is unavoidable, while he must

never cease battling against them. No matter if he did
know that his cooked beans had been shovelled from a
cart in which, a few hours before, the dead had been
piled up and taken away to the grave, — he couldn't
afford to get disgusted and reject the sustenance on that
account. He must eat the food and adapt himself and
his appetite to relish the dose, which is not so difficult
to a man when very hungry. There must be a general
closing up of the avenues of delicacy and sensibility,
and a corresponding opening of all that is cheerful and
truly hopeful in one's nature. I do not mean that hope
which buoys one up by unreasonable anticipations, and
which, when disappointed, becomes despair. It should
be a general, cheerful hopefulness, that builds no air-
castles of exchange, or speedy liberation by raids, but
sees hope even in the circumstances of misery, and
draws comfort and consolation from the thought that
things can be no worse. There must be a kind of
mental "don't-care" sort of recklessness of the future,
combined with doing what you can to comfort yourself
now, which is, after all, the preservation of a soldier in
thousands of cases. There is a kind of armor of indif-
ference which yields to circumstances, but cannot be pen-
trated by them. As soon as one gives way to melancholy despondency, as thousands naturally do under
such circumstances, the lease of such a man's life in
prison is not worth purchasing.

The occasion of so much sickness and death was found
in the causes enumerated, with the insufficiency in quan-

tity of food, its unsuitableness in quality, and the absence of all vegetables. The heating nature of Indian meal — the cob ground with the corn, also had its effects in producing an unhealthy condition of things. During July one could scarcely step without seeing some poor victim in his last agonies. The piteous tones of entreaty, the famine-stricken look of these men, their bones in some cases worn through their flesh, were enough to excite pity and compassion in hearts of stone.

Death by starvation and exposure was preceded by a mild kind of insanity or idiocy, when the mind felt not the misery of the body, and was unable to provide for its wants. We gave water and words of sympathy to wretches who were but a few degrees worse than ourselves. But there was danger when we gave food that we might starve ourselves, while that which we furnished to another would not preserve his life. If you allowed every sick man to drink from your cup, you were liable to bring upon yourself the terrible infliction of scurvy in the mouth, which was as much to be dreaded as death. Even a gratification of your keenest human sympathies thus became the potent cause of self-destruction and suffering to him who indulged in so great a luxury.

The terrible truth was, that in prison one could not attempt to relieve the misery of others more miserable than himself, without placing himself in greater peril. Was it wonderful that the cries of dying, famished men were unheeded by those who were battling with fate to preserve their own lives? If there were some who turned ears of deafness to distressed tones of entreaty, who forgot the example of the "good Samaritan" in their own distress, the fault and sin (if sin or fault there was under such torture and condition) were surely not upon their own heads, but upon the heads of those who had crowded into our daily existence so much of misery as to leave no room for the gratification of kindly sympathies, and had drowned out the finer sensibilities in the struggles with despair and death for self-preservation. Subjects of pity rather than of blame, they were not allowed the luxury of pity and sympathetic action. Yet many there were, surrounded by and suffering acutest torture, who moved like angels of mercy among suffering companions stricken by famine and disease.

It is a terrible thing to feel one's self starving; to brace every nerve against the approach of death, and summon to the aid of the body all its selfishness: yet men, in spite of the necessity of so doing in order to preserve life, assisted and soothed one another in hours of sickness, distress, and melancholy; and such had a reward in the consciousness of duty performed, of unselfish devotion, surrounded by famine and death — the bitter cup of misery pressed to their own lips, yet having still a care for others, under circumstances of trial when the thoughts of most men were turned upon themselves, and oblivious to others' woes amid their own misery.

Most prisoners, being only soldiers temporarily, have at variance two distinct elements of feeling, one springing from their habitual and the other from their temporary mode of life; one springing from peaceful associations, with the seclusions of home, or the luxury of the business activity of city life; the other from the more recent influences of the camp and battle-field. These incongruous elements are in constant antagonism. One moment it is the soldier, improvident and careless of the future, reckless of the present, laughing at discomforts and privations, and merry in the midst of intense suffering. Then it is the quiet citizen, complaining of misfortune, sighing for home and its dear ones, dreaming of seclusion and peace, yielding to despondency and sorrow. And this is perhaps fortunate, for at least there is less danger that the prisoner shall become improvident with the one element, or a miser dead to every feeling with the other. Most prisoners, in such misfortunes, are apt to indulge in a Bind of post-mortem examination of their previous life, to dissect that portion of their past history which is seldom anatomized without arriving at the conclusion that present misfortunes are nearly in all cases due to some radical error in their own lives. Misfortunes render some men reckless; others, on the contrary, become cautious through failure and wise through misfortune. And such, retracing in their leisure hours their paths of life, question the sorrowful spectres of perished hopes which haunt the crowded graveyards of the past. They draw

from the past nought but cold realities; they cut into
the body of their blighted life and hopes, and seek to
learn of what disease it died. This is rational; it is
instructive and courageous; but, unfortunately, it is not
pleasant. Better to light anew the corpse of the dead
past, to inwreathe the torn hair with blossoms, to tinge
the livid cheek with the purple flush of health, to en-
kindle the glazed eyes with eloquent lustre, to breathe
into the pallid lips the wonted echoes of a familiar voice,
which may discourse to us pleasantly of long departed
joys and of old happy hours. There is a piteous consolation in it, like the mournful solace of those who,
having lost some being near and dear to them, plant
the dear grave with flowers. It is this inward self which
is all his own that the prison leisure leads the speculative
captive daily to analyze. After a voyage of memory
over the ocean of the past, he returns to the sad present
with a better heart, and endeavors, from the newly-
kindled stars which have arisen above the vapory horizon of his prison life, to cast the horoscope of a wiser
future.

I have spoken of a mild kind of insanity which precedes death caused by starvation and brooding melancholy, in which the mind wanders from real to imaginary
scenes. Private Peter Dunn, of my company, was an
instance of this kind. At an early date of his imprisonment he lost his tin cup, which was with him, as
commonly was the case throughout the prison, the only
cooking implement. His blanket was also lost, and he

7

was left destitute of all shelter and of every comfort except that which was furnished him by companions who were sufferers in common with himself, and not overstocked with necessaries and comforts. Gradually, as he wasted away, his mind wandered, and in imagination he was the possessor of those luxuries which the imagination will fasten upon when the body feels the keenest pangs of hunger. With simple sincerity he would frequently speak of some luxury which he imagined he had partaken of. Suddenly a gleam of intelligence would overspread his face; he would speak of the prison, and say, "This is a dreadful place for the boys — isn't it? I don't enjoy myself when I have anything good to eat, there are so many around me who look hungry." And then, gazing in my face, said, in the saddest modulations I ever heard in human voice, "You look hungry too, Sarg." And then, sinking his voice to a whisper, added, "O dear! I'm hungry myself, a good deal." Poor, poor Peter! he soon died a lingering death from the effects of starvation and exposure. In the lucid moments that preceded death, he said, as I stood over his poor famine-pinched form, "I'm dreadful cold and hungry, Sarg." He again relapsed into a state of wandering, with the names of "Mary" and "Mother" on his lips; and the last faint action of life, when he could no longer speak, was to point his finger to his pallid, gasping lips, in mute entreaty for food!

Charles E. Bent was a drummer in my company, a

"When I was out, just now," he said, "my sister came and took it, and gave it to an angel." — PAGE 29.

fine lad, with as big a heart in his small body as ever throbbed in the breast of a man. He was a silent boy, who rarely manifested any outward emotion, and spoke but seldom, but, as his comrades expressed it, "kept up a thinking." I observed nothing unusual in his conduct or manner to denote insanity, until one afternoon, about sundown, one of his comrades noticed the absence of a ring commonly worn upon his hand, and inquired where it was. "When I was out just now," he said," my sister came and took it, and gave it to an angel." The next day, as the sun went down, its last rays lingered, it seemed to me, caressingly upon the dear, pallid face of the dead boy. His pain and sorrow were ended, and heartless men no longer could torture him with hunger and cruelty.

But while the minds of many became unsettled with idiocy or insanity, there were other instances where a vivid consciousness and clearness of mental vision were retained to the very verge of that country "from whence no traveller returns."

C. H. A. Moore was a drummer in my company — the only son of a widowed mother: all the wealth of maternal affection had been fondly lavished upon him. In him all her hopes were centred, and it was with great reluctance that she finally agreed to his enlistment. A soldier's life, to one thus reared, is at best hard; but to plunge one so young and unaccustomed even to the rudiments of hardships into the unparalleled miseries of Andersonville, seemed cruelty inexpressible. He was just convalescent from a typhoid fever when captured. In prison he gradually wasted away until he died. The day previous to his death I saw and conversed with him, tried to encourage and cheer him; but a look of premature age had settled over his youthful face, which bore but little semblance to the bright, expressive look he wore when he enlisted. He was perfectly sane, and conversed with uncommon clearness and method, as though his mind had been suddenly developed by intense suffering. His face bore an unchanged, listless expression, which, I have noticed in prison, betokened the loss of hope. He spoke of home and of his mother, but his words were all in the same key, monotonous and weary, with a stony, unmoved expression of countenance. On a face so young I never saw such indescribable hopelessness. It was despair petrified! And when I think of it, even now, it pierces me to the heart. His was a lingering death by starvation and exposure, with no relief from unmitigated misery. It seems to me that God's everlasting curse must surely rest upon those who thus knowingly allowed hundreds of innocent young lives to be blotted out of existence by cruelties unheard of before in the annals of civilized warfare. It seems to me that in the future the South, who abetted so great a crime against civilization and humanity, against Christianity and even decency, must stand condemned by the public opinion of the world, until she has done "works meet for repentance."

CHAPTER V.

Prison Vocabulary. — Punishment of Larcenies. — Scenes of Violence. — Destitution provocative of Troubles. — Short Rations. — More Fights. — Advantages of Strength of Body and Mind. — New Standards of Merit. — Ingenuity profitable. — Development of Faculties. — New Trades and Kinds of Business. — Cures for all Ills and Diseases. — Trading to get more Food. — Burden of Bad Habits. — Experience in Trade. — Stock in Trade eaten up by Partner. — A Shrewd Dealer destroys the Business. — Trading Exchange. — Excitement in the Issue of Rations. — A Starving Man killed. — His Murderer let off easy through Bribery. — Considerable Money in the Camp. — Tricks upon Rebel Traders in Prison. — Counterfeit or Altered Money disposed of.

THE prison had a vocabulary of words peculiarly its own, which, if not new in themselves, were novel in their significance. A thief, for instance, was termed a "flanker," or a "half shave," the latter term originating in a wholesome custom, which prevailed in prison, of shaving the heads of those who were caught pilfering, on one side, leaving the other untouched. Thus they would remain sufficiently long to attract universal attention and derision. The shaving was a less punishment in itself than its final consequences, for a fellow with half-shaven crown was lucky if he escaped a beating or a ducking every hour of the day. Where a thief had the boldness to steal in open daylight, and by a dash, grab and run, to get off with his booty, he was termed a "raider," which was considered one grade above the sneaking "flanker." The articles stolen were usually cooking utensils, or blankets, for the want of which, many a man died. Either epithet, "flanker" or "raider," hurled at a fast-retreating culprit, would insure a general turnout in the vicinity, to stop the offender. If the thief had shrewdness, and was not too closely pursued, he often assumed a careless appearance, mingled unperceived with his pursuers, and joined in the "hue and cry." Woe to him who attracted suspicion by undue haste when such a cry was raised; for although his errand might be one of necessity or mercy, he was sure to be hurt before it was ascertained that he was not the offending person, and his only consolation was in the fact of his innocence, or the thought that his head, if some sorer, was wiser than before.

Scenes of violence were continually enacted in the prison. Murders that thrilled the blood with horror were at one time of frequent occurrence, — of which we shall speak more particularly in coming pages, — perpetrated by bands of desperadoes who jumped Uncle Sam's bounties before they were retained in the firm grasp of military vigilance, and, when fairly caught, rather than fight were taken prisoners voluntarily. No's an hour of the day passed without some terrible fight — often over trivial matters — taking place in the stock ade. The reasons which provoked fights were not often plain; but one fact was ever apparent, viz., that hunger and privation did not sweeten sour tempers, or render the common disposition at all lamb-like. A piece of poor corn-bread, picked up in the dirt, a little Indian meal, or a meatless bone, which a dog or pig of New England extraction would turn up his nose at, would provoke violent discussions as to ownership, in which muscle, rather than equity, settled facts. Some of these personal encounters ended in a general fight, where all who were desirous of that kind of recreation took a part. It was quite a curious fact that when rations were scarcest in prison, fights were plentiest. In the absence of food, some took pleasure in beating each other. "I've not had anything to eat to-day, and would like to lick some varmint as has," said Kentucky Joe, a gaunt, half-starved, but never desponding fellow. "I'm your man," said Pat B., and at it they went, till Kentucky was beaten to his satisfaction, and acknowledged that "a 'varmint' who had eaten corn-dodger for breakfast was 'too much' for one 'as hadn't.'" The writer, seeing no fun in a muss, kept out of them, foreseeing misery enough, without a broken head to nurse. The great mass could ill afford to expend strength in such encounters, and it was usually easy to keep out of them without sneaking.

I have often, however, seen men who were weak with disease, and weak to such a degree that they could scarcely stand, engage in pugilistic encounters piteous to contemplate. I call to memory two almost skeleton men, whom I once saw engaged in fighting for the possession of a few pine knots! Bareheaded, in a broiling sun, barefooted, their clothes in tatters, they bit and scratched, and rolled in the dirt together. I left them, their hands clutched in each other's hair, — with barely remaining strength to rally a kick, — gazing into each other's eyes with the leaden, lustreless glare of famine stamped there — a look which I cannot describe, but which some comrade of misery will recognize.

The strong often tyrannized over the weak, and as we see it in all gatherings of men, the strong in physical health and in possessions kept their strength, while the many weak grew weaker and weaker, until they were crowded out of life into the small space grudgingly allowed them for graves. Each man stood or fell on merits different from those which had been valued by friends at home. He found himself measured by different standards of merit from those used in any of his previous walks of life. Rough native force or talent showed itself by ingenious devices for making the most of little. He who could make Indian meal and water into the most palatable form was "looked up to." He who could cook with little wood, and invent from the mud a fireplace in which to save fuel, was a genius! The producer of comforts from the squalid, crude material of life was respected as much as hunger would allow us to respect anything. He it was who got a start in the prison world, and managed to live.

It was desirable on the part of prisoners to follow some trade or occupation which should give to the individual means to purchase the few desirable luxuries which could be obtained of those who came into prison from among the rebels with permission to trade. By this method there were hopes of life, even if existence was misery. Yankee ingenuity was consequently taxed to the utmost to invent "from the rough" some kind of business that would pay — an onion, a potato, or an extra allowance of Indian meal per week. Under the fruitful maxim that "necessity is the mother of invention," it was surprising how trades and business started into life. Had these men been placed in a forest where raw material could readily be got at, I believe they would have produced every "item" of a city's wants, so well were we represented in the trades. The strivings for life were piteous, but often comical in their developments. Some traded their hats and boots, or a slyly-kept watch, for beans or flour, and with this elementary start began "sutlers' business." Another genius developed a process for converting Indian meal into beer, by souring it in water. And "sour beer," as it was termed, speedily became one of the institutions. This beer was vended around the camp by others, who pronounced it a cure for scurvy, colds, fever, gangrene, and all other ills the stockade was heir too, and they were many. You would at one part of the stockade hear a voice loudly proclaiming a cure for scurvy; you approach, and find him vending "sour beer;" — another proclaiming loudly a cure for diarrhœa; he would be selling "sour beer;" and so through a long catalogue of evils would be proclaimed their remedies.

One day I was almost crushed in a crowd who were attracted by a fellow crying aloud, "Stewed beans, with vinegar *on to um!*" The vinegar turned out to be "sour beer." Stuck upon a shingle I observed a sign which read, "Old Brewery; Bier for Sail, by the glass or bucketful, *hole sail,* retail, or no tail at all." I remember one ingenious fellow, who, with a jackknife and file and a few bits of wire, was engaged in getting into ticking order "played-out" watches, that had refused to go unless they were carried; and the ingenuity he displayed in coaxing them to tick was surprising. In one instance the watch tinker mentioned made for a friend of mine an entire watch-spring of whalebone, which set the watch ticking in such a tremendous manner, for a few minutes after being wound up, as to call forth the admiring ejaculation from the Secesh purchaser, "Gosh, how she does go it!" The watch stopped — *"rund* down," as the amazed Johnny afterwards said, "quicker nor a flash." You will readily understand that prisoners cared but little about watches except so far as they were tradable for Indian meal, hog, or hominy.

Another occupation was cooking beans and selling them by the plateful to such hungry ones as could afford to trade for them. Various were the means of "raising the wind" to obtain a supply to carry on the trade. Often some article of clothing, or buttons off the jacket, were traded for them. But a more common method was to trade the buttons or clothing for tobacco, and then trade tobacco for beans; for those addicted to the use of the weed would frequently remark that it was easier to go without a portion of their food, however scanty, than without their tobacco. In prison one thus paid the penalties of bad habits previously formed. One accustomed to the habit of taking a dram of something stimulating each day, died in prison for want of it. Habits, like chickens, "come home to roost," and were often the millstones that sunk their possessors into the hopeless misery which went before death. Thus, when only about half a pint of beans, uncooked, per day were issued, sometimes with a little bacon, men would lay aside a few each day to trade for tobacco.

The modes of selling were various; but the most common way of finding purchasers by those who had but a small capital of a few pints of beans, was to proceed to the principal thoroughfare, — for even here we were compelled to have paths unoccupied by recumbent men and their "traps," through a general understanding, or we should have continually trod on one another. Broadway, as we termed it, was the scene of most of the trading done in camp. The venders, sitting with their legs under them, like tailors, proclaimed loudly the quantity and quality of beans or mush they could sell for a stated price. Some would exultantly state that theirs had pepper and salt "on to

um;" and sometimes vinegar was cried out as one of
the virtues possessed by the vender of beans, and then
there would be a rush to see, if not to eat. Sometimes
I have seen on Broadway from fifty to seventy venders
of beans, who, together with small gamblers with
sweat-boards, on which could be staked five cents, and
hasty-pudding dealers and sour beer sellers, all of whom
sat on the ground, looking anxious, dirty, and hungry
enough to make the hardest part of their task a resist-
ing of the temptation to eat up their stock in trade.
I cannot refrain from narrating my own experience in
that line, it was so characteristic of experience common
to those who engaged in like speculations.

Clifton V. and myself possessed a joint capital of
an old watch, mention of which has been made, and a
surplus of one pair of army shoes, — for I went bare-
foot, disdaining to abridge the freedom of my feet when
it interfered with business. We invested them in beans,
which were, like those usually issued, possessed, previous to our possession, by grubs and worms. The terms
of our copartnership were, that he, "Cliff," was to do
the selling, while I and a companion named Damon
cooked, bargained for wood, and transacted the general
business of the "concern." Accordingly Cliff showed
his anxious face and raised his treble voice shrilly in
the market-place. The first day's sale brought us about
one pint of extra beans. The next day Cliff's hunger
got the better of his judgment and firm resolve to be
prudent, and he ate up near half our stock in trade,

which was vexatious; but I could not reprove him, seeing how cheerful it made him feel, and how sorry he said he really was. Besides, his full stomach gave him rose-colored views of the morrow's trade.

The morrow came, and Cliff made a "ten-strike," selling off all the beans I could cook, and was beside himself at the prospects of our having enough to eat "right straight along." The next morning I invested largely in beans, in all about three quarts, wet measure, and borrowed a kettle that would, cook about half of them, and paid for the convenience in trade. That day proved the ruin of the bean trade. Cliff came back despondently, declaring beans didn't sell; and the mystery was soon solved by the fact that on the south side of the branch they were issuing cooked beans. Whereupon, ascertaining beyond a doubt the truth of this, Cliff and myself sat down and ate one good square meal, did the same at supper time, finished them for breakfast next morning, and lived at least one day with full stomachs — a circumstance that seldom happened before or afterwards in our prison experience. Thus ended the bean trade.

After rations were issued, there would be a general meeting of a densely packed crowd, all trying to trade for something more palatable, or for that which they had not got. Some would cry out, "Who will trade cooked beans for raw?" "Who will trade wood for beans?" "Who will trade salt for wood?" while some speculator would trade little bits of tobacco for any kind of rations. The issue of rations was often a moment of fearful excitement. A crowd of five or six thousand, like a hungry pack of wolves, would fill the space before the gateway, all scrambling to get a look at the rations, as though even the sight of food did them good. At one time, during such a scene, one of the detailed men, who acted as a teamster, — and those so employed were always men that were loudest in blaming our government and "old Abe," and were insolent and well fed, — when one of the pack of hungry wretches put his hand out to clutch a falling crumb from the cart, the teamster beat his brains out with one blow of a club. He was tried by our stockade court of justice, (?) and condemned — to cart no more bread; owing, doubtless, to the fact of his having a few greenbacks, made in selling our rations.

Among the occupations of the prison was that of baker. The ovens were made of clay, kneaded and formed into bricks. The foundation was laid with those bricks while they were in a damp condition, being allowed to dry in the sun for two or three days, and then were ready as a basis for the oven. Sand was first carefully heaped upon the centre of the foundation, in shape of the interior of it, when done; over this mould the bricks were laid, and dried until the sand making the mould would bear removal, which was carefully done by the use of sticks, at the opening which was left for a door. A fire was then built inside, after which it was ready for use. There were only a favored few who got wood enough to consummate and carry on such an undertaking. The ovens described baked very good johnny-cake, and sometimes wheat biscuit. It was a convenience to be able to get rations cooked for three or four at halves. Thus our scanty rations often had to be diminished by one half, or eaten raw. There were others who followed the trade of bucket-makers, and very fair wooden buckets were made with no other tools than twine and a jackknife. As all water, with exceptional cases of those who owned wells, had to be brought from the brook, — often quite a distance for weak men to travel in the sun, — these were very desirable. There were several kettle-makers, who found material, somehow, of sheet tin and iron from the top of rail-cars, smuggled into prison by the rebels, who were fond of Yankee greenbacks. These were also a convenience to those who formed a mess, and made a saving of wood by cooking together. These kettles were made with no other implements than a common railroad spike. They were made in the manner government camp-kettles are made, by in-geniously bending the iron together in seams, in this manner rendering them water-tight without solder. Thus Yankee ingenuity developed resources where, at first sight, there seemed nothing but barrenness and misery. I never saw a friction-match in the stockade; I doubt if there were any; yet there were always fires somewhere, — how procured I could never understand, except on the supposition that they never went out.

I have entered thus minutely upon a description of these trades and occupations in prison, from the fact that it explains many apparently conflicting statements made by prisoners. While those thus engaged often got the means of subsistence, they were the exceptions of one to a thousand of the great mass of prisoners, who were daily perishing for want of food and from exposure. There was quite a sum of money circulating in camp, in the aggregate; but eventually it got into the hands of the Secesh, who were rabid for the possession of greenbacks. The rebels were constantly coming into the prison to trade, having first obtained permission of Wirz, the commandant of the "interior of the prison," as he was termed. They were fond of buying Yankee boots, watches, and buttons. All superfluous things, such as good caps, boots, &c., were freely traded in exchange for anything eatable, or for wood. One fact was quite observable — that when the Johnnies came in to trade the second time, they were sharper than they were at their first visit. The process of cutting their teeth was rather gradual; but after a while they would become a match at driving a sharp bargain with the sharpest kind of "Yanks," and prided themselves on what they termed Yankee tricks. Buttons were in great demand by them, especially New York and staff buttons, for which large prices were paid, and eagerly traded for.

On one occasion a Johnny came in to trade, who was evidently as unsophisticated and green as the vegetables he had for sale. He traded in the first place for a pair of army shoes, laid them down beside him, and while busy seeing to his "fixings," one of the boys passed the shoes around to a companion, who straightway appeared in front, and before the Johnny had time to think of anything else, challenged his attention for a trade. A trade was agreed upon, and the price paid, before the Johnny found out that though progressing in trade, he had but one pair of shoes. So, for safety of these precious decorations, he picked them up, and holding them in his arms, indignantly declared, "Durned if I can trade with yourn Yanks in that sort o' way, no how." We were, according to his exposition of the matter, "rather considerable right smart at picking up traps what wan't thar own." He was thus entertaining the boys with these original views, when one of our fellows, just to clinch what had been so aptly stated by the chivalrous representative, stepped up behind him and cut off four staff buttons, which adorned the rear of a long, swallow-tailed, butternut-colored, short-waisted coat. After executing this rear movement, he appeared in the crowd at the front, and offered them for sale. The Johnny took the bait, and traded his last vegetables for his own buttons, and started off highly pleased; and so were the boys. On the way out of prison our Secesh friend met a comrade, whose attention he called to the buttons, "like *u m* he had on the tail" of his coat, whereupon his comrade looked behind, and informed him that "thar was not a durned button thar," when our trading Johnny loudly declared, with a rich sprinkling of oaths, that "these yere durned Yanks had orter have their ears buttoned back and be swallowed."

An Ohio boy at one time set himself up in the provision business by altering a greenback of one dollar into one hundred. We considered it fair to take every advantage of them we could contrive, and it amused us to hear them gravely charge us with want of honesty. Says one of them one day to me, "I've hearn that yourn Yanks, down thar whar you live, make wooden pumpkin seeds, and I'll be dod rot if I don't believe I got some of um and planted, a year afore this war, for not a durned one cum'd up 'cept what the pesky hins scratched up."

CHAPTER VI.

Rations decreased and worse in Quality. — Crowded Condition of the Prison. — Heavy Rains and Increased Sickness. — Much Filth and Misery. — Hunger a Demoralizer. — Plots exposed for Extra Rations. — Difficulties of Tunnelling. — A Breath of Outside Air and New Life. — An Escape under Pretext of getting Wood. — Captured by Bloodhounds after a Short Flight. — Somethinglearned by the Adventure. — A Successful Escape believed to be possible. — Preparations for one. — Maps and Plans made. — A New Tunnelling Operation from a Well. — The Tunnel a Success. — The Outer Opening near a Rebel Camp Fire. — Escape of a Party of Twenty. — Division into Smaller Parties. — Plans of Travel. — Bloodhounds on the Path. — The Scent lost in the Water — Various Adventures. — Short of Provisions. — Killing of a Heifer. — Aided by a Negro. — Bloodhounds again. — Temporary Escape. — Fight with the Bloodhounds. — Recapture. — Attempted Strategy. — The Pay for Catching Prisoners. — Reception by Wirz. — Improvement by the Expedition. — Some of the Party never heard from. — Notoriety by the Flight.

THE last of June the rations became less in quantity, and worse in quality; which, together with the fact that the prison, originally intended for but ten thousand, was now crowded with over twenty thousand souls, with the incessant rains of the month, made our situation anything but comfortable. During this month it rained twenty-one days, almost without intermission. This stirred up the refuse garbage and dirt buried by those who were feeble and sick beneath the surface of the ground one or two feet. And whether at night, when we lay down, or in the morning when we sat upon our only bed and seat (the ground), it was miserably wet, dirty, and disagreeable with unpleasant odors. Neither could one get accustomed to, or be able to blunt the senses to, the existence of so much misery.

A great portion of my time from May to the last of June was spent in unavailing attempts at escape by means of tunnels. I was engaged in six, which were discovered by the prison authorities before their completion. Hunger is a great demoralizer, and there were men in prison who for an extra ration would inform the authorities of the prison of plots and plans in which they themselves were actively engaged. There, no doubt, was a struggle with hunger before it obtained mastery over them. Starve a man, and you stunt the growth of all his finer qualities, if you do not crush them out entirely. It changes the expression of his face; his mode of walking becomes loose, undecided; his intelligence is dimmed. Hunger blunts the keenest intelligence, and deadens susceptibility to wrong doing, and mere moral wrongs look small, or seem overbalanced, when placed by the side of food.

If you narrow down a man's purpose to sustaining his body — let his be a continual struggle for a foothold upon life, with uncertainty as to its results — give a man, in fact, crime with bread, on the one hand, and

SPOT.

This dog is a Cuban Bloodhound, and the only survivor of a pack of hounds (some of them, however, being the common Southern hounds) used by Captain Wirz at Andersonville Prison, Georgia, for recapturing escaped Union prisoners. Weight, 159 pounds; height, three feet; length from tip to tip, six feet four and one half inches. Taken from a photograph in possession of the publishers.

"Py tam!" said Captain Wirz to some fellow who had been detected tunnelling, "vy don't some of you Yankees get out? mine togs are getting 'ungry to pite you." Page 117.

on the other, integrity and truth with death — the thousand recollections of the old home, with the arms of a dear mother or wife or children that once encircled his neck — all these recollections bid him live. Consequently, it was difficult to trust men with secrets which might be sold for bread. Again, an impediment existed in digging tunnels in disposing of the earth excavated, in such a manner as not to attract suspicion and consequent detection. These were the potent causes of failure in all our tunnelling plans. The authorities were continually on the lookout for any trace of tunnelling. "Py tam," said Captain Wirz to some fellow who had been detected tunnelling, "vy don't some of you Yankees get out? mine togs are getting 'ungry to pite you."

I had been engaged on so many tunnels which were failures, that I began to regard them as an unprofitable speculation, yielding no prospects of a desirable nature. In this frame of mind, I often queried if there was not some method by which a tunnel might be successfully completed, and began to look round me for the material with which to practically solve so grave a problem. One day, by much "gassing" and manœuvring, I managed to get outside the stockade, under guard, with several of my comrades, to obtain wood. This was the first time since my imprisonment that I had got a breath of the sweet air, trod upon the green grass, scented the sweet fragrance of the wood, and heard the carolling of birds. It was like a new development of creation — some fairy land! The woods and verdant pastures all seemed so different from the terrible pen in which we had been confined for weeks, that nothing ever thrilled me with so strange a vigor and elasticity. I cannot express my feelings more than to say that I never had any previous ideas of how beautiful the grass and woods were until suddenly contrasted with the terrible dearth of that dreadful prison. My blood thrilled quick that morning to every breath that reached me in the cool wood, and every note of rejoicing freedom from the light-hearted birds found responsive echoes in my heart.

The guards were not very strict, seemingly more bent on trading with the prisoners than in preventing them from running away. I commenced picking up sticks, and thus gradually worked my way beyond them. All at once I found myself out of sight of the rebel sentinels, whom I left trading peanuts for buttons with other prisoners. For fear some guard might yet see me, I continued to pick sticks and bits of wood, thinking, if they found me so employed, this would deter them from firing at me, and lull suspicions they naturally might have that I was trying to escape. I looked around, and saw at a distance several of my companions, who had taken the hint, following me, picking sticks in the same manner. We got together, and, without saying a word, by mutual consent, dropped our wood, and ran like mad creatures through the woods for several miles. That night we travelled, with the exception of one hour, which was passed beneath a tree trying to get sleep, in the drenching rain. The next morning we were captured by bloodhounds while clinging to trees, and, more frightened at the dogs than hurt by them, were carried back to the prison, where we reluctantly took up our quarters again, after receiving a damning from the accomplished (?) "commander of the prison."

This adventure was one advantage to me. It showed me the way in which prisoners were hunted. I also learned the manner the guards were picketed on the outside of the prison, and fixed in my mind, by observation, the location of each. I got acquainted with one of the men engaged in hunting prisoners, and remarked to him that he would doubtless get a chance to hunt me again, and I would give him more of a chance "for travel and promotion," as we say to our raw recruits when enlisting them. This I said jocosely, not knowing what advantage it might prove to me in trying the same dodge again. Not long after, several of my friends tried the same method, and one was captured twenty miles from the prison while eating a hearty breakfast at a house where he was trapped. All this satisfied me that, with a few hours' start and with sufficient boldness, an escape was possible, in fact, almost certain, if unpursued by the dogs. Reflecting in this manner, I borrowed a map, which had been smuggled into prison, from which I traced on paper, previously greased in bacon fat to make it transparent and tough, a map of the portion of country needful for my project, with a scale of miles and points of the compass indicated on the same, besides possessing myself of all the information I could gather from numbers of prisoners who had from time to time been recaptured after escaping from prison. They all had their theories of throwing the dogs off the scent. One believed that red pepper rubbed upon the soles of the shoes would cause the dogs to abandon the trail; another had faith that fresh blood would have the same marvellous effect, and so on through the whole range of men who had been near successful in escaping. On one point, however, they all agreed, viz., that no dog could follow a man in the water on a log, or wading, any more than he could through the air, if flying.

While looking around in prison one day, hoping and wishing for something to "turn up" by which I might solve the grave question of escape, I observed an old well, partially dug, from ten to twelve feet from the dead line, which had been finally abandoned after digging over thirty feet without obtaining water. Here seemed an opening for several young men. And I thought the matter over until satisfied that a tunnel might be successfully completed if commenced in this well. One of my company had his "shebang"* near the well; and, as he was a trusty, enterprising fellow, I laid my plans before him, and finally we deter-

*Tent, spot, or blanket, or place of residence.

mined to go into the matter that night. We made a
rope from an old overcoat which he possessed, and tying
it around my waist, I was lowered into the well about
seven feet, not without misgivings that I might travel
the other twenty-five quicker than was good for my
health, by the catastrophe of the rope's breaking, — for
shoddy is doubtful material, — or its slipping from the
weak grasp of my confederate. I scooped with a half
canteen a place big enough to sit in. The next day
my comrade borrowed a rope, for the alleged purpose
of digging the well deeper; and that night we dug in
earnest, and made full eight feet. As daylight came
on, we stopped up the mouth of the tunnel with sticks
and mud, in such a manner that any one looking into
the well would not mistrust that there was a tunnel
being dug therein. Gradually we increased our numbers until we had twenty men at work, all of whom we
knew could be trusted, as they belonged mostly to our
battalion We organized four reliefs, each of which
were to dig in the tunnel two hours during the night.
This made eight hours' good labor, which, considering
that we could not commence very early at night, or
continue very late in the morning, for fear of discovery,
was doing well. The dirt excavated during the night
was tumbled into the well, and the next day we were
engaged, apparently, with the innocent task of digging
for water, — an almost hopeless task, — when in reality
our sole intentions were to keep the well from filling
up with the dirt excavated from the tunnel during the

night, without exciting suspicion. Many a time we
were joked while engaged digging out the well, on
tunnelling "through to China," the perpetrator of
the joke little suspecting that we really were tunnelling.

Finally, after almost incredible labor, for men in our
half-starved condition, we had got a tunnel ready to
open, nearly fifty feet long, extending near thirty feet
beyond the stockade, and dug with the rude implements
we had at hand, consisting principally of half canteens
and tin quart measures, such as every soldier carries
with him to cook his coffee in. By means of our rope,
one by one, on a dark, rainy night, we got into the well
and swung into the tunnel, one ahead of the other, on
our hands and knees, as if to play leap-frog. We then
commenced to open the tunnel, which was rather a delicate job. We were about six feet from the surface
of the ground, and digging up into the open air at
the further extremity of the tunnel was termed "opening the tunnel." This had to be performed with great
care, first, for fear of being discovered, and second,
there was danger of being smothered by the falling
earth. I had heard of one case where a tunnel was
opened in the middle of a picket fire; but it was told
that the tunnellers, nothing daunted, sprang out through
the fire; the guard, believing their patron, the devil,
had come to visit his Confederacy, ran away, leaving the
prisoners to escape. We were not ambitious to "pass
through the fire" in any such way, and were anxious

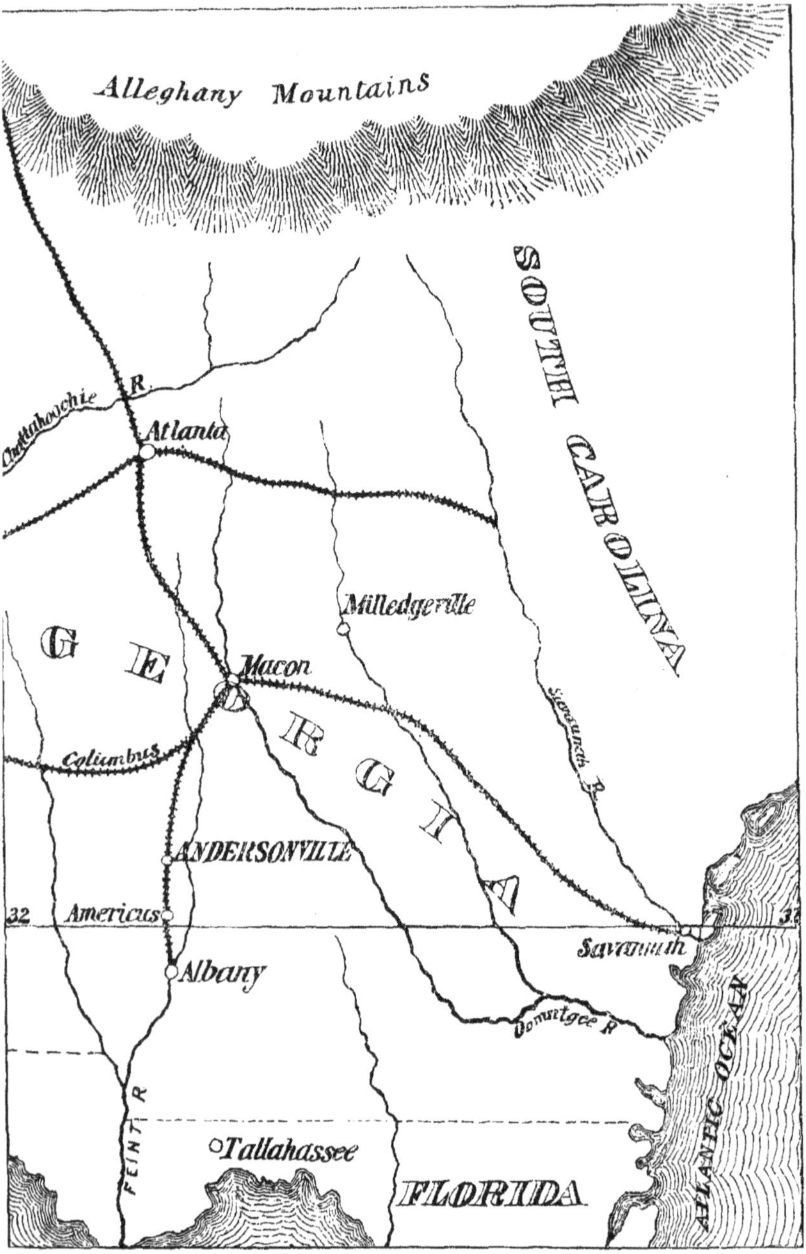
Alleghany Mountains
SOUTH CAROLINA
Chattahoochie R.
Atlanta
Milledgeville
GEORGIA
Macon
Columbus
ANDERSONVILLE
32
Americus
Albany
Savannah
Ocmulgee R
FEINT R
Tallahassee
FLORIDA
ATLANTIC OCEAN

only "to be let alone." We opened our tunnel after two hours or more of careful labor; and I, by virtue of having commenced the tunnel, had the privilege of sticking my head into the outer air first, and was not much pleased to see, sitting crouching in the rain, not a dozen paces from our opening, an outer picket guard, at a large fire. Had he not been so intent on keeping comfortable, he must have seen us, as we, one by one, crawled stealthily into the thicket near at hand. Once, when a twig broke, he made a motion to look up, and I thought we were "gone up;" but he merely stirred his fire, and resumed again his crouching position. As the last man came out, and, at a safe distance, we stood in whispered consultation, the hourly cry of the guard, "Twelve o'clock, and all is well," went round the stockade. We separated into parties of five, each to go in different directions, and, silently grasping each parting comrade's hand, we plunged into the gloomy pine forest, to make one effort for freedom.

I had fully considered for weeks all the difficulties of an escape. I would not venture going down the Flint River to the Gulf on account of the river's being picketed, and, besides, from the fact that there were several large fortified places to pass on such a route. Again, when we arrived at the Gulf, what were the prospects of falling in with any of our forces? After considering all the different points where I might reach our lines, I concluded there were less difficulties in the way of reaching Sherman's forces at Marietta than any other: the circuitous travel of one hundred and twenty miles, under favorable circumstances, would carry us through. The course I had marked out was very simple. If I tried to reach Sherman on the east side of Macon, flanking towards the sea-shore, I had many large places to pass, and such a course would throw us in contact with the many marauding forage parties which would naurally frequent that portion of the country. My plan was to go to the westward of Macon, in a north-westerly course, until the Chattahoochie River was reached, then following due north until the blue hills around Marietta could be seen, trust to fate and Sherman for deliverance.

These plans I had stated briefly to my comrades, who had adopted them, and looked upon me as a Moses, who was to lead them to the promised land. Travelling through the woods during the night, one of my four comrades got separated from the party. The next morning we reached overflowed portions of country, which indicated that we were near the Flint River. While debating as to the best course to pursue, one of my party declared he heard the hounds, which we soon found was an unpleasant fact. Not a moment was to be lost, and wading and swimming with almost frantic exertion soon brought us to the Flint River, the current of which, much swollen by freshets, was running swiftly. Getting upon logs, we floated with the stream for several hours, until we thought it sufficient to baffle the dogs from further pursuit. It was nearly noon, when, wet and exhausted, chilled with being so long in the water, we crawled upon the opposite shore, and were glad to run to get up a little warmth. As we emerged from the water, we found a sensation in the shape of an alligator, who lay just below us, like our floating logs.

That day we travelled incessantly through swamps, and woods, and water, which overflowed all the low portions of country. The only food which we had between us was a "pone" of johnny-cake, which we had starved ourselves to save in the prison. We had a pocket compass, which was intrusted to me, a small quantity of salt, and a butcher-knife, such as was issued to Massachusetts soldiers at Readville. Night came upon us, dark and rainy, and found us still travelling through the dark forest and wet swamps of the country. About twelve o'clock, seeing a bright illumination, which looked like a picket or a camp fire, just to the right, about a quarter of a mile from us, we went upon higher land to get an observation, and sat down on some fallen logs to consult in whispers as to what we had better do, about reconnoitring the light. Just then I was certain I heard something move in the log on which I sat. I sprang to my feet, with my club poised to strike — perhaps it was a bear. I challenged the log with the common expression among soldiers,

"Are you Fed or Reb?" "Yankee," came the reply; and emerging from the log, which for the first time I observed was hollow, came a human form, which, after shaking itself like a water spaniel, asked, in tones strangely familiar, "Well, boys, what next?" "Going to tie your hands, old fellow," said I, "until daylight shows enough of you to see if you look honest." "Well, well!" laughed our mysterious prisoner; "why, don't you know Tonkinson?" and sure enough it was our missing comrade. He had escaped the hounds like ourselves, by floating down the Flint River, and by a singular coincidence had fallen in with us again in the manner related: the hollow log he had selected for his hotel for the night. As he was a sharp fellow, and had a watch, he was quite a valuable addition to our party. When this surprise was well over, we held once more a consultation about the fire which had attracted our attention, before the incident narrated occurred. We concluded the safest and best way was to reconnoitre, in order to ascertain the nature of our neighbors, and see if danger was threatening us. We found it a camp fire near a tent, at which sat a solitary picket with his gun; it was on a cross-road, stationed, I suppose, to intercept prisoners. One of our number got near enough to have knocked him over, had it been desirable. At another time that night we heard voices behind us, but concluded it was some picket tent, of which there were many scattered over that part of the country.

About three o'clock that morning it stopped raining, and we lay down together under a tree, to get such rest as we best could. It was such lodging as we were accustomed to, and the three middle ones had some hopes of keeping warm. At daylight, stiff, and more weary than when we lay down, we resumed our journey through the wood. Our johnny-cake was eaten, and during the day we stopped only to pick a few berries, which grew in the woods. We got nothing else to eat during that day. Next day, about noon, we came upon some cattle browsing in the woods. We killed a little yearling heifer, one holding her by her horns while the other cut her throat with our sheath-knife. We cut the meat such as we desired and divided it among ourselves. The skin we cut into strips, with which, and with some of our clothes, we constructed rude haversacks, in which to carry our meat. We had no matches, or other method of kindling a fire, and of course ate our meat raw, with what little salt we had to season it.

Thus, day by day, we travelled incessantly, keeping away from the white men of the country, but receiving help and direction from the negroes. Our first confidence in negro aid was not brought about by any preconceived ideas, but by accident. We discovered it was possible to trust them, to some extent, from the following incident. One day we came accidentally upon some negroes working in the woods. We ran away quickly, thinking to get out of a bad scrape. One of them called after us, saying, "Don't be afraid, massa white man." Some idea that they might give us something to eat caused me to turn back. I advanced cautiously, and speaking to an old, white-headed negro, I said, "Uncle, I suppose you know what kind of fellows we are." "Well, I reckon," he replied, rolling up the whites of his eyes. "We are hungry, and want something to eat sadly." "Well," said uncle, "you does look mighty kind o' lean. Step into de bushes while I peers round to see if we've got some hoe-cake;" and off he trotted. We kept a good lookout to see that he did not betray us. But he came back with three pones, which he "clared to goodness" was "half they all had for de day." It was "right smart hard times in dem diggins." "Well, uncle," said I, "I suppose you know that Uncle Abe is coming down this way to set you all free when he gets the rebs licked." "Yes, yes," said the venerable negro, "I'se believe the day of jubilee is comin'; but, 'pears to me, it's a long time; looks like it wouldn't come in my time."

Bidding him God speed, we went on our way with lighter hearts at the thought that there were friends in the midst of our enemies. Some of the old negroes we met would shame the chivalry in point of humanity and good shrewd practical sense. One of my comrades who had escaped for three or four days, before this time, told me he met a negro in the woods with a gun and dog, who told him he had lived in the swamps for several years, defying the white man. He offered to take him, provide for, and keep him all winter in his hut. He refused, thinking to be successful in getting into our lines. And I was afterwards informed by some rebel officers that there was a negro who, to escape punishment, had run away from a plantation, and had subsisted in the swamps for a long time without being captured.

We were entirely out of provisions on the eighth day of our escape, and in the morning had halted in some low land in the woods near a clearing to pick raspberries, which grew in abundance. Suddenly one of our number, noted in our travels for his quick hearing, declared the dogs were after us. According to previous agreement, when we were satisfied such was the case, we separated, each running in different directions to give the dogs all the trouble we could, as possibly by this method some might escape. Nearer and nearer the dogs came. I jumped into a little brook which ran along through the low land, which was not wide enough to amount to much, as my clothes brushed the bushes on either side. But something must be done, and that quickly. Seeing ahead of me a live oak, whose branches overhung the brook in which I was running, I sprang and caught the ends of the extending limbs, and with more strength than I had supposed myself to possess, quickly threw myself on the branch, crawled towards the trunk, and went up near the top of the tree out of sight, and had just got my breath when a pack of the dogs, smelling the bushes, howling and yelping in a fearful manner, and snuffing the air, and two men on horses following the pack, came directly under the tree. Suddenly dogs and men started off in another direction, and I was not sorry to see them going. I sat in the tree, and heard them when they captured my comrades.

Another pack of dogs came around, and passed just to the left of my tree, and I was satisfied that my tactics had baffled them.

I had a good opportunity to observe, from my elevated position, the manner in which the horses followed the dogs. The men gave them a loose rein, and they followed the hounds, picking their way through the difficult places in the wood, and neighing in a manner which would seem to indicate that they loved the sport. The sound of the dogs grew fainter and fainter in the distance, until I was left in the tree to my own reflections undisturbed. Here I was. I had been without sufficient sleep for eight nights and days, almost continually drenched with rain. My hip was badly swollen with travelling; my feet bleeding, and clothes, by constant intercourse with brambles and cane-brake of the swamps, hung in picturesque tatters around me. Chilled, wet, and hungry, I got down from the tree paralyzed with sitting with my leg over a branch, shook myself, hopped around to get up circulation, congratulated myself warmly on being rather smarter than the rest of my crowd, and then sat down, taking out my note-book, in which I had kept a kind of a log, looked at my map, reckoned up the distance I supposed we had made per day, and the course we had been travelling, and judged myself from five to eight miles from the Chattahoochee River, near West Point, below Atlanta. Taking my course by the compass, I made a bee-line for the Chattahoochee River, which I determined should settle for-

"The next blow embodied a compliment to the whole pack, who had come yelling and snapping around me; and it laid one of them quivering just at the time the man following the dogs hove in sight." — Page 131.

ever the question between the dogs and myself. I afterwards ascertained that I had not varied five miles in my calculations, which was quite a feather, I thought, in my thinking cap.

When the dogs came upon us, it was about nine o'clock, and when I resumed my journey, it was about three o'clock in the afternoon. I had not the slightest idea but that those following the dogs had abandoned further pursuit, and thus felt easy. I had not gone more than two miles before I heard the dogs on my track, bellowing and yelling like wolves. In vain I looked for a convenient method to get out of this scrape; but the trees were pitch-pine, and had no branches nearer than twenty feet of the ground. In this extremity I saw just below me a Virginia fence, which I reached, and wrenching a stake from the fence for a club, I drew my coat sleeve down over my left hand, and thrust it out for the first dog which came up to bite at. He gave one jump at my extended hand, and just at that time I let the stake come down upon his ugly head in a manner which made him give one prolonged yell, and rub his head among the leaves in a way which seemed to take his mind from the business in hand. The next blow embodied a compliment to the whole pack, who had come yelling and snapping around me; and it laid one of them quivering just at the time the man following the dogs hove in sight, and sung out at the top of his voice, "Let go them thar dogs, you Yank, and get off the fence." I saw I was cornered, yet I did not feel like being bit up just to oblige him. So I replied by laughing at him, at the same time keeping the dogs off by a circular motion of my club, remarking that I should be happy to oblige him, but couldn't see the point of letting the dogs take a bite apiece out of my flesh. I had noticed during this time that he had been cocking and holding towards me a rusty revolver, which I mistrusted, by the way he acted, was not loaded.

After some parleying, he called the dogs off, remarking, "Well, I reckon yer are kind er tuckered eout, and I'll gin yer a little spell at breathin';" at which I politely thanked him. After some conversation, in which he confessed that he'd "worn the seat of his trousers a'most off toting around after us," I learned from him that the dogs were put on our track about two hours after our escape, but, owing to the rainy weather, did not follow very fast, and were baffled for a long time at the Flint River, but that, by taking two packs of hounds on opposite sides of the river, they finally regained our trail. Not knowing we had a compass, they had been surprised at the almost bee line we had struck in the woods of a strange country. After repented requests for me to "git into the path," which I told him I had no inclination for until rested, I finally complied. "Wal, I ll be dod rot," said he, laughing, "you take it as cool as though you had caught me, instead of my catching you." He was anxious for me to go "afore" him. I preferred, however, to walk as near him as possible, in hopes that he might get off his guard, and I might have the pleasure of helping him from his saddle by a quick lift of his leg, and thus gain a horse to pursue my travels under more favorable circumstances. But no such chance occurred. He informed me that he smelt a "pretty big rat," and had his "eyes open tight."

I was desperate, in spite of my seeming good nature, and went on the back track with as much reluctance as would a cat dragged by the tail over a carpet. I was once almost in the act of seizing his foot, when he caught my eye, and said, "No, you don't; yer needn't try yer Yankee tricks on me." Thereafter he kept me under range of his rusty revolver, and wouldn't allow me to come within ten feet of him. We soon reached the road and rejoined our companions, who were waiting at a cross-road with their captors.

I was informed, in my travels home, that the men employed in hunting us were all men who had been detailed from their regiments for that purpose. My captor, the head hunter, told me that he had done nothing for eighteen years but hunt "niggers." For every escaping Yankee caught, he shared equally with others thirty dollars. On excursions of the kind they sometimes killed men, but that was seldom done unless they had whiskey in the crowd. He informed me that my being captured was mere accident, as he had been out to a settlement to forage for something to eat, when returning, he had run upon my trail, and followed it up. His dogs were, he said, the best trained of any in Georgia, and would follow "nothing but humans." He used me very well indeed, and during the journey back to the stockade shared with me the food he purchased, and invited me to sit with him at table. He also paid me a rather doubtful compliment by saying, "If yer wer a nigger, I wouldn't take three thousand dollars for yer."

After a long, wearisome march backward of seventy-five miles, in which we had to keep up with horses and mules, we arrived again at the stockade headquarters. "Ah, py Got! you is the tam Yankee who get away vunce before!" was the first salutation of Wirz; and then, turning to the hunter, he said, "Vell, did you make de togs pite 'im goot?" "No," was the response. "Vell, you must next time." "If I must, I will," said the hunter; and I suspect he did, for I saw several, who were recaptured after that, frightfully bitten by the dogs.

After taking my name and the detachment I belonged to in prison, he turned savagely around to me and said, "Vell, vat you tink I do mit you?" "I am in hopes," I replied, assuming the first position of a soldier, "you will put a ball and chain on, and anchor me out here somewhere where I can get fresh air." "Ah, you likes it, toes you? Sergeant, take dis man to de stockade." Back I went to my comrades, among whom my blanket and some other things left behind had almost bred a quarrel. They were quite surprised to see me, and were glad that I brought with me a log of pitch-pine wood, which, through the kindness of Sergeant Smith, I was permitted to bring into the prison. On the whole, though my clothes were torn in shreds, and I was scratched with briers and bitten by the dogs, my health was better generally than when I left the prison. It was not long before I was tunnelling again, with what result will be hereafter shown.

Of those who escaped at the same time with myself, eight were captured the first morning after their escape, four got away some twenty miles, while the remaining three I have never since heard from. My unsuccessful escape gave me one advantage in prison; it brought me a flattering notoriety, which led to my being made a confidant in any plans of escape formed by those who were knowing to my adventure. I was sure to be posted in all tunnelling going on, and therefore, in my opinion, increasing thereby my chances for successful escape.

CHAPTER VII.

Increase of Prisoners, generally destitute. — Greater Suffering from
no previous Preparation. — Sad Cases of Deaths. — Rations growing
worse. — Bad Cooking and Mixtures of Food. — Almost untold
Misery. — Dying amid Filth and Wretchedness. — Preparing Bodies for Burial. — Horrible and Disgusting Scenes. — Increased
Mortality. — Rebel Surgeons alarmed for their own Safety. — Sanitary Measures undertaken. — Soon abandoned. — Scanty Supply
of Medicines. — Advantages of a Shower-bath. — Gathering up the
Dead. — Strategy to get outside the Prison as Stretcher-bearers. —
Betrayal by supposed Spies. — Horrors at the Prison Gate in the
Distribution of Medicines. — The Sick and Dying crowded and
trampled upon. — Hundreds died uncared for. — Brutality in carrying away the Dead. — The same Carts used for the Dead Bodies
and in carrying Food to the Prison.

D URING July prisoners continued to come into
prison at the rate of about one thousand per week.
These, with few exceptions, had previously been stripped
of their overcoats and blankets, and, in many instances,
had neither shoes stockings, nor jackets — nothing but
shirt and pantaloons to cover their nakedness. Numbers of the inmates of the prison had been prisoners at
Belle Island, and various other rebel prisons, for a year
or more, and of course in that time had got no additions
to their wardrobe, except such as their ingenuity could
devise. It was common to see prisoners without hat,

shirt, shoes, or pantaloons, their only covering being a pair of drawers. In this manner men became so burned by exposure to the sun, that their skins seemed tanned almost the color of sole-leather. The great mass who came into prison at this time had none of the advantages arising from gradual initiation, but were plunged into the depths of prison misery at once. Without the advantages of experience, with limited means of comfort, they were thrown into prison to struggle and sicken despondently, and die. Some twenty of my company died during the month. B. W. Drake, a lad about eighteen years of age, was a victim to despondency and starvation. His delicate appetite rejected the coarse, unsalted, unpalatable food of the prison. Without any particular disease, he wasted away to a mere skeleton, and finally died. Sergeant Kendal Pearson, of my company, also one of my mess, died during the month. He had been accustomed for many years to the moderate use of stimulating drinks. In prison, cut off from these, and with no proper nourishing food to take their place, he continually craved and thought of such things. In their place he would sometimes get a few red peppers, and make from them a hot drink, which seemed for a while to revive life and ambition within him; but gradually his strength grew fainter and more feeble, till he died.

In this manner they dropped off all over the prison: and one day you would see a man cooking his food, the next day he would be dead. The eighty-fifth New York,

who, it will be recollected, came into prison at the
same time with ourselves, was reduced in number by
death over one half. Our rations continually grew
worse, instead of better. For some of the last detachments formed in the prison, rice and beans were cooked,
and in the change around from cooked to uncooked
food, occasionally other detachments got the same; but
the food thus cooked was often fearfully dirty, caused
by the beans and rice never being cleaned before cooking, and from the flies which gathered on and in all
descriptions of eatables at that time of the year. The
rebels said that iron wire was so scarce that they
could not get it to construct sieves to cleanse the rice
and beans. Had they possessed a particle of ingenuity
or forethought, they might have winnowed them in the
wind. The simple reason seemed to be for so great
admixture of dirt, that they neither cared nor thought
the matter worth looking after.

The whole prison was now a scene of misery which
words cannot express, and which never was before, or
ever again will be seen. At night you are awakened,
your companion and friend dying by your side, his last
words of pathetic entreaty for food. "Don't tell mother
how I died," said a dying comrade to me; "it would break
her heart to know what I had suffered. I am glad she
cannot see how dreadful I look, she always loved to see
me so clean." "Wash my hands and face," said another of my comrades, when he knew he must die; "I
cannot bear to die dirty;" and as I washed his wan,

pinched face, and browned, thin hands, he smiled, spoke the name "mother," and died. His sensitive nature had ever shrunk from the vermin, filth, and dirt of the prison, so contrary to his habits of cleanliness and gentle breeding — he was anxious once more to be clean and die. Sad death-beds were all around. On the damp, hard ground, many a mother's darling, many a father's proud hope, breathed away a life which shut the light from some household — in some heart left sad throbbings. I am glad that no mother knows all the particulars of the miserable life, that preceded death in prison. I have been questioned by many mothers, who have lost a dear boy at Andersonville. If I seemed uncommunicative, and did not desire to converse with them, and should these pages meet their eyes, let them be assured it was not because I did not sympathize with them, or that my heart was not full, but because I could not bear to pierce their hearts by detailing misery which would only bring them keener pangs of sorrow.

There comes to my vision now, sitting in the soft twilight of this evening, listening to the village church bells, the form of one who died — miserably starved — at Andersonville. When I first made his acquaintance, he was a clerk at headquarters of our commanding general. In prison our acquaintance ripened into friendship, which ended only with death. I never can forget how fond his accents were when he spoke, as he often did to me, of his village home; described the winding slopes around the river's side, where he passed on his way to school or church; and, "Sarg," said he, while his intelligent eye would fire up with softened light, in which were mingled shadows of regret, "if it should please God to deliver me out of this misery, I would try and do nearer as mother wished me." He told me how in the long winter evenings he read to her while she peeled the red-cheeked apples before a blazing fire; and then he would exclaim, "What a contrast to this scene!" Again he would look around him, and say, in those far-off, dreamy, dreary tones often heard in prison, "I wish I had the scraps she throws to our dog and chickens," or "I wish I had the straw and house our pig gets." When he died, his last, faint words were, as he placed his well-worn Bible in my hand, "I shall not be needing this, or anything to eat, much longer. I have tried to live by that book; take it — may it prove to you, as it has to me, a last solace when every earthly hope has passed away."

I opened the book, and read in low, hushed tones from Psalm xxxiv.; and when I concluded the last verse, "The Lord redeemeth the soul of his servants; and none of them that trust in Him shall be desolate," he looked up, saying nothing, but with a smile of gladness, as though that trusting spirit was his. Shortly after he became delirious, and died that afternoon — one more victim to Andersonville.

The common mode of preparing bodies for the grave was by tying their two large toes together, and folding their hands one over the other. If the deceased had a hat, not needed by others, — which was seldom the case, — it was placed upon his face; otherwise the shrivelled cheeks, the unclosed eyes, and drooping jaw, as they were carried through the prison, presented a pitiable sight, which I will not enlarge upon.

It was when death became common as life; when the prison, reeking with deathly vapors, was crowded to suffocation with living victims; when, side by side with life, death walked with the prisoner, — it was then that inhumanity shuddered at its own cruel malice. Even rebel surgeons, accustomed to seeing all our sufferings, protested at last, and uttered complaints to the authorities, which will bear out all the statements ever made of Andersonville suffering. Under the influence of protests from various rebel sources, men were set at work to enlarge the stockade, and again an effort was made to fill in the cesspools of the prison; but these efforts to relieve our pitiful condition never seemed to be made in earnest, but were rather the result of fear that disease would spread into their own ranks outside the prison. These efforts, too, were soon abandoned, and matters relapsed into their old condition, growing worse and worse. "If Yellow Jack gets into this here place," said the rebel quartermaster to some of us, "it won't leave a grease spot on yer; and I can't say there'll be many left if he don't."

Medicines were issued in scanty quantities for a while, in July and August, but they seemed generally a played out commodity in the Southern Confederacy. They were variously crude in kind, and small in quantity. Bloodroot was used as an astringent; sumac berries were the only acid given for scurvy; blackberry root was given as a medicine for diarrhœa, and camphor pills were the standard medicine for various diseases. Personally I cared for none of these, as I ever placed but little faith in nostrums; but thousands of wretches, in hopes of prolonging life a little longer, crawled, and were carried, to the prison entrance where medicines were issued. "The best medicine, after all," remarked a rebel surgeon, one day, "for these wretches, is food;" and it was but little use to doctor starvation with herbs. But wholesome, nutritious food was more difficult to be obtained in prison than medicines, scarce as they were. I found one of the most efficacious remedies for the indescribable languor and weakness which result from insufficient food and scurvy to be cold-water shower-baths, taken morning, evening, and at noon. I usually showered myself by pouring cold water from my tin pail over my head and person while standing. Besides contributing to personal cleanliness, it had an agreeable, energizing action, without any of the depressing after effects produced by stimulating drinks. I do not think its influence in preserving life, in my case, can be much overstated. I practised daily bathing through all my imprisonment; and though sometimes the disposition induced by weakness and languor was greatly against exercise, yet I knew, from what I had seen, that

I must not give way if I hoped to live. Sometimes it seemed impossible for me to get to the "branch" to wash, and the water was often so filthy that it was not agreeable to use it even for bathing. Yet I always forced myself to creep to the brook and take a shower-bath. The effects were instantaneous, and sometimes seemed marvellous. I could always walk briskly back again up hill, and feel like a different man.

Looking back over the past, I can hardly imagine how I managed to live from day to day. Wood was so scarce that it was almost impossible to cook our food when it was issued raw, — as it was most of the time, in about half of the squads of the prison, who were supposed to have cooking apparatus. Every remaining root, where trees had been, was dug out with the rude implements of the prison. Every stump had claimants, who dug around it, and protected their rights from invasions by force. This, for men in our condition, was hard and wearisome work, as our implements were mostly inadequate to the task, under favorable circumstances, for stronger men. The stump and roots, after they were dug out, were cut up into small bits of three or four inches length and one inch thickness, — sometimes in more minute pieces, — by means of a jackknife, and often with merely a piece of blade without a handle. Occasionally an axe would be smuggled into prison by some mysterious means, and its possessor became a kind of prince, who levied tax upon all the surrounding miserables who required its use.

The dead were gathered up by detachments of prisoners, and laid in rows outside the stockade. In order to get wood, there was great competition to fill the office of stretcher-bearer, as there was sometimes a chance for such to pick up wood on their return. Hence it passed into a saying, "I swapped off a dead man for some wood." A stretcher was made for carrying the sick and dead by fastening a blanket to two poles, provided for the purpose, and then rolling up the blanket on the poles until about the width of those of the ordinary construction. As I have elsewhere instanced in these pages, sometimes men feigned to be dead, and were carried out by their comrades, each of the parties deriving advantage by the operation. Another sharp practice was, for four to carry out a dead man and only two return with the stretcher, which gave two a chance for escape and wood to the remaining; thus conferring mutual benefits. Nothing of this kind could be of long duration in practice, for by some method the Johnnies soon became posted in all our dodges. It was said, I know not with how much truth, every batch of prisoners sent into the "pen" were accompanied by a spy in U. S. blue, whom the others naturally trusted as a comrade. He found out all the secrets of the squad and reported them to Wirz. This, doubtless, will account for much seeming treachery among our own men. It does not seem possible that any amount of misery could induce comrades to betray one another, even for food. I class traitors as follows: First, bounty jumpers;

VIEW OF THE MANNER IN WHICH THE DEAD WERE INTERRED.

Taken from a Rebel Photograph. The bodies were laid in rows of one hundred to three hundred, and after the earth was thrown over them, a stake was thrust down to mark the place of burial. Page 144.

VIEW OF THE KITCHEN,

Which was a one-story shed, built of rough boards, one hundred feet in length, and less than fifty in width; it contained in the interior two medium-sized ranges, and four boilers of fifty gallons' capacity each.

second, enlisted prison convicts; third, men who dug tunnels for the purpose of discovering them to the rebels, gaining thereby an extra ration; fourth, spies sent in by the authorities.

Inside the stockade, near the gate, was often the scene of wildest horror. Here would be gathered together in the morning, waiting to pass out the gate to booths where medicines were distributed, the sick, creeping, often, upon their hands and knees, and those too sick to creep borne by feeble, staggering companions. Here, also, would be gathered the stretcher-bearers with their burdens of dead; all waiting, in a densely-packed throng of thousands, often in the rain, or sultry tropical sun, where not a breath of air stirred to revive the fainting. It was a rule, that no one, however sick, could be prescribed for or receive medicine unless first carried to the doctor. As it could never be ascertained on what day or hour medicines were given, day after day these suffering thousands would be turned away without medicines, after waiting for hours through the intense heat of the meridian sun. Often the sick, abandoned by those who carried them, would be left near the gateway, in the intense heat, where no air could reach them, and thus uncared for, die. This arose not so much from the want of feeling of comrades as from their inability to care for them. Those who bore stretchers often fell fainting, and died in that throng of waiting misery. One day, in July, twenty men died in less than four

10

hours among the crowd of dead and dying around the prison gate.

The numbers who went to the hospital outside corresponded with the numbers who died there daily. A police force of the prison dictated, with clubs, who were to pass first through the gate. The dead took the preference, followed by the sick on stretchers. Few of this throng got medicines. A great mass of the sick, rather than suffer the jamming and crowding, and rather than witness these depressing scenes of horror, remained, without trying to obtain what they came for; since, to pass through this truly horrible ordeal, to go through or stand among this crowd of dead, sick, and dying, was worse than the suffering it was intended to alleviate. I considered myself rather a tough specimen of a prisoner, but, after waiting, without success, for four successive mornings, to get out a comrade, I became confident, if I persised, I should be "carried out with my toes tied together" (which, in prison language, meant dead). Imagine two or three thousand men struggling, suffering, crowding together, to get through the gate, — all forms of death, disease, and sickness crowded and jammed together. Here the dead were crowding and jostling against the sick, and the sick, in their turn, jostling against and overturning the dead and dying.

From first to last, the system of dispensing medicines was productive of more suffering than it relieved. At such gatherings the stench arising from the dead and

dying was dreadful enough to make well men sick;
while the sight of men sick and dying, under the circumstances described, was sufficient to depress the
strongest heart with terror. The wan, pinched, famine-
stricken, dirt-clotted countenance of the poor sufferers,
the disgusting spectacle of dead men with unclosed eyes
and drooping jaw, the eyes and face swarming with
vermin, combined to make the scene one of the most
intense horror ever gazed upon by mortal eyes. One
of my battalion, a private in Company G, was carried
for two successive mornings to this gathering, and on
the third died, lying in the hot sun, without an effort
being made by the surgeons and attendants to obtain
shelter for him. Hundreds died in this uncared-for
manner, which was of too frequent occurrence to be
noticed or noted. One would naturally suppose such
spectacles enough to excite in hardened hearts emotions
of pity and remorse; but the chivalry gazed upon these
daily, unmoved, often remarking upon them, "Good
enough for the damned Yanks." Neither were the
dead and dying exempt from their abuse. I have
seen a dying man rudely tumbled from the stretcher
on which he lay, without the slightest heed being given
to his pleading entreaties for pity.

On one of the mornings when I was carrying the
sick, I saw an emaciated, sick man upon a stretcher;
his shrunken face and hands were covered with filth,
and begrimed with the pitch-pine smoke of the prison;
he had no clothing upon his wasted body save a pair

of army drawers, which had once been white; otherwise diarrhœa had rendered his condition too dreadful to be described to ears polite, or even to be gazed upon. One of the prison officers at that time crowded through the throng of the sick and the dead: while doing so, he forcibly pushed against this poor creature, who was uttering plaintive moans and cries for mercy, to which no heed was given. In the scramble which followed, the dying man was overturned, and, as he lay gasping in his last trembling agonies, the same officer or attendant passed again that way, and rudely thrust him with his foot from his path, saying, "One more Yank's gone to the devil." Sitting this evening before the crackling blaze of a New England's winter fire, and cheered by civilized comforts, I cannot repress a chill of horror and creeping sensations of shivering terror at its mere remembrance.

Such occurrences were too much a "matter of course" to be noticed, and I only instance this solitary, unknown dying man, among the suffering thousands of the prison pen, as an example of the fiendish hate and malice which pursued these patriots of the Union even when the doors of death were closed upon their starved, unburied forms!

Carrying away the dead to their final rest was but a horror in keeping with the scenes described, and a fitting climax to the life of misery which ended in the prison The dead that gathered during the day were placed in what was known as the dead house, — a rude

VIEW OF THE ANDERSONVILLE GRAVEYARD,

As the Rebels left it, containing the remains of nearly 14,000 victims to rebel barbarity.   Taken from Rebel Photographs in possession of the publishers.

"Carrying away the dead to their final rest was but a horror in keeping with the scenes described, and a fitting climax to the life of misery which ended in the prison."   Page 148.

shed frame, covered with bushes. From thence, each morning, they were taken, thrown upon a cart drawn by three mules, with a negro driver seated upon the middle one, over the ungraded field to the place of interment. The bodies were usually thrown, one upon the other, as high as could be reached; often the head, shoulders, and arms of one or more of the bodies protruding over the side and from the rear of the cart, or from under the dead piled above them, — the dropping jaw, the swaying head, undulating with each motion of the cart, the whole mass of bodies jolting and swaying, as a comrade expressed it, "like so much soft soap." It was said that from these carts maggots and vermin of various kinds could be scooped, after such an excursion, by the handful. In these same carts our rations were brought to us, shovelled in where the dead bodies had lain; and with flies, which gather, in a climate like Georgia, upon all eatables exposed, gave us food, when cooked, well mixed with everything which could be offensive and disagreeable. Death in prison, under such circumstances, was not always looked forward to with loathing or terror, — not always preceded by acute, though always with great suffering, — but was often hailed with tearful, trembling joy, as a message of freedom spoken to imprisoned men.

CHAPTER VIII.

Robberies in Prison. — Means taken to punish such Acts. — A Character. — Big Peter, a Canadian. — His Administration of Justice on Offenders. — Becomes a Ruling Power. — Missing Men and Rebel Vengeance. — Murders of Prisoners by Thieves. — A Police Force organized. — Courts established. — Trials of accused Murderess. — Conviction and Execution. — The Gang of Murderers, Thieves, and Bounty Jumpers broken up. — A Slight Tribute to Wirz, as only the Tool of Others. — Character of the Prison Police. — Not all Good Effects. — A Terror to the Good as well as Bad. — Sometimes the Instruments of Rebels.

F ROM the time we arrived in prison we were continually troubled and annoyed by having our scanty clothes, blankets, and cooking utensils stolen from us. There were so many temptations, and so few restrictions thrown in the way of the perpetration of theft, that it became an evil, at last, that must be checked. Stealing blankets from boys unaccustomed to hardships was downright murder; for, if no one extended the corner of his blanket to protect the unfortunate from the chill dews of evening and from the frequent rains, deprived thus suddenly, he was sure to sicken and die. Stealing cooking utensils reduced unfortunates, thus deprived, to the necessity often of eating their scanty rations without cooking, or of stealing or begging from others. Begging was as much out of fashion and good standing in prison as any place.

It was rumored around camp, from time to time, that raiders and flankers were organized for the perpetration of outrages, and of protecting themselves against the punishment of such acts. Although there was no definite organization among us, it was agreed upon that these villains should be promptly dealt with; that when any of the Plymouth prisoners could identify a "raider," or was attacked or robbed by one of them, he was to call out loudly "Plymouth!" when every one of the boys within hearing were to turn out to his assistance. In accordance with this agreement, we heard one morning the rallying cry, and captured a fellow who was caught in the act of stealing a blanket. The boys gathered around him, not knowing what to do with the Tartar now that they had caught one. He sat gnashing his teeth, threatening his captors with the vengeance of a band, which he said was formed for mutual thieving, if they should injure or inflict punishment upon him. Feeling some reluctance to proceeding against him, they were about to release him without punishment, otherwise than a few kicks, when a corporal of Company G, second Massachusetts heavy artillery, familiarly known in prison as "Big Peter," came into the crowd, and taking the raider fearlessly in hand, inflicted summary punishment upon him by shaving half of his head and face, giving no heed to the desperado's savage gnashing of teeth and threats of vengeance, except to thump his head at each beginning and repetition of them. After dealing out justice in this off-hand manner, and an administrative reminder (in the rear) from a pair of the heaviest of cowhides, the thief was released, with admonitions to sin no more.

This, I believe, was the first instance of formal punishment for such misdemeanors; and thereafter Big Pete, by virtue of these services, became the terror of evildoers. Pete exhibited so much courage at this time, and subsequently so much good sense and natural judgment, that he gradually became the administrative power for the punishment of offences committed. He performed for us the services of shaving, and in a dignified, impartial manner gave the culprit a trial, — hearing the statements of both sides before pronouncing judgment and inflicting punishment, both of which, however, were often condensed into the last act. Few exceptions were taken to his rulings, for who could object to the persuasive arguments of one who wore such heavy boots ?

The incident narrated was the beginning of a power in camp to punish offenders, which finally provided us with an effective police organization. Pete was an uneducated Canadian — a man of gigantic stature and great physical strength, of an indomitable will, great good nature, and with innate ideas of justice, in the carrying out of which, he was as inflexible as iron. A blow from his fist was like that from a sledge-hammer, and from first to last he maintained so great a supremacy in camp, that no description of the prison at that time would be complete without a sketch of him. His trials were often intensely grotesque and amusing to spectators, but not generally so to the culprit. I took pains to follow some of his trials, and I must say, in justice, I never knew him to make a wrong decision, though baffled in his purpose by ingenious lies. Through all the intricate lies, he had a talent for detecting them and sifting out the truth. Thus, at last, by common consent, if any one had complaints to make, he carried them to the "shebang" of Big Peter. He either went himself, or sent some of his adherents, who returned with the accused; witnesses were then summoned and punishments dispensed. Justice was being dealt out in this manner, when one morning it was announced — and to our sorrow we found it carried into practice — that our rations were to be stopped on account of men being missing from the stockade — supposed by the rebel authorities to have escaped by means of tunnels. Investigation led to no new discoveries, and after twenty-four hours' extra starvation, they were again issued as before, it being impossible to discover the missing men, or any modes by which they could have escaped.

About this time, the raiders, under the leadership of one Mosby, became exceedingly bold, attacked new comers in open daylight, robbing them of blankets, watches, money, and other property of value. Rumors of frightful import were circulated through the camp of men murdered for their blankets and money. After this, more men were missing at the morning roll-call, of whom there could be no reasonable account given. Under Big Peter a company was organized, armed with clubs, who proceeded to the shelter formerly occupied by the missing men. Inquiries being made among those who were living near, no information could be obtained, otherwise than the fact that outcries were heard during the night, and that there was a scuffle near; but scenes of disorder being common during the night, they had taken but little notice of them, since, as peaceable men, they wished to avoid all wrangling. Nothing at first could be found, in the shelter formerly occupied by these men, to excite suspicion . Most of the crowd had dispersed, when one of the men, on his hands and knees at the entrance, looking down into the grave-like hole which formed the principal part of the abandoned dwelling-place, saw a piece of blue cloth, partially covered with dirt. Seeing in this the element of a patch for the repairing of his shattered wardrobe, he pulled at it, and found it fastened in the ground. This excited his curiosity, also his desire for possession; and he began to dig and pull, until further progress was arrested, and he started back with horror at the unexpected appearance of a human hand. A crowd gathered around, and speedily a dead man was unearthed, whose throat had been cut in a shocking manner, and his head bruised by a terrible blow. In the same space, beneath him, was found another victim, with his throat cut. The news of these horrible murders spread through the prison, as if by telegraph, and a large crowd soon assembled around the scene of these atrocities. The police proceeded to the shelter of several notorious thieves and bad characters of the prison, and arrested them. Through information, or clew gained of one of these, they were induced to dig in the shelter of some of those arrested, which resulted in the discovery of money, watches, &c., in many cases identified as the property of the murdered men.

Rapidly after the perpetration of these cold-blooded atrocities, strong police forces were formed under Big Peter as chief of police. Afterwards a judge-ship was established in prison, and there were two regular practising attorneys, who took fees of Indian meal, beans, and small currency in payment for services rendered; and sometimes, it was said, bribed the judge and chief of police. In the case of Staunton, a big brute, and tool of the rebels, who killed a man, as mentioned in preceding pages, it was rumored that his money, procured by dicker with prisoners, obtained him a mild sentence and punishment. Not to digress further, the supposed murderers some fifteen in number, were arrested, and after gaining sufficient evidence, consent was obtained of the prison authorities for their trial. Besides this was obtained the privilege of conducting the trial under guard, in a building outside the prison. The accused were also held in custody through the kindness of Wirz, the commandant. A jury of men was empanelled, composed of prisoners just captured, who had never been in the prison, and who, therefore, could not have formed prejudices on either side. The trial lasted through a number of weeks. Competent men were appointed to defend the prisoners by the authorities. An able lawyer, an officer of the rebel guard, conducted the defence, afterwards stating to me that he had no doubt of the guilt of those who suffered punishment. The prosecution was conducted by men selected from among the prisoners. Six of these men were pronounced by a jury guilty of murder.

On the 11th of the month, Captain Wirz, accompanied by a guard, brought the prisoners into the stockade, where, on the south side, near the gate, and the scene of the murder, a gallows had been erected. Here he turned the offenders over to the prison police, with a short speech, in which he stated that they had been impartially tried and found guilty of atrocious murders, and that he left their punishment in the hands of the prisoners of the stockade. He then turned, and followed by his guard, left the prison. The police formed, in two ranks, a hollow square around the gallows; the ropes were arranged, and the guilty men ascended the scaffold steps. Up to this time the murderers did not seem to view the proceedings in a serious light, but rather as a joke. Leave was then given for them to speak, which they did, protesting their innocence, one or two calling upon their companions to do their duty, which, properly interpreted, meant that they wished to be rescued from the police. The ropes were adjusted about their necks, the bags were drawn over their faces, their hands pinioned, a hushed silence reigned in the camp, the drop fell, and five of the prisoners hung by their necks, swaying in the air; the sixth, nearest to the prison gate, sprang at the time, or before the drop fell, broke the rope about his neck, gained his feet, forced his way through the police and crowd, cleared his hands, ran swiftly, was pursued, beaten over the head, and recaptured, when the rope was again adjusted, his protestations of innocence were unheeded, and he was pushed from the drop, and hung with his comrades in guilt. Thus ended the lesson of retribution that put a stop to murders in prison, and broke up a gang of bounty-jumping desperadoes.

Let me here record, in justice to a man who has since met a similar fate, in retribution for crimes committed against Union prisoners, that I and many others of the prison were grateful to Henry Wirz for the privilege afforded us, to enable us to give the accused a fair, impartial trial. I have purposely avoided, in these pages, heaping unnecessary odium upon the head of one who, though guilty, I have good reasons to suppose was only the executive of a system devised by men high in rebel authority, and from whose orders no inferior could deviate. There never was a hanging conducted in a more orderly manner. There was no clamor of voices, but in silence and decorum befitting such a scene, thirty thousand men were its witnesses, Thenceforward raiding and flanking were of rare occurrence, and the police became one of the establishments of the prison. That the police did much to punish offenders and preserve order, cannot be denied. They were mostly of the class denominated "roughs," selected for their physical rather than mental qualifications, and in some instances became a greater evil than that which they were instituted to correct. They levied tax upon all trading stands and occupations in the prison, cudgelled men over the head for small faults, and whipped them upon the bare back, with a cat of nine tails, most of whom, however, deserved the punishments inflicted. Yet they would not tolerate any injustice done by others than themselves, unless they were well paid for not arresting offenders. Reserving to themselves the right (?) of doing injustice and committing abuses, they governed the camp and corrected all other abuses but their own.

I am sorry to record, that in the Florence (S. C.) military prison, when S. was acting chief of police, this kind of police force became for a while degraded tools in the hands of the rebels, and whipped men at their command upon the bare back for digging tunnels, &c., for which dirty service they were rewarded with extra rations. I have entered thus particularly into details which were needful that the general reader should have, that he may realize in some degree the position of a prisoner at Andersonville, and to show that anything originally devised for our welfare might be perverted to our misery.

CHAPTER IX.

Negro Prisoners. — Barbarous Amputations. — None but the Wounded
made Prisoners. — Their cleanly Habits. — Treatment. — Major
Bogle. — Bad Treatment of him as an Officer of Negro Troops. —
A Misunderstanding. — Andersonville a Prison for Privates, and
not Officers. — A great Project to break from Prison. — Two Thousand engaged in it. — The Project betrayed when nearly com
pleted. — Despondency at the Result. — Courage renewed prov-
identially. — Addition to the Stockade. — Much short Comfort from
the Enlargement. — A new Stock of Fuel soon exhausted. — Dis-
honorable Offers to Prisoners generally spurned by starving Men. —
Fidelity under extraordinary Circumstances. — Instances cited. —
Heroic Men. — New Methods of Operation. — These also spurned.
— Various Evidences of Devotion to Country.

IT was in July that I first noticed negro prisoners
among us, though they were, doubtless, there previous to that time. Scarcely any of them but were
victims of atrocious amputations performed by rebel
surgeons. It was said that none of the prisoners were
captured except the wounded. Those in the prison
were mostly New England men. Some of them had
been captured at the charge on Fort Wagner, when
Colonel Shaw was killed, and at the battle of Olustee,
Florida. I observed in the negro prisoners a commen-
dable trait of cleanliness. Indeed, I may safely say,
their clothes were, on an average, cleaner and better

patched than those of other prisoners of the stockade. Through exposure to the sun and rain, they were much blacker than the common southern negroes, and many were the exclamations of surprise among the guard at this fact. "The blackest niggers I ever saw," was the common expression on seeing them. I have said the negroes were mostly wounded and mutilated; when there had been a case of amputation, it had been performed in such a manner as to twist and distort the limb out of shape. When a negro was placed in a squad among white men, it was usually accompanied with the injunction, addressed to the sergeant of the squad, "Make the d—d nigger work for and wait upon you: if he does not, lick him, or report him to me, and I will." I never knew an instance, however, where a sergeant required of the black any service not usually allotted to others, and that in drawing and distributing rations.

Understanding that there was a major of colored troops in prison, I hunted him up, and found Major Archibald Bogle, who was formerly, I believe, a Lieutenant in the 17th Mass. infantry. He was captured at Olustee, after being severely wounded in several places He informed me that he formerly lived in Melrose, Mass. Since he came into the pen, he had been refused all medical and surgical treatment, though the prisoners detailed as hospital stewards had covertly afforded him aid, and dressed his wounds. He wore his uniform, and freely declared himself an officer of negro troops — a fact which all officers of negroes were not willing to own, by reason of the hard treatment received therefor from the rebels. His was an instance of the fact that a true gentleman remains the same amidst the most squalid misery and accumulated misfortunes. His intercourse with others was dignified, courteous, and urbane, as if in command of his regiment. There were many in prison, as there always has been in our army, who professed to despise negro troops, and have a contempt for their officers. Major Bogle was, at one time, I was informed, compelled to mess with his negroes; yet he always maintained his gentlemanly bearing and his self-respect, and commanded the respect of others amid all the accumulated misery of the "prison pen." Such were my impressions of Major Bogle.

Many loose statements have been made in print indicating that officers were as common among prisoners at Andersonville as enlisted men. With the exception of Major Bogle, there were no commissioned officers intentionally placed in Andersonville. Others were there by their own act; but the prison was intended for enlisted men only. At any time an officer of white troops could be sent to Macon, or some other officers' prison, by merely making a plain statement of facts which looked plausible. So much is required to be said, as there seems to be a great misunderstanding in relation to this matter; and it is my desire to write such a description of the prison that those who were prisoners at the time with myself will be the ones most

11

ready to testify to the truth of these pictures, crudely
drawn with pen and ink. Major Bogle, at one time,
was engaged in a tunnelling operation, in which he
plotted to release all the prisoners of the Stockade. It
failed through the treason of some one in the secret,
though it came near being a success. About the time
I became acquainted with him, an extensive plot was
formed to break the stockade. Over two thousand men
were pledged to risk their lives upon an effort to liberate the prisoners of the stockade. Here seemed the
choice before us, to die without an effort, amid all the
misery of the prison pen, or to die with our hands up-
lifted to strike one blow at our enemies, before death,
in an attempt to liberate ourselves and starving comrades. To no reasonable man did there appear at that
time to be any hope for life but in that manner. I
went into the project, I am willing to confess at this
day, having full confidence in our ability to achieve the
desired result, and with a feeling that it was better to
die in such an attempt than to die a miserable, loathsome death by gradual starvation.

Acting in concert, we set ourselves at work, and dug
tunnels up to the stockade; then the tunnel branched
off at right angles, running parallel with the stockade,
a shoulder of earth being left as a temporary support,
so that when a rush was made against the walls from
the outside, it would be thrown down in the places thus
mined. In this manner three portions of the stockade
walls were undermined — at least, I have reason to

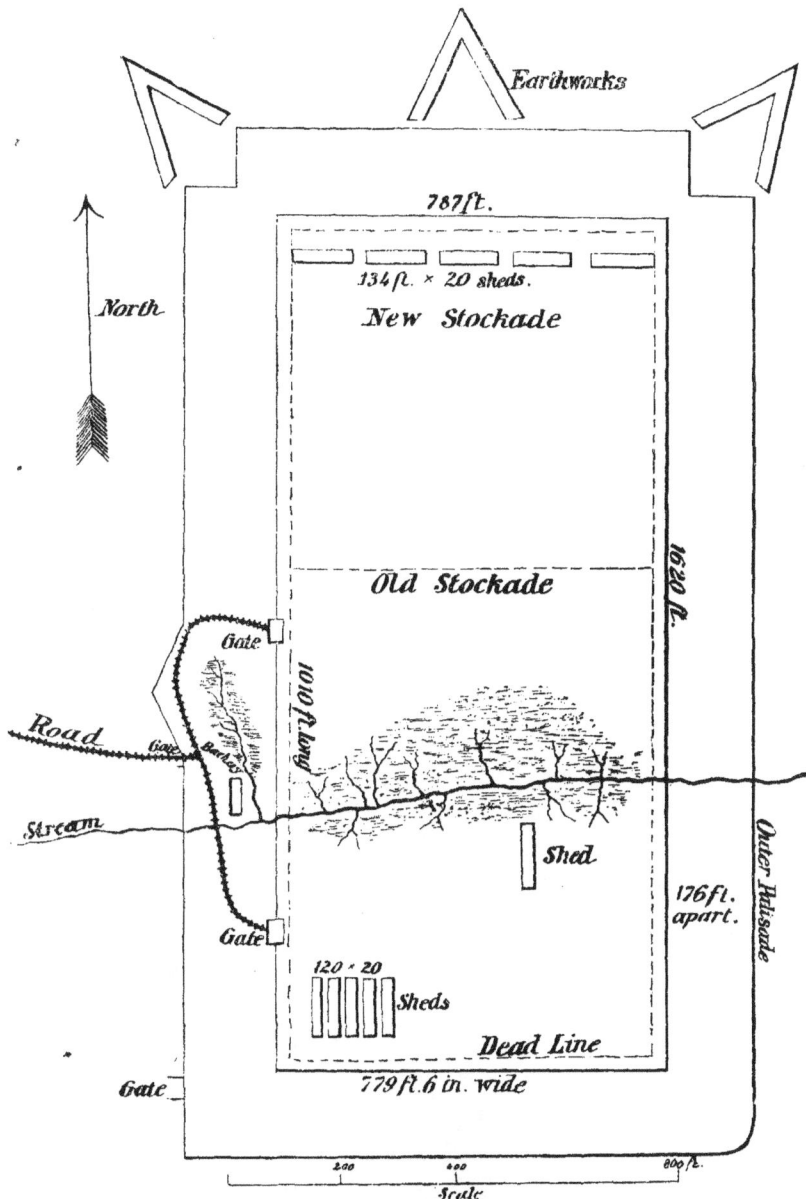

Earthworks

787 ft.

134 ft. × 20 sheds.

New Stockade

1620 ft.

North

Old Stockade

1010 ft. long

Gate

Road

Gate

Stream

Shed

176 ft. apart.

Outer Palisade

Gate

120 × 20

Sheds

Dead Line

Gate

779 ft. 6 in. wide

200   400   800 ft.

Scale

PLAN OF PRISON GROUNDS
ANDERSONVILLE,

Measured by Dr. Hambin.
Copy Right secured

suppose so, although I was engaged in digging and engineering on but one of them. Our plans were as follows: One detachment of prisoners was to break through on the south side, near the gate, and capture the reserve of the guard; another to break through on the north side, and, making a circuit of the stockade, capture the guard thereon; another party, breaking through on the south-west side, near the gate, was to capture the rebel artillery near headquarters, and use it according to circumstances, and make such capture of rebel officers as was possible; while prisoners outside, under detail, were to cut the telegraph wires. This achieved, prisoners were to be liberated, rations equally distributed, the cars seized, ammunition and arms placed in the hands of "the organization," and then, raiding through the rebel country, seize upon horses and other modes of transportation, and effect an escape to the Gulf. Such were our plans generally.

All was pronounced ready for the grand assault, and we were waiting with trembling expectancy, when a proclamation was read in prison, and posted in conspicuous places, stating that such a plan was known to be organized, and the commandant of the prison had full knowledge of all its details, even to the names of those concerned; and that, if we persisted in carrying it out, there would be great bloodshed, which he wished to avert. Such, in substance, was a proclamation signed by Henry Wirz. We had been betrayed by one who, we supposed, from every motive of interest, would keep the secret. Artillery was posted at various points, with men in position to use it: twice shots were fired over the heads of prisoners in crowds, while white flags mere placed all over the prison, as ranges for their artillerists. Thus ended the best-conceived plan for liberating the prisoners *en masse* during my imprisonment, and proved the assertion frequently made among the Kentucky boys, that "Everything in the Confederacy was drefful onsartain, and liable to bust."

After the repeated failure of long-cherished and hard-worked plans, which were to give liberty or death to the projectors, for once I became despondent and doubting, falling away from faith in ever getting out of prison otherwise than by dying. Dark clouds of despair gathered around me, and followed my feeble footsteps. Though I knew I was bringing upon myself the very fate I had been so long trying to avert; knew that such moods were productive of none but evil to him who entertained them; yet, for a time, it seemed impossible for me to rally from or shake them off. In this wretched condition of mind — prolific of none but pernicious results — I was, one day, creeping down the slippery pathway of the hill, which led to the brook-side. Everything around me looked foreboding; the dying men, who always encircled the quagmire of the prison, stretched out their withered hands in supplication for food, which I had no power to give; the dead, lying with unclosed eyes and dirt-stained, pallid faces, brought back to my heart, with startling force, the question, How soon shall I, like these, lie uncared for, dead, starved, after a painful life without a gleam of hope? The thought was maddening; reason was tottering; and, full of half-formed, desperate thoughts and gloomy resolves of ending at once that which seemed must be ended there in long and torturing misery by starvation, I saw lying at my feet a bit of waste paper. I said within myself, If there is anything on that paper — one word of hope — I'll take courage and live; otherwise — and here I clutched the paper, when the first words that caught my eye were these: —

> "Ye fearful saints, fresh courage take;
> The clouds ye so much dread
> Are big with *mercy,* and will break
> With blessings on your head!"

It was a portion of the leaf of an old hymn book. I never saw the hymn before nor since, and I may not have quoted it exactly; yet, had an angel from heaven assured me of my ultimate release from rebel hands, I could not, thereafter, have been more confident of my destiny. Never, after that, did my faith waver even for an instant. At another time, one of my companions, seeking for encouragement in his despondency, placed, at random, his finger between the leaves of his Bible; it rested upon the twelfth verse of the one hundred and fortieth Psalm: "I know that the Lord will maintain the cause of the afflicted and the right of the poor." Of course hope always construed such omens on our side to our advantage. Thus it was that the prisoner clung to every straw of hope. At various times, when I first went into prison, I had jocosely taken little bets of suppers, dinners, &c., as to the duration of our imprisonment, but always lost them, through the death of the other party.

During the last of July, or first of August, an addition was made to the stockade. This gave to the thirty-five thousand crowded into the space of ten acres more room by ten additional acres. The opening of the new stockade, as it was usually termed, was an event which contributed to the comfort of the prisoners in various ways. It gave them more wood, by the tearing down of the stockade walls, which had separated the new enclosure from the old, furnishing for a time a good supply. But, as the majority in prison had no means of splitting and cutting up the huge logs which formed the stockade walls, nor the instruments for digging up or cutting down the huge timbers, the bottoms of which had been solidly fixed into the ground some eight feet, and as but a limited number of the thirty thousand men could work at such employment at a time, the supply fell into the hands of a few who had the strength and implements to do the work. The stock, however, was soon exhausted, and wood became almost as scarce as ever. There were yet in the new stockade roots and stumps, which gave, for a while, to those who had the courage and strength to dig in the hot sun, a supply. But the larger number had neither

VIEW OF THE PRISON FROM THE MAIN GATE.

Reproduced from Rebel Photographs which were taken when about 35,000 men were here confined. Original Picture in possession of the publishers.

"During the last of July, or first of August, an addition was made to the stockade. This gave to the 35,000 crowded into the space of ten acres more room by ten additional acres." Page 166.

strength, courage, nor the implements, other than their
fingers, to dig with.

The reader, in considering our circumstances, must
always remember that the great majority of the imprisoned thousands had become so emaciated and weak by
continual exposure and starvation as to be scarcely able
to take advantage of any circumstance like the foregoing in their favor. There were always a few, perhaps one in two hundred, who formed an exception to
the great mass of sufferers. A few who had axes or
large wedges were able, in some cases, to lay in a large
supply of wood, but, as want increased, these did not
long retain possession. The police, vigilant in all matters of general interest to themselves, caused those thus
stocked to divide with the suffering thousands around
them, taking a good share for their own trouble. With
all the additional acres added to the prison grounds, we
were still crowded for room; and if I have not continually impressed the reader with our miserably cramped
condition, it was because one statement of such facts
seemed sufficient. For two or three weeks there was
a better supply of wood, but soon it was as scarce as
ever.

In spite of the sufferings endured, which I have but
feebly portrayed in the preceding pages, any offered
relief that involved dishonor to themselves, or reflected
diseredit on our government, was not favorably received
by the great mass of suffering men. At one time,
during a period of most intense suffering, rebels

from Macon and other large places came into the stockade, offering tempting inducements for prisoners to go with them, and work, during their imprisonment, at their trades. Shoemakers, carpenters, blacksmiths, and coopers were offered good food, clothes, and liberal compensation in greenbacks. Those who made this proposition were actually mobbed, and forced to leave the prison, by men who were on the brink of starvation, who had partaken of but one scanty meal during forty-eight hours. I observed, from time to time, in the different prisons where propositions were made of this nature, that a time was always selected when we were suffering the most for want of food. It was possible — and the fact speaks volumes in favor of the prisoners' fidelity to the government — they knew that at any other time such propositions would be rejected with contempt. The common sentiment among prisoners was, that it was as bad to assume the places of men who would thus be enabled to take muskets, as to use up arms themselves against their country.

David Robinson was a middle-aged man, a mechanic of Massachusetts, who had left a family at home dependent upon him for support, to fight the battles of the country. His son, a lad of eighteen years, a fine, manly fellow as ever gladdened a father's heart, had followed in his footsteps. When the proposition came to go out to work, and thus save the life of himself and son, he replied, "No! I know for what I enlisted, and have been fighting for; the boy and I will die, but we can never desert the cause." The boy died, in what manner I shall relate in coming pages. The father, broken in heart and health, lives to mourn his son. Yet he was only a New England mechanic, whom the terrors of death could not seduce from his country's cause. At another time the proposition was made to Corporal Gibson, of my company, an old man, who afterwards died at Charleston. The answer was heroic: "You can starve my body, but shall not stain my soul with treason!" Such were the men who died by thousands, and filled the begrudged graves dug by relentless foes.

During July and August efforts were persistently made by men among us, backed by the rebels, to get up a petition representing our condition, and asking our government to take action for our release. This was, in my opinion, at the time, and also that of a great majority in the prison, but an effort of the rebels to make the misery inflicted by themselves subservient to their own base purposes of forcing our government to their own terms. In prison, as elsewhere, there was a diversity of opinion, yet the almost unanimous voice was against forwarding such a petition. Sergeant Kellogg, I believe it was, who was captured at Plymouth, was asked to sign it. "No," he replied; "our government will do what is right. These are our enemies, trying to benefit their cause, not yours." Such was the language of starving patriots, and such was the force of words fitly spoken, that they were repeated through the prison in reply to those who asked for signatures. Thus, often sterling words counteracted evil influences!

The rebels have since made a virtue of having forwarded, through kindred tools, such a petition. They could look on and see the prisoner starve, and rejoice thereat, without lifting a helping hand, and the next moment forward a petition to our government, setting forth the misery which they were inflicting! Towards those of our own numbers who were forced by hunger to be their tools, we should be charitable, yet I believe it to be a fact, that those who signed that petition, were those who were suffering least in prison, — bounty-jumpers and deluded men, — men not in sympathy with the cause. The great mass repudiated the petition, and to-day, when the old flag floats over every foot of land once desecrated by rebels, I feel a thrill of pleasure, — melancholy though it be, — in contemplating those dark days when men starved and dying would not swerve from the right, that the cause for which they died has triumphed. And in coming days, the noblest monuments of sacrifices made for the nation's safety shall be those patriots' graves!

The more the prisoners were abused, the more fondly did their thoughts turn to the old flag, under which they had fought, and which was the symbol of happiness and plenty at home. "We have confidence in our government," was a remark often made in reply to accusations by the rebels that our government did not care whether

we starved or not. When I consider that this was the
common language of men suffering under miseries rarely,
if ever, paralleled in history; I cannot be astonished that
the Union exists to-day. I feel a conscious joy that
there was no act of mine, during a bitter imprisonment,
to disgrace that flag. In referring to the North, as
distinguished from the South, it was often spoken of as
"God's country," and the old flag as" God's flag.'
Such was the halo of glory with which all its associations seemed surrounded.

Incidents were of such frequent occurrence patheti-
cally illustrative of the prisoners' devotion to the glorious Stars and Stripes, that I will narrate one expressive
of the form this devotion often took. A color-sergeant
of one of the regiments captured at Plymouth, N. C.,
died some time in August. While his companions were
rendering the last services, — that rude preparation for
the grave already described, — they discovered his regimental flag, which he had so often borne in battle,
wrapped about his person. He had placed it secretly
there to shield it from traitor hands. He could not
bear that this loved symbol of his country's glory should
be desecrated by the hands of traitors. Reverently his
comrades gazed upon its folds, and silently, with tearful eyes, again restored it, as a fit covering for his
noble breast, to be buried with him. A glorious winding sheet for a patriot! Dying men clung to little
mementoes, such as a miniature flag, or the badge of
their army corps. But it was the general constancy

with which men ever clung through all their misery, with love to their country and its cause, which spoke more eloquently than any mere incident of their devotion, and the triumph of principles over circumstances of misery.

CHAPTER X.

H ERE, as in other prisons, a fearful epidemic
reigned, termed by old prisoners "Exchange on
the Brain." Frequent rumors of exchange were circulated designedly by the rebels, for the purpose of
quieting desperate men, and preventing the formation
of dangerous plots for release and escape. Often these
rumors seemed to have some foundation. Once the
priest who had charge of the spiritual development of
the prison commander, Wirz, came into prison, and

read a large concourse of prisoners, gathered to hear, extract from a paper purporting to give news of an exchange about to take place at Savannah. Prisoners coming in from Sherman's army brought news of a raid under Stoneman and McCook. The next news we heard was, that Stoneman's cavalry was fighting around Macon; and then it was announced by exultant Johnnies, that Stoneman and his whole army were captured. This was partially confirmed by men belonging to his force, coming in as captives. They informed us of the siege of Atlanta, and reiterated the former news of an exchange agreed upon; but when and where it was to take place, they had no information. When Stoneman was raiding towards us, with evident intentions of releasing the prisoners; when rumors came of his having arms for the prisoners, — which I have since ascertained to be true, — our hearts beat high with hope. Those who had previously had tendencies of Exchange on the Brain, went fearfully wild with release in the same place. A few, who had learned by bitter experience how uncertain every thing in Dixie was, while cheered by bright prospects, put but little real confidence in them. Some pinned their faith and hopes so implicitly upon a release, that they were unwilling to wait even a day, and when at last they found their hopes and faith disappointed, sunk into a despondency from which nothing could arouse them, and died. Rumors and statements of an exchange were so frequently made and backed by evidence which looked plausible, that the prisoners were expectant and despondent by turns during July and August.

These two months were the most terrible of and experienced by the general prisoners. Nine thousand were said to have died during that space of time. In one day in August, no less than one hundred and sixty prisoners died, and the average was over a hundred daily. From the 1st of February to the 16th of September, twelve thousand Federal soldiers, prisoners of war, were carried from the prison to the dead man's trench and the felon's burial. Many of the deaths were hastened by despondency. After an usual excitement about exchange, — especting to be called out to be released at any moment, — followed by disappointment, deaths were the most frequent.

Extreme heat, during July and August, was often followed by days dark with intermittent showers. On one occasion, during such a period, the ground was rendered so hot by the intense rays of the sun as to blister my feet by mere contact. This period of heat was followed by rain in such quantities as in a few hours to cause a freshet, which swept away the stockade where the brook entered and left the prison; and also swept away portions on the north-west side, by the flowing of the water down the hill-side. Wretched creatures all over the prison were crawling out of holes in the ground, in which they had burrowed, half drowned with the water which had suddenly filled them. Canteens, plates, bits of wood, blankets, spoons, pails, and hats,

were swept away down the hill-side, the prisoners
franticly rushing after their deserting goods and habitations. The only washing some of the poor fellows got
was on such an occasion. It was curious to observe
the different manner in which various individuals
accepted of such a dispensation. Some laughed, others
swore and abused fate, many screamed and cried as if
mad, while still others crouched in the rain, or saw the
whole scene unmoved, as if gazing on a panorama with
which they had no concern. I sat at such times crouching in the rain, my body bent up in a manner to bring
my knees, stomach, and head in close contact, between
which were folded and placed my jacket and ragged
blanket, — my back exposed to the rain, forming a kind
of roof to keep these valuables from the wet. But all
in vain such an effort. The force of the rain, running
down the hill-side, continually upset me, by under-
mining the sand beneath my feet, until at last losing
my blanket and philosophy, miserable and grotesque as
others, I went rushing and pitching after my tin pail
and blanket, caught up and carried away by the
torrent.

Large forces were thrown out to protect the portions
of stockade swept away by the flood, and keep the
prisoners from desperate attempts at escape. All night
under arms these forces were kept in position in the
rain, until the stockade was repaired. Night and day
artillery was manned, which commanded the broken
portions of the stockade, and every precaution taken

against the escape of prisoners. One great good resulted from this freshet. On the hill-side where the
stockade had been broken away, a spring was discovered, which supplied an abundance of pure water to the
prisoners, greatly in contrast with the filthy stream
which had been our only supply during the summer.

Shortly after the foregoing event, I became engaged
in a tunnelling operation, which came near proving
fatal to its projector. Tunnels did not usually cave in,
for these reasons: the top of the earth, after the tunnel
passed under the dead line, was interlaced by roots and
fibres, which formed sufficient adhesive power, in most
parts of the stockade, to keep the earth from caving in.
Besides, the earth was usually hard and clayey. In
this case, however, after we got beyond the stockade,
on the outside, we ran into sandy soil, where our misfortunes began. Two of us were digging, in the day-
time, when, in our rear, the tunnel caved in, and
effectually cut off our retreat into the stockade. Gradually it commenced falling upon us, filling our ears,
eyes, and mouths with dirt. There seemed to be no
release from our critical condition, except by digging
upward, which we commenced to do with fear and
trembling, as that operation was always attended with
great danger of being buried alive. Suddenly, down
came a mass of earth above us, which did not, as we
anticipated, bury us so deep but that we scrambled
out of it, shrieking with terror. The rebel guard at
that time, coming around with the relief, rescued us

from our peril — the only time I was ever glad to see a rebel.

During the last of August, rude barracks were in process of construction in the upper portion of the new stockade. This looked like preparations for winter, and gave us but little comfort, as these buildings consisted of roofs only, on uprights, and there was no prospect of more than a very few being accommodated by their use.

The weary, weary, dreadful days dragged slowly along, amid suffering and death in prison. September came. Over fifty of my company had died since the term of imprisonment began, which was not so large in proportion to their number as occurred in other companies captured at the same time with ourselves. The majority of our two companies were veterans — strong men, inured to hardships and exposure by a previous experience in camp and field. Scarcely any of my company died until after the middle of July; August swept them away by scores. The following is an incomplete, imperfect list of those who died: Wm. Arrington, Wm. Bessom, Nicholas Bessom, Chas. A. Bent, Wm. Brown, Winslow A. Bryant, B. G. M. Dyer, Wm. H. Burns, Geo. Combs, Peter Dunn, John Duffee, B. W. Drake, Geo. Edwards, Geo. Floyd, John Fegan, Cyrus B. Fisher, Patrick Flynn, James Henry, G. P. Reed, S. A. Smith, John Shaw, J. Thomas, James Wilson, C. O. Wilson, F. A. Stephens, G. Arrington, Pat. Henley, Charles Holbrook, Joseph Hoyt, Wm. H.

Haynes, Wm. Johnson, Michael Kelleher, Chas. A.
Moore, Wm. McGrain, Chas. Moss, John Milan, Ber
nard Mehan, C. M. Martin, John McDermot, John
Nevison, Benj. Phillips, Chandler Petie, Patrick Regan,
Wm. Wyman, Kendal Piersons, Wm. L. Gordon, and
others whose names I have lost.

Poor boys! Noble fellows! As I recall their names,
memory brings each face, pale with prison suffering,
before me. I cannot but have greater faith in human
nature from having known them. Dear comrades!
endeared to me by many sufferings! guilty of no
crimes; theirs was a death of lingering torture, to
which, in comparison, the devices of the Inquisition
would have been mercy. Victims of a relentless hatred which has not ceased with the war, your nameless,
crowded graves dot the prison burial-ground, and point
a solemn moral to the barbarities enacted there. To-day,
when the men of Georgia ask the rights they formerly
exercised, and among them the right of excluding the
negro from the ballot-box, I wonder those patriot
bones do not start from their crowded, shallow graves,
to bear testimony that, while living, every white man
of that locality banded with bloodhounds to prevent
their escape, forming a network of vigilance through
which it was almost an impossibility to break, and their
only dependence was in the blacks, — the Unionists alone
of that section, —who harbored them when it was a
peril to their lives, and gave them of their food when
they had but a bare subsistence for themselves. You

who sit by the quiet fireside and read these records of suffering, reflect, when you hear the clamorings of those who are trying to regain lost power, that they are those who, all over that southern land, by their silence consented, or by action indorsed, the barbarous treatment under which Union men lingered, suffered and died amid the tortures of starvation.

In September my last effort at gaining liberty by tunnelling was frustrated. Fifty men commenced a tunnel on a grand scale. It was nearly completed, and was the most perfect thing of the kind ever devised by the prisoners. It was commenced at the bottom of an old well, and two men could walk abreast from one end to the other. One of our number betrayed us to the rebel quartermaster for a plug of tobacco. Another of our companions saw them conversing, and, getting behind them, heard him propose to tell the quartermaster something important, if he would give him the tobacco. He ran and informed us in season for us to make ourselves scarce. After the tunnel was discovered, those engaged in it were naturally enraged, and, seizing the traitor, printed on his forehead, with India ink and needles, indelibly, the letter T. They were proceeding to worse punishment, when a rebel guard came into the stockade and carried him outside. In spite of evidence to the contrary, I have but little doubt he was a rebel spy, who had been sent in with other prisoners to betray us. Diligent inquiries were set on foot to find out who had punished the traitor in the manner described. To accomplish this, we were threatened with being starved into submission; but the rations, after being stopped for twenty-four hours, were again issued.

Rumors of exchange continued to pervade the prison. Men, crazy with the idea of freedom and home, wandered up and down the prison, clinging to every rumor, like drowning men to straws. The excitement was made worse by the extravagant rumor circulated around camp by the rebel quartermaster and the priest, who was said to be Wirz's confessor! The excitement increased daily, and men were expecting at any moment to be called out. Many were called, but it was to that bourn from whence no traveller returns: many were released, but the herald of their freedom was the grim messenger, Death!

At last, after repeated rumors had prepared the prison for their purpose, orders came for certain of the detachments or nineties, as they were termed, to be ready to leave the prison. We were told that there was a Federal transport fleet off Savannah, waiting for us. To all in prison this seemed the dawn of freedom, and the most incredulous believed. Kentucky Joe, who always protested that everything was "dreadful onsartain in Dixie," became a convert, and had exchange on the brain. Every one clamored for a chance, and feared to be left out of the exchange. Ninety after ninety went out of prison rejoicing, and faintly cheering. It was cheering which brought tears to the eye, so puny and weak did it come from the poor, weak, starved fellows. But

> "The hollow eye grew bright,
>   And the poor heart almost gay,
>   As they thought of seeing home and friends again."

I never hear that song without its recalling that scene. Men who had been brought by suffering to the very verge of idiocy, or who for months had been smitten with almost hopeless melancholy or despair, as these sounds came at last dimly to their ear, like remembrance of a dream, their glorious import, "going home," burst upon them. They staggered to their feet, and were carried, by the pressure of a dense crowd, outside the prison, feebly cheering, or regardless of the presence of rebels, joined in the chorus of

> "Rally round the flag, boys, rally once again."

My ninety had got orders to be ready, and I was in a tremor of excitement, when one of my comrades sent for me, saying he was dying. My heart sank at thinking of the suffering, dying men who must stay behind and perish. My heart almost reproached me for being glad, when companions who had stood by my side in days of battle were suffering — dying, with none to care for them, — without sister's or mother's hand to soothe them, without food, and with no shelter from the pitiless rain and sun.

I went, and found John Nevison stretched on the

poor remains of his blanket, dying. How often the poor fellow, true to a stubborn Scotch nature, had rallied, and tried to live! "I am glad you are going home, Sarge." (His generous heart had room for joy at others' good fortune even in death.) "I wish you to send word to my mother" (Mrs. Margaret Nevison, Newcastle, England, on the Tyne); "tell her I enlisted to fight against slavery — for my adopted country. Tell her all about me!" Poor fellow! I understood him; he wished me to tell her he had done his duty. Comrade in battle, I can testify that none stood up in fight more manfully than John Nevison — he who so often had sung, with pathetic voice, the song,

> "Comrades, will you tell me, truly,
> Who shall care for *mother* now?"

I now understood why he sung that song with so much feeling. He never before had spoken of his mother. Poor John! enshrined in the hearts of comrades, you lie in your nameless grave among the victims of Andersonville; and

> "Who will care for mother now?"

I took his poor, thin hand in mine, and pledged him I would do all he wished. I forgot his address for a time, but in the delirium of a fever recalled it, though many other forgotten things were not again brought to mind.

I was waiting for my turn to come to get out of

prison. Every subterfuge was resorted to to go with the lucky ones. Those who had means bribed; those who had none "flanked," and were rewarded ofttimes with broken heads, for others became savage at the idea of being cheated out of their chance, and the police exercised anything but a protecting influence upon the unlucky heads of flankers. Those who tried their wits received often a reminder upon their brain, not as a test of its quality, but as a check to its further exercise. Men were crying at the gate, as we went out, at being defrauded of their chance by some audacious flanker. I went at last, rejoicing at what appeared to be the day of deliverance. As I passed rebel headquarters, I saw Sergeant Smith, who, it will be remembered, was one of my captors when I escaped at one time from Andersonville. "Well, Smith," said I, "there are no bloodhounds after me this trip homeward." The Sergeant shook his head (it seems to me, sorrowfully, when I recall it now) to see us thus elated by delusive hopes of "going home," destined, O, in how many cases, never to be realized ! We reached the depot, were divided into squads of sixty, and crowded into box cars. We were full of hope, however, and kept saying, "Well, we shall have room enough soon." Our rations had been previously placed in each car — a piece of corn-cake about the shape and size of a brick. We were told these were our rations for three days' journey. One of my comrades, J. W. D., desperately resolved to preserve a piece of the bread to carry home as a curiosity; but hunger got the better of the poor fellow's resolve, and I saw the last crumb disappearing before the afternoon of our second day's journey.

During the first day, three men died in the car where I was. My bread lasted me two days, as I was careful not to eat too much at a time; yet it was considerable trouble to have it around — a continual temptation to myself and to others. We arrived at Macon the afternoon of our first day's travel. The vigilance of the guard was here redoubled, and the fact excited our suspicion that there was to be no exchange, after all. As we passed through Macon, one of Stoneman's men pointed out to me the bullet marks on the buildings and fences made by our advance just before his capture. We had been suspicious that we were going to Alabama, but our hearts rose within us as the cars took the direction for Savannah. A negro informed us that "Captin Sherman" had taken Atlanta, and was making for Macon as "tight as he can come." This looked like removing us to a place of security rather than an ex change; still, we were hopeful that we were to be exchanged to prevent our capture. As we neared Savannah, and changed our guard, the officer of the new guard came up, and we made inquiries of him as to our destination — if we were to be exchanged. He replied by candidly stating that we were to be placed down on one of the islands, under fire from the Federal guns. Several men were shot, on our route from Savannah to Charleston, while trying to escape from the cars. We caught sight of our fleet in the distance, as we passed over the bridge leading to Charleston, — and our hearts thrilled with a savage kind of joy, when we heard the shell from our batteries, shrieking over the city. We termed them Gilmore's errand boys, or Gilmore's morning reports on the condition of rebeldom.

At last the cars were halted in the streets of Charleston, and citizens, negroes, and soldiers, thronging the streets, peered curiously into the cars, to get a look at the Yanks. It appeared to me, then, that they wore a haggard, care-worn look. The only hopeful face of the group was some old negress, who had kept fat and jolly on the idea of Uncle Abe's coming soon. Said one citizen to another, in my hearing, "They are all foreigners — ain't they?" This riled me not a little, and I replied, saying, "You recollect the Plymouth prisoners who passed through these streets in April?" "Yes, perfectly; a very fine body of men," said he. "These are the same men; your government has starved all semblance of men out of us." "You are a foreigner?" said he, looking sneeringly and critically at my dilapidated wardrobe and dirty face, which had been guiltless of washing for the three days of our journey. "No, I belong to Massachusetts!" I proudly replied. He seemed much shocked, either at the fact of our condition, or that any one should not be ashamed to hail from Massachusetts.

It was just before sundown when we were formed in line, and marched through the back streets of Charles-

ton. The effects of the siege were visible upon every
hand, but we were informed that the damage done was
really worse than mere appearances indicated. The
shell made only an irregular hole through the exterior
walls, whereas the interior of buildings where shell had
exploded was often a mass of ruins, It was no figure
of speech, but a reality, that grass was growing in
the streets of the proud but doomed city which first
raised its defiant hand against the Federal government.
The shell and shot from Gilmore's batteries had a
civilizing influence over its people, for in no place were
we so kindly treated by citizens and soldiers as in
Charleston. Women and children looked pityingly
upon us, and such expressions as "Poor fellows!"
"Too bad!" &c., showed pity and sympathy for our
condition, which we had never before experienced in
the Confederacy.

I noticed that those citizens whose dress betokened
that they belonged to the better classes wore often a
sober, subdued look, which, during my experience in the
war, I had observed as the result of much anxiety,
mental suffering, and loss of friends. I addressed one
of these as we were waiting on the street — "Ain't you
folks about sick of all this fighting?" "We are tired
of it, dreadful sick of it," said he, while he vainly tried
to keep back the tears that ran down his face; "but we
are going to fight you'un Yanks just as long as we kin."
Noble stuff — worthy of a more decent cause.

Finally, just as the sun was setting in an ocean of

beautiful clouds, we arrived at our destination on the "Fair Ground," or "Race Course," in the rear of Charles ton, where were about five thousand of the Andersonville prisoners, who had preceded us. The situation was pleasant; the green grass, to which our sight had been unused for many weary months, met the eye with refreshing pleasantness. The situation was better than we had anticipated, though we were disappointed in not being placed down on the islands, where we could see the flash of friendly artillery, or perchance the old flag, for no one who has not had such experience can understand the longing of our hearts for the old flag, and for familiar sights.

CHAPTER XI.

Imprisonment on the Fair Ground. — Improved Condition. — Hard. Tack and the Fear of losing it. — Tin Pail stolen. — Great Misfortune. — Loss of Caste by it. — Kindness of Women. — Ludicrous Tumbling into Wells. — Gilmore's Morning Reports welcomed. — The Dead Line again. — Continued large Mortality. — Want of Hospital Accommodations. — Good Offices of Sisters of Charity. — The Issue of Rations. — More Variety, but not of Quantity. — Expedients to obtain an Increase. — The Rebels baffled in Counting. — Honorable conduct of Colonel Iverson. — Scarcity of Wood. — Sad Cases of Destitution. — Shocking Condition of the Writer. — Effects of Scurvy. — Death while waiting for Food. — Decreased Rations. — Plans for Escape. — A Trial at it. — Recaptured. — A warm Fire. — Sent to the Workhouse. — Improvement on the Camp. — Discovery of interesting Papers. — Sent back again to Prison. — A new Partnership. — Rations getting worse. — Further Attempts to bribe Prisoners to Disloyalty. — Starved and insane Men consent. — A Speech and its good Effects. — The picturesque Appearance of the Orator. — Yellow Fever. — Ludicrous Incidents. — Leave Charleston. — Journey to Florence. — Another Attempt to escape.

THE Fair Ground proper, when seen under favorable circumstances, must have been a beautiful spot. It contained an area of about forty acres, surrounded by dense overhanging trees, interwoven by ivy, laurel, and honeysuckle, forming an almost impenetrable foliage. Aside from a distant view, we were not allowed any of the enjoyments which such shade and beauty could confer. We were placed in the centre of the Fair Ground, with no shade or habitations, except, such as we might construct from our garments or ragged blankets; but there was a cool breeze from the ocean, and the sound of bells and the rattle over pavements came pleasantly to the ear. The sight of green foliage refreshed the gaze of miserable men, for a long time unused to pleasant sights and sounds.

The night of our arrival, three "hard-tack" were issued as rations, for twenty-four hours, to each man, and we were in the third heavens in anticipating such luxurious rations each succeeding day. That night, after devouring two of my "hard crackers," I lay down to rest with the remaining one in my tin pail, under my head, for my morning's breakfast. I found it impossible to keep my mind from the hard-tack long enough to get to sleep, supposing sonic one would steal it while I was slumbering: the thought was maddening. Vainly I endeavored to divert my mind from craving hunger, by saying the multiplication-table. It was "no go." That hardtack was so fascinating! Hunger, and fear of losing it, got the better of the contest with sleep, and I could bear no more. Arousing myself, I devoured that "infantry square," in one time and several motions, not down in the tactics. I never remember of enjoying any food, however luxurious, as I did that hard cracker.

I mention this incident, insignificant in itself, as illustrative of how little it took to elate or depress men in our condition. That night, however, I met with the great misfortune of my imprisonment. Some vagabond stole my little tin pail, which, I may say without exaggeration, had been my best friend during the preceding months of my captivity. It had been such a convenience to myself and companions, that few, who have not been prisoners, can understand how great a loss it was. Used by one and another, sometimes it was not off a fire during the day, except long enough to change hands.

I was reduced, by this misfortune, thenceforward through my imprisonment, to the unpleasant alternative of borrowing cooking utensils, or of eating my rice, flour, or Indian meal raw. It took so little in prison to make one's circumstances indescribably miserable, that this really was an overwhelming misfortune. The loss of a fortune at home could not have so affected my well-being or "good standing" among companions. From one accustomed to confer favors on others, I became dependent, and begging and hunting, often for whole days, for some one willing to loan me a tin quart to cook in.

On the morning following, the people of Charleston came in flocks to see the Yankees. A majority of these were women. Some few came with food to sell, but were not allowed to trade over the guard line with prisoners. Others, actuated by pity, watched for chances, and, when the rigor of the guard was relaxed, threw cakes, potatoes, or some like luxuries, over the guard line among the wretched creatures who gathered waiting for luck to favor them in some manner. The food thus thrown in was, however, but a drop in that Maelstrom of human miserables, who, actuated by hunger, struggled madly among each other for its possession. After a time, this feeding of the common prisoners was stopped, and the women were told to confine their manifestations of pity to the hospital, which was situated outside of the prison grounds, in our rear. Many a poor fellow, who otherwise would have died, lives to bless the women of Charleston. May those whose hands were thus lifted in pity never be stricken down with that hopeless hunger which they sought so kindly to relieve!

The next evening we received as rations two "hard-tack" per man, and a rarity of about two ounces of fresh meat, — which last was, so far as I observed, eaten raw throughout the camp at one sitting. Thus it was that we were inclined to be pleased with the change in our situation, in spite of disappointment about exchange. During the first two weeks, I had not been fortunate enough to get the means of constructing shelter. One day, when wood was being brought to the camp for the use of the prison, I accosted an officer, whom I saw around camp, and requested him to get me three sticks from the wood-pile, that I might construct a shelter from the sun by raising my blanket upon them. Contrary to my expectations, he at once kindly complied with my wishes, and I was made happy with the means of constructing a "shebang." Upon subsequent inquiry, I found this officer to be Lieutenant-Colonel Iverson, in command of the camp. He had very strong prejudices against Yankees, but was inclined to do all within his limited power to better the condition of the prisoners.

At Charleston we obtained a kind of brackish water, by digging shallow wells from six to ten feet deep. In a short time, so easy were they to dig, they became so plenty as to be annoying and inconvenient to the pedestrians around camp. Plenty of water, coupled with the fact that, about twice a week, we got a small piece of soap, caused clean faces to become more common than ever before in prison. The inconvenience above mentioned was so great that one could not walk around in the evening without being precipitated into a well. Thus many a fellow took an extemporized bath, in which his feet and legs, or head and shoulders, got the uncontemplated benefit of water. Under such disadvantages, night-walking became unpopular and unpleasant.

Each morning, about sunrise, shell from the guns of the Federal batteries down the harbor would begin to burst over a prominent steeple of the city. The report of the gun which sent the missile could not usually be heard. These were termed, among the prisoners, Gilmore's morning reports. Sometimes a shell would burst over the Fair Ground, which would be received with great enthusiasm among the prison boys, and with demonstrations of applause, such as, "Bully for the Swamp Angel," &c. Some days the bombard-

13

ing would be very active, and we could hear in the
city the dull thud, and the ripping and tearing, as the
shell penetrated or burst in buildings. As may be supposed, it was diverting to us to see and hear these evidences of retributive justice going on among our foes.
If one had fallen in our very midst, I have no doubt
our boys would have cried, "Bully!" so welcome,
always, were these evidences of the nearness of friends.
The people of Charleston seemed to have got accustomed to them to such a degree that, during the
heaviest bombardment of September, when none cared
to stay in the lower portion of the city, the boys were
unconcernedly flying their kites. I counted eighteen
kites up while one of the heaviest bombardments was
going on. Fires were of such frequent occurrence,
resulting from shells, that the fire department became
almost as important as that of the military.

On the first week of my confinement at Charleston,
our old enemy, the dead line, was introduced. A negro, superintended by the "irrepressible" white man,
was sent around camp, turning a furrow with a plough
and its mule attachment. This was the line which to
overstep was death to the prisoner. None but those
prisoners in comparatively good health had been sent
from Andersonville. For quite a time an effort seemed
to be made to relieve our misery; but the great mass
had been starved and exposed to sun and rain too long to
be benefited by anything short of a most radical change.
Hence men died about as fast, in proportion to their

numbers, as at Andersonville. Scurvy, diarrhœa, and fever swept the prisoners off in vast numbers.

The place dignified by being called "the hospital," did not contain a single tent, the only shelter being, here and there, blankets raised on sticks, which were inadequate protection from rain or sun. Colonel Iverson, who, I believe, was, for a time, in command of the prison, made strenuous efforts for our benefit. A sutler was appointed for the camp, who was not allowed to ask of prisoners higher prices than asked in the city. This was a convenience to those who had money, but the great majority had none. The sutler's store of goods contained but few varieties — black pepper, unground, turnips, sweet potatoes, and baker's bread. Ten dollars in Confederate money for one in greenbacks was the general rate of exchange; and this was obtained through the Sisters of Charity, who visited us, doing acts of kindness to the suffering, bringing clothes and food, carrying messages to our officers, prisoners in the city, and bringing the reply. To people so cleanly we must have been objects of disgust. The vermin, visible upon all prisoners, could not have been pleasant to refined persons, unaccustomed to such misery. Our dirt-begrimed, half-naked persons must have been revolting, yet no word or look from these kindly Sisters showed shrinking or disgust. I have seen them bending in prayer or in offices of mercy over almost naked creatures, whom disease and filth had rendered indescribably loathsome, never, by word or look, showing other feeling than pity, and never making the object of their care feel humiliation or shame. Their kindly address of "My poor child!" fell pleasantly on the ear. No importunities could vex them, and I do not remember of having heard an utterance of impatience from their lips. I may have been prejudiced, at first, against these Sisters of Charity, but certainly their acts were truly Christian, worthy of imitation by all on like occasions.

As I have said, gangrene, diarrhœa, and scurvy raged terribly in camp, notwithstanding our improved condition. It was about the third week of my stay at Charleston, I was told that Corporal Gibson, of my company, whom I have mentioned in preceding pages, lay dying. I found this brave man lying in the hot sun, with no shelter or attendant. Said he, "I could have lived to get out of the hands of any savages but these; they are too cruel for an old man like me to expect from them anything less than death." The untold sufferings this man endured, — who once had refused to purchase freedom and life as the price of treason, — retaining clearness of mind until the moment of death, was but one instance among the many daily occurring in prison. A young soldier, who at one time had been clerk of Company G, second Massachusetts heavy artillery, died during the same week at Charleston. In his last moments he continually said, "I should be willing to die if I could have enough to eat, and die at home." Thus longings for home and food and thoughts of death were often bitterly crowded together.

For convenience in issuing rations, the prisoners were divided into detachments of thousands, and then subdivided into hundreds. There were sergeants of thousands and sergeants of hundreds, and a chief sergeant over the whole. These divisions were to facilitate the issue of rations, and the sergeants were selected from among the prisoners, and were often chosen by them. Much trouble, first and last, occurred in prison from the rebels never being able to count the prisoners correctly. We were often counted, but with no satisfactory results. There were, throughout the prison, so many hungry men — whose wits seemed to sharpen in proportion to their hunger — continually devising ways to get "extra feed," that it was not strange that the rebels frequently found themselves issuing more rations than there were men in prison. By judicious management, ingenious Yankees contrived to belong to two or more squads, and draw rations for each without exciting suspicion. Upon one count the rebel sergeants found they had issued five hundred more rations than there were men in camp; and even by exercise of the greatest care in these countings, they would often be cheated two or three hundred men, through the dexterity which prisoners had acquired of shifting from one squad to another, and getting counted twice. Once, while en deavoring to count us, Colonel Iverson was so baffled by the tactics, that he dismissed the matter for the day, good naturedly declaring that we were "heavy dogs."

At last, in despair of finding out the exact number

of Yanks in any other manner, they marched the prisoners out into the open space, and kept us standing in line until counted; but even here, where any cheat seemed certain of being detected, and though threatened with punishment if we played Yankee tricks on them, the men of the rear rank were managed in such a manner that, in our detachment, a little over nine hundred men contrived to count up a thousand. The officer counting us mistrusted something wrong, and recounted us twice, without detecting the cheat, but expressed his distrust in a kind of a stage aside, saying, "You'n Yanks are the doggondest fellows I ever did count." The rebels in this transaction reminded me of Cuffee, who, being asked by his master if he had counted all the pigs, replied, "Yes, massa, all 'cept a little speckled one; he run'd round so I couldn't count him." They never succeeded to their liking in making us come out straight.

About this time Colonel Iverson detected the sutler in two offences: first, of receiving greenbacks in pay ment for goods, — a criminal offence in the Confederacy, — and, second, charging the prisoners exorbitant prices in trading. Whereupon he confiscated the greenbacks, to be used to obtain comforts for our sick, and forced him to conform to the schedule of prices in the city. The following were, with little variation, the prices charged in Confederate money: Bread, one dollar her loaf; sweet potatoes, ten dollars per bushel; three flat turnips, one dollar; black pepper. ten dollars per ounce. Taking into consideration the fact that one dollar in greenbacks would bring ten dollars in Confederate money, it made the schedule of prices extremely reasonable to those who were lucky enough to have money. There were, however, only a very few fortunate ones who had managed to conceal money, and get into prison with it. Those who had been captured during the summer in the vicinity of Richmond underwent strict searches, and were robbed of their money, watches, and other valuables by the authorities, who pretended that they would again be restored when their imprisonment was over. Whatever may have been their intentions at the time, I never knew of but one instance where such promises were fulfilled, and that was in the case of Colonel Iverson, who had taken away greenbacks to the amount of many hundred dollars, and when the prisoners were released, restored the money. The great majority of prisoners had not a cent in their pockets, nor a pocket to put it in if they had a cent. To such the sale of the delicacies mentioned was nothing but an aggravation. If potatoes had sold for five cents a bushel, not more than one man in a hundred of the prisoners could have purchased a peck.

After giving us hard-tack for a few days, raw rations were issued in prison in very small quantities, in which the rebels seemed to have adopted a plan to make variety take the place of quantity. Rations for each man per day were for a time as follows: Two heaped spoonfuls of rice, two of flour, one of beans, and one of hominy. I remember it more particularly, as one of my comrades, who acted as a squad sergeant, usually divided the rations with a common teaspoon. Sometimes this estimate would fall short, but rarely, if ever, overrun. Wood was issued in quantities of about one common cord wood pine stick for twenty men per day. But its issue was very irregular. Sometimes none would be given for weeks. There was, however, a good excuse for this, for all the wood had to be brought a long distance on the cars, and then brought in teams to the prison ground. As there was a scarcity of rolling stock in those parts, this was a better excuse than could be found at Andersonville, where the prison was surrounded by a dense pine forest.

Many of the prisoners were destitute of cooking utensils, and could not borrow; and either from want of strength to run round, or getting discouraged by failures, after repeated rebuffs upon application for such favors, they would eat their rations raw, or go without. A young fellow belonging to the eighty-fifth New York independent battery, named Myers, had nothing in which to draw his rations, but a boot leg, into which he had fitted a wooden bottom. He had no cooking utensil, and ate his rations from this boot leg, without a spoon, day after day, uncooked, sometimes stirred up in a little water. This miserable being camped on the ground near the place I occupied. He scarcely ever lay down at night without wishing that he might never awake. It did, indeed, require more courage to live than to die. At last, after days and nights of lingering torture, his prayers for death were answered. Near me, one morning, I found his cold and lifeless form stretched upon the ground. He had died, his eyes closed as if in sleep. I noticed something clasped in his hand, and stooped to examine it. It was the likeness of a beautiful girl, and on the back was written in a delicate female hand, "To William, from Sarah" — a whole history of love, disappointment, and death, in brief. When I reflected that each man among the thousands dying around me had histories similar in their griefs, and loves, and longings for home, and when I considered the bitter pangs of dying men uncared for among worse than barbarians, it seemed too much of human misery for contemplation or utterance.

One day, when some Sisters of Charity came into the prison limits, — no very agreeable task for a cleanly female, — one of them remarked, in apology for not having got some article which she had undertaken to obtain for one of our number, that the firing was so heavy that it was not safe to venture down in the part of the city where such things were sold. These kindly Sisters attended to all alike without ever inquiring our creed, or appearing to think they were doing anything more than a duty.

My physical condition at this time was worse than at any time during my captivity. My clothes were in tatters, scurvy had drawn up the cords of my legs, and from the same cause my teeth were almost dropping from my jaws; my gums and mouth were swollen, and it became difficult to eat the most common food. My bones ached so intensely at times that I could find no more appropriate name for the pain than "teethache" in them. Something must be done. I must make continual efforts, or go down to the dogs' death many were suffering around me. So I used to wander around camp, picking up potato peelings from the mud and dirt, which some "well-to-do" fellow had thrown away. These I washed, and ate raw; and I have no doubt they did me much good. Once or twice, I was lucky in obtaining some turnip-tops, which I cooked, and enjoyed hugely. But there were thousands of hungry men on the lookout for these delicacies as well as myself, and therefore it took continued and persevering efforts for me to get a nibble once a week. This vegetable food checked the scurvy, and kept it at least within bounds.

The hospital was at last moved into one corner of the prison grounds. One day it was rumored that vegetable soup would that day be issued to the sick of the prison. A man who could crawl was not considered sick. A poor sick fellow near begged me to take his dish and draw some for him. This I undertook to do, and after waiting some hours I got the soup, and returned quickly to the sick man. He was sitting on the ground, his hands clasped, and his head upon his knees. I spoke to him, but he did not answer. I touched his hand — raised it — it fell lifeless from my grasp; he was dead — died while sitting, waiting for food in this mournful position. It was quite common for men to die thus suddenly. In my squad I was knowing to several instances of men's drawing their rations, and dying an hour or two afterwards. I took the dead man's place in eating the soup, for however sorry I was for him, I was too hungry to refrain from relishing the food. That afternoon, with a full stomach, I felt like patronizing everybody.

About the last of September, we learned from our guard that five or six thousand rebel prisoners had been landed on one of the islands, in possession of our forces, in Charleston harbor, to occupy a stockade built for that purpose. This, perhaps, explained the reason why we were not put down under fire ourselves.

I had often, when low in health, and restless under the restraints of captivity, turned over in my mind the probabilities of an escape. The rations of the prison were steadily growing less in quantity, and the extreme negligence or the purposed plans of the rebels kept us frequently for twenty-four hours without food. Restlessly seeking some mitigation of these sufferings, it appeared to me possible that some dark night I might crawl on my hands and knees through and beyond the guard. There was great danger of being shot, But there were other terrors in prison which would thus be left behind. I made a copy of a map of Charleston and vicinity, determined to try my luck the first dark, rainy night, favorable to such an undertaking. My plans were vague and general, the idea of getting to the water, and obtaining something to float upon down the harbor in the night, being uppermost; or, if I did not get a boat or a log, to get into the city, and trust to some of the German people for a suit of clothes or concealment. At any rate my condition might be bettered, and could scarcely be made worse.

Under the inspiration of these ideas, one rainy night in September, making a confidant of no one, I crawled beyond the guard. I could hear their measured tramp, and one stood so near to me that I could hear him breathe. Indeed, I thought myself perceived, when he wheeled upon his heel and walked his post in another direction, giving me a good opportunity to creep by. I got to a safe distance from the sentinel, then rising to my feet, ran towards the north part of the Fair Ground, forced my way through the dense foliage which enclosed it, when there burst upon my vision with lurid glare, ahead and about me, a number of camp fires, around which soldiers gathered. "Halt!" came the sharp salutation, close on my left. I heeded not the command, but ran, steering midway between two fires. "Halt!" "Halt!" simultaneously came the order from right and left of me. Still I ran on. Bang! bang! bang! rang the report of three or four rifles, aimed true enough for me to hear the angry z-z-z-z-t of the bullets as they whispered death around my ears. Close upon me, right ahead again, came the order, "Halt!" I halted, answering the summons, "Who goes there?" which rapidly followed the command, "Halt!" by replying, "A friend." "Yank, surrender!" laughingly called out the sentinel. I obeyed promptly, as I heard him bring his musket to a full cock, with an ominous click, and saw uncomfortably near me the gleaming of the polished musket. All this occurred in less time than I have taken to relate it. "What in dog-gond-ation was yer tryin' to do?" interrogated the Johnny. "Trying to pick up some warm quarters," I responded, as I walked to the fire and commenced warming myself. "Reckon yer found it durned warm, when the Charleston Guards commenced to blaze at yer, old hoss!" laughed my captor. I tried to show my contempt by saying, "O, that's nothing when one is used to it." "I reckon I'd er let daylight through yer, before yer got used to it, if yer hadn't stopped 'bout as yer did." I laughed at him, thinking it best to take things easy, while he called the officer of the guard. "Well, I'll be durned," said he, slapping my shoulder as a compliment, "if yer arn't right smart, for a Tank, any way." While waiting for the officer of the guard, one of the sentinels gave me a hard cracker, and my captor presented to me a generous slice of "sow-belly," which, I couldn't help thinking, was an ample reward for the risks I had run. The officer of the guard came up, and began to question me as to how I got beyond the sentinels of the prison grounds. "Bribed them," replied I, not caring what answer I made, so long as I did not give him any information. He looked at me from head to foot, seriously, for a second, then, as if struck with my picturesque costume of rags, smiled and chuckled, as if intensely amused, and said, "They must have tooken a mighty slim bribe."

I slept by the warm fire, under guard, that night, and the next morning was sent to the workhouse, in the city. This building was of brick, built on three sides of a square, with two towers, one of which, I noticed, had been split down, by collision of solid shot or shell, from top to bottom. Under the arched ways of the building, which led from the yard, were two rudely-constructed ovens, used by the officers for cooking their food. In the building were the quarters of Federal officers, The windows were heavily grated. In the yard was a high lookout tower, from which could be seen the jail-yard adjoining. I staid here two days, congratulating myself on my improved quarters, which, in contrast with the Fair Ground, were very comfortable, though I was not allowed inside the building, and I was only fearful of being sent back to the Race Course. While prying around in the archways of the building, I found, in one corner of a dark doorway, a bundle of documents which threw light upon the purpose for which the building had formerly been used, and the manner in which slaves were committed for punishment. The following is a sample of a few in my possession: —

"Master of the Workhouse: Receive Jerry, and put
him in sol. con.   ROB. ROWAND.

    Aug. 14, '56."

                           "July 10, '58.

"Master of Workhouse: Receive the girl, Mary, give
her (15) fifteen paddles, and return to me.

                           SAM'L WATSON."

"Master of the Workhouse: Give Hulda 5 paddles,
put her in confinement 12 hours, and return to me.

    Jan. 20, '56.   J. RICKER."

On the morning of the third day, to my great disgust, I was sent to the Fair Ground, under guard. I
kept pretty still about my adventure, being a little
ashamed of not escaping after so many trials, and my
comrades merely remarked that they hadn't seen me
around for a day or two, and did not know but that
I had had my "toes tied together." That day I hunted
up Jesse L., who was formerly a comrade in the engineer corps, and re-formed a kind of partnership, which
had been, for a time, suspended — to sleep under the
same shred of a blanket, cook, hunt vermin together,
and take turns watching each other's traps, while one
was in quest of potato peelings or drawing rations.
Jesse was a good-natured fellow, who was accustomed
to say of himself that he could "scarcely draw breath
on the rations he drew, and was running down so fast
he couldn't run around." He was capable of laughing
at any amount of misery, and baffled and held death at

arms' length by ingenious devices; and his "devil-may-care" temperament, which nothing could daunt, and his irrepressible drollery, which would bubble up from the midst of misery, made him a desirable companion, to lighten the loads of despair which hung around us like a pall of midnight darkness.

Colonel Iverson had left the command of the camp, and we were miserably starved and neglected, having, often, the mockery of uncooked rations issued us, when there was not a chip or stick in the whole camp with which to cook. It was during one of these periods of extra starvation, when we had not had food for forty-eight hours, when the strongest men among us, through weakness, staggered and fell in endeavoring to walk, that a well-dressed officer from the city rode to the entrance, as it was termed, where rations were usually issued, and made to the prisoners there congregated, waiting in hopes of receiving rations, the proposition to go out and work. The following, as near as I can recollect, was the substance and manner of his proposition.

"We wish you to work down on the islands, under guard, as prisoners; it is work which any of you can do — which, as soldiers, you have been accustomed to. You won't have to take a musket: there are none compelled to go; but those, after what I have said here, who do volunteer to go, will be made to perform the work required of them, whether they like it or not. In return, we will give you rations of flour, meat, rum, and tobacco."

Ah, well do I remember that the very mention of fresh meat and flour was enough, almost, to craze me at that time. I remember how wishful and longing those poor fellows looked. Yet I had seen so much of their constancy under suffering, that I was not prepared to hear them clamor as they did to go out and work for food. It was a cruel temptation. The poor fellows had become childish, and knew not what they were doing. Said an old Belle Island prisoner, standing at my side, "Some one ought to speak to these men; they are crazy with hunger." Under an uncontrollable impulse, I clambered upon an empty rice cask, and commenced to speak. "Wait," said the officer, addressing me, "until I leave." After this he said, "All those who wish to avail themselves of the opportunity, may go and get their traps, and be ready about dark to leave the prison." He bowed to me, and saying, "You can now listen to your friend," withdrew a short distance out of camp, sitting on his horse, where he could hear what was said.

My theme had in it inspiration. I think I never did, nor ever shall, speak with such effect as then. I commenced by saying, "This rebel officer has honorably stated what he requires of you. You understand that he wishes you to dig rifle pits for our enemies, though he has not squarely said so. However honorable it may be for him to make this proposition to hungry, suffering men, it is treason for you to accept." I then spoke to them of their *homes,* of their friends, of the *cause,* and

14

the pride they would feel when, some day, they should again stand under the old flag, true men, not traitors. I closed by saying, "I, too, am starving: it is the work of our enemies. You can see written all over me 'Long imprisonment.' We are famishing, but let us show our enemies that we are not hirelings, but patriots; that we can die, but will not be dishonored. Is there one here, after suffering for so glorious a cause, that will band himself with traitors?" "No," "No," "No," "Go on," "Go on," came the answers, like a pæan of victory, from the lips of starving men — truly a victory of truth over death.

It was said some went out that night, after dark. I did not see them, and can only wonder that the desire for life was not strong enough to prompt more to go. Many, who had clamored to go, when the officer first made the proposition to them, came up to me, and, with tears, thanked me — thanked me for keeping food from their lips at such a price. Poor, noble fellows! One of my company boys was among the number, and said, "It was the right kind of talk, Sarge;" and tears streamed down his shrunken cheeks as he said, "I suppose I shall die before I get out; but I had better, for I couldn't look mother or sis in the face after being a traitor." Poor, noble fellow! he did die not a meek from that day, and, as his pale face rises unbidden to memory, I can scarce but reproach myself that words of mine prevented him from saving life at even such a price. "My heart rose up in my throat," said another, "at thought of the Stars and Stripes, and I wouldn't go for a brigadier-general's commission in the Home Guards."

Imagine me as an orator, clothed in picturesque rags. My wardrobe consisted of a pair of pants, remnants of a shirt, which hung in tatters from the neck-band, and an old torn hat, which looked like a letter A, rent by a dog. My pants were full of holes — so many mouths eloquent of misery. A decently-dressed, better-fed prisoner would not, perhaps, have affected my comrades by words so easily. It was because I was one of them, suffering with them, that they listened so earnestly and responded so eloquently. Their hearts were right, and needed only a monitor.

Sunday afternoons were holidays among the negroes of Charleston, and, dressed in their best "clo'es," they came to get a "peek" at the Yankees. They acted like overgrown children, and, when the Secesh artillerists pointed the guns towards them, as if to shoot, they ran screaming away.

During the last of September, two citizen prisoners of our number went down Charleston Harbor on the rebel flag-of-truce boat, expecting to be paroled or exchanged. One of them was paroled, and, as no arrangements could be made for the disposal of the other, he was brought back. In sight of the old flag and the friendly uniform, and then to be dragged again to an imprisonment which was to end — when or how no one knew — how great a disappointment! The poor

fellow pined away, lost courage, and soon died. Better
for him had he never sailed down the harbor, with high
hope of liberty, that pleasant morning.

About this time it was rumored that the yellow fever
had made its appearance in camp and in the city. But
there were so many rumors continually in circulation
among us, that we knew not what credence to give
them. October came, and we were told that a removal
of the prisoners would at once be commenced. A number of cases of the yellow fever had occurred in town,
and humanity, no less than the sanitary condition of the
city, demanded our removal. I would have been willing to remain behind and take the risks, as, on the
whole, our condition was liable to be worse at any
other place than here.

A detachment of prisoners was sent away the first of
October, and about two thousand every two days continued to be sent off, until the camp was cleared. On or
about the seventh day, all the remaining squads of the
prison, except the hospital department, were ordered to
be ready to move on the morrow. About dark a pint
of beans, a half pint of Indian meal, and a few spoonfuls of rice were issued to each man, for three days'
rations. We got no wood to cook it with. That evening Jesse and myself cut into small pieces the sticks
used to raise our blanket on, and, obtaining half of a
canteen to cook in, commenced to prepare our rations.
First, we boiled the beans, — of course without salt or
pork; and, as we had no means of taking them with

us, and were hungry, ate them, for convenience and
to keep them safe from pilferers. Then we boiled
our rice, and, stirring up the Indian meal with it,
cooked a johnny-cake in our canteen. All around us,
gathered in anxious groups, were men engaged in similar occupations, and the casualties happening were
curiously ludicrous. Men were continually falling into
the shallow wells around them. It being the last night,
the prisoners used such fuel as they had liberally, and
indulged quite freely in pitch-pine torches. Every moment or two might be heard a "chug" and splash, which
proclaimed that some wandering star had fallen from
its orbit into a well. The position was more vexing
and comical than dangerous. I had been not a little
amused at seeing others precipitated into wells, and had
made up my mind that I would keep out of them. How
fallible are all resolves! While creeping on hands and
knees, and not thinking of the proximity of wells, I
was suddenly precipitated head foremost into one about
six feet deep. Jesse caught me in the act of scrambling
out, and, as I sat rubbing the sand out of my hair, and
trying to keep the water from running down my back,
he commenced to poke fun at me. "Ben in bathin',
old fellow? Better stand on yer head, and let it drain
off," said he, referring to the moisture, elevating his
torch, so as to get a better view, and stepping back,
chuckling. Suddenly, splash went something, and
Jesse was invisible: he had disappeared into the recesses
of the earth. It was then my turn to laugh. Thus

we made merry over our misery, which, ordinarily, would have dampened the fun of most people. Was it not as well to laugh as cry?

The morning dawned, and found our rations cooked into a mysterious, black-looking substance, which we called a johnny-cake. We fell into line when the order came, in a hurry to see what fate and the Johnnies would do with us next. We were speedily marched to the northern entrance of the Fair Ground, where, after going through with a good deal of the usual counting, we were packed on board of box cars, and went slowly on our way in a northerly direction.

As the cars were leaving Charleston we caught a glimpse of the Federal officers, who were embarked on board of box cars, *en route,* as I afterwards understood, for Columbia. Along on the railway, for quite a distance out of Charleston, were families of white people, living in box cars, having their beds, and kitchen furniture, and stoves therein. This I had noticed in all my transportations through Secessia. At Macon and other points it was quite as common as on the double and turn-out tracks near Charleston.

Our route from Charleston to Florence was unmarked by extraordinary occurrences. There were several men shot by the guard, while trying to escape by jumping from the cars while in motion. At every stopping-place those of our number who had died during transportation were left along the route for burial. A dickering trade was kept up along the way between the guard, who were stationed on the top of the cars, and the prisoners. At one place where we stopped to wood up, while the vigilance of the guard was relaxed, I slyly got off the cars and crept under the platform of the depot, and was much chagrined when one of the Johnnies came along and stirred me out of my hiding-place, with admonitions "to git into them thar cars."

CHAPTER XII.

Imprisonment at Florence. —An affecting Scene. — Inhumanity of
Rebel Authorities. — The Stockade similar to that at Andersonville
— Precautions against Tunnelling. — Disrespect of Rebels to their
Chief. — Poor Shelter. — Afterwards improved. — Suffering from
Cold. — Scanty Rations. — Woodcutters detailed. — Dreadful An-
noyance by Vermin. — Police organized under Big Peter. — The
Force perverted to bad Purposes. — Despondency at the Pros-
pects. — Further Attempts to purchase Treason.— Despair has its
Effects. — An Apology for the poor Fellows. — Their Hope of Escape while in Rebel Service. — Some of them shot as Deserters. —
Sublime Heroism. — Colonel Iverson again. — A Brutal Under
officer. — Good News. — The Arrival of Clothing. — A scanty
Supply. — The Hospital flanked for a good Meal. — The Clouds
breaking. — More Food. — Statement of Colonel Iverson that Food
was limited by Orders. — Interest in Presidential Election. — Vote
by Prisoners. — Majority for Lincoln.

I T was pitch dark and raining furiously when we
arrived at Florence, our destination. We were
marched into a field, and took up our quarters among
the hillocks, where had once been a cornfield. Water
and mud combined to make the ground an uncomfortable bed that night. During the night a large number
died. Willard Robinson, who had been complaining
some few days, died that night while lying under the
same blanket with his father. The morning dawned,
and the unhappy parent found his son lifeless by his side.

Smitten with grief, the father sat by the side of his dead boy, who had shared with him the perils of battle, and had been a companion in all the misfortunes and miseries of imprisonment. That father, who had more than once refused to purchase life by dishonor, would see that son no more. It was agonizing, but harder still the sequel. We went to the officer of the guard, and entreated for permission to bury the body. This poor boon for the father was refused. We then asked that the father might have the privilege of seeing him buried. This, too, was refused us. Their ears were deaf to the father's pleading — their eyes were blind to his tearful sorrow. The father spread the poor remnants of his handkerchief over the face of his dead son, folded his dear hands — it was all he could do. With a heart breaking with grief, he turned to leave him there, never to meet until the glory of a brighter morning should bring them together.* Not daring to look behind lest we should see rough hands stripping the dear body, we turned and commenced our march for the prison, — about a third of a mile distant.

At last a "stockade" similar to that of Andersonville loomed up before us. We were marched through the gates, which were closed upon us, to be opened, perhaps, never again during life. We were assigned to a portion of the stockade, and set ourselves at work to better our condition. The prison, like that of Andersonville,

* This was the last of several young boys who joined our company from the same New England village — South Scituate.

was situated on two hill-sides, with a branch of muddy water running through the centre, embracing, in all, about twenty acres. To prevent tunnelling, on the outside a ditch was dug, the dirt from which was thrown against the stockade, forming a kind of walk around the entire prison, which brought the top of the stockade breast high to the sentinels, who constantly walked their posts. These sentinels did not seem to have the fear of Jeff or the Confederacy before their eyes, as, when at night the hourly cry went round, they often closed their "— o'clock, and all is well," with a poetical flourish of their own— "And old Jeff's gone to h—l." "What regiment do you belong to?" I inquired of one of them on the morning of my arrival. "I belong to the fifth Georgia; Cheatham, he's our adjutant." I afterwards found out who Cheatham was — a comical, jolly grayback as ever graced the Confederacy.

Four others, with myself, formed a mess, and commenced constructing a shelter. For this purpose we dug a hole in the hill-side, about three feet deep. Two sticks were then set into the ground, across which was tied a third for a ridge-pole. Over this was stretched an army blanket. The front and rear ends, of course, were open, as we had nothing with which to stop them up. When it rained, we sometimes stopped up one end with our garments. In this grave-like place four human beings lodged, kept their "traps," and called it their home. We found sufficient wood for cooking purposes by peeling the bark from the stumps of trees, while those who had the implements cut and dug at the stumps for fuel. A week or two after my arrival, I obtained permission to go outside the prison under guard, and get material for completing our apology for a tent, and returned rejoicing with as much untrimmed pine brush as I could drag. We stripped off the pine pins, and put them in at the bottom of our shelter, making a very aristocratic bed, which few in prison enjoyed. We then patched up the rear of our "shebang" with pine limbs, which made altogether quite comfortable quarters, compared with what we had formerly enjoyed. But we needed all this, and more too, to make up for want of circulation and vitality in our scurvy-stricken bodies, and for the inclemency of a South Carolina winter, which, however sunny the South is said to be, was very cold. I never suffered more with cold than at this time. The days were usually quite warm, but, from sundown to ten o'clock in the morning, it was, to our poorly clad, emaciated bodies, bitterly cold. My clothes, which I have before described, were full of holes, and my feet were bare. The frost in the mornings was like snow on the ground, and often, through fear of freezing or being chilled to death, barefooted men walked up and down the prison all night, longing, through intense suffixing, for morning to come. Often, in the dead hours of midnight, I walked the frosty ground, pierced with the sharp winds which mercilessly sought out every hole in my scanty

wardrobe, and the next day took my revenge by sleep-
ing in the sunshine to make up for lost sleep.

From the day of my arrival in camp, I commenced
making use of hard wood ashes and water to clean and
rinse my mouth, and soon had the satisfaction to know
that it was counteracting the effects of scurvy. Our
rations at this place were as scanty as at Charleston.
Our divisions for the issue of rations were the same.
In no place did prisoners suffer so intensely, and yet in
no prison was the commanding officer so inclined to
make us comfortable. Nothing, however, short of a
complete change in their mode of living could now
benefit the majority of prisoners. A large number
of men, after a few weeks, were paroled to remain
outside the prison during the day to cut wood for the
use of the camp, while our police were urged by the
colonel commanding into building log shelters for those
of the sick who could not help themselves, and made
to keep the prison quite clean and orderly.

As it was impossible to obtain water without going
into the mud and water over knee before getting to the
branch or brook which was the only supply of the
prison, there were men who made a business of obtaining water for others, the common fee for so doing being
a "chaw of tobacco." "Who wants a pail or canteen
of water for a chaw of tobacco?" was as common a
clamor as "Have a hack?" "Have a hack?" at our
metropolitan railroad stations. Near the brook a hundred or more men would be gathered, who would feel

repaid for half a day's waiting, wading, &c., with one or two diminutive chews of tobacco. Sometimes might be seen men around camp selling the proceeds of these labors for rations.

During the summer we had been annoyed with flies, mosquitos, fleas, and all such kindred plagues. As cold weather advanced, we got clear of these; but a greater annoyance set in, little dreamed of. The vermin, not troublesome in warm weather, now, as the cold set in, took the benefit of the warmth of our bodies, swarming from our blankets and the ground upon our persons. Night or day there was no peace with them; they would not be still. Scratching only pleased them; for, where the skin was once started, they went to work eating into the flesh. The results were frightful, loathsome sores. I have seen sick persons whose flesh was eaten almost to the bone. I cannot, however, say whether the vermin ate the flesh, or only produced the irritation followed by scratching, which may have caused the sores. However disgusting such details, it is necessary that I should record them in order that the general reader may understand our condition.

At Florence the police organization, as I have intimated, was again revived under Big Peter as "chief of police." Their offices consisted in seeing to the police duties of the camp, guarding against the perpetration of nuisances, constructing shelter, procuring fuel for those not able to help themselves, and the carrying out of the dead. Under these arrangements, the camp became clean and orderly, wood was more regularly divided and dealt out, and the dead cared for more decently than before. There can be no disputing that they accomplished much good. But even this organization was perverted into a tool of the rebels for detecting the work on tunnels, and punishing those who dug them by thirty stripes upon the bare back with a cat-o'-nine-tails. "Big Pete" becoming prostrated with a fever, a gigantic, ignorant brute, with neither the good sense, good humor, nor the disposition to deal justly, which were characteristic of Peter, took his place as "chief of police," and under his misrule cowardly acts were perpetrated upon prisoners. Those who incurred the displeasure of the rebels, or their tool, the "chief," were tied to a whipping-post, and were mercilessly punished upon the bare back with that classic instrument, a cat-o'-nine-tails. Sergeant English, of a New York regiment, had once been instrumental in bringing this big brute before the prison tribunal at Andersonville for the murder of one of his company or regimental boys. On some trivial excuse, the chief brought Sergeant English to the whipping-post, and, before even a form of trial was through with, and while yet his hands were pinioned behind him, struck him repeatedly in the face with his clinched fist. It was only through the instrumentality of Lieutenant Barrett, of the prison, that he got a trial, and, nothing being proved against

him, he was released. Sergeant English then said he
would have justice; and I only wonder that S. has
never since been brought to trial for his brutal outrages
against prisoners.

In November the cold became so intense, our rations
so inadequate for the maintenance of health, the prospects of an exchange before the close of the war so
vague, and the chances for life so uncertain, that the
strongest heart recoiled at thoughts of the future.
Broken in health and spirits, they cast despairingly
around them in search of some means by which to
escape from the impending doom which threatened
them. Terrible were those days and nights of torture
and death, from which there seemed no release. Most
of the prisoners whose hearts had been buoyed so long by
hope of exchange, parole, or deliverance by raids, now
sank in despondency. Taking advantage of this hopelessness among prisoners, a recruiting station for the
Confederate army was opened near the stockade, the
officers of which came into prison for recruits. There
were some among us so hopeless, so lost to every
feeling but hunger, that they bartered their honor for
food, and took the oath of allegiance to the detested
Confederacy. Let those who blame them consider that
these men had been suffering the torments of Andersonville, Belle Island, Salisbury, Charleston, and Millen,
for many dreary months, and now before them was a,
hopeless winter, without clothes to cover their nakedness, food sufficient to preserve health, or blankets

to wrap themselves in at night. Some, considering an oath taken at such a time not binding, went out only to risk their lives in an escape. Jimmy, a boy about fifteen years of age, had no blanket or cooking utensils. He was continually obliged to beg for the use of them from some one more fortunate. In his destitution, he had to walk nights to keep from being chilled completely through, which, with men in prison, was usually followed by death. His life was crowded with inexpressible misery. For weeks brave Jimmy endured these miseries. He had refused at Charleston to go out and work; but at last the tempter prevailed: he went out, took the oath, had enough to eat for one week, and was shot, it was said, while trying to escape the next.

Many died rather than stain their lips with the dishonor of such an oath. D. P. Robinson, whom I have twice before mentioned, had it urged upon him thus to save his life. His answer was, "My boy is dead. I shall go with the boy." Simple words, yet heroic. "Death rather than dishonor" has been sub-limely uttered by orators and novelists, but never was its import so heroically realized as in many instances like those daily occurring in prison. I was, however, sometimes grieved to see men in comparatively good health going out to take the oath, men who possessed a blanket or overcoat. N. L. and A. H., men of my battalion, were of this number, in spite of promises made to me a few moments before. When my back was turned they went out to the recruiting office. So great was the indignation of the prisoners at the conduct of such men, that the rebels had continually to protect them by a guard. The rebels had no respect for them, and distinguished them from the genuine graybacks by the significant term of "Galvanized Yanks." It was true that a few under terrible suffering, with death looking them in their faces, took the oath as the last hope of life. Yet I cannot but be amazed at the general constancy with which starving men repudiated such conduct while surrounded by suffering and death. There are but few instances recorded where men exposed to such temptations so resolutely acted, suffered, and died for the right.

The hero who gives his life for a cause, while shouts of comrades cheer his heart, thrilling with grand emotions, is looked upon with admiration. But he who suffers gradual starvation, temptation, and despair, for many, many weary months, and at last seals his devotion with death, is he not the truest hero? Many a one lies to-day in his prison grave, which bears no name or mark to tell how he died, or what he suffered, or how true he was to the cause for which he renounced home, happiness, and life; but a grateful nation will recognize and remember in coming time the devotion which has done so much to perpetuate and preserve national life and honor.

Lieutenant-Colonel Iverson was in command of the prison, and a lieutenant named Barrett had the super-

15

vision of its interior. He was a rough, green, conceited brute, who never spoke without blasphemy, and never gave a civil word, or did a kind deed for any prisoner — a man with as few of the elements of good in his nature as I ever knew. I have always wondered that a man like Iverson tolerated such a coarse brute. I cannot account for it unless I take as an explanation an expression which I once heard him utter: "Barrett is just rough enough to scare the Yankees, and make them stand round." It was a task Iverson was too kind-hearted to take upon himself. Iverson paroled eight hundred men to cut wood for the prison, and continually urged upon our police, to whom he gave extra rations, the building of shelter, &c., for the destitute. But this took time, and meanwhile hundreds were dying. It was not life, it was mere existence.

From the time I made my escape from Andersonville I was troubled with aching limbs, which, after my release, terminated in paralysis of my legs, and left side, from which, I have not as yet recovered sufficiently to walk without a crutch.

About the first of November came the joyful announcement that clothes had arrived from Charleston, sent by our Sanitary Commission. The excitement among the prisoners was very great, and a hundred at a time were marched to the prison entrance, to be inspected and supplied according to their merits of raggedness. But the supply was inadequate to make us anything like comfortable. Some poor creatures,

who for months had been without blanket or coat,
got one, robed themselves in it straightway, and
lay down, as if they had reached at last their ideal
of comfort. The police did much to distribute these
articles of clothing where they justly belonged. I
had no shirt. Some shreds simply, hanging from the
neck-band, proclaimed that my person had once rejoiced
in such an article. I had no shoes, and holes formed
the principal part of my breeches. All my ingenuity
could not make my wardrobe break joints to cover my
nakedness. Yet there were so many worse off than
myself that I was justly overlooked until the last.
When it became certain that no more urgent cases
were to be supplied, then I got a cotton shirt. This
I was lucky enough to swap for a red flannel one, in
the possession of which I was positively happy for a
time.

Somewhere near this period the south-west corner of
the stockade was separated from the main prison for a
hospital. Here rude barracks were built, and outsiders,
not regularly admitted, were kept out by a police force
detailed from the prison. Once I escaped their keen
eyes, and flanked into the hospital, where a friend gave
me such a stomachful of wheat bread and sweet potato
soup that its very remembrance gladdened me for
weeks. Thus slowly the clouds began to break, and
luck turned in my favor. There were men in prison
who bought four or five sweet potatoes of the rebel
sutler, and, cooking them, sold enough to buy again,

and get one for themselves. One morning I drew In
dian meal for my ration, and traded it for a sweet
potato. This was not so much in bulk as the half pint
of meal, but the potato seemed to do me more good;
and thereafter, when I could, I traded off my rations
for sweet potatoes, under which diet, and my habit of
daily bathing, if I did not gain strength, I managed to
keep what little I had. Sergeant Charles Stone, of a
Maine regiment, gave me at this time about a dozen
potatoes. I shared them with comrades, and as the
irrepressible Jess described it afterwards, "The way
we walked into those potatoes" would have made the
reader smile to behold.

At one time officers came into the prison, covertly
buying greenbacks of the prisoners. As they went out
of prison, Colonel Iverson caused them to be arrested,
seized upon the greenbacks, and devoted the money so
obtained to buying potatoes for the sick prisoners. I
state these facts from a sense of justice towards a man
who showed consideration for prisoners. Though Iverson did harsh things through his red-headed brute tool,
Barrett, such as hanging men by the thumbs, &c., in
the main he intended to deal justly by the prisoners,
which had been unusual in my prison experience. He
once stated to me that the men would get more food if
he was not positively limited by the quantity and quality
issued to him for that purpose. He could issue no more
than he had.

Before the presidential election at the North, the rebels evinced intense interest in its result. They were anxious for McClellan's election over Lincoln, or, at least, for Lincoln's defeat. To test the sentiments of the prisoners, and thus form some estimate of the manner the States would go in the pending election, on the day of election two bags were placed on the inside of the stockade. Those who were in favor of Lincoln were to put a black bean into a bag, and those for McClellan were to vote white beans, which were provided for this purpose. We were marched by hundreds, and deposited our ballots. It was understood that if a majority of votes were cast for Little Mac, we should get extra rations that day. The result of the ballot was about fifteen hundred for McClellan and six thousand for Lincoln. There were about ten thousand men in the camp, but all did not vote. The rebels were disappointed at the result. When the vote was declared, the prisoners gathered at the place of election, cheering and singing patriotic songs, and Colonel Iverson forbade their being interrupted.

CHAPTER XIII.

Philosophy of Humor in Suffering. — Natural for Men to seek for Sunlight. — Smiles and Tears. — Lightness of Heart. — Jesse L. a Sample. — His comical Demeanor. — Jess as a Pair of Bellows. — A queer Remark. — Dealing out Rations. — All Eyes on the Meal-bag. — Squeezing the Haversack. — Eyes big with Hunger. — Jesse's Tactics. — Raising the black Flag.— More Truth than Poetry.— Jack E. — Herbert Beckwith. — Jess cooking under Difficulties. — Scurvy. — Combination of Disease, &c. — Torturing Memories. — Character developed by Suffering. — Arthur H. Smith. — A Break. — Death of Comrades. — A Political Creed. — Escape by Bribery. — Coincidences. — Instances of them. — December, 1864. — A Call for Clerks. — Colonel Iverson's Surprise.

U NDER the circumstances described in the foregoing chapters, it may seem to the general reader inconsistent with human nature that those so situated should see and realize anything like the grotesque and humorous in the kind of life which, as prisoners, we endured. This is true as applying to the many; but gleams of wit and fun were all the more striking when contrasted with the dark background of prison misery. In reading these pages, it may sometimes appear to critical readers, that the author has exhibited too great a disposition to indulge in levity or humorous delineations, to satisfy them that he was, after all, so great a sufferer, and that the horrors of prison life, as depicted, were not overdrawn, or, at least, exceptional in their application. Human nature remains the same under all conditions, and, though modified by circumstances, must act itself out, strange though some of its phases may appear. Humanity is complex and curious as a study, especially when seen under extraordinary circumstances, where the conventional courtesies of etiquette, which mask the character of most men in the common conditions of society, are dropped, or cast aside unknowingly from its features.

There is a physical and mental disposition, common among most men, when their condition is overcast by the gloomy shadows of misery and want, to seek for and enjoy some ray of the sunshine to which they may have been accustomed, however little there may be. So, in our prison sufferings, if we could sometimes get glimpses of anything like, or even suggestive of, the sunlight of other and better circumstances, amid the gloom of our squalidness, we were inclined to enjoy and appreciate it, though the elements from which the gayety or humor would be produced, were often, perhaps, more properly causes of agonizing tears than of hilarity or glee. Lamentations and laughter, mingling together, as is frequently seen in children, were phenomena sometimes witnessed among the prisoners. In this manner the one element mitigated the keenness of mental and physical sufferings produced by the other, without which, often, the one, if not beyond endurance, would have proved much harder to bear. In this way Nature sometimes kindly tempers the winds of adverse circumstances to the shorn lambs of wretchedness. There are several causes contributing to produce this condition of mind, but first among them is the disposition to make the best of one's circumstances, practicalizing the old adage, "It is no use to cry for spilt milk."

All reflective minds seem intuitively to assume that nothing can be gained by taking gloomy views of unhappy circumstances, over which they have no control; that it is better to be merry than sad; better the laugh should well up from a sinking heart than to give expression to groans of despondency, for these outward expressions are oftentimes instrumental in producing a joyous or saddened condition of mind. To one whom Nature has gifted with much buoyancy or lightness of heart, who has, perhaps, a keen appreciation of the ridiculous, there are no circumstances where the combinations of the ludicrous are so often possible as in the midst of the most extreme misery. There seems, amid such scenes, to be but one step from the tragic to the laughable, and the transition is so readily and easily made from the one to the other, without change of scenery or character, that feelings of mirthfulness and lamentations not unfrequently mingle in the same utterances. This is, seemingly, typical of their relations, and symbolizing the narrow division which, once overstepped on either side, readily produces either of the two extremes. The squalid and ill-conditioned circumstances of the peasantry of Ireland seem to have given them a love for drollery and an appreciation of the humors, conceits, and vagaries which will often spring up and group themselves around great poverty.

There were usually two opposites of character continually mingling together in prison, one borrowing gloom from the future, the other more hopeful, with tendencies constantly uppermost to laugh at the ridiculous and comical, seen gleaming through the clouds of despondent wretchedness. Blessed was he who retained this happy disposition; who, forgetful, for the moment, of himself, could still find in his heart the elements of mirth and humor. It increased his chances of life, when others, of opposite mould of character, were almost sure to die. Jesse L. whom I have more than once alluded to in this narrative, was a fine sample of this phase of character — a man whom no amount of suffering from short rations and cold could dampen or dismay. If he ever entertained serious thoughts, he kept them to himself, or made them known in so droll a manner as to make one laugh in spite of hunger and other miseries. A certain comical grimness in his physiognomy was heightened by a dirty face, where, perhaps, a few tears, shed over others' misfortunes, or a smoky fire, had worked lines of queer and grotesque import, which an artist's pencil rarely could have imitated or excelled. On one momentous occasion, when a dish of mush trembled in the balance and was found wanting, for the need of fire to cook it, Jess desperately turned himself into a pair of bellows and, thus engaged, blew about all the strength and wind out of his half starved body, until, at last, despairing of obtaining any flame, he looked up, coughed, and, with an inimitable grimace, said, "Look'ere, Sarge; just help me — can't you?" Seeing how fruitless he had been in developments, I modestly disclaimed having any ability in the blowing line. "Well," said Jess, winking and coughing with smoke, "you might put one hand on my stomach and the other on my back, and squeeze a little more wind out of me at that smoke."

The dealing out of rations for a squad of twenty men was an interesting daily performance, spiced with hunger and an anxiety on the part of each to get as much if not more than his comrades. On such occasions, in my squad Jesse usually officiated with a spoon, dealing around, in regular order, one spoonful of meal and then another, until it was all given out. At times it of course overran more than even spoonfuls to the whole, sometimes half of us getting one more than the rest. This was equalized by commencing to deal out the rations where, on the day previous, they left off giving the extra spoonful. Each man had a number, by which, at ration time, he was known. During such a performance, the meal-bag, or haversack, was the focus of all the twenty eyes interested in its fair distribution. Dead silence reigned throughout the squad. More solemnity and anxiety could not have been infused into any other transaction of our life than was given to this matter, so near our hearts. Great interest was usually shown in having the bag, or haversack, in which was contained the meal, well shaken and scraped of its contents. One day the flour which was issued went but little over three heaping spoonfuls apiece, and hungry eyes were turned to that common centre, the meal-bag. Jesse turned the haversack, shook it, and scraped it with desperation, knitting his brow, then, looking grimly around on each silent, anxious face, with a twitch at the corners of his mouth, and in a snuffling tone said, "Boys, yer eyes won't have to be very big to be bigger than your bellies, if they feed us this 'ere fashion long."

At another time some hungry customers persisted in critically examining the bag (after Jess had got himself into a sweat in scraping it until not a speck remained which would have proved a temptation to a pismire), to see that it contained no more meal. Jess threw the bag towards them, remarking, "If yer can look any meal inter that 'ere bag, I wish you'd give a look inter my stomach!"

As winter advanced, in common with other prisoners, Jess experienced great trouble from those tormentors of our flesh, the vermin. Almost continually during the day he had his nether garment off, engaged in a war of extermination, when, as he expressed it, he raised the black flag, and gave "no quarters" to the enemy. Drury, a quizzical fellow of our acquaintance, came upon the busy Jess thus engaged, and remarked,

"Now, old feller, you seem to be at them about all your time." "Yes," said Jess, suspending operations for a while, to scratch his back, "it's a pooty even thing; me and these fellers take turns." "How so?" inquired D. "Why," quietly remarked Jess, with a droll snuffle, "I torment them all day, and they torment me all night!" "In that remark, O Jess, was condensed more vigorous truth than poetical *licence,*" remarked D., as he walked away, leaving the undaunted Jess still "at um."

Damon, another comrade of mine, shared, in common with the rest of us, a very spare diet. One day, after being diligently engaged in compressing his pantaloons around him, in order to keep them on, for the want of suspenders for that essential purpose, with a long-drawn sigh, shook his head, and remarked, "There's one consolation: if I keep on growing slim in this way, there'll be cloth enough in this pair of breeches to make two pairs, which will give me a chance for winter." The idea was so amusing that laughter was irrepressible.

On another occasion I noticed my hungry comrade Beckwith eating a suspicious-looking substance, which bore a close resemblance to raw dough, rather than bread. "What, Beck., eating your flour raw?" I inquired, just to see what he would say. "Raw? Yes! exclaimed he, with mingled tones of indignation and humor; "I shouldn't wonder if 'twas just the thing to stick to my ribs and make me fat." Thus it was that starving, suffering men, while battling for life, laughed at fate, and threw their jokes in the face of famine and wretchedness.

On first entering the Florence prison I saw Beckwith almost daily. He always met me with the same brave smile, and with a quick, merry sparkle of his fine blue eye. I remember his jocular expression used to be, when we met, "Hey, old boy! what der you think of this — don't you? Tall living, perhaps you believe." But there came a change: his steps grew more and more feeble; his blue eyes looked their merry smile no more. He lived to reach Annapolis, and died without the longed-for sight of loved friends and home, where and among whom he had hoped to lie down and be at rest. Brave comrade! poor fellow! farewell! No more shall loved ones gaze upon thy merry, soul-lit face; no more will ring thy light, full-hearted laugh.

How many faces, like his, pale with dreadful suffering, come up like ghosts in households throughout the land, bringing to anguished hearts wails of bitterness and sorrow, which nothing can heal in this life! How hard the task, among our northern homes, to forget or forgive those who committed the crimes which mercilessly starved and tortured helpless men and youth, sent from every village of the land! At Andersonville, Florence, Charleston, and Belle Isle, their bones are an attestation of a stain which no future can ever wash from the garments of the South.

I one day found Jack E. intently engaged in stretching the remnants of an old shirt across two mud walls, built up like a dog kennel, leaving a space between almost large enough to admit two persons when lying down. Jack was whistling away, as though well satisfied with the manner in which things were progressing, when I remarked that I couldn't see the use of the old shirt, as it would neither keep out cold, wind, or rain. "Well," said Jack, stopping suddenly in his whistling, with a puzzled gaze fixed on his "shebang," then looking up, with a triumphant grin, "I don't suppose it will; but won't it strain some of the coarsest of it?"

During a rainy spell at Florence, at one time it became almost impossible to start a fire, and wood produced, at best, little besides smoke. The persistent Jess, under these circumstances, was indefatigable in his efforts to choke down the smoke and blow up the fire. Being defeated time after time, at last perseverance was rewarded. The little fire blazed, and Jess's face glowed with eager satisfaction as he held extended over the coals a split canteen, containing a concoction of flour and water, which the poor fellow's stomach was sorely in need of. He was at the height of satisfaction, when some clumsy fellow, in passing, stumbled and fell, putting out the fire, and sitting in the identical canteen, and on the contents of which poor Jess had centred his ambition and appetite. With one blow the prospects of Jess for a supper and a fire had disappeared. The strain on his nerves was too much; he burst into tears, and from tears to a discordant wail of chagrin, disappointment, and hunger. But, seeing the destroyer of his hopes, Venus-like, rising from a small sea of paste, his sense of the ludicrous was awakened, and Jess, bursting from a howl of sorrow and dismay to laughter, exclaimed, "Old fellow, if you'll set over that fire till it bakes, I'll go halves with you."

It was often piteous to see men struggling with despondency, hunger, and cold, in an attempt to preserve life. Men whose half-clad bodies were chilled through were to be seen moving feebly around during the night, uttering agonizing wails and moans, in an attempt to keep up circulation, and retain life in their wasted bodies. I recollect some half a dozen naked forms, out of which the likeness of human beings had been starved, with chattering teeth, groping around in prison, without a shirt to their backs, their gaze idiotic, and their speech confused and incoherent. Staggering feebly, they fell and died by the brook-side and in the sloughs of the quagmire, or by the dead-line. All human language fails to depict these scenes, and their very remembrance chills my blood with horror.

No imagination can picture the wretchedness of the hospital at the camp. Not one half of its inmates had their senses; their bodies begrimed with dirt, their limbs swelled and discolored with scurvy, or covered with the filth of diarrhœa, they lay often on the bare ground, in the rain, without shelter or blanket to cover their nakedness. Could the scenes occurring in prison be depicted and understood by the North in all their horror, the spirit of revenge would, I fear, have been aroused,

and have gone forth in a war of retaliation and exter
mination against the South. How hard, alas! it is to
comprehend scenes of wretchedness which elsewhere
have no known parallel in the history of suffering men

I have never seen a description given of the effects
upon the human system of a meagre diet of entirely
one kind of food. At Florence no vegetable food was
ever issued, or meat, with three exceptional cases, to
any but the hospital inmates. Our rations had more
variety than we obtained at Andersonville, usually consisting of wheat flour, hominy, rice, or Indian meal.
Dr. Hamlin, in his learned dissertation on Andersonville, assumes that to the scarcity of food were entirely
owing those aggravated forms of scurvy with which the
prison was reeking. This, no doubt, contributed in
producing them, by weakening the system and giving
less power to the body to throw off the influence of disease; but, in my opinion, it was the entire absence
of vegetable food, together with want of variety, which
caused such unusually dreadful cases of scurvy.

The tendency of scurvy to bring out old diseases,
and to reproduce and render chronic any weakness to
which the system had a previous tendency, is also, I
think, but little understood, as one of its effects. I believe the diarrhœa in camp, which, in a majority of
cases, produced death, was only one of the aggravations
of this disease, seizing upon that portion of the physical system which was weakest. Scurvy in the mouth
produced scurvy in the bowels, which was followed by

a general disorder of those functions. Old diseases, which were supposed to be eradicated, were revived by its influences, such was its tendency to seize upon the weaknesses of the system. I have of these matters, it is true, no scientific knowledge; but, having been witness to its workings in thousands of cases, I merely make the statement as a result of my observations on the subject.

It was true that starvation and mental despondency blended with so many forms of physical horror as to make it difficult to trace the distinct action of any particular disease. At Florence, as at Andersonville, the combination of them all produced feeble-mindedness and often insanity, which never partook in their character of fierceness, but were rather characterized by timidity of demeanor and incoherence of speech, in which often were mingled piteous tones of entreaty, low and tremulous with weakness; sometimes gleams of intelligence lighting the stony eye, or thrilling the voice with a wail of hopeless despair. No pen can picture or language express it; only those who are familiar, to their sorrow, with these scenes, will recognize the full import of my meaning. I seldom recall, willingly, these pictures of wretchedness; but they are too indelibly impressed upon memory, by the fierce brand of suffering, to be forgotten. Those sad, wailing voices, those clutching, restless hands, those pinched, despairing or meaningless faces, — all unbidden come back to me, with the horror of reality. Perhaps it

16

might be better to let such memories slumber in their prison homes but they seem to rise reproachfully, and bid me speak. I am almost glad that language fails to convey half my meaning, for the hearts of parents and kindred would freeze with terror could they but see those loved ones in all their hopeless wretchedness.

Revenge is not tolerated in the light of our high, ennobling civilization; but when I behold the South, stricken and suffering from fire, famine, and the sword, as one of the results of the awful civil contest just closed, I seem to see the hand of God's retribution seeking out and visiting her crimes with chastisement. If in coming times, as in the past, she shall sin against the moral ideas of the age, or if we, as then, become participants in her crime, so shall we reap, with her, the punishment of those crimes.

There was a phase of character developed by prison life which was neither joyous nor sad in its outward expression, seemingly a quiet bracing of every nerve, and the concentration of all the powers of mind and body against disease and death, in which men neither laughed, nor smiled, nor cried, nor could anything move them from their impervious calmness of demeanor. Not even an exciting rumor of exchange, or prospect of speedy deliverance, seemed to start them from their impenetrable placidity. Imbued with a quiet inflexiblenees of purpose, — and that to *live,* — they calculated every chance of life in each moment of time, yet never seemed to feel disappointment or passion. Like a rock in mid-ocean, lashed by the storm, they stood unmoved by the passions and longings that swayed and actuated the great mass of tortured mortality. I recall to mind one of this mould of character.

A comrade informed me one morning that S. was dying. I visited him, and found him suffering great bodily pain; but not an expression of it disturbed the calmness of his face. It was simply in the vice-like compression of his lips, and the convulsion of his limbs, that could be detected his great suffering. His hands were poor and wasted, seeming to be, simply, a parched skin drawn over angular bones. "Do you think you will live through it?" I asked of him. "Yes, I know I shall live as long as any one who does not get more rations than I do."

I did not believe him at the time; but, in spite of my unbelief, he lived, and is living still. He had a philosophy of his own in economizing life. He did not allow any passion or excitement to use up his vitality. He had a system of exercise, and, seemingly, was engrossed with profound reflections on his condition, studying himself and his circumstances to solve the problem of how he could best prolong life. I once asked him if he got down-hearted at the prospects. His reply was an index to his character: "No — there'd be no use in that;" as if his inflexible will controlled even the action of his mind, in that one purpose of living. Men of this iron mould were rare. It is uncommon, indeed, as a phenomenon, to see one possessing such stoical determination, such steady, unfaltering nerves while battling for a foothold on life.

Sergeant Arthur H. Smith was a man who had something of this composition. Always quiet, determined, and undemonstrative, he took the hardships of prison life with dogged grimness of purpose, — as if to extract all the life there was from the food to be had, and infuse it into bone and muscle, for purposes of endurance. It was this calm, ceaseless persistence and inflexible purpose which were requisite qualities for carrying men through the quicksands of death which surrounded us. When Smith first came to Florence, he was sent out to gather wood for the prison. The guards did not have their muskets loaded that day, and, had they been, they were nearly as liable to go off the wrong end as the right one. Noticing all these facts, Smith commenced to organize "for a break." Suddenly, to the surprise of the Johnnies, about half of their prisoners filed quietly in another direction, as if acting under orders; and so I suppose they were — from Smith. By the time the grayback sentinels began to understand the Yankee trick, the prisoners mentioned had scattered in all directions through the woods, and were not attentive to the repeated invitation of their guardian graybacks to "halt, thar!" It must have shocked the Johnnies' ideas of propriety to see the Yanks scampering off with so little notice. Smith was out on the "rampage" two or three weeks, but was finally captured in the vicinity of Wilmington. He had found friends among the black men, evidence of which he carried on his person, in the shape of some increase of flesh, and in a full suit of coarse gray clothes, and a shirt, made, I should think, from an old carpet. He came into prison with the same stoical demeanor and persistence of purpose standing out in his face — that of living and enduring to get home; which, it is needless to say, he achieved. He was my companion from Annapolis to Massachusetts, and lives to-day, shattered in health, but not shaken in the resolution to live as long as possible.

Sergeant Attwood, another comrade, was a man of opposite tendencies, with something of changefulness in his moods and disposition. He was, perhaps, as noble-hearted and brave a fellow as ever stood at a gun. Elated or depressed easily by good news or the reverse, his was not the temperament to endure the horrors of prison life. He sank under it, and, I believe, died at last amid the despondency and gloom of the prison.

Baxter, of Company G, went the same way, though he got his parole, and was on his way North. Shattered in mind and body, he roused himself at the prospect of going home, made the effort, and died. I recollect asking him, at one time, what he thought of the southern chivalry. His answer had in it food for thought, which, though it may be indigestible in these lenient times, was the spirit evoked by the barbarous usage of prisoners. "I have made up my mind," said he, "to one creed, political and religious, to govern my conduct when I get out of prison." "What creed is that?" I inquired. "To hate what they love, and love what they hate. I shall be sure, then, to be on the right side." If the future is to be a repetition of the past, I think his creed a safe one for the guidance of the North. But let us charitably hope that, now the great moral cause of southern inhumanity is removed, wrong ideas may also be revolutionized and supplanted by new ones.

At Florence the difficulty of escaping was increased by a deep ditch, already described, encircling the entire prison. This made tunnelling difficult and unprofitable, as it carried the tunneller, at best, but just beyond the stockade, where getting from the ditch would, under ordinary circumstances, attract or draw the fire of the guard. Yet men got out, by bribing the sentinels, and making their escape, with assistance, over the stockade.

One lucky fellow, who was the possessor of a watch, with several others, made his escape in this manner, and succeeded in getting into the Federal lines. I afterwards met him at the North, accidentally, on the train from New York to Boston, and had from him the particulars of his adventures. He and his comrades fell in with others who were escaping, formed a party establishing him as a leader, travelled nights, and slept in the woods daytimes. When set upon by dogs, they killed an entire pack of them, resumed their journey, reached the chain of mountains in North Carolina, and travelled on the table-lands of these elevations. At two or three different times they met white men, and, knowing it impossible to trust them, — although they, in each case, protested that they were Union men, — the alternative lay before them of killing them, or disposing of them in some manner so as not to endanger their own safety. Therefore they bucked and gagged them securely, and left them in the woods to their fate. It was hard that no other course was left to them, but desperate men, who had endured prison suffering, were in no mood to temporize under such circumstances. I wish I remembered and could give this man's name, and the full details of his escape, as narrated to me. It deserves to be put on record. My meeting him, in the manner described, was one of those singular coincidences which are stranger than the inventions of fiction. Many such coincidences and meetings occurred in my prison life. I will instance a few.

Jesse L., whom I have mentioned in these pages, was an old comrade in the engineer corps, in which I first enlisted. From the time of my first capture I had not seen him until I met him at Andersonville. Two men whom I had known at Belle Island very intimately, I met again during my second imprisonment. One of them I saw for the first time when we embarked on the flag-of-truce boat at Charleston. I sat down in the only place I could find, looked around at the man next to me, and thought I detected something familiar in his face: thinking him one of my casual acquaintances at Florence, I accosted him, when, to my surprise, he claimed to be one of my old Belle Island associates. At one time, in Florence, a German met his brother, whom he had not seen since he left home in the old country, some five years before.

The month of December was cold and gloomy, its chilly winds wailing through those long, bitter nights, like a requiem for the dead. The frost-whitened ground, which lay like a shroud over the prison; the various dreadful forms of despair, insanity, disease, and death; the shivering, half-clad beings, wandering with plaintive moans and chattering teeth up and down the prison, impress me now with terror, as one of the darkest times of my prison life. I can never think of that time without thanking God, with a full heart, for deliverance. As it is darkest just before dawn of day, so there is a gloom of circumstances sometimes preceding the light of happier days.

The rebel adjutant came into camp one day, looking up clerks to work upon a register of the prisoners, a copy of which was to be sent to our government in return for a like compliment conferred by them. I wrote my name and detachment, and handed it to the officer of the guard. In the afternoon, an orderly came into prison, and inquired for me. I accompanied him to the colonel's quarters, which was a log house, in which were a fire-place and two or three pine tables. At one of these sat a youngish, rather under middle sized man, dressed in gray. He looked at me with surprise, and said, with something of pity in his voice, "My poor fellow, can you write?" I took up a pen, which lay upon the table, and wrote upon a slip of paper a simple sentence, signing my name, rank, &c. The colonel drew it towards him, looked it over a moment, and said pleasantly, "Very good; that will do. Go into the prison and get your traps, and I will set you at work." "I have no traps," said I. "No cooking dishes?" "No!" It appeared to strike him as very strange. "Well," said he, "I'll feed you well out here." "I cannot agree to do writing," said I, "except for the prison." He looked up as if angry, and said, abruptly, "What difference does it make to you?" I said nothing. "Well, well, your Yankeeisms shall be respected, said he."

CHAPTER XIV.

I SIGNED a parole of honor, agreeing not to go beyond prescribed limits without a pass. That night I got a glorious supper of fresh beef and white bread, of which, however, I did not dare to eat as much as I wished for fear of the consequences. I slept in the Adjutant's cabin before a fire, and certainly thought myself altogether a lucky fellow. The next

morning Adjutant Cheatham, of the fifth Georgia, gave
me from his wardrobe a shirt and pair of drawers, which
I considered very clever in one who had so poor a
supply himself. Said he, apologetically, "I did have
quite a lot of clothes when I came here, but I gave
them all away to the bloody Yanks who were running
around in thar" (pointing to the prison) "like yourself." I sent my former wardrobe into the prison to
one of my comrades, and thus disposed of my vermin,
or most of them. Still I had no shoes, or any other
articles of clothing, except the said drawers and shirt;
but they were woollen and warm, and I tingled all
over with pleasant sensations from having again a full
stomach and warm clothes. I went at once to work
making up a dead register. This register showed,
when completed, that over seventeen hundred Federal
soldiers, prisoners of war, had died in this prison since
its establishment, the last of September, 1864. The
prison had never numbered over fifteen thousand men,
and a good portion of the time five thousand would
have covered the number contained therein. Many of
the dead were marked "Unknown." What a burden
of sorrows, disappointed hopes, and miseries were embodied in that word! Their names, their history all
unknown, uncared-for, they died. Some mother, wife,
father, or sister mourns them, or vainly waits for their
coming. Each sound of footsteps at the door may
cause their hearts to throb with expectancy; but no
more in life shall they behold those faces which once

gladdened the household. "Sick and in prison," they lingered and died, unknown.

Another lot of goods came from the Sanitary Commission, *via* Charleston, for distribution among prisoners during the middle of October. A guard was placed over them, and a Federal officer, who by mistake had got into the prison, was taken out and paroled for the purpose of taking charge of and distributing the goods among prisoners. Boxes also came through for several prisoners. The instructions were, that all boxes were to be examined, to see that they contained nothing contraband. The Colonel commanding undertook the task. The first box opened had a little pocket Bible, and on the fly leaf was written the name of the prisoner, with the words, "From your mother." As if this incident had roused some tender recollections of his own home, the Colonel turned quickly away, saying, "Put on the cover again, and let the poor boy have his box just as his mother packed it." Of the Sanitary goods I got a good suit myself, and had a chance to send my drawers and shirt into the prison for friends. The Colonel and Adjutant were very jealous of any of the paroled men having communication with the other prisoners. I had now been out at work on the register over a week, getting enough to eat, if I had dared to eat it. I had to exercise continual vigilance in regard to eating, and nothing but the most absolute self-control enabled me to keep from eating too much. I had had experience of this kind before, when released from Belle

Island, which was of great value to me. As it was, I scarcely passed a day without intensely griping pains and vomiting. At this time, too, I began to have my first symptoms of paralysis, and often collapsed in a heap while walking along, by my legs giving way from under me.

During my second week on parole, two rebel mail agents came to Florence, with about thirty thousand letters for the different prisons of the Confederacy. As the prisoners had been shifted around so much since imprisonment, it was impossible to tell exactly where they were. I was set to work to help distribute these letters, and look up the names on the register. Often the persons would be found to be dead; whereupon Colonel Iverson instructed me to write to their friends, informing them of the fact. While thus at work, it had never occurred to me that there might be letters for myself, until I came upon two. These letters informed me that all my friends were well, and though they were rather old, they encouraged me, and relieved many anxieties. Certainly, thought I, if fortune favors in this manner, I shall get out of prison before the war is over. Receiving these letters revived passionate longings for home and friends, which had been crushed for months under the accumulating miseries and mere struggle for foothold upon life.

The office where I wrote and lodged was the quarters of Lieutenant-Colonel Iverson, which I have once described. Paper was a scarce commodity, and we were not expected to make a very generous use of it. Cheatham, the rebel Adjutant, had before the war been a cashier in a bank. He was very kind to his Yankee boys, as he termed us, and was quite an able business man. The Adjutant had taken most of the young boys from the prison, and put them in a camp by themselves, providing them with much better rations than the stockade got. In this manner, about one hundred boys, from twelve to fifteen years of age, were cared for. He had one or two fine-looking little fellows around the office, whom he made great pets of. The Adjutant was very droll and humorous sometimes, and was never so happy as when he could get Eddy Knapp and another Yankee boy at dancing, or singing negro and comic songs. He used gravely to tell the women down in the village that these boys were Yankee girls, and at one time so completely humbugged them into the belief, that, prompted by curiosity, these Secesh dames one day made a visit to the prison headquarters, and commenced quizzing the Adjutant about his supposed girls, when the Adjutant, who had instructed the boys what to say, had their hair parted in the middle, and introduced them at the headquarters. The women asked them, "Be you Yankee girls?" "Yes, ma'am," was the answer. "Where do you stop o' nights?" "O, right in here with the Adjutant." Whereupon each Secesh dame took her snuff stick, which she had sat chewing, from her mouth, and sat in blank amazement, and when the Adjutant was out, said among themselves,

"This Cheatum is a drefful man." These women afterwards wished to look over the stockade at the prisoners,
and were so lost to all Christian feeling and decency as to
say, as they saw the emaciated creatures of the prison,
"Good enough for them Yanks; they needn't have cum'd
down to fight we'uns." Cheatham was a humane fellow,
generous in his impulses, yet a rebel of the darkest dye,
for all that. "Gol ding it," he used to say, "the Yanks
have got a powerful spite 'gainst us, and we have got
everything 'gainst them, and the best way is to fight
until it's knocked out of each other."

I often had a chance of seeing the "five Georgia"
and other rebel regiments in line. Their dress was a
medley of all the dry goods of the Confederacy, and
their drill in the manual of arms embraced every description of infantry tactics, from Scott to Hardee.
Some of the rebel privates one day passed headquarters,
and said one to the other, "Good quarters, arn't they,
Jim?" "Yes," responded Jim, "and full of them
devilish Yanks." The Adjutant heard the remark, and
turned to me, and said, "You see how jealous our folks
are when we do any kindness for you Yankees." I
have no doubt that the Colonel and Adjutant had to put
up with many caustic remarks from rebel soldiers and
citizens, whenever it was known they showed mercy
or favor to the starving, dying thousands under their
charge. "To tell the truth," said Cheatham," I wouldn't
have one of you Yanks to work on that register, but
my rebs have no tact for business. They can fight like

the devil, but don't take to reading or writing, or such things." This was a tacit acknowledgment of the superiority of the Yankees in point of intelligence. It was full as rare to see a Yankee private who could not write, as it was to see a rebel who could.

While distributing the mail, of which I have spoken, the rebel general, Winder, made his appearance at the prison. He was a man apparently about sixty years of age, dressed in homespun Secesh citizen clothes, butternut-coat and gray pants, tall, spare, and straight in figure, with an austere expression of face, a firm, set mouth, a large Roman nose, like a parrot's beak, and a cold, stony, stern eye. I overheard a conversation, which took place on the morning of his arrival, between him and Colonel Iverson, who stood just under the cabin window, near where I was writing. Said Winder, in sharp, abrupt tones, "Colonel Iverson, I can't have all these Yankees running around outside the prison. What are they doing?" The Colonel explained that it was necessary, in order to provide the prison with wood, and to erect shelter for the sick. "No necessity," said Winder, abruptly; to which Iverson responded in a tone of remonstrance and entreaty, "General, the prisoners, in spite of all I have done, or can do, are starving." "Let them starve then!" said Winder, in sharp, angry tones, putting a stop to further conversation. In about an hour afterwards, Iverson came in with a pale, anxious, troubled look upon his handsome features, and walking nervously back and forth in the office, gave the Adjutant instructions to write the order sending back all paroled men except those at work in the office, and a few others, to the prison.

I mention this incident, as I think it furnishes the key to the general inhumanity with which prisoners were uniformly treated in all the rebel prisons. First, public sentiment South forbade to prisoners civilized usage; second, the inflexible Winder was in general command of all the Confederate prisons, and received orders direct from the chief actors in the rebellion. Winder afterwards died of disease contracted at Florence military prison, and thus poetical justice was dealt out. Mr. Christian, the rebel mail agent, related to me an instance of General Winder's severity and moroseness of temper. "In some battle around Richmond, a Brigadier-General was captured with other prisoners. Winder stood giving orders for the disposal of the prisoners. The Brigadier-General, in fawning tones, said, "Ah, General, what are you going to do with me ?" Winder turned abruptly on his heels, replying in his sharpest tones, "Hang you, sir."

Several times I had conversations with Iverson and the Adjutant in relation to the treatment of prisoners, and in regard to slavery, in which my natural hastiness often got the better of my caution, and I expressed myself pretty freely. The Colonel defended the use of a deadline, saying it was copied from our prison regulations, and very gravely stated that the Federal treatment of

17

rebel prisoners was as bad as theirs. "The treatment,' said he, "on both sides is cruel." He instanced the treatment of prisoners at Fort Delaware, and said some of the boys of his regiment had been there, and that they did not get enough to eat, though he admitted it was through the rascality of the officers in charge of the distribution of rations. "They had tents," said I. "Yes," said he, angrily, "but we don't have any for our own men," and closed the conversation by going out. Some of my comrades, engaged in writing on the register with me, said, "Sarge, the Colonel has got his mad up, and you'll be sent into the stockade." Iverson stood only just outside, overheard the remark, and coming in at the door, indirectly reproved the speaker, by coldly saying, "I never think less of a man who has convictions which are not changed by his circumstances. I can trust such men." There were no men among the prisoners whom the Colonel had such contempt for as the "Galvanized Yanks." He treated men with severity when they intimated that they wished to "take the oath." He would say roughly to them, "You are traitors on one side — you will turn traitors to us the first chance you get; I can't endure a man who does not fight from principle." To Union men, who belonged to southern states, he was very vindictive and harsh, often calling them d—d traitors, asking them some-times what they were fighting against their country for ?

The Colonel's estimate of Yankee integrity and

intellect was a very low one. He was very much prejudiced against them, and refused to see that the general physical and mental condition of the prisoners was owing to long suffering. He would sometimes say in my hearing, of some poor creature who had had all his humanity starved out of him, "Now, look at him; he don't know so much as one of our niggers." I once overheard a conversation between him and a citizen. "These Yanks," said he, pointing to a squad of prisoners, "are just like our niggers; you can't trust most of them out of sight." Noticing that I heard him, with true gentlemanly instinct, he stopped in his remarks. When I got a little ahead of him in any remark, he would say, "Sergeant, you are the dog-gondest stubborn Yank I have got," or, "You are a heavy dog," and then closed the conversation by walking off.

Adjutant Cheatham used to delight in telling humorous incidents, and would even mimic his favorite rebels in all their grotesqueness. Unlike most rebels, he was free from the negro accent or patois, but would assume it with great drollery when he was mimicking the "South Caroleneans." I will not vouch for the truth of the following incident, which he used to relate in a manner which would have made a mule laugh. "I was out the other morning," said he, "and saw a guard drill that knocked all my ideas of that performance. Groups of men were standing around their huge fires — the mornings were quite cold — when one of the

South Carolinian officers came up, and pushing away a
big fat fellow who had tied a tarred rope into his belt to
make it reach round him, said, 'Eph, git from afore
me, for I'm a-cold,' and proceeded to warm his rear by
elevating his coat tail on his hands. Then looking
around upon the group, he said, 'Now, boys, git into
two ranks like tater ridges, for I'se a goin tu fling yer
into fours.' After getting them into two ranks, he
gave the order to 'right dress;' but the line didn't suit
him. Eph, especially, gave him trouble. 'Eph, Eph,
stick yer stomach in thar.' This Eph endeavored to
do; but when his feet were in line his stomach pro-
truded way beyond, and when his stomach was in line
his feet were in the rear rank. Getting vexed at this,
he pulled out his sword, and drew a crooked mark
in front of the company, saying, 'Gol ding it, if yer
can't right dress, come up ter that scratch.' They did
this very satisfactorily, when he commenced to drill
them. The first order was, 'Two ranks inter four
ranks, double smart, right quick, git!' But in this
manœuvre they got mixed up so bad that it wasn't
tried again. He then commenced to drill them in the
manual of arms. The person addressed as Eph
seemed to take unkindly to this military drill, and his
Captain addressed him in pathetic tones of remonstrance: 'Eph! Eph! I've told yer four times to bring
that gun ter a tote, and yer hain't done it. Eph, yer
have acted the plum fool!' Addressing the Sergeant
of the relief he said, 'Put this 'er Eph on guard near

the swamp, where Cheatum won't see him.' And,"
said Cheatham, "without seeing me, away went the
relief at route step, with arms in all positions but the
right ones."

During the second week out on parole, about thirty
men belonging to one of our merchantmen, captured
just off New York harbor by a rebel cruiser, were
brought into the prison. Iverson paroled the officers,
but turned the common sailors into the prison to take
their luck with the prisoners. The officers, who had
enough to eat and good clothes, thought outside life
about the hardest of anything they ever heard of, and
were much surprised when I told them I thought they
ought not to grumble, when men inside the stockade
were starving. Two officers, Lieutenant Luke and
Lieutenant J. Laughlin, were captured while trying to
escape from Columbia, and brought into Florence
prison about this time. Lieutenant Laughlin was
captured in the same battle with myself, and as I was
personally acquainted with him, I slyly gave him
clothes, and went to the Colonel, at risk of being sent
into the stockade again, and interceded for good
quarters and food for them, which were given.

The last of November, orders came from General
Hardee to commence making out parole rolls for the
sick and wounded prisoners at Florence, who were to
be sent to Charleston, at the rate of two thousand
every other day. I, with others, went to work upon
these paroles. What a joyful day it was to those men

as at last they realized that they were going home, and with trembling, eager hands they signed their parole of freedom! I was at work making out these parole rolls, when a poor creature came with tottering steps to the table, and tried to sign his name. "You'll have to write my name," said he; "I'm not the man I was when you and I were captured at Plymouth." I looked up and recognized in this shattered wreck of humanity a Sergeant who belonged to Company G, second Massachusetts heavy artillery. I left my writing to another clerk, while I helped the poor fellow to my log hut, and gave him warm drink and food, and my blanket to lie on. The poor fellow tried to thank me, but broke down, crying like a child. He was not very coherent in his speech. He could only say repeatedly, "Do you think we're going home?" I assured him of the fact, and left him to resume my duties. Afterwards, when I returned, he was gone. He must have died on the way to Charleston, as I could never ascertain that he reached his home.

Day after day I wrote on the parole rolls, trying to see my way clear to get away with the sick and wounded. Men were hourly dying before headquarters. Mr. Christian, the rebel mail agent, repeatedly said, as he saw the poor fellows come out, feebly trying to cheer, that it was the saddest sight he ever beheld. I was instrumental in getting several of my comrades out of prison on the parole list, and finally summoned courage to make application in my own behalf, when I was told to be contented or go back to the stockade.

After quite a delay in transportation, an order came from General Hardee, to have fifteen hundred prisoners ready for transportation on the afternoon of the next day. The names were placed on rolls, giving rank, regiment, and company, after which the prisoners signed their names, or made their marks. These rolls were in triplicate, and each roll contained, I believe, about three hundred names. Like our army rolls, no erasures were allowed. When the order came I asked the Adjutant if I could put my name down on the rolls. He turned away, muttering something, and I proceeded to put my name down among the paroled. I then made out triplicates for the rolls, containing about three hundred names each, and anxiously awaited results. An officer commenced calling the rolls, each man stepping out into line as the names were called. The decisive moment at length arrived. My name was called. I laid down my pen, took my hat and stood in line. "Here! here!" exclaimed both the Adjutant and Colonel, in chorus, "what does this mean?" "I thought you told me," said I, with feigned surprise, "that I could go home with this squad, Adjutant." The Adjutant laughed, the Colonel looked pleasant, and I took courage. "Well," said Colonel Iverson, after a pause, "you can go; but you must confess that it is a d—d Yankee trick." When at last I left, on my way to the cars, the Adjutant said, "I'm glad for you; I intended

you to go soon. I expect next you will be telling the
Yankees what a d—d rascal Adjutant Cheatham was."
And here I am telling all about him.

I left Florence that night. We were stowed on top
and inside box cars. We travelled all next day, and
arrived in Charleston about twelve o'clock next night.
It blew hard, and was bitterly cold, when we were
ordered off the cars, and had rations of hard-tack
given out to us. Prisoners here and there lay
dead and dying. It seemed too sad, when so near the
promised land, that they should die. It was very cold
the next morning, when we were on our march to the
flag-of-truce boat; but what did we care for that?
Were we not going home once more to see friends, and
the dear old flag we had so often fought under, and
which, God willing, we would fight under again?
The wind was too heavy for the flag-of-truce boat
to go, and reluctantly we were obliged to leave her;
and from thence we were marched to Roper Hospital.
From here, however, we were sent to the workhouse
yard, which I have described in preceding pages. For
two days we waited here, losing courage. Many lost
hope, and many lay dead and dying around us.

The rebel commissary came in the evening to the
workhouse yard. I inquired of him when we should
be sent to our transports. His answer was encour-
aging; and in course of conversation he asked me
where I belonged. I answered, "Massachusetts." "So
do I," said he, extending his hand; "I belong to

Massachusetts." I inquired what part. "Marion," was the reply. I was acquainted there, and soon found I knew several of his friends. He took me and several friends out with him, and gave us quarters in Roper Hospital, which were very good. While at this hospital I came upon some letters. One of them was addressed to the board of physicians in charge, asking what disposal was to be made of the hospital if the city fell into Federal hands. This letter was dated just at the time of our first attack on Charleston, and shows that the rebels were not so confident at that time of withstanding the assault as they afterwards were.

We had been in Charleston three days, anxiously waiting, when the fog, which had been very dense, cleared away, and orders for our removal, together with ambulances, came to the hospital to move the sick to the flag-of-truce boat. Those not able to walk were brought out and laid on the sidewalk, where some of the poor fellows died. Peter Jones, one of my company, died thus. "It is hard," said he, sorrowfully. They were the last words he uttered.

While these men lay gasping on the sidewalk, a woman came to the red-headed surgeon, who superintended their removal, and asked permission to give the poor sick fellows some soup she had for them. He rebuked her severely, saying, "If you have any such thing to give away, give it to our boys, down on the Island. You show," said he, "what side you are on." Her reply was, "Anything for humanity's sake, doctor;

let me give these poor men something to eat." While she was thus occupying the attention of this Confederate ogre, she had sent some children around on the flank, who provided the sick with soup and gruel. The surgeon raved when he found himself outflanked and outwitted by a woman.

About three o'clock that afternoon, we were again on the wharf, near the flag-of-truce boat. What a joyful moment! yet it seemed too good to be true. We, who had been so used to being deceived, were incredulous to the last moment. As we stood on the wharf, the commissary whom I have mentioned came up to me, and, shaking hands, said in a tremulous undertone, "I'd give anything to be in your place, going to Massachusetts." Dear, proud old Massachusetts! thy children can never, wherever their footsteps wander, forget thee! At last we sailed down the harbor — were in sight of our dear old flag — at last were lashed to our receiving ship, were on board, and, thank God for his mercy, were again under the old flag. How our tear-dimmed eyes gazed at its folds, and we, with solemn, sobbing voices, said, "Thank God! thank God!" The link that bound us to the terrible past was broken; the gaunt forms, the famine-stricken faces of those who survived, and the torturing memories they will ever have of those dark days of death and despair, attest how cruel and merciless were those who had charge of rebel prisons.

I arrived at Annapolis on the 16th of December,

1864, and was soon at home among friends, where, upon my arrival, I was attacked with typhus fever, and the only sight I could bear upon the walls of my sick room during my delirium, was that emblem of our country's honor and glory, the Stars and Stripes. To-day, though broken in health, and perhaps crippled for life, I record these sufferings as a remembrance to coming generations, and dedicate these pages to the memory of the living and the dead, who in the "great struggle" have suffered or died in prisons, and upon well-fought battle-fields, for our country's preservation and honor.

APPENDIX.

---oo;o;oo---

"We, the undersigned, having been informed that Mr. Warren Lee Goss has written a book narrating his experience and observations in rebel prisons during the late civil war, which work may contain statements not readily accepted by some persons as true, desire unhesitatingly to testify that, from long personal acquaintance, we know him to be a gentleman of undoubted veracity and unquestionable integrity.

I. W. RICHARDSON, 68 Cornhill, Boston, Attorney at Law
I. N. RICHARDSON, "   "   "
R. I. ATTWILL, Boston Daily Commercial.
C. B. WOOD, Town Clerk and Treasurer of Middleboro'.
S. B. PRATT, Editor and Proprietor Middleboro' Gazette.
W. H. WOOD, Judge of Probate Plymouth County.
L. A. ABBOTT, Pastor of Baptist Church, Middleboro'.
S. B. PHINNEY, Editor and Proprietor Barnstable Patriot
            and Collector of Port of Barnstable."

The following is from surviving comrades: —

"We, the undersigned, prisoners at Andersonville and other rebel prisons with Warren Lee Goss in 1864, take pleasure in bearing testimony to his unimpeachable truthfulness as a man, and to his honor and bravery as a soldier. In hours of sorest trial in those dreadful prisons (the horrors of which have been but one half told), when all finer sensibilities were pinched out of most of the men by hunger, sickness, and dread, he was ever a kind, patient, and faithful friend. Though suffering himself the common lot of hunger, exposure, and torture, he ever found time to comfort the sick and soothe the dying. When others sank, their hearts appalled by the prospects before and around them, his unfaltering courage upheld and cheered them. We are sincerely gratified at this opportunity of expressing our appreciation of his merits, and are pleased that so worthy a comrade and so kind a friend has taken upon himself the task of giving to the world an account of those days of suffering, despair, and death, when the strongest hearts were appalled with terror, and found hope and refuge only with God.

Residence

S. J. EVANS, Sergt. Co. H., 2d Mass. H. A., Providence, R. I.
G. T. WHITCOMB,   "   "   N. Bridgewater, Mass.
S. F. SULLIVAN,   "   "   Lynn,   "
S. T. MEARA,   "   "   Salem,   "
J. W. DAMON,   "   "   Boston,   "
W. S. OAKMAN,   "   "   Charlestown,   "
J. T. McGINNIS, 1st Sergt. Co. C., 5th U.S. Vols., Boston."

"The following is from the descriptive rolls of Warren Lee Goss, Acting Sergeant-Major Battalion, Second Massachusetts Heavy Artillery, on file at Washington: —

"'Warren Lee Goss was a prisoner at Andersonville, Georgia, Charleston and Florence, South Carolina, and other rebel prisons. During the action at Plymouth (where captured) he behaved with great bravery.'

(Signed)   "O M. FISH, 1st Lieut. Co. H.,

2d Mass. H. A., Commanding Company."

———

In the city of Washington at the time of the Wirz trial, there being survivors of Andersonville Prison present from all parts of the country, an organization was formed called the "Andersonville Survivors' Association." The following letter is from the President of that body: —

"I am glad some one has at last undertaken the task of writing an account of life in rebel prisons. I am sure you are acquainted (to your sorrow) with all the minutiæ of the subject. I am especially gratified that an old comrade, whom I have always found of unflinching integrity in all the trials of a soldier's life, — one who enjoyed the confidence of his officers, and esteem and love of comrades, — should assume a task like this. All returned soldiers who were acquainted with you testify to your kindness, bravery, and faithful friendship in those scenes of horror which were the accompaniments of prison life.

"PATRICK BRADLY,

"President Andersonville Survivors' Association.

" MILFOBD, December 17, 1866."

The physician who attended the author after his arrival from prison, testifies to his physical condition as follows:—

"Immediately after the arrival of Warren Lee Goss from rebel prisons, I was called to see him professionally, and found him completely prostrated, suffering from scurvy, chronic diarrhœa, and cerebrous typhus fever, all of which were, beyond doubt, the effects of privations and inhuman treatment while incarcerated in those loathsome prisons; as also paralysis of the limbs, from which he has not as yet recovered.

" WILLIAM P. CROSS, M. D.

"BOSTON, December 18, 1866."

———

"I have had an acquaintance for several years with Mr. Warren Lee Goss, and cheerfully testify that I know him to be a gentleman of sterling integrity and worth. During the war he has performed good and patriotic services for the country.

"Last winter he delivered in this county lectures of unusual interest, giving details of his experience in the army, for which he received the thanks of our people.

"S. B. PHINNEY,

"Editor and Proprietor Barnstable Patriot.

"BARNSTABLE, December 1, 1866."

———

Colonel Archibald Bogle, Thirty-fifth United States Colored Troops, sends the publishers the following:—

"MELROSE December 27, 1866."
"Messrs. LEE AND SHEPARD,
"Publishers, Boston.

"Gentlemen, — I have read over one hundred of the proof pages of a book written by Warren Lee Goss, Esq., entitled 'The Soldier's Story of Captivity.' I have peculiar pleasure in saying I formed an acquaintance with the author at Andersonville in 1864. I am but too familiar with many of the scenes which he depicts, and unhesitatingly testify that, so far as I have read, his descriptions of scenes of prison life are written with rare fidelity to truth, without exaggeration, and with a candor and straightforwardness which I am sure cannot fail to meet the warm appreciation of those who survived the terrors of that prison, and claim the highest consideration of every reader As such I commend it.

"I am, gentlemen,

"Very respectfully,

"ARCHIBALD BOGLE."

WE, the undersigned, who were companions or acquaintances of Warren Lee Goss at Andersonville and other rebel prisons, having read the book written by him, entitled "The Soldier's Story of his Captivity at Andersonville, Belle Isle, and other Rebel Prisons," certify to the general truthfulness of the work, and also to many of the particular incidents narrated. Some of the scenes depicted, which did not come under our immediate notice, we know to have been of very frequent occurrence. The picture is in no respect overdrawn; on the contrary, language would fail to convey to the reader a just appreciation of the terrible agony suffered, and the appalling scenes constantly witnessed by us.

ARCH. BOGLE, late Col. 35th U. S. C. T., Melrose, Mass.

EDWARD F. CAMPBELL, late 2d Lieut. 2d Mass. Heavy Artil., Cambridge, Mass.

S. J. EVANS, late Qr. Master Sergt. 2d Mass. Heavy Artil., Providence, R. I

ARTHUR H. SMITH, late 1st Sergt. 2d Mass. Heavy Artil., Chicopee, Mass.

JOHN F. McGINNIS, late 1st Sergt. 5th U. S. Vol. Inf., Boston, Mass.

PIERCE PENDERGHAST, late 1st Sergt. 5th U. S. Vol. Inf., Boston, Mass.

S. T. MEARA, late Sergt. 2d Mass. H.Art., Salem, Mass.

WILLIAM H. SHIRLEY, late Sergt. 1st Mass. Heavy Artil., Salem, Mass.

S. F. SULLIVAN, late Sergt. 2d Mass. H. Art., Lynn, Mass.

J. W. DAMON, late Sergt. 2d Mass. H. A., Boston, Mass.

C. F. RILEY, late Sergt. 2d Mass. Heavy Artil., Randolph, Mass.

GEORGE T. WHITCOMB, late Corp. 2d Mass. Heavy Artil., North Bridgewater, Mass.

THOS. H. MANN, late Cp. 18th Mass. Vol. Inf., Ionia, Mich.

P. DALEY, late of 2d Mass. H. A., Milford, Mass.

P. FITZSIMMONS, late of 2d Mass. H. A., Milford, Mass.

MICH. CONNIFFE, late of 2d Mass. H. A., Milford, Mass.

PETER PREW, late of 2d Mass. H. Artil., Milford, Mass.

WM. SMITH, late of 12th Mass. Vol. Inf., Milford, Mass.

PATRICK BRADLEY, late of 2d Mass. H. A., Milford, Mass.

DEXTER D. KEITH, late of 2d Mass. H. A., Randolph, Mass.

"They never fail who die
In a great cause.   *   *   *
They but augment the deep and sweeping thoughts
Which overpower all others, and conduct
The world at last to Freedom."   *Byron.*

NAMES

OF THE

UNION SOLDIERS

BURIED AT

ANDERSONVILLE.

NAMES

𝕵𝖚𝖓𝖎𝖔𝖓 𝕾𝖔𝖑𝖉𝖎𝖊𝖗𝖘 𝖇𝖚𝖗𝖎𝖊𝖉 𝖆𝖙 𝕬𝖓𝖉𝖊𝖗𝖘𝖔𝖚𝖛𝖎𝖑𝖑𝖊.

THE following is a complete list of the names of the Union soldiers who died at Andersonville, Georgia, as far as can be ascertained, together with their rank, the numbers of their graves, the regiments and companies to which they belonged, the dates of their decease, and the diseases of which they died, arranged alphabetically by states and by names.

The numbers prefixed to the names denote the graves. Persons numbered below 12367 died in 1864; those numbered above, in 1865. The rank of sergeant is indicated by a section mark (§), that of a corporal by a double dagger (‡), next after the names; all persons whose names are not so marked were privates, unless otherwise particularly stated.

The diseases of which they died are abbreviated as follows:—

Abscess	abs.	Diarrhœa	dia.	Hemorrhoides	hes.	Pneumonia	pna.
Anasarca	ana.	" acute	dia. a.	Hepatitis	hep.	Remittent Fever	r. f.
Ascites	asc.	" chronic	dia. c.	Hydrocele	hye.	Rheumatism	rhm.
Asphyxia	asa.	Diphtheria	dip.	Hydrothorax	hyx.	Rubeola.	rua.
Bronchitis	brs.	Dysentery	dys.	Icterus	ics.	Scorbutus.	scs.
Catarrh	cah.	" acute	dys. a.	Ictus Solis	i. s.	Small Pox	s. p.
Cathisnetice	cas.	" chronic.	dys. c.	Intermittent Fever	i. f.	Syphilis	sys.
Cerebritis	ces.	Enteritis	ens.	Laryngitis	las.	Typhoid Fever	td. f.
Congestive Chill	c. c.	Epilepsy	epy.	Marasmus	mas.	Typhus Fever	ts. f.
Congestive Fever	c. f.	Erysipelas	ers.	Nephritis	nes.	Ulcus	uls.
Constipatio	con.	Gangrene	gae.	Phthisis	phs.	Vulnus Selop	v. s.
Debilitas	des.	Gastritis	gas.	Pleuritis	pls.	Wounds	wds.

ALABAMA.

No. of
Grave.

7524 Barton, Wm, 1 cav, L, Sept 1, scs.
2111 Berry, J M,§ 1 cav, A, May 17, dia. c.
4622 Belle, Robert, 1 cav, E, Aug 3, dys.
5505 Boobur, Wm, 1 cav, E, Aug 13, dia.
8425 Brice, J C, 1 cav, L, Sept 11, scs.

8147 Guthrie, J, 1 cav, I, Sept 8, scs.

2514 Henry, P, 1 cav, F, June 26, pna.

996 Jones, Jno F, 1 cav, K, Mar 15, ana.

No. of
Grave.

4715 Mitchel, Jno D, 1, A, Aug 4, scs.

5077 Ponders, J, 1 cav, H, Aug 8, dia.
5763 Panter, R, 1, L, Aug 15, dia. c.
6886 Patterson, W D, 1, K, Aug 25, dia. a.
2504 Prett, J R, 1, F, June 26, dia. a.

10900 Redman, W R, 1 cav, G, Oct 14, scs.

4731 Stubbs, W, 1, I, Aug 4, brs.

CONNECTICUT.

2380 Anderson, A, 14, K, June 23, dia. c.

3461 Batchelder, Benj, 16, C, July 17, dia. a.
3664 Baty, John, 16, C, July 19, dia. c.
7306 Brunkissell, H, 14, D, Aug 30, dys.
2833 Brennon, M, 14, B, July 3, dys. c.
3224 Burns, John, 7, I, July 12, dia.
10414 Blumly, E, 8, D, Oct 6, scs.

545 Bigelow, Wm, 7, B, April 14, dia.
11965 Ball, H A, 3, B, Nov 11, scs.
12089 Brookmeyer, T W, 8, H, Nov 18, scs.
12152 Burke, H, 16, D, Nov 24, scs.
12209 Bone, A, 1, E, Dec 1, scs.
10682 Burnham, F,‡ 14, I, Oct 11, dys. c.
10690 Barlow, O I, 16, E, Oct 11, dys. a.
10876 Bennett, N, 18, H, Oct 13, scs.

(275)

5806 Brown, C H, 1, H, Aug 15, dys.
5919 Boyce, Wm, 7, B, Aug 17, dys.
6083 Bishop, B H, 1 cav, I, Aug 18, dys.
6184 Bushnell, Wm, 14, D, Aug 19, ces.
1763 Bailey, F, 16, E, Sept 4, dys.
2054 Brewer, G E, 21, A, June 16, dia. c.
5596 Burns, B, 6, G, Aug 14, brs.
5632 Balcomb, 11, B, Aug 14, dia.
5754 Beers, James C, 16, A, Aug 15, dys.
1636 Birdsell, D, 16, D, Oct 28, scs.
4296 Blakeslee, H, 1 cav, L, July 30, ana.
3900 Bishop, A, 18, A, July 24, dys.
1493 Besannon, Peter, 14, B, June 2, dia.
2720 Babcock, R, 30, A, July 1, scs.
2818 Baldwin, Thomas, 1 cav, L, July 3, pna.
2256 Bosworth, A M, 16, D, June 21, dia. c.
5132 Bougin, John, 11, C, Aug 8, dys.
5152 Brooks, Wm D,‡ 16, F, Aug 9, dys.
5308 Bower, John, 16, E, Aug 11, scs.
5452 Bently, F, 6, H, Aug 12, dia.
5464 Bently, James, 1 cav, I, Aug 12, scs.
4830 Blackman, A,‡ 2 art, C, Aug 6, scs.
7742 Banning, J F, 16, E, Sept 3, dys.
8018 Ballentine, Robert, 16, A, Sept 6, dys.
12408 Bassett, J B, 11, B, Jan 6, '65, scs.
12540 Bohine, C, 2, E, Jan 27, '65, rhm.
12620 Bemis, Charles, 7, K, Feb 8, scs.

3707 Chapin, J L, 16, A, July 21, '64, i. f.
3949 Cottrell, P, 7, C, July 25, dia. c.
3941 Clarkson, —, 11, H, July 25, scs.
4367 Culler, M, 7, E, July 31, dia.
4449 Connor, D 18, F, Aug 1, scs.
4848 Carrier, D B, 16, D, Aug 6, dia. c.
6060 Cook, W H, 1 cav, G, Aug 18, ces.
6153 Clark, H H, 16, F, Aug 15, dys.
6846 Clark, W, 6, A, Aug 25, dia.
5799 Champlain, H, 10, F, Aug 15, dys.
336 Cane, John, 9, H, April 2, dia.
620 Christian, A M, 1, A, April 19, dys.
775 Crawford, James, 14, A, April 28, dia. c.
7316 Chapman, M, 16, E, Aug 30, scs.
7348 Cleary, P, 1 cav, B, Aug 31, scs.
7395 Campbell, Rob't, 7, E, Aug 31, dia.
7418 Culler, M, 16, K, Aug 31, dia. a.
7685 Carver, John G, 16, B, Sept 3, dys.
7780 Cain, Thomas, 14, G, Sept 4, dia.
9984 Crossley, B, 8, G, Sept 29, scs.
10272 Coltier, W, 16, B, Oct 3, dia.
11175 Callahan, J, 11, I, Oct 19, scs.
11361 Candee, D M, 2 art, A, Oct 23, scs.

25 Dowd, F, 7, I, March 8, pna.
7325 Davis, W, 1 cav, L, Aug 30, dys.
2813 Davis, W, 10, E, Aug 3, ana.
3614 Damery, John, 6, A, July 20, dia.
7597 Diebenthal, H, 11, C, Sept 2, dia.
8568 Donoway, J, 1 cav, A, Sept 12, dys.
8769 Dutton, W H, 16, K, Sept 14, dys.
5446 Dugan, Chas, 16, K, Aug 12, scs.
11339 Dean, H, 16, H, Oct 23, scs.
11481 Demmings, G A, 16, I, Oct 24, scs.
11889 Downer, S, 18, C, Nov 7, scs.
11991 Demming, B J, 16, G, Nov 13, dia.

3481 Emmonds, A, 16, K, July 17, td. f.
4437 Easterly, Thomas, 14, G, July 31, dia. c.
4558 Earnest, H C, 6, I, Aug 2, gae.
7346 Ensworth, John, 16, C, Aug 31, scs.
7603 Edwards, O J,‡ 8, G, Sept 2, dia.
8368 Evans, N L, 16, I, Sept 10, scs.
11608 Emmett, W, 16, K, Oct 28, scs.
12442 Eaton, W, 6, F, Jan 12, '65, dia. c.

186 Fluit, C W, 14, G, March 27, dia.
1277 Francell, Otto, 6, C, May 22, dia.
2612 Fry, S, 7, D, June 28, dia.
4444 Fibbles, H, 16, G, Aug 1, dia.
4465 Fisher, H, 1, E, Aug 1, dys.
5123 Florence, J J,‡ 16, C, Aug 8, dys.
5382 Fuller, H S, 24, H, Aug 11, scs.
5913 Frisbie, Levi, 1 cav, G, Aug 17, dys.

5556 Fogg, C,§ 7 K, Aug 13, dys.
8028 Feely, M, 7, I, Sept 6, scs.
9089 Filby, A, 14, C, Sept 18, dia. c.
10255 Frederick, John, 7, A, Oct 3, scs.
12188 Fagan, P D, 11, A, Nov 28, dys.

3028 Gordon, John, 14, G, July 7, dia.
4096 Gray, Pat, 9, H, July 27, phs.
4974 Grammon, Jas, 1 cav, K, Aug 7, scs.
4005 Gulterman, J, mus, 1, E, July 26, dec.
5173 Gilmore, J, 16, C, Aug 9, dia.
7057 Gallagher, P, 16, D, Aug 28, dia.
7337 Gott, G, musician, 18, Aug 30, dys.
7592 Goodrich, J W, 16, C, Sept 2, scs.
7646 Graigg, W, 16, B, Sept 3, dys.
9423 Guina, H M, 11, G, Sept 21, dia.
10300 Grady, M, 11, B, Oct 4, scs.
10397 Gladstone, Wm, 6, K, Oct 6, dys.

49 Holt, Thomas, 1 cav, A, March 15, pls.
2336 Hughes, Ed, 14, D, June 22, dia.
3195 Hitchcock, Wm A, 16, C, July 12, dia.
3448 Hall, Wm G, 1, K, July 17, dys.
3559 Holcomb, D, 14, D, July 18, dia.
1350 Hilenthal, Jas, 14, C, May 25, dia.
3033 Haskins, Jas, 16, D, July 8, dia. c.
5029 Hollister, A, 1 cav, L, Aug 8, dia.
5162 Hally, Thomas, 16, F, Aug 9, dia.
5352 Hanson, F A, 15, I, Aug 11, ana.
6695 Hodges, Geo, 1 cav, H, Aug 24, dia. c.
4937 Harwood, G, 15, A, Aug 7, ana.
6964 Hoyt, E S, 17, B, Aug 27, dia.
7012 Hull, M, 16, E, Aug 27, scs.
7380 Holcomb, A A, 16, E, Aug 31, dia.
7642 Haly, W, 16, D, Sept 3, dys.
7757 Hubbard, H D, 16, D, Sept 4, gae.
8148 Hubbard, B, 16, A, Sept 8, dys.
8403 Haywood, 18, E, Sept 11, dia. c.
8613 Heath, J,§ 16, K, Sept 13, scs.
9129 Hall, B, 16, G, Sept 18, ana.
9369 Heart, W, 11, F, Sept 20, scs.
9981 Hurley, R A, 16, I, Sept 29, dia.
12086 Hibbard, A, 18, D, Nov 18, scs.
12117 Hancock, W, 14, G, Nov 22, dys.
12163 Hudson, Chas, 11, C, Nov 26, scs.

9340 Islay, H, 11, Sept 4, scs.

737 Jamieson, Charles, 7, D, April 26, dia.
5221 Johnson, John, 16, E, Aug 10, dys.
7083 Johnson, G W, 11, G, Aug 28, dys.
7365 Jamison, J S, q m s, 1 cav, Aug 31, dia.
7570 Jones, John J, 16, B, Sept 2, dia.
7961 Jones, James R, 6, G, Sept 6, dia.
8502 Johnson, F, 1, D, Sept 12, gae.
11970 Johnson, C S, 16, E, Nov 12, scs.
12340 Johnson, W, 16, E, Dec 26, scs.

1590 Kingsbury, C, 14, K, June 3, pna.
5186 Klineland, L, 11, C, Aug 9, scs.
6374 Kempton, B F, 8, G, Aug 21, dia. c.
6705 Kershoff, B, 6, H, Aug 25, dia. a.
6748 Kelley, F, 14, I, Aug 25, rhm.
7749 Kalty, J, 1 cav, L, Sept 3, dia. a.
8065 Kimball, H H, 7, H, Sept 7, dia. a.
8866 Kohlenburg, C, 7, D, Sept 15, scs.
10233 Kearn, T, 16, A, Oct 2, dia. a.

3401 Lendon, H, 16, D, July 16, dia. c.
5893 Lastry, J, 10, I, Aug 16, dia. c.
5499 Lewis, J, 8, E, Aug 12, dia. c.
6124 Leonard, W, 14, H, Aug 19, dia. a.
7912 Levanaugh, Wm O,§ 16, C, Sept 5, dys.
7956 Linker, C, 8, G, Sept 6, dia. a.
9219 Lewis, G H, 7, G, Sept 19, scs.
10228 Lee, — farrier, 1 cav, F, Oct 2, dia. c.

74 Mills, W J, 6, D, March 20, rhm.
119 McCaulley, Jas, 14, D, March 20, dia.
2295 Miller, Charles, 14, I, June 21, dia. a.
3516 McCord, P, 16, G, July 18, td. f.
3644 Miller, A, 14, D, July 19, scs.
3410 Mould, James, 11, E, July 16, td. f.

1892 McGinnis, J W, 15, E, Aug 17, ens.
4079 Miller, D, 1 cav, E, July 27, dia.
4417 Messenger, A, 16, G, July 31, dia
4492 McLean, Wm, 11, F, Aug 1, scs.
4595 Marshall, B, 8, H, Aug 3, dia.
5238 Mickallis, F, 16, F, Aug 10, dia. a
5328 Miller, H, 16, A, Aug 11, dys.
6342 Malone, John, 16, B, Aug 22, dia.
6426 Messey, M, 7, E, Aug 22, scs.
6451 McGee, Thomas, 11, D, Aug 22, dys.
6570 McDavid, Jas, 1, K, Aug 23, i. s.
6800 Meal, John, 11, D, Aug 25, dys.
6902 Mape, George, 11, B, Aug 25, dia. a.
6240 Marshall, L, 8, H, July 20, scs.
7547 Moore, A P,‡ 1 cav, H, Sept 2, dia. c.
7852 Miller, F D, 16, B, Sept 5, des.
8150 Modger, A, 10, I, Sept 8, wds.
8446 Mathews, S J, 16, K, Sept 11, scs.
8501 Meyers, L, 1 cav, Sept 12, scs.
9170 Merts, C, 11, C, Sept 18, scs.
9821 Milor, W,§ 14, F, Sept 20, dia.
10595 McCreieth, A, 14, H, Oct 10, scs.
10914 McKeon, J, 7, H, Oct 14, scs.
11487 Murphy, W, 16, C, Oct 26, scs.
11538 McDowell, J, 11, D, Oct 27, dys.
12134 Montjoy, T, 5, C, Nov 23, dia.

5044 Nichols. C, 16, G, Aug 8, dys.
6222 Northrop, John, 7, D, Aug 20, ces.
7331 North, S S,§ 1 cav, D, Aug 30, c. f.
10895 Nichols, M, 7, I, Oct 14, scs.

4565 Orton, H C, 6, I, Aug 9. rhm.
7511 Olena, R, 1 cav, E. Sept 1, scs.
8276 Orr, A, 14, H, Sept 14, scs.

2960 Pendalton, W, 14, C, July 6, scs.
3808 Pompey, C, 14, B, July 24, dia.
4356 Parker, S B, 10, B, July 31, dia. a.
3803 Phelps, S G, 1, H, July 22, td. f.
4934 Pimble, A, 16, I, Aug 7. dia.
5002 Plum, James, 11, G, Aug 8, des.
5386 Patchey, J, 1 cav, I, Aug 12, dia.
7487 Post, C,‡ 16, K, Sept 1, dia. a.
7688 Potache, A, 7, G, Sept 3, din. a.
9248 Phillips, J I, 8, B, Sept 19, scs.
9444 Padfrey, Sylvanus, 8, H, Sept 21, dia.
9533 Painter, N P, 7, C, Sept 22, scs.
10676 Puritan, O, 1 cav, L, Oct 11, scs.
11616 Peir, A, 7, D, Oct 28, wds.

2804 Ruther, J,‡ 1 cav, E, July 3, pna.
2871 Reed, H H, 2 art, H, July 4, dia.
3674 Risley, E,‡ 10, B, July 20, dia.
4636 Reins, Wm, 11, I, Aug 3. dia.
5902 Ross, D, 10, K, Aug 16, dia. c.
6400 Robinson, H, 21, K, Aug 21, scs.
6796 Ringwood, R, 14, J, Aug 25, dia.
8078 Reed, John, 7, B, Sept 7, din. a.
8170 Richardson, C S, 16, E, Sept 9, scs.
8345 Ray, A, 11, G, Sept 10, scs.
7310 Reed, Robt W, 7, A, Aug 30, dia.
8602 Roper, H, 16, G, Sept 13, ana.
10029 Robinson, J W, 18, D, Sept 29, dia.
10196 Richardson, D T, 16, G, Oct 2, scs.

10416 Reynolds, E, 1, E, Oct 6, dia.
12031 Rathbone, B, 2, A, Nov 15, '64, scs.

4 Stone, H I, 1 cav, A, March 3, dys.
234 Smith, Horace, 7, D, March 29, dys.
2405 Seward, G H, 14, A, June 24, dys. c.
2474 Stephens, E W, 1 cav, L, June 25, ts. f.
3010 Scott, W, 14, D, July 7, scs.
3026 Sutcliff, B, 21, G, July 7, dia. c.
3041 Stuart J, 7, July 8.
3522 Smith, J, 14, I, July 18, dia. c.
3598 Sherwood, D, 1, D, July 18, dia. a.
4212 Smith, C E,‡ 1 cav, L, July 27, dia.
4316 Straubell, L, 11, C, July 30, dia. c.
4555 Straum, James, 2 art, D, Aug 2, dia.
4722 Sullivan, M, 16, D, Aug 4, dia.
4802 Steele, Sam, 14, C, Aug 6, dia. c.
5385 Shults, C T, 14, I, Aug 12, dys.
5563 Stino, P, 16, K, Aug 13, dia.
5712 Steele, Sam, 16, C, Aug 15, dia.
5725 Smith, S, 7 B, Aug 15, scs.
6734 Steele, James M, 18, F, Aug 25, dia.
7070 Stephens, B H, 14, Aug 28, dia.
7975 Smith, Henry, 5, H, Sept 6, scs.
8088 Short, I. C, 18, K, Sept 7, scs.
8235 Smally, L, 16, E, Sept 9, scs.
9304 Starkweather, E M, 1 cav, L, Sept 20, dys
9435 Sutliff, J, 16, C, Sept 21, dia.
9648 See, L, 1, G, Sept 24, gae.
9987 Sling, D, 7, F, Sept 29, dia.
10138 Schubert, K, 16, K, Oct 1, dia.
10247 Sparring, T, 7, K, Oct 3, dia.
10476 Steele, H, 16, F, Oct 7, dys.
10787 Stauff, J, 1 cav, L, Oct 12, dia.
12005 Swift, J, 1, K, Nov 14, dia.
12288 Smith, J T, 7, D, Dec 13, scs.

541 Taylor, Moses, 14, E, April 14, brs.
4443 Thompson, Wm T, 14, I, Aug 1, dia.
5427 Thompson, F, 14, A, Aug 12, dia. c.
5479 Tibbels, Wm, 16, G, Aug 12, dia.
7723 Treadway, J H,‡ 15, E, Aug 3, dia. a.
10035 Tisdale, Ed F, 1 cav, B, Sept 29, scs.
10142 Taylor, J, 14, I, Oct 1, scs.
11089 Turner, H, 11, A, Oct 18, scs.

3107 Valter, H, 14, A, July 10, ans.

401 Winship, J H, 18, C, April 6, dys.
2158 Weldon, Henry, 7, E, June 19, dia. a.
2601 Warner, E, 1 cav, E, June 28, dia.
5543 Wikert, Henry, 14, C, Aug 13, dys.
5222 Wright, C, 16, B, Aug 10, dys.
4649 Wheely, James, 10, G, Aug 3, dia.
5675 Wenclell, John L, 16, E, Aug 14, gae.
6138 Way, H C, 16, K, Aug 19, dia.
6918 Wigglesworth, M L, 2 art, H, Aug 26, scs
6024 West, Chas H, 16, I, Sept 6, ts. f.
9028 Williams, H D,‡ 16, F, Sept 17, scs.
9265 Wheeler, J, 1 cav, M, Sept 19, scs.
9512 Ward, Gilbert,§ 11, Sept 22, dys.
10033 Weins, John, 6, K, Sept 29, dip.
12600 Ward, G W, 18, C, Feb 6, '65, scs.

6394 Young, C S,‡ 16, C, Aug 21, '64, pna.

DELAWARE.

8612 Aiken, Wm, 7. G, Sept 15, scs.

5529 Boice, J, 4, Aug 13, din.
7016 Brown, J H, 2, I, Aug 27, dia. a.

1709 Callihan, Jno, 1, B, June 7, dia. c.
2608 Conoway, F, 1, K, June 30, dia. c.
4394 Conley, J H, 2, F, July 31, dia. a.
2253 Connor, G, 1 cav, D, Dec 9, scs.
10868 Conner, C, 2, F, Oct 13, scs.
11245 Cunningham, K, 1, F, Oct 13, scs.

6217 Donahue, H, 2, D, Aug 20, scs.

6677 Emmett, W, 1, K, Aug 24, ans.

2091 Field, S, 2, D, June 17, ans.

9004 Hanning, H, drum, 2, F, Sept 17, scs.
8346 Hills, W, 2, K, Sept 10, dia. c.
5504 Hobson, W, 1 cav, E, Aug 13, dia. a.
9839 Hudson, G W,§ 2, Sept 27, scs.
11634 Hussey, J R, 1 cav, D, Oct 28, scs.

790 Joseph, W C,‡ 1, E, April 28, dia. a.
5346 Jones, H, 2, B, Aug 11, dia.

11410 Kinney, M, 1, D, Oct 24, scs.

8292 Laughlin, R M, 1, C, Sept 9, scs.
483 Limpkins, J H, 2, D, April 9, dia. c.

5956 Maham, Jas, 2, C, Aug 17, td. f.
8972 Moxworthy, Geo, 2, D, Sept 16, dia.
9580 Martin, J, 1, G, Sept 23, dia.
9943 Manner, C, 2, K, Sept 28, dia.
1671 McCracklin, H, 1, B, June 6, dys.
1570 McKinney, J, 1, F, Oct 27, scs.
12407 McBride, 2, F, Jan 6, '65, scs.

9450 Norris, Clarence, 1 cav, L, Sept 21, dia.

6307 Peterson, P, 4, F, Aug 20, dia.
8743 Piffer, W, 2, F, Aug 14, des.

7551 Reitter, G, 2, F, Sept 2, dys.
11534 Riddlor, H A, 1, H, Oct 27, scs.

6618 Saurot, John, 2, E, Aug 23, dia. a.
6479 Sholder, Ed, 2, H, Aug 22, dia. c.
6593 Simble, Wm, 1 cav, C, Aug 23, dia. a.
12707 Sill, James, 2, K, Feb 28, '65, scs.
5764 Smith, E E, 2, E, Aug 15, dia. a.

276 Taylor, Robt, 1, G, March 31, pna.
8082 Thorn, H I, 2, D, Sept 8, dys.
9324 Tilbrick, E L, 1 cav, L, Sept 20, dia. a.

11981 Warner, G, 2, K, Nov 13, scs.
10302 Wilds, J, 2, K, Oct 4, scs.
198 Wilburn, Geo, 2, G, March 27, brs.

DISTRICT OF COLUMBIA.

8449 Boissonnault, F M, 1 cav, H, Sept 11, scs.

11700 Clark, Theodore, 1 cav, I, Oct 31, scs.

11180 Farrell, C, 1 cav, E, Oct 19, scs.

5736 Gray, G S, 1 cav, K, Aug 15, dys.

9463 Pillman, John, 1 cav, D, Sept 21, scs.

6873 Ridley, A C, 1 cav, M, Aug 26, dys.

11716 Russell, T, 1 cav, D, Nov 1, scs.

6847 Stretch, J, 1 cav, G, Aug 25, des.
8189 Sergeant, L,§ 1, G, Sept 8, dys.
11742 Stanhope, W H, 1, I, Nov 2, dia.

12457 Veazie, F, 1 cav, K, Jan 15, '65, dia.

8172 Winworth, G, 1 cav, G, Sept 8, dys.
8807 Wiggin, Nat, 1 cav, M, Sept 15, scs.
10301 Wilson, W, 1 cav, E, Oct 3, scs.

ILLINOIS.

8402 Adams, H F,§ 17, E, Sept 11, scs.
12430 Adder, W, 30, C, Jan 4, '65, dia.
3840 Adlet, John, 119, K, July 23, dia. c.
8249 Adrian, F, 9 cav, E, Sept 9, scs.
5876 Akens, C,‡ 78, F, Aug 16, dia.
8381 Albany, D, 22, D, Sept 10, scs.
1264 Aldridge, A, 16 cav, L, May 20, dia.
8127 Alexander, B, 123, B, Sept 8, scs.
1423 Allen, R C, 17, I, May 28, dia.
10762 Alf, H, 89, A, Oct 12, dys.
2400 Allison, L J, 21, B, June 24, dys.
6710 Anderson, A, 19, K, Aug 24, scs.
10242 Anderson, A, 98, E, Oct 3, scs.
9946 Anderson, W, 89, C, Sept 28, scs.
10271 Anthony, E, 3, E, Oct 3, dia.
7339 Armstrong, R, 89, A, Aug 30, scs.
12792 Arnold, L, 137, I, March 18, '65, scs.
10979 Atkins, E, 6, C, Oct 15, scs.
9733 Atkinson, James, 14 cav, D, Sept 25, dys.
11777 Atwood, A, 23, G, Nov 3, scs.
8046 Augustine, J, 100, I, Sept 6, ana.

3709 Babbitt, John, 7, K, July 21, scs.
2598 Babcock, F, 44, G, June 28, pna.
3783 Bailey, P,§ 38, B, July 22, ana.
12530 Baker, James, 25, H, Jan 26, '65, scs.
2892 Baker, John, 89, B, July 4, pna.
3308 Baker, Thomas, 16 cav, M, July 14, dia.
1034 Bales, Thomas, 2 art, M, May 11, ana.
5848 Barber, C F, 112, I, Aug 16, des.
3829 Barclay, P, 42, I, July 23, dia. c.
12758 Barnard, W, 14, F, March 12, '65, dia. c.
10480 Barnes, Thomas, 135, F, Oct 7, dia.
8458 Barnet, J, 120, I, Sept 11, gae.
8762 Barrett, A,‡ 25, A, Sept 14, dia.
12687 Bass, J, 2 cav, C, Feb 22, '65, dia.
977 Basting, C, 47, B, May 9, dia.
3275 Bathrick, J, 1 cav, A, July 14, dia.
4618 Batsdorf, M, 93, F, Aug 3, i. f.
3603 Bayley, Frank, 16 cav E, July 19, dia. a.
11917 Beaver, M, 29, B, Nov 8, scs.
11652 Beard, J, 14 K, Oct 30, scs.
1870 Beal, John, 78, June 12, dia. c.
6644 Bear, D, 93, B, Aug 28, scs.

4573 Beck, J, 21, G, Aug 2, dys.
411 Beliskey, J, 16 cav, D, April 7, dia.
1230 Bender, George, 12, C, May 20, dia.
5242 Bennet, A, 16, B, Aug 10, dia.
6412 Benning, John, 6 cav, G, Aug 22, dia.
3345 Benstill, John, 27, H, July 15, dia.
10653 Benton, C W, 29, B, Oct 11, scs.
8188 Berlizer, B, 16 cav, F, Sept 8, scs.
10681 Best, William, 88, E, Oct 11, scs.
4315 Black, John,§ 31, A, July 30, wds.
2904 Black, J H, 21, E, July 5, scs.
1665 Blanchard, L,‡ 16 cav, D, June 6, ana.
1983 Bloss, P, 21, A, June 15, pna.
11085 Bodkins, E L, 103, D, Oct 18, scs.
2890 Bogley, J E, 21, D, July 4, dia.
12456 Bohem, J, 14 cav, B, Jan 14, '65, scs.
9899 Boles, William, 89, C, Sept 27, scs.
10795 Bolton, N P, 100, B, Nov 4, scs.
10791 Boman, J, 108, D, Oct 12, scs.
3008 Boorem, O, 64, B, July 7, dia.
1262 Borem, M, 35, G, Feb 9, 65, pls.
11921 Bouser, G, 89, F, Nov 8, scs.
5475 Bowden, W, 9, F, Aug 13, scs.
5046 Bowen, A O, 113, C, Aug 8, dys.
5943 Bowman, E, 123, F, Aug 17, scs.
9328 Boyd, B F, 6 cav, B, Sept 25, dia.
11678 Boyd, H P, 14, I, Oct 31, scs.
1971 Boyd, J E, 84, B, June 15, dia.
10984 Boyer, J,§ 14, H, Oct 16, dia.
11729 Boyle, F, 4, B, Nov 1, scs.
12840 Bradford, D, 85, C, April 25, '65, dia.
4259 Branch, J, 38, C, July 29, scs.
1815 Brandiger, F, 24, K, June 10, dia.
1619 Brannock, C,§ 79, K, June 4, dia.
1578 Brayheyer, H, 7 cav, M, June 3, pna.
3940 Breft, James, 88, K, July 24, scs.
1669 Brewer, Henry,§ 24, C, June 6, dia.
6421 Brewer, H, 78, F, Aug 22, scs.
3264 Bridges, W H, 30, K, July 13, des.
9570 Bridges, W J, 122, F, Sept 23, dia.
1613 Bridewell, H C, 38, D, June 4, dia.
2367 Brinkey, Morris,§ 16 cav, L, June 25, cas.
3056 Britsnyder, J, 65, G, July 9, dia.
2927 Brockhill, J, 4 cav, M, July 5, dia.

8717 Brookman, J E.‡ 44, I, July 21, dia.
8911 Brothers, D, 48,†H, Sept 16, scs.
9350 Brown, A F.§ 73, C, Sept 20, dia.
12450 Brown, H, 15, F, Jan 14, '65, scs.
5978 Brown, J, 73, B, Aug 17, ces.
9011 Brown, J H, 12, F, Sept 17, dia.
5924 Brown, J M 29, B, Aug 17, ens.
6836 Brown, William, 1 cav, G, Aug 26, dys.
8962 Brown, William, 16, C, Sept 16, ana.
6256 Bryant, William C, 107, A, Aug 20, scs.
10763 Briden, E, 35, E, Oct 12, dys.
5785 Buck, B F, 30, I, Aug 15, wds.
4963 Buchman, 16 cav, H, Aug 7, dys.
10888 Buckmaster, J, 79, C, Oct 13, scs.
12362 Buffington, B, 74, F, Dec 30, dia.
5457 Burdes, G, 89, A, Aug 12, i. f.
4299 Burrows, J, 90, L, July 30, dia.
7055 Burns, John, 100, K, Aug 28, dia.
5936 Burns, H.§ 16 cav, D, Aug 17, scs.
526 Burr, W B, 112, E, April 13, dia.
11858 Burton, O L, 35, I, Nov 6, scs.
11858 Butler, H J, 89, D, Oct 10, scs.
10362 Butler, N,‡ 89, D, Oct 5, scs.
8776 Butler, J, 89, A, Sept 14, dia.
11668 Button, A R, 79, E, Oct 30, scs.
9824 Butts, John, 22, F, Sept 27, dia.
626 Byres, George, 65, B, April 19, '65, dia.

12348 Cadding, J C, 89, B, Dec 27, scs.
6356 Callahan, C, 39, F, Aug 21, dia.
6505 Campbell, J M, 120, G, Aug 22, '65, dia.
10026 Capell, C, 87, D, Sept 29, dia.
10257 Capsey, J,‡ 90, D, Oct 3, scs.
3556 Carl, C C, 38, H, July 18, dia.
666 Carroll, J, 3, H, April 22, ts. f.
7037 Carroll, J Q,‡ 78, I, Aug 27, scs.
3393 Carren, O, 38, H, July 16, ana.
6693 Cairrt, Robert, 113, D, Aug 24, dia.
446 Cault, Albert, 116, A, April 9, pna.
1844 Castle, F, 103, E, June 10, dia.
7502 Center, E R, 115, H, Sept 1, dys.
3907 Charles, R J, 5 cav, M, July 24, dia.
6109 Chase, E S, 23, C, Aug 18, scs.
9095 Chattenay, S, 82, H, Sept 18, scs.
10459 Clienly, S, 79, A, Oct 7, scs.
4319 Chitwood, Thos C, 16 cav, H, July 30, dia.
3205 Chlunworth, Wm, 9, G, July 12, dia.
10551 Choate, Wm, 6 cav, D, Oct 10, scs.
9935 Chunberg, A, 89, G, Sept 28, scs.
6935 Christiansen, J, 82, F, Aug 26, ana.
7868 Clancey, J W, 38, E, Sept 5, gae.
504 Clark, A E, 16 cav, M, April 12, pna.
7760 Clark, C, 51, K, Sept 4, dia.
9560 Clark, C, 29, B, Sept 23, dys.
8834 Clark, F J, 6 cav, B, Sept 15, scs.
12672 Clark, R, 114, F, Feb 18, '65, dia.
5143 Clark, Wm, 14 cav, K, Aug 9, dys.
9925 Cleaver, M, 3 cav, H, Sept 28, scs.
8750 Cleggett, M,‡ 36, I, Sept 14, dys.
5787 Cline, John, 12 cav, I, Aug 15, dia.
1726 Cline, M, 14, B, March 4, '65, dia.
12051 Cline, T, 15, E, Nov 16, scs.
2287 Clusterman, —, 16 cav, D, June 21, dia. c.
2048 Coalman, H, 16 cav, June 15, dia.
2753 Colbern, M, 73, I, July 1, dia.
2244 Colburn, Thomas, 16 cav, G, June 20, dia.
5597 Colburn, William, 16 cav, G, Aug 14, scs.
300 Cole, John, 112, E, April 1, dia.
7211 Cole, W H, 112, A, Aug 29, dia. c.
6971 Coller, John, 6, B, Aug 27, dia.
256 Collins, Wm, 93, G, March 30, ts. f.
1198 Coddington, M J, 93, G, May 18, dys.
11719 Compton, H H, 21, K, Nov 1, scs.
2933 Cooret, D, 78, F, July 5, dia.
4683 Covey, J, 38, I, Aug 4, scs.
2758 Corey, O C, 106, D, July 1, dia.
6738 Cornelius, Jas, 9 cav, H, Aug 24, dia.
3856 Corwin, J, 7, cav, K, July 24, dia.
3677 Corwin, J V, 6 cav, L, July 20, dys.
6091 Cotton, J,‡ 100, H, Aug 18, i. s.
9704 Craig, G, 23, B, Sept 25, scs.
9307 Craig, J, 38, I, Sept 20, scs.

12506 Craig, 2 art, B, Jan 22, '65, dia.
9704 Craig, S, 23, B, Sept 25, scs.
10087 Craig, F, 9, K, Sept 30, scs.
1974 Crandall, W M, 93, A, June 15, dia.
2329 Crane, M, 23, E, June 23, dia. c.
2253 Crawford, Wm, 16 cav, K, June 21, dia.
10912 Crelley, C W, 29, B, Oct 14, ana.
4879 Cook, G P, 16 cav, L, Aug 6, dia.
12433 Crosbey, J, 90, C, Jan 11, 65, scs.
1417 Cross, E, 111, C, May 27, brs.
8859 Cross, J D, 14 cav, I, Sept 15, wds.
7982 Cross, J T, 21, D, Sept 6, scs.
6744 Crouse, J.§ 16, I, Aug 24, dys.
2032 Cruse, J, 79, D, June 15, dia. c.
2179 Creman, George, 24, C, June 19, dia.
10026 Cupell, C, 82, D, Sept 29, dia.
10257 Cupsay, J,‡ 90, D, Oct 3, scs.
3887 Curtis, A, 16, D, July 24, dia.

8626 Dake, G,‡ 100, D, Sept 13, dys.
4663 Dalby, James, 73, H, Aug 3, dys.
1826 Darling, D W, 93, B, June 10, scs.
10961 Darum, J J, 112, I, Oct 15, scs.
356 Davis, And, 112, A, April 2, dia.
8553 Davis, C, 112, E, Sept 12, scs.
10603 Davis, J, 113, D, Oct 10, scs.
4150 Davis, W, 16 cav, M, July 28, dia.
4048 Davis, H,§ 38, A, July 27, dys.
12311 Delancey, L D, 2 art, F, Dec 9, scs.
7013 Day, W F, 111, H, Aug 27, wds.
9073 Decker, C, 7 cav, M, Sept 17, dia.
4608 Decker, J P, 119, C, Aug 3, dys.
7150 Demos, B F, 78, F, Aug 29, dia. c.
2497 Denhart, W, 16 cav, K, June 26, dys.
4422 Denioo, E.§ 79, B, July 31, dia.
7514 Deming, Joseph, 31, D, Sept 1, scs.
12660 Denton, E,‡ 15, B, Feb 16, 65, dia.
2231 Detreeman, D.§ 44, E, June 20, scs.
5165 DePue, J W, 16, C, Aug 9, scs.
352 Derans, G W, 21, B, April 2, dia. a.
2365 Drieks, Henry, 89, C, June 23, dys.
12547 Dilley, A, 15, E, Jan 28, '65, pna.
1314 Dobson, M.§ 3 cav, H, May 23, dia.
8187 Dock, C, 9 cav, H, Sept 8, scs.
3834 Dodd, G W, 21, F, July 23, ts. f.
4207 Dodson, R B, 6 cav, B, July 29, dia.
2867 Dooley, James, 16 cav, L, July 4, r. f.
1441 Doran, W H, 78, I, May 28, ana.
1103 Donen, C, 6, I, May 15, dia.
1727 Dowd, J W, 38, G, June 8, dys.
1343 Dowdy, John, 16, K, May 24, brs.
10143 Dowell, J W, 112, K, Oct 1, scs.
10496 Downer, A, 24, H, Oct 8, scs.
12436 Doyle, P, 65, H, Jan 11, '65, wds.
12476 Doyle, J, 112, I, Jan 17, '65, wds.
5053 Drake, R R, 34, H, Aug 8, dia. c.
10332 Dresser, C, 24, G, Oct 4, dia. c.
9678 Drum, G, 89, Sept 24, scs.
3123 Dudley, J W, 89, F, July 10, ana.
2666 Dumond, P, 35, E, June 29, dia.
9947 Dunn, Alexander, 75, A, Sept 28, scs.
12496 Dunsing, A, 30, C, Jan 21, dia.
9037 Dyer, J C, 30, D, Sept 17, scs.
12686 Drew, E, 53, D, Feb 20, '65, rhm.

209 Eadley, Levi, 26, H, March 28, dys.
8045 Easinbeck, M, 100, D, Sept 6, dia.
10909 Easley, W A,‡ 21, G, Oct 14, scs.
5992 Eastman, Wm, 36, F, Aug 17, mas.
4962 Edwards, C D, 51, K, Aug 7, dys.
8084 Elliott, Ed, 92, B, Sept 7, dia.
9703 Ellis, William, 26, G, Sept 25, dia.
9734 Ellison, W, 14 cav, F, Sept 25, dia.
2249 Elslin, James, 112, E, July 24, ana.
4502 Emery, J, 22, K, Aug 1, dia.
4979 Emerson, J, 16 cav, L, Aug 7, scs.
9717 Erb, J, 9, C, Sept 25, dia.
12628 Ermains, F, 14 cav, M, Feb 14, '65, dia.
214 Errickson, C, 16 cav, M, March 28, cab.
2211 Ench, W, 29, H, June 20, asa.
11727 Enrow, W, 7 cav, M, Nov 1, dys.
2936 Evans, J, 9, C, Sept 25, dia.

8166 Newberg, H, 22, F, Sept 8, dia.
299 Newbery, Wm, 2 art, M, April 1, pna.
5778 Newby, E, 123, A, Aug 15, dia. c.
8129 Newlan, H, 25, B, Sept 8, scs.
4896 Nicely, F, 82, A, Aug 6, dia.
6945 Nichols, L C, 14, F, Aug 26, scs.
7847 Nicholson, R H, 123, B, Sept 4, dia. a.
7086 Nugent, T, 108, E, Aug 28, dia. c.
12460 Nully, C, 120, A, Jan 15, '65, scs.

6519 Obevre, O B,‡ 112, C, Aug 22, dia. a.
10851 O'Brian, D, 89, C, Oct 13, scs.
11274 Ochley, Wm, 24, K, Oct 20, scs.
3847 O'Connor, M, 2, F, July 24, scs.
1921 O'Dean, Thomas, 78, F, June 14, dia. c.
1533 O'David, H, 9, A, June 1, dia. c.
7751 O'Donnell, 34, I, Sept 3, scs.
3609 Odom, W, 9, G, July 19, scs.
1502 Oglesby, D, 16 cav, M, May 31, dia. c.
1214 O'Keefe, M, 2 art, G, May 19, dia.
7856 Olderfield, J R, 6 cav, B, Sept 5, des.
9196 Oley, O S,‡ 21, I, Sept 18, dia. c.
10042 Oleny, A, 108, K, Sept 29, dia. a.
9885 Olson, J, 112, K, Sept 27, scs.
6098 Olson, J, 89, D, Aug 18, dia. c.
30 O'Neil, D, 16 cav, K, April 19, s. p.
10469 Osborn, J W, 9, H, Oct 7, dia. c.
6774 Oss, 89, D, Aug 25, dia. a.
4123 Ottway, D, 8 cav, A, July 28, dys.
8414 Owens, C, 120, Sept 11, dia.
10279 O'Mine, D J,‡ 9 cav, E, Oct 3, scs.

5541 Padon, C, 12, F, Aug 13, dia.
6095 Paine, S, 88, B, Aug 18, scs.
3408 Paisley, F F, 120, E, July 16, dys.
6301 Parshall, J M, 114, A, Aug 20, dia. c.
6303 Partridge, W J,§ 30, F, Aug 20, wds.
12357 Parkhurst, B, 14, H, Dec 30, scs.
12677 Patterson, F J, 14, F, Feb 19, '65, dia. c.
393 Penny, James, 14 cav, D, April 6, dia. c.
12707 Penny, W, 114, F, Feb 26, '65, dia. c.
7700 Peeter, H M, 107, C, Sept 3, dia.
2621 Perkins, A E, 89, A, June 28, ts. f.
4853 Perry, George, 89, G, Aug 6, i. f.
9313 Perry, J, 9 cav, G, Sept 20, dia. c.
3953 Perry, N, 1 cav, B, July 18, des.
12179 Peterson, J B, 112, I, Nov 27, ana.
1686 Pettas, Wm, 65, I, June 6, dia. c.
5889 Pettijohn, J, 21, F, Aug 16, dia.
12594 Philbrook, A,§ 17 cav, F, Feb 5, '65, dia. c.
410 Phillips, Wm,‡ 16 cav, L, April 6, dia.
4887 Pierce, Charles,‡ 16 cav, H, Aug 6, scs.
1506 Pierce, W B, 8 cav, H, May 31, dia. c.
3764 Place, S, 44, F, July 22, dys.
10059 Plamerly, H, 14, D, Sept 30, scs.
3679 Porterlange, Wm, 24, K, July 24, dia.
1862 Pollard, F, 127, A, June 12, dia. c.
9602 Post, George, 7 cav, L, Sept 23, dia. a.
5783 Powell, A, 122, C, Aug 15, dia.
3058 Powell, D, 16 cav, K, July 9, dia. a.
3422 Powers, James, 44, C, July 16, dia.
23 Preston, C W, 8 cav, M, March 8, pna.
6007 Price, J M, 79, D, Aug 17, dia. c.
9059 Prickett, F, 30, E, Sept 17, scs.
12597 Pratt, W, 16, F, Feb 6, '65, dia. c.
10893 Prime, D, '?3, K, Oct 14, scs.
7972 Puck, John 122, D, Sept 5, scs.
1143 Puhrer, Fred, 27, A, May 16, dia.
10412 Pyner, T, 89, D, Oct 6, scs.

1053 Quinn, P, 52, A, Oct 8, scs.

3039 Ralston, John, 79, I, July 8, r. f.
1011 Ramsay, J C, 21, B, May 10, dia.
1765 Ramsay, A B, 45, K, June 9, dia.
12763 Ramsey, T J, 79, A, March 12, '65, scs.
10772 Randall, C F, 124, I, Oct 12, scs.
8578 Rankin, W A,‡ 3 cav, I, Sept 12, dia. a.
12680 Ransom, J, 4 cav, B, Feb 19, '65, dia. a.
7604 Reany, J H,§ 6 cav, B, Sept 2, dia. c.
5968 Redmont, John, 112, H, Aug 17, dia. a.
8571 Reed, A, 98, I, Sept 12, dys.

3496 Reed, D, 26, H, July 18, scs.
12324 Richardson, T, 34, E, Dec 23, scs.
1616 Richards, H, 79, I, June 4, scs.
3809 Rickold, W, 16, G, July 23, scs.
2836 Rictor, Charles,‡ 82, H, July 3, dia.
8632 Ripley, J, 9, B, Sept 13, gae.
7748 Ritter, D, 14 art, D, Sept 3, dia. a.
2074 Roberts, W W, 16 cav, I, June 17, ana.
8410 Robinson, E H, 36, A, Sept 11, ana.
4460 Robinson, H B,§ 6 cav, B, Aug 1, dia.
6080 Robinson, J B, 79, A, Aug 18, ces.
10751 Roder, F, 16 cav, G, Oct 12, scs.
2596 Rodenberger, N, 96, E, June 29, scs.
10184 Roferty, J G, ? cav, H, Oct 1, dia. a.
747 Rodgers, O, 12, A, April 26, dys.
1807 Rogers, Silas, 65, D, June 10, dia. c.
7228 Rogers, George, 16 cav, G, June 29, dia. c.
528 Rolla, E J, 103, G, April 13, dia.
4389 Rosecrans, H, 113, A, July 31, ana.
11473 Ross, J W, 45, F, Oct 26, dys.
8465 Ross, Thomas, 113, K, Sept 11, scs.
306 Rudd, Eras,§ 100, K, April 2, dia.
1294 Rudd, F, 16 cav, L, May 23, dia. c.
2557 Ryan, M, 89, A, June 27, phs.

2000 Saddle, M, 27, G, June 15, ana.
9345 Saler, J B,§ 14, F, Sept 20, dia. a.
10512 Sandler, L,‡ 19, D, Oct 8, dia.
11289 Sargeant, M,§ 14, K, Oct 22, scs.
1902 Savage, P P, 13, June 13, dia. c.
9915 Sauin, B, 36, C, Sept 28, scs.
7558 Schrider, D, 23, A, Sept 2, dys.
7163 Schrider, John, 44, K, Aug 29, dia. c.
3493 Schannoller, C, 24, H, July 17, dys.
10359 Schurtz, W, 44, F, Oct 5, scs.
1573 Scitaz, Victor, 16 cav, L, June 3, dys.
11077 Scott, H, 28, G, Oct 17, scs.
4524 Scuyner, N,‡ 64, G, Aug 2, wds.
12034 See, S, 11, G, Oct 15, scs.
1787 Seeley, Charles, 44, G, June 10, dia. c.
9325 Sem, C, 8 cav, D, Sept 20, dia. c.
4872 Serens, R B, 112, I, Aug 6, dys.
1333 Setters, Geo H, 38, G, May 24, dia. c.
12827 Seward, R, 61, E, April 8, '65, dia.
5350 Seybert, A J, 39, E, Aug 11, scs.
9322 Shadrach, G H, 7 cav, C, Sept 20, dia. c.
1661 Shanbach, Ed, 44, E, June 6, ana.
8861 Shark, L F, 113, D, Sept 15, dia. a.
12149 Sharp, A, 7 cav, B, Nov 24, scs.
2579 Sharp, A H, 22, A, June 27, dia.
1899 Sharp, E D T, 89, June 13, dia.
2647 Shaw, J, 89, E, June 29, dys.
7315 Shaw, Joseph, 98, D, Aug 30, scs.
4135 Sheeby, John,§ 42, G, July 28, dia. c.
8386 Sherwood, J F, 16 cav, I, Sept 10, dia. c.
7270 Shields, J A, 6 cav, E, Aug 30, scs.
12046 Siebert, H C, 7 cav, M, Nov 16, scs.
10441 Siffle, H, 7 cav, M, Oct 7, scs.
2430 Silkwood, H M, 89, D, June 24, epy.
1717 Silter, John, 16 cav, L, June 9, ana.
12713 Simmons, W D, 42, H, March 1, '65, dia.
7630 Simmons, C, 14, D, Sept 2, dia.
12834 Simmons, M A, 42, H, April 17, '65, dia.
309 Sipple, A, 107, E, April 2, dia.
12390 Skinner, H, 14, C, Jan 4, '65, dia. c.
10082 Skinner, Wm, 16, G, Sept 30, scs.
2585 Slasher, H,‡ 96, E, June 28, scs.
10663 Slick, P, 9, E, Oct 11, dia. c.
9402 Smith, C W, 16, K, Sept 24, dia.
5960 Smith George, 53, E, Aug 17, dys.
362 Smith John B, 7 cav, L, April 2, dia.
12566 Smith, J S, 115, D, Feb 1, '65, des.
10866 Smith, N P, 28, G, Oct 13, scs.
10975 Smith, O, 114, H, Oct 15, scs.
4659 Smith, William, 16 cav, M, Aug 3, gas.
8223 Snyder, B, 6 cav, B, Sept 8, dia.
8079 Sommers, W, 40, F, Sept 7, dia.
2165 Soms, C, 82, A, June 19, dia. c.
4283 Spangler, H J, 16 cav, L, July 30, dia.
9092 Spindler, W, 113, F, Sept 18, dia.
11359 Sprulock, A, 79, F, Oct 23, scs.
4598 Sprague, W, 8 cav, K, Aug 3, dia.

INDIANA.

1759 Barra, John, 65, H, June 9, dia. c.
2016 Burnett, Wm, 6 cav, G, June 15, dia.
2191 Buckhart, E, 27, F, June 19, dia.
2222 Brasier, S, mus, 19, I, June 20, dia.
2299 Bumgardner, 44, D, June 22, dia.
2458 Barrett, E, 42, I, June 25, dia. c.
2874 Bowman, John, 42, C, July 4, dia.
3044 Bruce, J W, 5 cav, M, July 8, dia. c.
3359 Broughton, D, 7 cav, K, July 15, dys.
3366 Bricker, J, 68, C, July 15, dia. c.
4027 Barton, J F, 52, G, July 26, dia. c.
4035 Ballinger, Robert, 39, I, July 26, scs.
4251 Bonly, James, 81, C, July 29, dia.
4479 Baker, J, 9, G, Agu 1, scs.
4563 Baker, D W, 13, B, Aug 2, dia.
4948 Bayer, F, 129, H, Aug 7, dys.
5089 Brenton, J W, 29, I, Aug 8, scs.
5093 Bowlin, Wm, 53, G, Agu 8, wds.
5220 Barton, E, 2 cav, G, Aug 10, scs.
5275 Busick, W A,‡ 101, F, Aug 10, dia.
5442 Bryer, P, 81, K, Aug 12, scs.
5590 Bohems, Philip, 79, A, Aug 14, dia.
5690 Baker, I P, 7 cav, H, Aug 15, dia.
5794 Boom, W P, 31, F, Aug 15, scs.
5981 Barton, George, 130, F, Aug 17, dia. c.
6163 Brookers, J M, 112, E, Aug 19, dys.
6410 Brown, J M, 66, F, Aug 22, scs.
6518 Bartholomew, I, 99, A, Aug 22, dys.
7370 Bamgroover, J A, 101, H, Aug 31, dia.
7794 Barnes, Thomas M, 5 cav, B, Sept 4, dys.
8314 Babbitt, W H, 29, I, Sept 10, dys.
8397 Bassinger, H, 14, C, Sept 10, dia.
8519 Boyd,, W F, 125, F, Sept 12, ana.
9098 Bartley, S, 88, I, Sept 18, scs.
9548 Bray, T E, 79, K, Sept 23, scs.
9708 Brown, J,§ 1 cav, A, Sept 24, dia.
9777 Birch, T A, 58, L, Sept 26, scs.
9793 Bozell, J F, 40, B, Sept 26, scs.
9846 Bixter, D, 5, B, Sept 27, scs.
10350 Blackaber, Wm H, 42, I, Oct 5, scs.
10939 Benton, L, 30, H, Oct 14, scs.
11559 Bennett, R N, 72,DF, Oct 27, scs.
11604 Bemis, J M,‡ 87, F, Oct 28, scs.
11919 Brown, D, 128, B, Nov 8, dys.
11930 Bailey, George, 72, A, Nov 8, scs.
12019 Bennet, A, 29, G, Nov 15, scs.
12128 Booth, J, 32, E Nov 22, scs.
12294 Bennett, C, 6, H, Dec 15, scs.
12486 Barrey, H, 66, I, Jan 19, '65, scs.
12504 Balstrum, J, 93, F, Jan 22, '65, scs.
12596 Branson, E, 57, A, Feb 6, '65, Pna.

301 Charles, James, 6, G, April 1, dia.
625 Connell, P, 6 cav, M, April, 19, dys. c
634 Claycome, S A,§ 66, G, April 20, dia.
1117 Cox, Joseph, § 42, B, May 15, dia.
1146 Carter, Henry, 2, C, May 16, pna.
1172 Curry, J W, 30, F, May 17, dia. c.
1463 Currier, Win, 87, K, May 30, dia.
1523 Crest, J D, 31, F, May 31, dia. c.
2254 Carpenter, O C,‡ 29, D, June 21, dia.
2307 Cottrell, M,§ 6 cav, G, June 22, ana.
2776 Cooley, A, 38, C, July 2, pna.
3043 Clark, W, 82, C, July 8, dys.
3922 Connolley, D, 9, I, July 25, dia.
4192 Cox, S, 66, E, July 28, dia.
4917 Clifford, H C 7 cav, I, Aug 6, scs.
5262 Courtney, J F, 2 cav, L, Aug 10, dys.
5654 Collar, E, 130 G, Aug 14, scs.
5660 Crews, E M, 5 cav, A, Aug 14, dys.
5901 Clark, A, 54, A, Aug 16, dia. c.
6208 Chrichfula, S, 93, A, Aug 19, gae.
6477 Croane, J J, 22, C, Aug 22, scs.
6646 Cornelius, E, 58, B, Aug 23, scs.
6926 Carnahan, A W,§ 6, E, Aug 26, dys.
7383 Carpenter, S, 66, I, Aug 31, scs.
7726 Callings, W, 120, F, Sept 3, dia.
7737 Cramer, A, 30, H, Sept 3, des.
7899 Cheny, James, 7, cav, I, Sept 5, dys.
9051 Crumton, R, 101 I, Sept 6, dia.
8108 Crazen, J, 53, G, Sept 7, scs.
8133 Crager, J, 13, C, Sept 8, c. f.

8144 Cooper, ?, 80, E, Sept 8, dia.
9294 Christman, J E, 6 cav, G, Sept 19, scs.
9535 Collins, G, 56, F, Sept 22, dia.
9980 Connett, Daniel, 130, F, Sept 28, scs.
10084 Conel, J, 13, D, Sept 30, dia.
10905 Callan, M, 35, B, Oct 13, dia.
11423 Cafer, J H, 87, K, Oct 24, scs.
11631 Cummings, J W, 93, F, Oct 28, scs.
12062 Clark, M, 101, B, Nov 17, dia.
12173 Cannon, A, 42, F, Nov 26, scs.
12213 Cregs, Wm, 5 cav, E, Dec 3, scs.
12415 Collins, W A,§ 5, G, Jan 8, '65, scs.
12559 Calvert, G F, 8 cav, I, Jan 30, '65, dis. ?
4234 Curry, W F, 4 cav, I, July 29, dia. c.

426 Dummond, J H, 65, F, April 7, dia. a
508 Davis, J M, 66, ? April 12, dia.
964 Darker, Wm, 12, C, May 8, ana.
2205 Denny, John, 44, E, June 19, dia.
3157 Detrich, C, 29, K, July 11, dia.
3419 Dusan, J, 6, D, July 16, dia. c.
4021 Develin, E, 35, K, July 26, pna.
4029 Decer, P, 32, K, July 26, scs.
4124 Dill, C P, 42, F, July 27, dia.
5255 Davis, K, 13, D, Aug 10, dia.
5367 Dunben, M, 36, E, Aug 11, scs.
5420 Delup, Z S, 13, D, Aug 12, scs.
5681 Dallinger, W C, 38, E, Aug 14, dia.
6147 Denton, Philip, 81, D, Aug 19, '65, scs.
6834 Downey, S M, 116, I, Aug 25, scs.
6944 Dowell, W L, 6, C, Aug 26, dys.
9638 Dunlap, W, 30, A, Sept 24, scs.
10010 Downs, J R, 5 cav, I, Sept 29, dys.
10435 Dane, Andrew, 36, I, Oct 6, scs.
10446 Dignon, L, 35, B, Oct 7, dia.
10916 Dawson, L F, 29, I, Oct 14, scs.
10954 Dial, R, I, B, Oct 14, dia. c.
12087 Daffendall, P H, 58, D, Nov 18, scs.
12172 Davenport, J, 6 cav, I, Nov 24, scs.
12236 Delashment, F,§ 14, B, Dec 6, scs.
12533 Duckworth, J, 85, F, Jan 27, '65, scs.
12545 Dawley, J, 73, I, Jan 27, '65, rhm.
12580 Dawson, J, 124, D, Feb 3, '65, pls.
9236 Diver, O, 19, F, Sept 19, gas.

916 Evans, G H, I cav, A, May 6, dia. c.
917 Edwards, G H, mus, 6, G, May 7, dia. s
1083 Ellis, H C, 6 cav, D, May 14, dia.
1279 Evans, W, 75, I, May 22, r. f.
1346 Eskridge, Oakley, 29, D, May 24, dia. c.
1994 Edwards, J W, 38, G, June 15, dia. c.
2481 Esenthal, F, 5 cav, D, June 25, dia. c.
4075 Eaton, W H, 58, B, July 27, dia. c.
4953 Ecker, J, 39, I, Aug 17, ana.
5076 Evans, J, 6 cav, I, Aug 8, dia.
7917 Ells, D, 20, I, Sept 5, dia. c.
11320 Elston, F, 9, B, Oct 22, scs.
11429 Estelle, E W,§ 2 cav, L, Oct 24, scs.
11712 Eldridge, E, 38, Nov 1, scs.
11774 Earl, D,‡ 2 cav, B, Nov 3, scs.
12285 Emmons, W, 5, D, Dec 14, scs.

1482 Frecks, F, 35, D, May 30, dia.
1808 Fitter, B, 66, I, June 10, dia.
2143 Fike, Tobias, 30, D, June 18, dia.
3014 Fitzgerald, I, 30, D, July 7, dia.
3453 Fescher, D, 32, E, July 17, scs.
3637 Fuget, W, 3 cav, C, July 20, dys.
8379 Fields, N, 6 cav, F, Sept 10, scs.
8547 Fenton, I, 72, D, Sept 12, scs.
8766 Forward, S, 8 cav, I, Sept 14, ana.
9847 Forshua, W, 75, H, Sept 27, scs.
10509 Farmingham, W C, 14 cav, K, Oct 8, scs.
11311 Fanier, F, 6 cav, I, Oct 22, scs.
11526 Fish, C, 2 cav, H, Oct 26, scs.
12012 Falkerson, J,§ 93, B, Nov 14, i. f.
12144 Francis, F, mus, 93, Nov 24, scs.
12320 Fross, John,§ 5 cav, D, Dec 24, scs.
12728 Felnich, H, 10, F, March 4, 65, dia. c.

98 Graham, Wm, 6, G, March 22, pna.
322 Gladman, H, 110, B, April 2, pna.

1048 Goodwin, Wm, 2 cav, M, May 12, ana.
1165 Grimes, F O, 66, I. May 17, dys.
1215 Garver, John, 29, F, May 19 dia. c.
1312 Gullsen, William, 7 cav, L, May 23, dia. c.
1594 Griffin, William, 6 cav, I, June 3, rhm.
2337 Gray, D L, 22, I, June 22, ts. f.
2386 Guthrie, W B, 80, C, June 24, dia. c.
2418 Gillard, Wm, 120, C, June 24, r. f.
3573 Gibbons, W T, 128, I, July 19, dia.
4179 Gould, Wm, 66, E, July 28, scs.
4273 Gilbert, H A,§ 2 cav, K, July 29, dia.
4347 Galliger, Wm, 7, B, July 31, dia.
4901 Gerard, H, 35, G, Aug 6, ana.
6189 Goodwin I, 20, F, Aug 19, dia.
6398 Gordon, W M, 74, G, Aug 21, scs.
6493 Goodridge, E,‡ 94, H, Aug 22, dia. c.
7298 Grass, C, 32, H, Aug 30, scs.
7321 Gray, H F, 2 cav, H, Aug 30, scs.
7698 Gerber, I, 30, C, Sept 3, dia.
8546 Galliger, P, 58, C, Sept 12, scs.
8791 Gagham, Wm, 35, K, Sept 14, scs.
9112 Green, S, 72, E, Sept 18, wds.
9114 Gillan, J, 29, F, Sept 18, scs.
10782 Griswold, Thomas, 2, F, Oct 12, scs.
11409 Gordon, J W, 13, D, Oct 24, scs.
11581 Greenwood, W, 3, C, Oct 28, scs.
12216 Grant, H G, 5, G, Dec 3, dia.
12398 Garnett, T, G, E, Jan 5, '65, scs.
12483 Green, Wm, 39, E, Jan 19, '65, scs.

630 Hollar, John, 5 cav, I, April 19, dia. c.
879 Henick, Wm, 30, F, May 4 dys.
1953 Hall, L S, 117, C, June 14, dys.
2118 Hilliard, J, 116, D, June 17, dia. c.
2130 Hodges, J, 7, C, June 18, pna.
2379 Hustin, James. 74, B, June 23, dia.
2392 Hodges, S, 9. F, June 24, dia.
2629 Humphrey, I, 3, C, June 28, dia.
2768 Hendricks, J, 2 cav, C, July 2, rhm.
2768 Higgins, M P, 3 cav, C, July 2, dys.
2793 Hodges, W J, 6, F, July 2, scs.
2812 Hillman, H, 65, G, July 3, ana.
2974 Hamilton, James, 7, K, July 7, dia.
3289 Hine, S, 68, A, July 14, dia.
3507 Hodgen, J W, 80, G, July 18, des.
4487 Hanger, L S, 65, A, Aug 1, dia.
5362 Hart, J R, 88, H, Aug 11, scs.
5678 Hittle, B, 6 cav, L, Aug 14, scs.
5695 Helville, N C, 20, G, Aug 16, dia.
5872 Heah, jacob, 20, G, Aug 16, dia.
6076 Hearne, John, 5 cav, F, Aug 18, scs.
6198 Hershton, A, 4, M, Aug 19, dys.
6491 Hendrick, I, 129, H, Aug 22, scs.
7031 Hartsock, I, 30, A, Aug 27, dia.
7790 Hunter, J M, 42, F, Sept 4, des.
7837 Hammond, G W,‡ 65, D, Sept 4, dia.
7903 Halfre, J A, 32, A, Sept 5, dia.
7971 Hamilton, P S, 7, E, Sept 6, scs.
8091 Hughes, W H,‡ 81, D, Sept 7, dys.
8347 Hart, A, 7, A, Sept 10, dia.
8541 Haft, M, 4 bat, Sept 12, ana.
8681 Hunter, H, 42, F, Sept 13, scs.
8778 Haynes, W, 30, G, Sept 14, ana.
8836 Higgins, John W, 3 cav, C, Sept 15, scs.
8967 Holloway, J, 5 cav, M, Sept 16, dia.
9083 Hubbner, F, 4 cav, E, Sept 18, dia. c.
9329 Hurst, R V,‡ 36, B, Sept 20, scs.
9429 Higgins, W E, 53, H, Sept 21, wds.
9911 Haghton, J, 2, D, Sept 28, ana.
9933 Harrington, O, 30, I, Sept 28, dys.
10123 Hoffman, J, 80, C, Oct 1, pna.
10293 Hunstler, W H,§ 38, E, Oct 4, scs.
10522 Hoagler, N C, 39, E, Oct 8, scs.
10613 Harris, W C, 13, D, Oct 10, dia. c.
10820 Hector, E, 13, D, Oct 12, scs.
11231 Haskins, H, 99, A, Oct 20, scs.
11243 Hasfle, J, mus, 1, F, Oct 21, scs.
11790 Hill, R, 14, D, Nov 4, scs.
12249 Hamilton, D, 13, B, Dec 9, scs.
12536 Hall, H H, 2, E, Jan '65, dia.

6444 Ihn, C, 129, B, Aug 22, '64, scs

8963 Igo, T,‡ 4, E, Sept 16, dia.

670 Johnson, Isaac, 5, C, April 22, dys.
1931 Jennings, C,‡6 cav, I, June 14, dia. c.
2212 Jackson, John, 22, C, June 20, dia.
2353 Jones, Wm M, 63, D, June 23, dia. c.
3311 Jasper, Wm, 38, I, July 10, scs.
5245 Judd, Henry,§ 2, D, Aug 10, scs.
6172 Julerso, H, 2 cav, D, Aug 19, mas.
6311 Jones, H C, 5, C, Aug 20, scs.
7100 Jones, A, 88, I, Aug 28, dia.
9948 Johnson, J, 7 cav, A, Sept 28, scs.
12517 Jones, J, 120, C, Jan 24, 65, rhm.
12799 Johnson, H, 40, C, March 19, '65, dia. c.

417 Kistner, George, 42, B, April 7, des.
618 Kinnan, A, 56, G, April 18, dia.
858 Ketchum, G W,§ 5 cav, I, May 3, dia.
2036 Kelley, John,§ 5 cav, June 15, dia.
2407 Kennedy, Amos, 2, H, June 24, dia. c.
1908 Kelso, E O, 3 cav, C, June 13, dia. c.
2527 Kanga, J, 74, E, June 26, r. f.
3047 Kennedy, J W,‡ 3, I, July 8, dia.
4024 Keys, Wm, 72, E, July 26, des.
5149 Keiler, W J,§ 4 cav, H, Aug 9, dys.
5253 Kocher, T, 29, I, Aug 10, scs.
5722 Kern, W, 25, H, Aug 15, ens.
6596 Kelly, John, 32, C, Aug 23, scs.
7085 Kames, J, 128, F, Aug 28, dia.
8621 King, D, 81, A, Sept 13, scs.
10689 Keller, I, 49, B, Oct 11, dia. c.
12278 Kuling, I, 79, A, Dec 12, scs.
12587 Keef, P,‡ 10 cav, C, Feb 4, '65, dia.

1041 Lewis, J, 6, H, May 12, '64, dia. c.
1239 Lawrence, R J, 30, G, May 20, dia. c.
1261 Lower, N G, 116, I, May 21, dia.
2615 Lewis, James, 65, F, June 28, dia. c.
2745 Luff, C, 58, I, July 1, dia. c.
3029 Lewis, J, 3 cav, C, July 7, scs.
3767 Lannon, J S, 128, F, July 22, des.
3890 Lawrence, D, 80, A, July 24, dia.
4548 Lyons, Wm, 35, A, Aug 2, scs.
5014 Lee, John, 3 cav, C, Aug 8, dys.
5585 Lawson, Willam, 75, A, Aug 14, scs.
5616 Lawyer, James, 80, B, Aug 14, dys.
6775 Lyons, Wm, I, E, Aug 25, dia.
7162 Lowery, D, 2 cav, G, Aug 29, dia.
8607 Lunger, A, 7 cav, M, Sept 12, scs.
9256 Liggett,—, 52, G, Sept 10, scs.
10508 Lewis, R, 7 cav, C, Oct 8, dia. c.
11152 Lash, J, 101, B, Oct 18, scs.
11715 Lakin, A, 7 cav, Nov 1, scs.
12250 Lawrence, B T, 42, D, Dec 9, scs.

130 McCarty, John, 66, D, March 23, i. f.
631 Mullen, James, 6 cav, G, April 19, dia.
746 Masters, Wm, 65, G, April 26, dia.
841 Milton, John, 18, C, May 1, dys.
903 Mytinger, Wm, 117, F, May 5, dia. c.
954 Milburn, J, 6, K, May 8, dia.
1090 Moore, Peter, 6, I, May 14, dia. c.
1405 Miller, Jacob, 74, E, May 27, dia.
1516 Martin, George,§ 3 cav, C, May 31, dia.
1860 Merritt, H, 30, G, June 12, dia. c.
2240 Mitchell, J J, 30, D, June 20, dia.
2397 Milliken, S L, 1 cav, G, June 24, phs.
2511 Moneyhon, B, 38, D, June 26, dia. c.
2608 Marsh, J, 88, D, June 28, dia. c.
5 Moodie, Z, 117, K, March 31, s. p.
3387 Mank, E, 80, E, July 16, dia. c.
3633 Marlit, J, 80, H, July 20, scs.
3884 Mulchy, A, 3, July 24, dia. c.
4010 Mercer, John, 12, F, July 26, dys.
4388 Malshy, F, 14, cav, A, July 31, dia.
4959 McDale, R, 19, A, Aug 7, dia.
5562 Manihan, J, 38, D, Aug 13, dia.
5618 Mageson, J, 7 cav, A, Aug 14, ts. f.
5703 Mensome, S,§ 42, E, Aug 15, dys.
5713 Monroe, S, 33, F, Aug 15, scs.
5767 Montgomery, R, 80, F, Aug 15, dys. c.
5863 Michael, S, 7, I, Aug 16, dia.

9093 Simmons, J, 84, I, Sept 18, dia.
9252 Sharp, D M, 13, E, Sept 19, scs.
9546 Sharpless, W, 43, G, Sept 23, dia.
9623 Smith, S B, 17, F, Sept 24, dia.
9807 Skeels, W, 65, A, Sept 26, dia.
10790 Smith, George, 131, D, Oct 12, dys.
10949 Smith, I, 39, I, Oct 14, scs.
11006 Sioat, G W,§ 44, B, Oct 16, scs.
11187 Seigferd, G H, 4 cav, I, Oct 19, dia.
11427 Swietzer, J, 2, G, Oct 24, scs.
11842 Shaw, W R, 99, B, Nov 5, wds.
11969 Shoe, G W, 74, E, Nov 12, scs.
11984 Steamer, F, 29, F, Nov 13, scs.
12113 Scarff, F, 6 cav, D, Nov 21, scs.
12381 Starke, M S, 93, D, Jan 2, des.
12492 Salts, H C, 4 cav, F, Jan 20, dia. c.
12582 Smith, D H, 12 cav, H, Feb 3, dia c.
12615 Sides, G, 66, A, Feb 8, pls.
12666 Smure, C, 2 cav, G, Feb 17, dia. c.
12724 Stewart, E B, 38, E, March 3, scs.
12809 Staley, G W, 72, A, March 24, dia. c.
2625 Sattershwait, A, 82, I, June 28, scs.

518 Tenher, James, 117, I, April 13, dia. c.
3778 Tunblora, B, 65, B, July 22, dia.
3791 Thompson, T, 6 cav, C, July 22, dys. a.
4733 Tooley, G W, 42, H, Aug 4, scs.
5065 Truman, L H,§ 6 cav, G, Aug 8, scs.
5403 Taylor, N, 63, I, Aug 12, wds.
6509 Tooley, W R,‡ 42, H, Aug 22, dys.
6719 Todd, T, 6, B, Aug 24, hep.
7096 Thomas, H D, 42, I, Aug 28, ana.
7442 Taylor, George H, 4 cav, M, Sept 1, dia. c.
8495 Trumble, D A, 30, A, Sept 11, dia.
8525 Taylor, E, 25, I, Sept 12, dia.
10438 Thomas, M, 2 cav, Oct 6, dys.
12337 Tucer, B, cit, Nov 26, scs.
12609 Terhune, C, 9 cav, A, Feb 7, pls.
10219 Tasnahet, Charles,§ 33, E, Oct 2, scs.

10356 Underwood, P, 7 cav, C, Sept 5, scs.
10760 Upton, F M, 52, A, Oct 12, scs.

1717 Voit, T, 6 cav, K, June 8, dia. c.
5363 Venome, James, 30, K, Aug 11, dia.
6250 Vanose, J, 93, B, Aug 20, ces.
7691 Verhouse, D, 42, A, Sept 3, scs.

135 Windinger, J, 117, G, March 24, r. f.
886 Walters, J H,‡ 6 cav, G, May 5, i. f.

934 Williams, A, 6, G, May 7, dia. c.
1194 Wright, Samuel, 6 cav, I, May 18, dia.
1776 White, P, 6 cav, C, June 9, dia. c.
1812 Wise, Eli, 88, D, June 10, dia.
1918 Warren, E, 65, H, June 14, dia.
2107 Williams, F, 38, F, June 17, dia. c.
2242 West, E, 7 cav, H, June 20, dia.
2363 Woodward, W W, 29, A, June 23, dia. c.
2417 Wilson, J N, 75, G, June 24, dia. c.
2467 Warden, I, 44, B, June 25, dia. a.
2554 Warren, E, 37, I, June 27, pna.
2670 Ward, J, 79, F, June 29, ana.
2900 Wyn, W E, 13, D, July 5, dia.
2929 Wislake, I, 116, I, July 5, dys. c.
2934 Wicks, L, 6 cav, H, July 6, dia.
4528 Whitehead, J, 29, I, Aug 2, dia.
4639 Winship, James, 36, K, Aug 4, scs.
4826 Witt, T, 125, D, Aug 5, dia.
5399 Wade, C, 81, K, Aug 12, dys.
5547 Waynin, J H, 4 cav, I, Aug 13, dia.
6132 Washburn, R H, 6 cav, A, Aug 19, scs.
6405 Winders, A, 120, I, Aug 21, des.
6524 Wagner, M, 5 cav, I, Aug 22, scs.
7184 Winters, F W, 84, C, Aug 29, dia.
7191 Wagoner, E, 42, A, Aug 29, scs.
7349 Witzgall, John, 2, D, Aug 31, scs.
8943 Weiber, Charles, 13, F, Sept 16, scs.
9228 White, W, 7, E, Sept 19, dia.
9316 Watkins, J, 81, A, Sept 20, dia. c.
6418 Wellington, H, 129, I, Sept 21, dia. c.
9501 Wilson, J B, 6, E, Sept 21, dia.
9998 Wagner, F, 7, D, Sept 29, dia.
10648 Ward, J, 29, G, Oct 11, scs.
11141 Whitehead, N B, 5 cav, L, Oct 18, scs.
11424 White, R B, 6, D, Oct 24, scs.
11602 Walters, J, 5, I, Oct 28, scs.
12708 Winebrook, P, 35, B, Nov 18, scs.
12316 Werper, J, 32, E, Dec 20, scs.
12341 White, J, 7, A, Dec 26, scs.
12462 Wells, J M, 13, D, Jan 16, scs.
12497 What, J, 93, B, Jan 21, pls.
12737 Wade, W, 10 cav, M, March 6, dia. c.
3837 Weltz, Ira,§ 4, B, July 23, dia. c.
6000 West, S N,‡ 7, B, Aug 17, dia.
9920 Williams, J A,§ 38, C, Sept 28, scs.

5055 Younce, Charles A, 7 cav, I, Aug 8, dys.
5838 Yorker, Daniel, 28, B, Aug 16, ens.

1540 Zuet, J, 65, H, June 1, des.

IOWA.

5560 Allen, N, 3, K, Aug 13, dia.
8974 Ankobus, L,‡ 6, I, Sept 17, dia. c.
9472 Ashford, A W, H, C, Sept 21, wds.
11784 Alderman, W W, 31, F, Nov 4, scs.
11896 Austin, Wm, 3 cav, A, Nov 7, dia.

1293 Bartche, C P, 5, K, May 23, dia.
1570 Bingman, W H, 39, H, June 3, dia.
5276 Blanchard, A, 7, A, Aug 10, dia. c.
6164 Bursford, M, 7, F, Aug 19, dia.
7779 Baird, J J, 26, H, Sept 4, dia.
8265 Buckmaster, F, 15, K, Sept 9, dia.
9301 Buell, J, 4, D, Sept 20, dia.
9456 Boylan, C, 14, G, Sept 21, dia.
9691 Boles, M B, —, I, Sept 24, dia.
10749 Bellings, J, 5, B, Oct 12, scs.
11334 Blakely, Geo, 3, G, Oct 23, wds.

167 Collins, Henry,§ 4, G, March 26, dia.
328 Chenworth, Wm, 4, K, April 2, dys.
4582 Cromwell, G W, 27, F, Aug 2, dia.
5101 Cooper, S, 5, B, Aug 9, scs.
5244 Cox, E E,‡ 5, G, Aug 9, dys.
5620 Cox, W A, 5, G, Aug 14, dia.
?999 Coder, E, 31, E, Aug 17, dia.
6378 Cox, H, 5, I, Aug 21, scs.
?804 Clamson, Henry, 26, I, Aug 23, dia. c.

6848 Collins, M, 3, L, Aug 25, dia.
8062 Culbertson, S,‡ 5, H, Sept 7, dia.
8352 Crow, B, 4, E, Sept 10, dys.
9784 Coles, J W,§ 8, K, Sept 26, dia. c.
9820 Cobb, E, 3 cav, C, Sept 26, dia. c.
10037 Cramer, J M, 5 cav, B, Sept 29, dia. c.
10901 Chapman, J, 3, G, Oct 14, gae.
12230 Chamberlain, J B, 8 cav, A, Dec 6, wds.

2903 Davis, S, 3, E, June 30, dia. c.
4206 Davis, J, 15, D, July 29, wds.
9229 Davis, H, 17, A, Sept 19, scs.
4675 Dermott, L, 5, G, Aug 4, scs.
6849 Discol, S, 26, I, Aug 25, dys.
9852 Dingman, W, 31, D, Sept 27, scs.
11098 Denoya, W H, 5, M, Oct 18, des.
11753 Dutlin, S, 4, Sept 28, scs.
12245 Durochis, Wm, 12, H, Dec 8, scs.
12657 Derickson, W W,‡ 8 cav, M, Feb 15, dia. c.

262 Ennis, Wm, 4, B, March 31, dys. a.
11414 England, G, 9, F, Oct 24, scs.

3705 Field, Jacob, 5, K, July 21, dys.
4503 Farnsworth, S, 2, N, Aug 1, ana.
1316 Forney, James M, 10, K May 23, dia.
7715 Fru, J, 10, Sept 8, dia.

7878 Frederick, J A, 16, C, Sept 5, dia.
8380 Frussell, G W, 6, D, Sept 10, scs.
10048 Fordson, Michael, 16, H, Sept 29, dia.
11078 Fener, J W, 3 cav, B, Oct 17, scs.
12711 Ferguson, A W, 15, A, Feb 28, uls.

750 Gain, L, 6, C, April 26, ts. f.
1484 Gender, Jacob, 5, I, May 30, dia. c.
5004 Gentle, G, 4, G, Aug 8, dia. c.
5836 Gunshaw, C, 26, Aug 16, mas.
10511 Gray, J, 11, C, Oct 7, dys.
10366 Gothard, J, 8, G, Oct 11, scs.

5461 Harris, J, 8 cav, H, Aug 13, dys.
8106 Hastings, J,§ 11, B, Sept 7, dia.
9379 Hird, D,‡ 3, G, Sept 20, wds.
9417 Hudson, M, 16, B, Sept 21, dia.
2168 Huffman, R J, 5, H, June 19, dys.
862 Heeller, A, 5, D, May 3, brs.
1633 Harper, D, 7, K, June 5, des.
1816 Hurlay, J, 8, H, June 11, dia. c.
12749 Hubanks, C,§ 17, H, March 8, des.

10360 Ireland, J S, 5 cav, H, Oct 5, wds.

4461 Jones, C, 4, B, Aug 1, scs.
8656 Jenks, G A,§ 8, C, Sept 13, dia. c.
9401 Jones, J, 5, C, Sept 21, dia. c.

3204 Kolenbrander, H, 17, K, July 12, dia.
7 King, Alexander, 17, H, April 5, s. p.
6464 King, E, 2 cav, C, Aug 22, wds.
3560 Kesler, F, 4, B, July 18, dys.
5378 Kennedy, B, 16, I, Aug 11, wds.
11281 Knight, J 11,§ 9, I, Oct 22, gae.

892 Lambert, Chas,‡ 39, K, May 5, brs.
2045 Littleton, J, 5, June 15, dia.
7959 Lord, L, 13, G, Sept 6, des.
8263 Lanning, A, 13, I, Sept 9, scs.
9438 Lowdenbeck, N, 5, B, Sept 21, ana.
10224 Lowelenbuck, D R, 5, B, Oct 2, dia.
10881 Layers, W, 5, E, Oct 14, scs.
11752 Luther, J,‡ 9, B, Nov 2, scs.
12629 Littlejohn, L D, 4 cav, B, Feb 10, dia. c.

257 Moore, John, 39, H, March 31.
307 Myers, M, 4, K, April 2, dia.
450 Moon, James, 39, H, April 9, dys.
1192 McMullen, James, 4, C, May 18, i. f.
1317 Miller, F, 5, H, May 23, dia.
1472 McCameron, W, 4, A, May 30, r. f.
2027 McAllister, A P, 14, E, June 15, dia.
3423 McNeil, J W, 11, I, July 16, dip.
4804 Moore, Wm, 13, A, Aug 5, scs.
5445 Murray, J J, 17, I, Aug 12, scs.
6167 McCall, Thos, 8 cav, M, Aug 19, mas.
6815 Merchant, Wm, 13, G, Aug 25, dia.
6878 Maynard, J D, 4, B, Aug 26, dys.
7143 McDonald, D B,§ 5 cav, M, Aug 29, dia.
8120 McClure, Z,§ 16, C, Sept 8, scs.
9274 Martin, S S, 11, G, Sept 19, scs.
9585 Mann, J, 16 Sept 23, scs.
?11? Miller, J, 5, D, Oct 1, scs.
10827 McCoy, G B,‡ 5, G, Oct 13, dia.
10950 Mercer, John, 4, C, Oct 14, scs.
11745 Miller, E,‡ 31, D, Nov 2, scs.
12484 Martin, J B, 5, B, Jan 19, rhm.
12561 Macy, C S, 8 cav, C, Jan 31, dia.

6959 O'Conner, P, 26, D, Aug 27, dia.
9509 O'Verturf, P W, 5, H, Sept 22, scs.
12169 Osborn, F L, 16, A, Nov 26, scs.

1972 Peterson, J, 76, E, June 15, ana.
2869 Palmer, L H, 9, D, July 4, ana.
6209 Phillpot, C P, 31, B, Aug 19, dia.
9370 Putnam, O, 27, F, Aug 20, scs.
10270 Pitts, J, 16, I, Oct 3, dia.
10297 Pugh, A,‡ 8, M, Oct 3, scs.
10413 Parker, D, 4, I, Oct 6, scs.

18 Rule, Y A, 10, A, April 12, s. p.
1796 Ryan, Charles, 5, G, June 10, pls.
1820 Richardson, John, 2 cav, I, June 11, dia.
1951 Ratcliff, J, 4, I, June 14, des.
5878 Reed, R, 16, I, Aug 16, dia. c.
6572 Robinson, D, 13, G, Aug 23, wds.
7400 Rice, H M, sut's clerk, 9, Aug 31, scs.
9413 Riley, M, 5, A, Sept 21, ts. f.
9483 Reeves, S J, 9, D, Sept 21, des.
10015 Reed, C, 2, C, Sept 29, scs.
10017 Rogers, L, 4, F, Sept 29, scs.
12264 Russel, E, 4, G, Dec 12, scs.
12287 Raiser, A, 8, C, Dec 14, scs.

451 Stout, John, 5, A, April 9, pna.
599 Shuffleton, J, 5, H, April 17, pna.
641 Seeley, Norman, 9, B, April 20, pna.
2712 Smith, R F,‡ 10, H, July 1, dia.
2845 Shutter, J, 30, K, July 3, dys.
3060 Sparks, M J, 5, K, July 9, dys.
4178 Sutton, S, 5, H, July 28, ana.
4773 Smith, Charles,‡ 20, F, Aug 4, scs.
5410 Starr, C F, 30, H, Aug 12, pna.
5892 Sheddle, G, 16, C, Aug 16, dia. c.
7954 Seins, Wm, 3, D, Sept 6, dia. c.
8200 Smith, J, 13, A, Sept 8, dys.
9209 Smith, O, 5, D, Sept 19, scs.
9125 Sherman, J W, 3, I, Sept 17, dia. c.
9234 Spears, J, 5 cav, H, Sept 19, scs.
9367 Smith, D, 3 cav, B, Sept 20, dia.
11789 Shaw, W H, 5, H, Nov 4, scs.
12729 Smice, W, 16, E, March 4, dia. c.
10884 Sayres, W, 5, E, Oct 14, scs.

1981 Taiping, Wm, 5, K, June 15, pna.
3986 Thopson, M, 5, G, July 25, dys.
6687 Tivis, C, 5, A, Aug 24, scs.
9720 Tonune, B, 4 cav, M, Sept 25, scs.
11708 Thier, A F, 3, Nov 1, scs.

10351 Voke, John C,‡ 5, E, Oct 5, scs.

1674 Whitman, O R,‡ 5, E, June 6, dia. c.
2161 Wells, F,§ 5, I, June 19, dia. c.
2213 Withsrick, A K, 9, K, June 20, scs.
2855 Wolf, B F, 8, E, July 4, dia.
4916 Wolfe, J H, 2, C, Aug 6, scs.
6934 Wheelan, J,§ 26, D, Aug 26, dys.
8101 Walworth, C,§ 5, K, Sept 7, scs.
8131 Woolston, S P,§ 13, H, Sept 8, dia.
9221 Ward, O R, 3, I, Sept 19, ana.
9486 Wagner, Joseph, 13, E, Sept 21, scs.
9727 Wersbrod, Y, 31, A, Sept 25, scs.
10818 Wilson, P D, 10, G, Oct 13, scs.
10942 Woodward, J, sut, 9, Oct 14, scs.
11114 Whiting, J, 5, H, Oct 18, scs.
11141 Whitehead, N B, 5 cav, L, Oct 19, scs.
12741 Wen, C, 57, C, March 6, dys.

KANSAS.

1614 Freeman, F J,§ 8, F, June 4, dia. a.

1935 Gensarde, Thos, 8, A, June 14, dia. c.

12127 Sweeney, M, 1, H, Nov 22, scs.

11139 Weidman, W, 8, B, Oct 19, dia. c.
1663 Williams, C A, 8, A, June 6 dys.

KENTUCKY.

329 Allen, Sam'l S,‡ 13, F, April 2, dia. c.
674 Alford, George, 11 cav, B, April 22, sys.
1575 Anderson, S, 11 cav, D, May 3, dia.
8385 Adams, J D, 1 cav, I, July 16, dia.
3759 Ashley, J M, 1 cav, L, July 22, scs.
4723 Allen, Wm,‡ 11 cav, C, Aug 4, scs.
4894 Atkins, A, 39 cav, H, Aug 6, ana.
6093 Aughlin, J A,‡ 18 cav, B, Aug 18, scs.
6720 Arnett, H S, 13 cav, A, Aug 24, dia.
10514 Adamson, Wm, 15 cav, K, Oct 8, scs.
11759 Adams, J L, 27, G, Nov 3, scs.
12426 Arthur, D, 4, G, Jan 9, dia. c.
12528 Ayers, E, 52, A, Jan 26, pls.
12703 Ayers, S, 52, A, Jan 26, dia. c.
12593 Arnett, T, 4 cav, F, Jan 5, dia. c.

193 Bow, James, 1 cav, March 27, pls.
261 Burrows, Wm, 1 cav, K, March 31, dia. c.
366 Byerly, Wm, 11 cav, E, April 2, rua.
379 Baker, Isaac, 1 cav, H, April 5, dia. c.
413 Basham, S, 12 cav, E, April 7, dia. c.
419 Button, Ed, 11 cav, D, April 7, dia. c.
608 Burritt, B, 6 cav, D, April 18, dia.
609 Bloomer, H, 4 cav, G, April 18, dia.
803 Baker, A W, 3 cav, C, April 29, dia. c.
832 Boley, Peter, 12, L, May 1, dia.
891 Bird, W T, 11 cav, H, May 5, dia.
857 Bailey, A W, 14, G, May 2, dia. c.
1167 Burton, Tillman, 1 cav, F, May 17, scs.
1200 Butner, L B,§ 6 cav, I, May 18, dia.
1263 Bell, P B, H cav, I, May 21, dys.
1362 Barnett, James, 8 cav, H, May 25, dys.
1566 Baird, Sam'l J, 12 cav, D, June 2, dia.
1789 Bishop, D L, 11 cav, A, June 10, dia.
2022 Bowman, G, 11 cav, D, June 15, dia. c.
2423 Bray, H N,‡ 9 cav, H, June 24, phs.
2529 Buchanan, S, 12 cav, F, June 26, dia. c.
2760 Ball, David, 11 cav, B, July 2, dia. c.
3087 Beard, John C,§ 1 cav, C, July 9, dia. c.
3228 Brophy, M, 5 cav, I, July 12, dys.
3433 Bailey, F M, 4 cav, G, July 17, scs.
3909 Banner, J, 11 cav, C, July 24, dia. c.
3998 Bridell, S,‡ 3 cav, F, July 26, dys.
4562 Booth, Z,§ 16 cav, E, Aug 2, scs.
4653 Barger, George, 5 cav, I, Aug 3, dia.
4835 Baker, Wm, 3 cav, I, Aug 6, ana.
4971 Bigler, A, 6 cav, B, Aug 7, scs.
5471 Bailey, J H, 11 cav, A, Aug 12, dia. c.
5644 Branan, H, 1 cav, G, Aug 14, dys.
6576 Boston, J, 27 cav, E, Aug 23, scs.
6727 Bottoms, J M, 1 cav, H, Aug 24, dys.
9551 Brinton, W J,§ 11 cav, C, Sept 23, ana.
9568 Barnett, A, 12 cav, K, Sept 23, scs.
9628 Brown, J, 10 cav, I, Sept 24, dia.
9740 Boyd, M, 13 cav, A, Sept 25, dia.
10147 Baft, W, 5, G, Oct 1, dia.
10202 Byron, H M,§ 1 cav, I, Oct 2, scs.
10451 Bill, B S, 1 cav, K, Oct 7, pna.
10816 Bodkins, P,‡ 1 cav, K, Oct 12, dia. c.
10859 Bagley, T, 11 cav, Oct 13, scs.
11052 Brickey, W L, 4, F, Oct 17, gae.
12256 Baldwin, J W, 11, H, Oct 21, dia.
11303 Brown, E W, 4, F, Oct 22, scs.
11491 Barber, T, 4 cav, H, Oct 26, scs.
12006 Brannon, J, 3, B, Nov 13, scs.
12304 Beatty, R, 5, B, Dec 18, dia.
12333 Barnes, J, H, D, Dec 25, scs.
12360 Brodus, O, 11 cav, A, Dec 30, scs.
12421 Britton, J, 45, F, Jan 9, scs.
5098 Bowman, Henry, 11 cav, F, Aug 9, dia. c.
12777 Balson, L, 12, B, March 15, dia. a.

11483 Cranch, J P, 10, D, Oct 26, scs.
240 Conler, Wm, 14, I, March 20, dia.
484 Caldwell, Wm, 12 cav, I, April 9, dia.
509 Cook, Theod, 12 cav, D, April 12, dia. c.
672 Colvin, George, 11 cav, D, April 22, dia.

877 Christmas, J, 11 cav, F, May 4, dia.
966 Collague, M, 12 cav, E, May 8, dia.
1268 Cash, Philip, 1 cav, I, May 21, pna.
1600 Cole, W C, 1 cav, C, June 4, dia.
1676 Christenburg, R I,§ 12 cav, G, June 6, dys.
1687 Calliham, Pat, 11 cav, A, June 6, scs.
1856 Clane, H, 11 cav, E, June 12, dia. c.
2152 Clinge, W H, 40, A, June 18, des.
2293 Cox, A B, 6 cav, I, June 21, i. f.
2339 Chippendale, C, 1 cav, B, June 22, dia. c.
2446 Carlisle, J, 6 cav, I, June 25, dia. c.
2823 Cummings, J, 11, F, July 3, dia.
2912 Cleming, Thos, 18, I, July 5, dia. c.
3184 Carter, W, 11 cav, H, July 11, dys.
60 Cristian, John, 4 cav, C, July 4, s. p.
4044 Clark, A H, 11, I, July 27, dia.
4809 Chapman, 11, H, Aug 5, dia.
6387 Coulter, M, 23, B, Aug 21, pna.
9835 Conrad, R P, 4, B, Sept 27, scs.
11179 Clun, W H, 11 cav, L, Oct 19, scs.
11486 Chatsin, W M, 6 cav, H, Oct 26, scs.
12447 Carcunright, 4, C, Jan 13, scs.
12700 Cook, J P, 4, G, Jan 26, ana.
2223 Corbitt, Thos, 5, A, June 20, dia.
8113 Coyle, C, 11 cav, I, Sept 7, scs.
4740 Chance, A J, 1 cav, C, Aug 5, ana.

421 Dupon, F, 12, G, April 7, pna.
1388 Delaney, M, 11 cav, I, May 26, dia.
1414 Dugean, J R,§ 12 cav, K, May 27, dys.
1568 De Barnes, P M, 11 cav, C, June 2, dia.
1627 Demody, Thos, 1 cav, H, June 4, dia. c.
1867 Drake, J H, 12 cav, G, June 12, ana.
2736 Davis, B, 5, C, July 1, dia. c.
23 Duncan, E, 12 cav, G, April 15, s. p.
3623 Dodson, E, 39, H, July 20, scs.
27 Derine, George, 1 cav, I, April 17, s. p.
3924 Davis, G C, 12 cav, F, July 25, des.
3966 Derringer, H, 11 cav, I, July 25, dia. c.
4510 Dulrebeck, H, 11, E, Aug 1, dia. c.
4556 Delaney, H, 4 cav, H, Aug 2, dys.
5088 Dounty, P, 5, F, Aug 8, dys.
5899 Daniel, R, 9, F, Aug 18, dia.
11405 Disque, F,§ 6 cav, G, Oct 24, scs.
12280 Duland, D W, 3, K, Dec 13, scs.
12623 Dannard, W, 4, D, Feb 9, dia. c.
2684 Dipple, S, 4, E, Feb 21, dia. c.
1109 Dinsman, H, 4 cav, E, May 15, dia. c.
2805 Davis, J P, 13, A, July 3, dia.
2117 Davis, C, 6 cav, D, June 31, scs.

639 Eodus, James, 1 cav, F, April 20, dia.
1174 Edmiston, J W, 11 cav, A, May 17, dia. c.
1439 Edwards, H S,‡ 8 cav, K, May 27, dia. c.
2544 Emery, J, 10, G, June 27, ts. f.
5341 Errbanks, J, 1 cav, A, Aug 11, dia.
12277 Esteff, J, 1 cav, L, Oct 22, dia.
1447 East, R, 1 cav, G, May 29, dia.

384 Falconburg, I K, 1 cav, A, April 5, pna.
2540 Fleming, R, 4 cav, D, June 27, dia. c.
3640 Forteen, John, 8, A, July 20, dia.
4344 Fenkstine, M, 1, D, July 30, dia.
6763 Featherstone, J, 6, C, Aug 25, i. f.
7068 Fritz, J, 4 cav, G, Aug 28, dys.
10280 Funk, J, 1 cav, I, Oct 4, wds.
11549 Frazier, C R, 23, H, Oct 27, wds.
11720 Fletcher, T, 17, E, Nov 1, dia. c.

1612 Gritton, G, 11 cav, D, June 4, dia. c.
1618 Graves, G, 18, C, June 4, dia. c.
1841 Gritton, M, 11 cav, B, June 11, dia. c.
2583 Gibson, John, 6 cav, L, June 27, dys.
3630 Griffin, B, 11, E, July 20, dia.
3663 Glassman, P, 4 cav, B, July 20, dia.
3888 Gouns, J M, 4, H, July 24, dia.
4438 Gather, M, 4 cav, F, July 31, dia.

19

5779 Gullett, A, 45, K, Aug 15, ana.
7197 Green, J B,§ 11, I, Aug 29, dia.
7817 Grabul, B, 1, F, Sept 4, ana.
8049 Gury, J, 4, H, Sept 6, scs.
8903 Gray, C D, 20, G, Sept 18, scs.
9318 Gett, John,§ 40, G, Sept 20, dia.
9950 Gill, W J, 11 cav, H, Sept 28, scs.
10053 Gower, J C, 13, A, Sept 30, scs.
10650 Gibson, A, 8 cav, K, Oct 10, scs.
10831 Grulach, J,§ 4, K, Oct 13, scs.
11910 Grimstead, J R, 1, E, Nov 8, scs.
12022 Griffin, R, 11, E, Nov 15, scs.
1235 Gregory, H, 12 cav, D, May 20, dia.

81 Hanns, J B, 12, K, March 20, pna.
237 Holloway, Richard, 4, I, March 29, ts. f.
289 Harley, Alfred, 40, K, April 1, dia. c.
292 Hood, G, 5 cav, F, April 1, dia.
348 Hammond, J W, 1 cav, G, April 2, dia. c.
376 Harper, J, 1, C, April 5, dia. a.
402 Harlow, Harvey, 13, I, April 6, dys.
614 Hess, Wm F, 12 cav, M, April 18, dys.
643 Hendree, A,§ 11, F, April 20, brs.
1023 Hillard, Geo, 11, D, May 11, ts. f.
1127 Hoffman, C, 11 cav, E, May 15, dys.
1584 Hughes, Thomas,§ 9, G, June 3, ana.
1760 Hennesy, J, 28, D, June 9, dia. c.
1878 Hundly, Geo W, 4 cav, June 12, dia.
1956 Hazlewood, J H, 18, G, June 14, dys.
1990 Hamner, A, 9, B, June 15, dia.
2490 Huison, J W,§ 9, B, June 26, pna.
2705 Hillard, S, 1 cav, I, June 30, dia. c.
3239 Henderson, J, 18, B, July 12, dys.
26 Hooper, Samuel, 11 cav, D, April 16, s. p.
3944 Hooper, J, 1 cav, D, July 25, scs.
3994 Hickworth, J, 45, D, July 26, dia.
4313 Hall, J H, 1 cav, C, July 30, dia.
4420 Hammontius, P, 6 cav, L, June 31, dia.
4970 Hayner, E, 1 cav, D, Aug 7, scs.
5059 Haines, J, 12 cav, D, Aug 8, scs.
5091 Harrington, C, 15, K, Aug 8, scs.
5793 Hatfield, L, 1, F, Aug 15, ana.
6193 Hendrie, Wm, 11 cav, F, Aug 19, scs.
6801 Hardison, G, 23, I, Aug 25, r. f.
8032 Hise, P, 4, I, Sept 6, dia.
8111 Hicks, P, 11 cav, F, Sept 7, scs.
8181 Heglen, C, 4 cav, I, Sept 8, dys.
9376 Hanker, R, 18, F, Sept 20, scs.
9599 Hyrommus, Jas, 11 cav, D, Sept 23, dia.
10683 Halton, S M, 2, K, Oct 11, scs.
11054 Halligan, J, 4, A, Oct 17, ana.
11095 Hall, F, 1 cav, F, Oct 18, scs.
11132 Hazer, John, H, I, Oct 18, scs.
11251 Harter, F, 12 cav, M, Oct 21, dia. c.
12293 Hays, J F, 5, A, Dec 15, scs.
12518 Hasting, J, 4, H, Jan 24, scs.
12638 Hudson, B F, 4, A, Feb 11, dia. c.

5734 Inman, John, 24, A, Aug 15, dia.
9757 Isabell, J M, 3, H, Sept 25, scs.
11392 Inman, W, 11 cav, D, Oct 24, scs.
12203 Isabel, A, 1, K, Dec 1, scs.

649 Jackson, John, 45, D, April 20, ana.
2679 Jeffries, Wm, 1 cav, A, June 30, dia.
5229 Jacobs, John W, 4 cav, I, Aug 10, scs.
7294 Johnson, A, 10, H, Aug 31, scs.
7371 Jenkins, S, 6 cav, A, Aug 31, dia.
7594 Justin, J, 39, F, Sept 2, ana.
7754 James, W, 5, K, Sept 4, dia.
9654 Jarvis, W D, 12, D, Sept 24, dia.
11000 Jordan, J, 5 cav, B, Oct 16, dys. c.
11143 Jones, D, 1 cav, L, Oct 18, scs.
12541 Jones, J, 16, E, Jan 27, dia.

87 Kennedy, Jas, 11 cav, E, March 21, dia. c.
191 Knotts, Fred, 11 cav, E, March 27, ts. f.
926 Kessmer, John, 12 cav, I, May 7, dia.
1045 Kennedy, S B, 39, B, May 12, dia.
1173 Keiling, M, 11 cav, D, May 17, pna.
3928 Keystone, C, 6, E, July 25, dia.
4921 Kenndsy, A,‡ 1 cav, A, July 6 dia.

5553 Knapp, Thomas, 6 cav, M, July 13, scs.
5925 Kressler, P, 4 cav, K, July 17, dia.
12265 Knapp, J, 5 cav, B, Dec 12, scs.

48 Lenniert, L, 1, K, March 15, brs.
310 Lambert, R, 11 cav, F, April 2, dia.
1135 Lay, Wm, 11 cav, D, May 16, pls.
1726 Lossman, A, 4 cav, E, June 8, dia.
1802 Larger, W, 1 cav, L, June 10, dys.
1912 Ledford, J A, 16, B, June 13, dia. c.
2109 Little, J, 1, D, June 17, c. f.
2352 Lononey, B, 1 cav, K, June 23, ana.
2654 Lutherland, H, 32, G, June 29, dys.
2668 Lasper, Otto, 15, H, June 29, dia. c.
2837 Lublett, M L, 13, E, July 3, ts. f.
3340 Leville, Thomas, 4, D, July 15, dys.
3398 Lee, S, 1 cav, A, July 16, scs.
3658 Loy, W B, 8 cav, L, July 20, ana.
3776 Lanhart, J, 6 cav, G, July 22, dia.
3839 Lowry, Jas W, 12 cav, G, July 23, dia. c.
6024 Lewis, T, 2 cav, C, Aug 18, scs.
7132 Landers,—‡ 36, I, Aug 28, dia.
7934 Luster, W, 1 cav, B, Sept 5, dia.
8487 Luttman, Thomas, 6, K, Sept 11, scs.
8634 Little, J F, 12 cav, D, Sept 13, dia.
11870 Lindusky, G, 11, G, Nov 6, scs.
12175 Ledwick, A, 7, C, Nov 27, scs.
9175 Lord, Wm, 20, G, Sept 18, scs.

271 McMannus, Saml, H, D, March 31, dia. c.
369 Miller, John, 3, A, April 5, pls.
525 McDougal, W C, 14, K, April 13, hye.
796 Mills, John, 1, H, April 29, dia. c.
991 McClure, P, 11 cav, C, May 10, dys.
1222 Marshall, Wm, 5 cav, I, May 19, dia. c.
1380 Montgomery, W A, 5 cav, H, May 26, dia. c.
1391 Moreland, H, 1 cav, F, May 26, dia. a.
1969 Merix, J, 45 cav, D, June 14, dia. c.
2024 Morton, W, 7 cav, I, June 15, ana.
2137 Meldown, D, 11 cav, E, June 18, dia. a.
2669 Miller, W C, 27 cav, A, June 29, dia.
3152 Mitchell, James, 12 cav, C, July 11, dia.
64 Mullins, W W, 1 cav, H, Aug 8, s. p.
3418 Morgan, J, 4 cav, D, July 17, dia. c.
4513 Masters, J, 11 cav, A, Aug 1, scs.
4550 McDonald, J, 4 cav, I, Aug 2, dys.
4646 Mitchell, R M, 17 cav, E, Aug 3, dys.
5691 Mooney, Pat, 11 cav, G, Aug 15, dia.
7951 McCarty, E, 5 cav, K, Sept 6, dia.
8455 McCarty, John, 6 cav, K, Sept 9, scs.
8685 McCarter, W, 9 cav, B, Sept 13, scs.
9239 Munch, J, 28 cav, F, Sept 19, cah.
9498 Macary, C, 11 cav, M, Sept 21, gae.
9711 Moore, Wm, 12 cav, D, Sept 24, dia.
7336 Martin, F P, 12 cav, D, Aug 30, scs.
10170 Marshall, L, 1 cav, F, Oct 1, dia.
10460 Mills, George, 4 cav, H, Oct 7, scs.
11455 Murphy, W M, 2 cav, H, Oct 25, scs.
11478 Miller, E, 4 cav, I, Oct 26, scs.
12466 Miller, J, 4 cav, K, Jan 16, rhm.
12491 Meyers, J, 4 cav, C, Jan 20, dia.
12720 Meach, A J, 1 cav, A, March 3, des.
12764 Morgan, F,‡ 3, I, March 12, wds.

212 New, Geo W, 1 cav, F, March 28, pna.
447 Neely, B W, 1 cav, G, April 9, dys.
63 Nelson, John, 1 cav, D, July 19, s. p.
7693 Northeraft, J, 6 cav, H, Sept 3, scs.
9230 Newton, A,‡ 4 cav, H, Sept 19, dia.

2499 O'Bannon, Wm, 11 cav, B, June 20, dia c.
2513 Oper, L, 4 cav, B, June 26, dia. c.
11943 Owen, W,‡ 1 cav, L, Nov 9, scs.

1178 Pott, J, 7 cav, C, May 17, scs.
1905 Porter, J F, 18 cav, June 13, pna.
3654 Pulliam, J, 2, July 20, dys.
4220 Plyman, Wm, 39, D, July 27, dia. c.
5761 Pally, S C,§ 12 cav, B, Aug 15, dia. c.
6616 Phelps, Wm E, 6 cav, F, Aug 23, dia.
6632 Pruils, W H, 1 cav, F, Aug 23, scs.
7222 Pope, Frank,‡ 5 cav, B, Aug 29, scs.

8070 Pott, Samuel, 4 cav, G, Sept 7, dys.
8207 Patterson, J, 2 cav, B, Sept 8, dys.
9299 Phelps, F M,§ 11 cav, I, Sept 20, dia.
10249 Partis, J R, 1 cav, F, Oct 3, scs.
12220 Pace, John, 3 cav, G, Dec 4, scs.
12327 Purcell, J, 1 cav, G, Dec 23, scs.

2144 Queata, J, 11 cav, E, June 18, dia.

452 Rurves, E,§ 4 cav, F, April 9, des.
577 Roberts, R, 12 cav, H, April 16, dia.
590 Ramay, Lester, 39 cav, H, April 17, dys.
637 Raberie, Geo, 1 cav, A, April 20, pna.
825 Richardson, M,‡ 3, H, May 1, pna.
1097 Runs, T, 11 cav, H, May 14, dia.
1193 Russell, Jacob, 12 cav, B, May 18, dia.
1355 Ritter, B B, 6 cav, L, May 25, dia.
1555 Rose, R C,‡ 6 cav, B, June 2, scs.
1571 Rogers, W, 1, F, June 3, dia. c.
2463 Reve, F N, 11, F, June 25, dia.
2751 Reilly, Thos, 1, D, July 1, dia. c.
4018 Ramsay, Robert, 45, A, July 26, dys.
4482 Robertson, H, 11 cav, D, Aug 1, des.
4549 Rodes, James, 1 cav, F, Aug 2, dia.
4919 Rockwell, W W,‡ 1 cav, C, Aug 6, ana.
5775 Roberts, L, 1 cav, K, Aug 15, scs.
5967 Rieff, R, 1 art, Aug 17, scs.
5976 Roberts, Andrew, 1 cav, K, Aug 17, dia. c.
6274 Readman, W, 11 cav, I, Aug 20, mas.
7215 Rogers, Henry, 12 cav, A, Aug 29, dia.
10124 Robuy, F, 15 cav, E, Oct 1, scs.
11369 Racine, P, 12 cav, M, Oct 23, scs.
11583 Ryan, W, 1 cav, I, Oct 28, scs.
11642 Riddle, J H, 1 cav, I, Oct 30, scs.
11644 Rogers, Wm, 2 cav, I, Oct 30, scs..
11873 Rusby, J, 2 cav, F, Nov 6, scs.
12828 Rice, P D,§ 3, I, April 9, dia. c.
1202 Ruble, Leander,‡ 11 cav, D, May 19, dia. c.
4106 Rankin, J H,§ 18 cav, G, July 27, dia.

213 Simpson, W, 1 cav, C, March 28, pna.
277 Sims, Geo,§ 40, I, March 31, pna.
567 Summers, W H, 11 cav, D, April 15, pna.
797 Smith, Geo, 13 cav, G, April 29, ana.
925 Sallac, Geo,‡ 11 cav, C, May 7, dia. c.
995 Smith, Wm A, 4 cav, K, May 10, dia.
1003 Smith, H, 16 cav, B, May 10, dys.
1101 Smith, R C, 1 cav, I, May 14, dys.
1180 Schafer, J E, 4 cav, A, May 18, dia.
1500 Stempf, Lewis, 12 cav, G, May 31, dys.
1659 Sutherland, J E,§ 1 cav, C, June 6, dys.
1681 Sebastian, J W, 45, C, June 6, dia.
1691 Sanders, J S, 12 cav, E, June 7, dia.
1708 Stine, C, 4 cav, K, June 7, dys.
1716 Sandfer, Jno, 11 cav, B, June 8, dia. c.
1811 Summers, Wm, 11 cav, D, June 10, dia.
1827 Sweeney, M, 5 cav, I, June 11, dia.
1952 Shirley, John, 28 cav, E, June 14, dia. a.
1964 Stanley, C O, 17 cav, E, June 14, dia.
2063 Salmond, P, 18 cav, H, June 16, scs.
2094 Shanks, W L, 6 cav, B, June 17, dia.
2766 Show, J, 11 cav, I, July 6, dia. c.
44 Smith, John, 2 cav, I, May 13, s. p.
51 Shaggs, I P, 11 cav, G, June 2, s. p.
3402 Shuman, J, 4 cav, A, July 16, dia.
4258 Smith, B,‡ 5 cav, A, July 29, dia. c.
4829 Schmal, Andrew, 4 cav, B, Aug 6, dys.
4831 Schottsman, F,‡ 1 cav, D, Aug 6, dia.
4976 Snyder, H M, 10 cav, B, Aug 7, scs.
5297 Smith, W H,‡ 27, E, Aug 11, dys.
6260 Stevens, P L,§ 12 cav, G, Aug 20, ts. f.

6280 Schrausburg, R, 1 cav, K, Aug 20, scs.
8226 Stimett, J, 6 cav, K, Sept 9, scs.
8487 Sutton, Thomas, 6 cav, A, Sept 1, scs.
8827 Shulds, J, 2 cav, K, Sept 15, scs.
10154 Sanders, B, 4 cav, F, Oct 1, dia.
10673 Sheppard, T L, 5 cav, H, Oct 11, dia.
11456 Sapp, B, 1 cav, B, Oct 25, scs.
11898 Selors, W H, 1 cav, C, Nov 7, scs.
12556 Stewart, E, 4 cav, A, Jan 30, scs.
10197 Sawney, Wm, 5 cav, H, Oct 2, scs.

253 Taylor, Thos,‡ 11 cav, H, March 30, dia.
391 Thrope, H, 1 cav, B, April 6, dia. c.
781 Tucker, Wm, 12 cav, I, April 28, dia. c.
1009 Travis, Geo, 16 cav, E, May 10, dia.
1628 Truney, J, 11 cav, C, June 4, dia. c.
2116 Tutune, J,§ 11 cav, A, June 17, scs.
2371 Tudor, Ab'm,‡ 11 cav, A, June 23, dia. c.
3701 Tullor, G W, 28, A, July 21, cah.
5424 Tabu, Silas, 27, D, Aug 12, dia.
6234 Templeton, W H,‡ 11 cav, B, Aug 20, dys.
6257 Tapp, George, 13 cav, I, Aug 20, scs.
6508 Tracy, Jas, 11 cav, L, Aug 22, dia.
6956 Thorp, J, 4 cav, K, Aug 26, scs.
7205 Tucker, Robt, 17 cav, G, Aug 29, scs.
10028 Tucker, J A, 15 cav, A, Sept 29, scs.
10398 Thornburg, R, 2 cav, G, Oct 6, ts. f.
10588 Tussey, E D, 24 cav, A, Oct 10, scs.
10809 Terry, Wm, 1 cav, A, Oct 12, scs.
10892 Thomas, W E,§ 11 cav, G, Oct 14, scs.

10657 Vandevier, J, 11 cav, C, Oct 11, dia.

278 West, John C, 11 cav, E, March 31, ts. f.
494 White, A, 6 cav, K, April 12, dys.
735 Wallar, M R, 16 cav, C, April 24, dys.
1125 White, John, 11 cav, D, May 15, dys. c.
1706 Westfall, J, 4 cav, D, June 7, dys. c.
1734 Wickles, John, 40, K, June 8, dia. c.
1745 Walsh, J E, 6 cav, L, June 8, dia.
1894 Wright, John E,‡ 1 cav, June 13, dia.
2199 Wheelan, Jas, 18 cav, C, June 19, dia.
2584 White, C, 1 cav, H, June 27, ana.
2901 Wiser, R M, 1 cav, K, June 30, dia.
40 Ward, F W, 1 cav, A, May 3, s. p.
4374 Warren, W P, 34 cav, K, July 31, dia.
4624 Wallace, H, 14 cav, E, Aug 3, dys.
4697 West, P H, 6 cav, K, Aug 3, dia.
15057 Webb, J, 6 cav, F, Aug 8, scs.
5762 Welch, T C, 5 cav, G, Aug 15, dia.
5790 Walsh, John, 6 cav, H, Aug 15, dia.
6101 White, W E, 1 cav, E, Aug 18, dia. c.
6121 Winfries, W S, 3 cav, A, Aug 19, dys.
6893 White, S A, 17 cav, G, Aug 26, dys.
7038 Willser, J, 11 cav, I, Aug 27, scs.
7694 Wells, John W, 12 cav, C, Sept 3, wda.
8533 Wallace, J,§ 11 cav, K, Sept 12, dia.
9258 Warner, D, 12 cav, A, Sept 19, scs.
9541 Wicog, S, 4 cav, I, Sept 23, dia.
9636 Wagoner, H,‡ 4 cav, I, Sept 24, scs.
10770 Warner, Thos, 15 cav, F, Oct 12, scs.
10898 Walton, J J, 8 cav, A, Oct 14, scs.
11749 Willit, M, 4 cav, I, Nov 2, scs.
12279 Weasett, A, 1 cav, D Nov 13, scs.

904 Yocombs, H, 11 cav D, May 5, phs.
1166 Yoam, J, 10 cav, D, May 17, cah.
2689 Yeager, L,§ 11 cav, [?], June 30, dia.
3757 Yeast, R, 1 cav, I, July 22, cah.

5257 Zertes, G, 4 cav, G, Aug 10, ana.

LOUISIANA.

6778 Kimball, Jas, 2 cav, A, Aug 25, con.

MAINE.

2604 Anderson, John, 19, I, June 28, dia. c.
8093 Allen, A, 32, K, July 10, dia. c.
7024 Arnold, E W, 17, G, Aug 27, dia. c.

  22 Butler, C A, 3, K, March 7, pna.
 269 Brown, E M, 5, G, March 31, dia.
3953 Buner, A E, 31, E, July 25, scs.
6211 Bachelor, P,§ 3, K, Aug 19, dia. c.
9162 Baker, James, 17, H, Sept 18, dia. c.
10669 Ballast, J, 19, G, Oct 11, scs.
7663 Bartlett, H, 17, C, Sept 3, i. s.
7255 Barney, G S, 32, I, Aug 30, scs.
6683 Bean, G W, 8, C, Aug 24, des.
6603 Bennett, L, 1 art, Aug 23, dia.
9097 Berry, C H, 6, H, Sept 18, scs.
7645 Bigelow, C, 19, H, Sept 3, scs.
5290 Blaizdell, H, 8, F, Aug 11, scs.
12055 Boren, W, 16, I, Nov 16, dia.
9408 Bowden, —, 7, A, Sept 21, dia.
4776 Braley, J, 3, E, Aug 4, dia.
5015 Briggs, J C, 19, F, Aug 8, scs.
8542 Brinkerman, L, 9, D, Sept 11, scs.
8247 Broadstreet, C B, 1 cav, B, Sept 9, dia. c.
6811 Brown, J, 8, G, Aug 25, dia. c.
11980 Bryant, C D, 16, E, Nov 13, dia. c.
5719 Bullsen, E T,§ 5 cav, B, Aug 15, ens.
5757 Bunker, S A, 1 art, A, Aug 15, scs.
8474 Burgen, A, 4, I, Sept 11, scs.

7017 Cardoney, C, 17, G, Aug 27, dia.
7746 Carlen, M, 1 cav, F, Sept 3, dia.
8374 Carr, J, 19, E, Sept 10, scs.
6246 Cariton, J S, 31, D, Aug 19, dia. c.
5989 Chase, F W, 1 art, D, Aug 17, dia.
2316 Clark, James, 1 cav, C, June 22, dia.
8143 Clark, P M,§ 1 cav, C, Sept 8, dia. c.
10376 Clark, L, 19, D, Oct 5, dia.
10421 Clayton, E B, 1, F, Oct 6, scs.
  28 Cohan, D, 3, K, March 7, pna.
6950 Conder, W H, 16, G, Aug 26, brs.
8037 Conley, W, 5, F, Sept 6, dia.
3943 Cook, James, 4, D, July 25, ts. f.
8433 Condon, D H, 20, K, Sept 11, scs.
 425 Craw, H, 3, B, April 7, pna.
12061 Cressy, N F, 11, G, Nov 17, scs.
10936 Cromwell, S R,‡ 1 art, M, Sept 14, scs.
11211 Cromwell, W H, 19, D, Oct 20, scs.
8625 Curtiss, John, 16, I, Sept 13, scs.
12367 Cutts, O M, 16, D, Jan 1, scs.
  80 Cutter, A, 20, E, March 20, dys.
5171 Cross, Noah, 1 art, A, Aug 9, i. s.
8581 Crosby, W, 4, A, Sept 12, dys.

8445 Davis, D, 3, C, Sept 11, scs.
 227 Davis, Wm L, 20, E, March 29, dia.
5615 Dougherty, Thomas, 8, G, Aug 14, dys.
6612 Donnell, F, 8, E, Aug 23, dia.
9624 Downes, J, 8, G, Sept 23, dia.
1359 Doyle, Wm, 6, D, May 25, dia. c.
5481 Drisdale, F, 1, H, Aug 13, dia.
4425 Duffy, A, 3, G, July 31, ana.
6415 Dugan, D, 32, A, Aug 21, scs.
6438 Dunning, S P, 29, G, Aug 21, dia.
7240 Dunnie, G, 5, G, Aug 29, ana.
6357 Dye, John, 1 cav, E, Aug 21, scs.
5035 Dittener, H, 20, A, Aug 8, scs.

10608 Eckhard, H, 7, C, Sept 10, scs.
7212 Edwards, N S, 1 cav, F, Aug 29, dia.
8538 Ellis, A, 2 art, H, Sept 11, dia.
1877 Emerson, H H, 3, June 12, scs.

2628 Farewell, E, 31, E, June 28, dys.
8401 Ferrell, P, 6, H, Sept 10, scs.
4765 Fish, Wm, 7, A, Aug 5, dys.
5243 Flags, J B, 5, K, Aug 10, dys.
  69 Flanders, L G, 20, E, March 19, dia.

1989 Foley, John, 19, E, June 15, dia.
2362 Forrest, Thomas, 1 cav, E, June 23, dia.
2482 Foster, A,‡ 6, K, June 25, dia. c.
8145 Foster, E R, 16, C, Sept 8, dia.
7073 Foster, Samuel, C, 16, K, Aug 28 r.
6191 Frisble, L, 7, C, Aug 19.
10957 Fitzgerald, Joseph, 8, E, Oct 14, scs.

5907 Gardner, W H,§ 4, Aug 16, scs.
12515 Gibbs, R, 19, K, Jan 23, dia.
2906 Gilgan, W, 7, C, 5, July 5, dys.
6107 Goodward, A, 1 art, I, Aug 18, dia.
5580 Goodwin, M T, 8, F, Aug 14, dia.
4141 Grant, G, 1 art, F, July 28, dia.
7391 Grant, Frank, 16, F, Aug 30, car.
8392 Griffith, S, 8, G, Sept 10, dia. c.
9190 Gunney, C, 31, A, Sept 18, dia.
10031 Gunney, J F,§ 1, 1, Sept 29, scs.
11823 Gilgrist, —, 31, E, Nov 5, scs.

8306 Hammond, J, 19, G, Sept 10, ana.
12343 Harris, J S, 1, F, Dec 26, dys.
3506 Hassen, H, 7, G, July 18, dia.
3274 Hatch, J S, 3, G, July 13, dys.
6112 Hatch, S,§ 8, F, Aug 19, scs.
9311 Heath, B, 3, F, Sept 20, dia.
4174 Heninger, —, 19, July 28, des.
12349 Hopes, H, 19, D, Dec 27, scs.
7474 Howard, D H, 17, D, Sept 1, dys.
3844 Howe, Samuel W, 1, K, July 23, dia.
7186 Hoyt, A D, 3, K, Aug 29, dia.
3237 Hudson, W, 17, E, July 12, dia.
8797 Hughes, Wm, 31, K, Sept 15, scs.
9652 Hamphrey, —, 3 cav, L, Sept 24, scs.
3484 Hunkey, B, 1, L, July 17, dia. c.
4703 Henley, D, 8, G, Aug 4, dys.

5355 Ingols, L, 16, H, Aug 11, i. s.
9389 Ingerson, P, 7, J, Sept 20, dia.

11489 Jackson, A J, 17, J, Oct 26, scs.
10619 Jackson, R, 7, B, Oct 10, scs.
10710 Jackson, R W, 7, D, Oct 11, dia.
12602 Jerdan, J, 19, F, Feb 6, rhm.
7385 Johnson, B, 7, K, Aug 30, scs.
5849 Jones, Wm, 19, E, Aug 16, ens.
10243 Jory, G F, 8, F, Oct 3, scs.

11586 Kellar, J, 19, J, Oct 28, scs.
8237 Kelley, L, 11, D, Sept 9, dia.
3313 Kennedy, W, 17, G, July 14, dia.
6169 Kilpatrick, C, 3, C, Aug 19, des.

5366 Ladd, C, 6, I, Aug 11, dia. c.
8350 Lamber, W, 17, K, Sept 10, dia.
11707 Levitt, H, 19, A, Nov 1, scs.
7967 Lincoln, A, 16, I, Sept 6, scs.
10931 Littlefield, C, 1 cav, F, Oct 14, scs.
6340 Lord, Geo H, 3, B, Aug 21, dia.
5549 Ludovice, F, 13, F, Aug 13, scs.
 490 Lowell, B, 4, G, April 12, dia. c.

9426 Macon, L, 8, A, Sept 21, dia.
 709 Malcolm, H M, 16, A, April 24, ers.
6606 Marshall, B F, 1, H, Aug 23, dia.
12122 Maston, A, 19, D, Nov 22, scs.
10392 Mathews, James, 32, F, Oct 14, scs.
12011 Maxwell, J, 8, E, Nov 14, scs.
3679 McFarland, G, 3, G, July 21, ana.
9538 McGinley, J, 7, A, Sept 22, scs.
2200 McKinney, G, 3, I, June 19, dia.
12084 McFarland, E S, 8, I, Nov 18, scs.
4391 Medealf, Oliver, 8, H, July 31, dia. c.
12768 McFarland, W,‡ 19, K, March 13, scs.
5200 Melgar, J, 7, A, Aug 10, dia.
5614 Messer, C R, 7, F, Aug 14, scs.
9399 Miller, C J, 1 cav, B, Sept 21, scs.

2002 Miller, J O, 2, D, June 15, dia.
7578 Mills, M, 1, Sept 2, dia.
2808 Moore, Charles W, 8, B, July 3, dys.
11042 Moore, G, 18, D, Oct 17, scs.
7273 Moore, J D, 1 cav, B, Aug 30, scs.
6940 Moore, W C, 7, A, Aug 26, scs.
8118 Moyes, F, 32, F, Sept 8, dia.

7046 Newton, C, 9, K, Aug 27, ana.
1507 Nickerson, D, 4, F, May 31, dia. c.
8020 Nolton, H, 7, B, Sept 6, ana.

2131 O'Brien, W, 16, A, June 18, dia. c.
6325 Opease, S, 19, Aug 21, des.
143 Osborn, A J, 8, March 24, dys.
10866 Owens, O H, 10, Nov 6, scs.

3710 Parker, A, 1 cav, E, July 21, dia.
7979 Parsons, James W, 16, D, Sept 6, dia.
9362 Patrick, F, 14, F, Sept 20, dia.
2272 Peabody, F S,§ 5, I, June 20, dia.
12543 Pequette, P, 4, G, Jan 28, scs.
1486 Perkins, D, 1 cav, I, May 31, dia.
5197 Perkins, T, 1, H, Aug 10, scs.
6911 Peters, H, 4, E, Aug 26, scs.
12056 Phillbrook, F, 1 art, A, Nov 17, dia.
2064 Phelps, W H, 1 cav, H, June 16, dia.
3436 Pinkham, U W, 1 art, A, July 17, dia.
1361 Pottle, A E, 1 cav, I, May 25, dia.
5698 Pratt, A M, 1 cav, L, Aug 15, wds.
8441 Pulerman, G, 16, D, Sept 11, scs.
12410 Prescott, C, 19, H, Jan 7, dia.

7785 Richardson, C, 31, L, Sept 4, scs.
6762 Richardson, J K, 8, G, Aug 24, scs.
10465 Richardson, W M,‡ 1 cav, B, Oct 7, dys.
5522 Ricker, Wm,‡ 1 cav, D, Aug 13, dys.
8480 Ridlon, N, 7, D, Sept 11, scs.
900 Riseck, R, 3, I, May 5, ana.
3921 Roberts, H, 19, K, July 25, dia.
5236 Rowe, L, 1, A, Aug 10, dia.
166 Rosmer, Frank, 4, C, March 26, dia.
5796 Ruet, 11, 2, H, Aug 15, dys.
8557 Russell, G A, 1 cav, E, Sept 12, scs.

5450 Sampson, E, 1, F, Aug 12, scs.
4532 Sawyer, Enos, 1 art, H, Aug 2, dia.
3182 Sawyer, John, 31, K, July 11, i. s.
11462 Shorey, S, 1 cav, K, Oct 20, scs.

2243 Simmons, G F, 6, K, June 20, dia.
3159 Smith, W, 9, K, July 11, dia. c.
3331 Smith, W A, 6, F, July 14, dia.
1782 Snowdale, F, 4, C, June 10, dia. c.
9974 Snower, S C, 19, A, Sept 28, dia.
1998 Springer, H W, 36, A, June 15, dia.
4596 Steward, G, 20, H, Aug 3, dia.
11562 St Peter, F, 19, F, Oct 27, scs.
7001 Swaney, P, 19, F, Aug 27, dia.
199 Swan, H B,‡ 3, F, March 28, dys.
1936 Swan, F, 3, F, June 14, ana.
8682 Thompson, F, 9, E, Sept 13, scs.
10455 Thompson, John, 3, E, Oct 7, dia.
621 Thorn, E, 9, I, April 19, dys.
10928 Toothacre, J, 7, G, Oct 14, scs.
1106 Turner, C C, 4, E, May 15, dia. c.
5090 Tufts, J, 32, C, Aug 8, dia.
11875 Taylor, G, 9, C, Nov 16, scs.
12322 Tuttle, D L, 32, F, Dec 20, scs.
12196 Tuttle, L S,‡ 32, F, Nov 30, dia.
12706 Thorndie, W B,‡19, I, March 2, scs.

6245 Valley, F, 32, K, Aug 19, dia.
3335 Venill, C, 32, G, July 15, dia.

7226 Walker, A B,‡1, K, Aug 29, dia.
3894 Walker, M C, 5, I, July 24, des.
7722 Wall, A, 1 cav, K, Sept 4, dia.
5942 Walsh, Thomas, 20, H, Aug 17, scs.
6750 Watson, B, 7, K, Aug 24, dys.
10558 Webber, Oliver, 3, A, Oct 9, dia.
4559 Whiteman, A M,‡ 5, I, Aug 2, scs.
1648 Whitcomb, T O, 4, F, June 5, dia. c.
6251 Whittier, J K P, 32, C, Aug 19, brs.
10445 Willard, W, 20, B, Oct 7, scs.
7711 Williams, C, 6, G, Sept 3, des.
6900 Wilson, George, 32, C, Aug 26, dia.
3639 Wilson, G W, 16, H, July 20, ana.
3132 Willey, D H, 19, E, July 10, dys.
3860 Winslow, E, 1, A, July 24, scs.
5512 Winslow, N L, 4, K, Aug 13, des.
6372 Wyman, A, 32, C, Aug 21, scs.
2095 Wyman, J, 16, A, June 17, dia.
12470 Wyer, R, 3, K, Jan 16, dia.
12043 Wright, C, 1, G, Nov 16, scs.

178 Young, E W,§ 3, H, March 26, des.
6369 Young, J, 3, H, Aug 21, scs.
8140 Young, J W,‡ 8, I, Sept 8, scs.

MARYLAND.

850 Allen, W H, 1, H, May 3, dys.
1928 Anderson, Wm, 2, C, May 11, dys.
1379 Aikens, A, 1 cav, I, May 26, dia. c.
1928 Adams, Jas T, 6, H, May 14, dia.
10288 Abbott, D E, 2, D, Oct 4, scs.
2325 Archer, H, 1, I, Dec 24, scs.

112 Babb, Samuel, 8, I, March 23, brs.
288 Berlin, Jas, 2 cav, F, April 1, pna.
472 Beltz, W W, 2, H, April 9, dia. c.
1086 Bowers, A, 1, I, May 14, dia. c.
1455 Brown, Augustus, 2, G, May 29, dia. c.
1487 Braddock, Wm, 2, D, May 30, dia.
1549 Buck, H, 1 cav, B, June 1, dia.
1644 Buckley, Geo, 9, B, June 5, dia. c.
2404 Bennett, C B, 1, D, June 24, dia. c.
3268 Brant, D B, 2, H, July 13, dia. c.
4602 Betson, James, 1 bat, A, Aug 3, scs.
5261 Ball, J A, 2, B, Aug 10, scs.
5525 Brown, J C, 1 art, B, Aug 23, scs.
6540 Brown, E R, 2, C, Aug 13, scs.
7727 Brown, E, 2, D, Sept 3, dys.
8975 Buckley, A M, 1, B, Sept 17, dia.
11184 Beale, R, 1 cav, D, Sept 19, scs.
11761 Buckner, George, 2, K, Nov 3, scs.
11620 Bell, J R, 8, D, Oct 28, scs.
12373 Bloom, J,‡7, F, Jan 1, pls.
12639 Book, C, 8, G, Feb 19, dia.

54 Carpenter, Wm, 2 cav, I, March 17, dia.
304 Cook, Lewis, 9, E, April 1, dys.
469 Coombs, E A, 9, I, April 9, dia.
524 Carter, Wm, 2, C, April 13, pna.
728 Cury, W H, 9, F, April 25, dia.
1357 Carl, J M, 6, E, May 25, dia. c.
1371 Cabbage, C H, 2, H, May 25, dys.
2012 Cullin, John, 2, D, June 15, dia.
4182 Crasby, M, 1, G, July 28, dys.
4620 Carter, John, 2, A, July 3, dia.
5036 Carr, Wm, 1 cav, D, Aug 8, dia. c.
5063 Childs, G A, 9, I, Aug 8, dia. c.
5826 Crisle, J, 6, G, Aug 16, dys.
8008 Crouse, W A, Coles' cav, E, Sept [?], dia.
8035 Conway, Wm E, 4, E, Sept 6, dia.
8266 Crabb, H, 4, E, Sept 9, dia.
8357 Coon, H S, 1, E, Sept 10, dia.
8618 Crouse, A J, 1 cav, A, Sept 13, dia. c.
10600 Collins, D, 1, C, Sept 10, dia. a.
12395 Callahan, P, 1, F, Jan 4, dia.

181 Duff, Chas,‡ 8, A, March 27, pna.
1410 Dunn, John,‡ 9, H, May 27, dia. c.
2396 Davis, Thomas, 9, June 24, dia.
3912 Drew, C, 35, B, July 24, dia.
4138 Dennis, Benj, 2, A, July 28, dia.
4211 Davis, G, 1 cav, F, July 29, scs.
6510 Dickwall, Wm, 2, F, Aug 22, dia.

8199 Deller, F, 1, E, Sept 8, dia.
6788 Dennisseu, T, 42, 1, Aug 25, dia.

8428 Ellis, C, 4, D, Sept 12, scs.
10410 Eli, W, 7, C, Oct 6, scs.

3849 Fecker, L, 2, I, July 24, scs.
1321 Fairbanks, J E, 9, C, May 23, dia. c.
2559 Francis, J,‡ 2, K, June 27, r. f.
2600 Feage, F J, 2, H, June 28, dia.
2824 Farrass, Jas, 7, G, July 2, dys.
6016 Frantz, F, 2, H, Aug 17, ana.
7404 Fink, L, 2, H, Aug 31, des.
9290 Frederick, J E, 9, I, Sept 19, scs.
12752 Freaere, W, 8, A, March 10, scs.

1271 Gordon, A B, 9, E, May 22, dys.
2138 Gerard, Fred, 1 cav, B, June 18, dia. c.
3013 Green, Thos, 2, D, July 7, dia.
3789 Gregg, F, 2, I, July 22, dia.
6072 Gilson, J E,§ 1 cav, C, Aug 18, scs.
6731 Ganon, J W, 2, K, Aug 24, dia.
12735 Goff, John, 1, I, March 6, dia. c.

1767 Honck, J,‡ 2, H, April 27, dia.
826 Hickley, John, 9, G, May 1, ana.
1625 Howell, L H, 1 cav, M, June 4, dia. c.
1720 Hoop, H, 2, I, June 8, scs.
2357 Hickley, J S, 2, H, June 23, dia. c.
2494 Hidderick, H, 1, I, June 26, dia.
2978 Hite, J E, 2, I, July 7, dia. c.
3864 Hering, P,§ 2, C, July 24, scs.
4767 Hank, Thomas, 1 bat, D, Aug 5, scs.
5292 Hilligar, 1, E, Aug 11, dia.
5408 Hood, John, 8, C, Aug 12, scs.
5917 Holmes, L, 2, H, Aug 17, dys.
6484 Hour, S, 8, E, Aug 22, dia.
6504 Harris, J E, 1, A, Aug 22, dia.
7434 Hazel, J, 9, C, Sept 1, dys.
8165 Himick, F, 1 cav, E, Sept 8, r. f.
8398 Hall, J, 7, D, Sept 10, dia. c.
9932 Holden, J, 9, C, Sept 28, dys.
11109 Hakaion, F, 2, K, Oct 18, scs.
12422 Hoover, J, 2 cav, C, Jan 9, scs.

2895 Isaac, Henry, 2, H, July 4, dia. c.

93 Jones, David, 1 bat, A, March 22, dia.
669 Jenkins, M, 2, A, April 22, dia. c.

460 Keplinger, J, 2, H, April 9, dia.
544 Keefe, Lewis, 7, F, April 14, pna.
7242 Kirby, J, 9, F, Aug 29, dys.

1019 Laird, Corbin, 1 cav, F, May 11, dia. c.
1956 Lees, W H, 2, C, May 13, i. f.
3913 Louis, J,§ 2, B, July 24, dys.
11385 Little, D, 2 cav, K, Oct 24, scs.
12361 Lebud, J, 1 cav, D, Dec 30, scs.
12667 Lambert, W, 1, I, Feb 17, scs.

206 McCarle, Jas, 1 cav, B, March 28, dia. c.
471 Moland, B, 2, F, April 9, dia. c.
896 Myers, Noah, 9, G, May 5, dia.
1190 McGuigen, S K, 1 bat, D, May 18, dia.
1307 Myers, L S, 1, B, May 23, dia. c.
1797 Moore, Frank, 9, A, June 10, c. c.
1898 Moffitt, Thos, 6, June 13, dia. c.
2059 Martz, G H, 2, H, June 16, ana.
8429 Machler, C S, 1 bat, A, July 17, dia.
3797 McKinsay, Jno, 2, I, July 22, dia.
4051 Miller, F, 6, C, July 27, scs.
4146 Mathews, F, 8, G, July 28, dia.
4881 Macomber, John, 1 cav, B, Aug 6, dia.
6170 Marvin, J, 2, H, Aug 9, scs.
6757 Moon, J J, 1, D, Aug 25, scs.
7281 McCullough, J, 1, I, Aug 30, scs.
7827 McLamas, J, 7, C, Aug 30, dys.
8043 Markell, S, 2, H, Sept 6, dia.
10150 Munroe, J,‡ 4, H. Oct 1, dys.

10861 Markin, W, 1, F, Oct 13, scs.
11547 Mathews, J, 8, Oct 27, scs.
12608 McMiller, J A, 1, E, Feb 7, scs.

91 Nice, Jacob, 5 cav, M, March 2, pna
371 Nace, Harrison, 9, H, April 5, pna.
9752 Norris, N, 1, I, Sept 25, scs.

153 Pool, Hanson, 2, H, March 25, phs.
7590 Porter, G, 1, I, Sept 2, dia.
7981 Pindiville, M, 7, H, Sept 6, scs.
5069 Papple, D,‡ 2, H, Aug 8, dys.

252 Rusk, John, 9, E, March 30, dia.
918 Russell, A P, 2, C, May 6, dys.
1606 Rodh, Simon, 9, E, June 4, dia.
1901 Robinson, J, 9, June 13, dia. c.
2350 Rynedollar Wm, 1 cav, D, June 23, dia c.
6599 Reed, Thos P, 1 art, B, Aug 23, dia. c.

155 Seberger, F, 9, F, March 25, c. f.
317 Scarboro, Rob't, 9, I, April 2, pna.
478 Suffecol, S, 1, I, April 9, dia. c.
718 Sinder, John, 2, H, April 24, dia.
899 Snooks, W, 9, E, May 5, dia. c.
1205 Spence, Levi, 9, D, May 19, ana.
1272 Scarlett, Jas, 1, D, May 22, dys.
1926 Smith, Ed,§ 9, I, June 14, dia. c.
2004 Stafford, John, 9, G, June 15, dia.
2361 Shipley, W, 9, G, June 23, dia. c.
2489 Schineder, J, 1 bat, B, June 26, dia.
5797 Smith, John, 1 cav, B, Aug 15, dys.
6751 Shelley, B, 2, F, Aug 24, scs.
6816 Shiver, G H,‡ 1, C, Aug 25, scs.
6919 Stull, G E, 1 cav, D, Aug 26, dia. c.
7580 Shilling, Wm, 2, K, Sept 2, dia. c.
7833 Stolz, 7, K, Sept 4, dia. c.
8296 Smitzer, J, 1, D, Sept 9, scs.
8716 Segar, Chas, 6, F, Sept 14, scs.
9309 Snyder, F, 2, K, Sept 20, dia.
9451 Stratten, J A, 1 art, C, Sept 21, dia.
10215 Shafer, J N, 1 cav, A, Oct 22, dia.
11159 Samon, L W, 1, I, Oct 19, dia. c.
11160 Speaker, H, 1, F, Oct 19, scs.
12195 Spaulding, J, 4, C, Nov 29, dia.
12704 Smith, G C, 1, I, Feb 26, scs.

149 Tyson, J T, 9, D, March 25, pna.
1022 Tysen, J T, 9, I, May 11, dia. c.
677 Turner, Wm F, 1 cav, D, April 22, dys.
1029 Turner, A, 1 cav, B, May 11, pna.
1356 Tindle, E,‡ 9, K, May 25, dia. c.
1377 Turner, C, 9, E, May 26, dia. c.
7872 Thompson, J, 13, I, Sept 5, scs.
8689 Thompson, John, 2, S, Sept 14, dia.
9246 Tucker, 2, D, Sept 19, scs.
9335 Tindell, Win, 11, B, Sept 20, scs.
11450 Tilton, J, 1 cav, F, Oct 25, dia.

1583 Ulrich, Daniel, 9, I, June 3, dia.

1305 Veach, Jesse, 2, H, May 23, dia. c.
8269 Viscounts, A J, 1 art, E, Sept 9, dia. c.

78 Wise, John, 9, D, March 20, dia.
21 White, Wm, 9, C, March 7, dys.
553 Widdons, D, 1, E, April 14, dia.
597 Webster, Samuel,‡ 9, G, April 17, dia.
1171 Wharton, Samuel, 2, F, May 17, dia. c.
2275 Worthen, Wm, 9, C, June 20, dia. c.
4748 West, M, 4, D, Aug 5, scs.
9409 Weaver, George, 1, B, Sept 21, dia.
11587 Witman, D, 13, D, Sept 28, scs.
12147 Wolfe, H, 1, B, Nov 24, scs.

455 Yieldhan, R, 9, C, April 9, pna.

1060 Zeck, Wm J,‡ 7, E, May 13, des.
3223 Zimmerman, Chas, 9, E, July 12.

MASSACHUSETTS.

?247 Hay, Wm, 2 art, H, July 13, ts. f.
5789 Haymouth, N, 2 cav, M, Aug 15, scs.
4209 Haynes, Charles E, 2 art, H, July 29, dia.
8604 Hayes, P, 37, A, Sept 23, dia.
3508 Heart, John, 28, G, July 18, dia.
7416 Hebban, Thomas, 28, B, Aug 31, dia.
3168 Henrie, E W, 17, H, July 14, dia.
5606 Henry, D, 16, H, Aug 14, dys.
4604 Henry, J, 2 art, K, Aug 3, dia.
1093 Hermans, John, 11, G, May 24, dys.
7297 Hervey, George W,‡ 33, I, Aug 30, scs.
6242 Higgin A, 23, B, Aug 20, ts. f.
4906 Hill, F, 9, I, Aug 6, dia.
1740 Hills, J B, 2 cav, G, June 8, dia.
11762 Hillman, G, 16, H, Nov 3, scs.
6056 Hines, S, 59, C, Aug 10, dys.
9223 Hitchcock, J C, 27, C, Sept 19, dia.
6907 Hogan, Pat, 2 art, G, Aug 26, dys.
6067 Hogan, S, 19, E, Aug 18, dia.
9260 Hoit, D, 19, B, Sept 19, scs.
4811 Hoitt, J F, 2 art, D, Aug 5, dia.
6228 Holbrook, Charles, 2 art, H, Aug 20, ana.
6826 Holden, Pat, 2 art, G, Aug 25, r. f.
1986 Holland, P, 17, I, June 15, dia.
905 Holland, Pat, 11, C, May 5, dia.
4816 Holmes, S, 12, I, Aug 5, scs.
8712 Holt, E K, 1 art, Sept 14, scs.
6716 Holt, T E, 22, H, Aug 24, ana.
8575 Howard, C, 24, C, Sept 12, dia.
10864 Howard, James, 59, D, Oct 13, scs.
7025 Howe, C H, 36, G, Aug 27, scs.
222 Howe, E H, 36, H, May 29, dia.
3871 Howe, John W, 24, B, July 24, scs.
5973 Hubbard, E, 34, B, Aug 17, dia.
11045 Hubert, G W, 27, I, Oct 17, scs.
11960 Hunt, J, 84, D, Nov 11, scs.
4323 Hunting, John W, 25, I, July 30, dia.
12299 Hartshaw, L E, 56, A, Dec 16, dia.
6161 Hyde, N L, 2 cav, B, Aug 19, scs.
5470 Hyde, Richard, 39, E, Aug 13, scs.

3487 Jackson, N S, 1 art, K, July 17, dys.
3501 Jackson, N S, 17, K, July 17, dia.
8429 Jackson, Wm R, 2 cav, B, Sept 11, scs.
5733 Jaquirius, C, 57, D, Aug 15, dia.
2308 Jaynes, H, 59, G, June 22, ana.
10561 Jeff, M, 16, I, Oct 9, scs.
5915 Jeffrey, A, 58, B, Aug 17, des.
9951 Jewett, E, 27, I, Sept 28, dia.
12820 Jewett, G, 4, A, April 11, dia.
5473 Johnson, M, 34, G, Aug 13, scs.
5850 Johnson, R A, 19, G, Aug 16, dys.
3684 Johnson, Wm, 2 art, H, July 21, dia.
10702 Jones, J, 59, E, Oct 11, dia.
603 Jones, John, 2 cav, M, April 18, dys.
8875 Jones, N P, 32, F, Sept 16, dia.
6054 Jones, Thomas, 11, A, Aug 18, scs.

6183 Kavanaugh, Jas, 32, K, Aug 19, des.
8658 Kelley, Charles, 3 art, C, Sept 13, scs.
6579 Kelley, Henry, 20, E, Aug 23, scs.
9983 Kelley, M, 2 art, H, Sept 17, scs.
6275 Kelsey, E, 27, D, Aug 20, mas.
6712 Kempton, E, 2 art, G, Aug 24, pls.
5708 Kennedy, Wm, 59, F, Aug 15, scs.
6529 Kenny, J, 3 cav, G, Aug 23, scs.
8252 Kent, S, 27, H, Sept 9, dia.
12490 Kerr, Wm,§ 56, D, Jan 20, scs.
6036 Keyes, J C, 2 art, G, Aug 18, scs.
868 Kice, Thomas, 2 cav, B, May 3, r. f.
296 Kilan, M,§ 17, I, April 1, pna.
4544 Kimball, A, 1 art, B, Aug 2, des.
1754 Kinnely, F,§ 17, E, June 9, dia.
12813 Kluener, F, 27, A, March 25, des.
554 Knapp, David, 2 art, M, April 14, dia.
3842 Knight, —, 25, A, July 23, wds.
11119 Keephart, M, 2 art, E, Oct 18, scs.
5037 Kuppy, H, 1 art, K, Aug 8, dia.
8648 Krote, Huer, 20, G, Sept 13, scs.

12549 Langley, L F,§ 28 B, Jan 28, scs.
??35 Lain, S, 12, I, Aug 24, dia.

10885 Lane, J H,§ 23, Oct 13, scs.
9738 Latham, W, 25, K, Sept 25, dia.
8835 Lathrop, W O, 58, C, Sept 15, scs.
2175 Laurens, John, 23, E, June 15, dia.
9621 Leach, C W, 20, I, Sept 23, dia.
2781 Leary, D, 2 cav, A, July 2, dia.
7707 Leavey, W H, 12, A, Sept 3, dys.
7210 Lecraw, W H, 1 art, G, Aug 29, dia.
7548 Leonard, W E, 59, H, Sept 2, dia.
7725 Leonard, I G, 1 art, K, Sept 3, scs.
7798 Lewin, Charles, 19, I, Sept 3, dys.
2448 Lewis, F, 2 art, G, June 25, dia.
10068 Lewis, G G, 2 art, G, Sept 30, scs.
4082 Lewis, L, 5 cav, L, July 27, dia.
10750 Lewis, L, 1 art, A, Oct 12, dys.
5401 Lindsay, J, 18, A, Aug 12, scs.
12413 Liswell, L, 27, F, Jan 8, dia.
8748 Livingston, R, 39, C, Sept 14, dia.
1156 Lochien, Joel, 1 cav, E, May 16, dia.
480 Lohem, E D, 18, H, April 9, dys.
3163 Lombard, B K, 58, A, July 11, cah.
12256 Loring, G, 20, A, Dec 10, scs.
10744 London, Ed, 22, G, Oct 11, scs.
8437 Lovely, Francis, 25, I, Sept 11, scs.
3217 Lovett, A W, 39, E, July 12, scs.
3175 Lowell, George, 22, E, July 11, dys.
9957 Lucier, J, 2, G, Sept 28, dia.
4090 Lugby, Z, 2 art, G, July 27, dia.
8593 Lyons, E, 27, I, Sept 12, scs.
3683 Lynch, John, 56, K, July 21, dia.

7521 Macey, Charles, 18, I, Sept 1, dys.
4264 Macomber, J, 20, H, July 29, dia.
4034 Mahan, E, 56, I, July 26, dia.
3383 Marintine, G H, 18, I, July 16, dys.
9940 Mann, N C, 16, saddler, F, Sept 28, scs.
6220 Mansfield, D R, 58, G, Aug 20, ces.
503 Marden, G O, 17, I, April 12, r. f.
1350 Mariland, W H, 17, D, May 25, dia.
7147 Marchet, C, 28, F, Aug 29, dia.
8450 Martin, C M, 2 art, H, Sept 11, ana.
6272 Maxwell, M, 1 art, I, Aug 20, mas.
5060 McAllister, J,‡ 17, Aug 8, dys.
7823 McCaffrey, J, 27, E, Sept 4, dia.
3835 McCloud, J, 56, K, July 23, dia.
9942 McCord, G, 32, H, Sept 28, scs.
12176 McCorner, J, 19, F, Nov 27, scs.
8905 McDavle, J, 8 art, M, Sept 15, dia.
6162 McDermott, J, 2 art, B, Aug 19, scs.
4409 McDevitt, Wm, 25, E, July 31, dia.
9439 McDonald, R, 18, D, Sept 21, dia.
430 McDonnell, P, 2, B, April 8, pna.
7459 McDonough, P,‡ 25, E, Sept 1, dia.
1984 McGiven, J, 22, K, June 15, dia.
6375 McGovern, B, 34, D, Aug 21, dia.
2652 McGowen, John, 2 art, H, June 29, dys.
5280 McGowen, Wm, 12, A, Aug 11, dys.
4260 McGoneyal, R, 16, K, July 29, dia.
5124 McGuire, A, 58, D, Aug 9, dys.
6460 McHenry, James, 2 art, G, Aug 21, scs.
6544 McIntire, H, 1 art, K, Aug 23, dia.
11531 McKarren, E, 1 art, I, Oct 26, scs.
11849 McKenny, B, 34, A, Nov 5, dys.
6358 McKinzie, George, 27, I, Aug 5, scs.
5223 McKnight, B, 2 cav, A, Aug, 10, scs.
3174 McLaughlin, E,§ 9, C, July 11, ts. f.
10030 McMasters, 71, A, Sept 29, dia.
3675 McMillan, Jas, 24, B, July 20, dys.
522 McNamara, 17, I, April 13, dys.
5185 McNaury, R, 27, I, Aug 9, dia.
11381 McNulty, P, 2 art, G, Oct 24, scs.
5194 McWilliams, W, 77, D, Aug 10, scs.
7586 Medren, W, 20, G, Sept 2, scs.
5808 Mehan, B, 2 art, H, Aug 16, ana.
1434 Melan, A, 18, F, May 28, dia.
9735 Melvin, S, 1 art, K, Sept 25, dia.
2269 Meritt, M, 27, C, June 20, pna.
1358 Merriman, W H, 17, D, May 25, dia. c.
9117 Messers, W, 1 art, B, Sept 18, dia.
9597 Mesters, E, 34, H, Sept 23, scs.
6286 Meyer, J, 1 cav, K, Aug 20, dia.
8631 Miland, John, 2 art, H, Sept 13, scs.

11514 Millard, P S, 19, G. Oct 26, scs.
1219 Miller, A, 28, F, May 19, dia.
4329 Miller, J M, 11, A, July 30, ts. f.
10169 Miller L, 20, Oct 1, scs.
4050 Miller, Joseph,§ 57, C, July 27, dia.
7178 Millrean, M W,‡ 2 cav, E, Aug 29, ana.
9539 Milton, C, 21, A, Sept 22, dia.
8506 Mitchell, W C, 23, A, Sept 11, scs,
11867 Mitchell, F, 14, A, Nov 6, scs.
11771 Mitchell, John, 19, C, Nov 3, dia.
8343 Mittance, L, 20, G, Sept 10, scs.
4053 Mixter, G L, 1 cav, E, July 27, dia.
6235 Monroe, J, 2 art, M, Aug 20, dia.
2456 Morgan, C H, 27, H, June 25, r. f.
8017 Morgan, Pat, 23, B Sept 7, scs.
3160 Moore, A, 56, C, July 11, dys.
5490 Moore, C A, mus, 2 art, N, Aug 13 dia.
10593 Moore, M, 57, A, Oct 10, dia.
3411 Moore, P, 18, F, July 16, dia.
3990 Morris, N G, 1 art, July 26, dys.
1004 Morris, R,§ 28, F, May 10, dys.
9627 Mortimer, L, 19, E, Sept 24, scs.
8272 Mortor G H, 42, C, Sept 9, dia.
5360 Morton J, 34, A, Aug 11, dia.
6982 Moss, Charles, 2 art, H, Aug 27, dia.
12516 Moulton, H, 15, F, Jan 23, dia.
12619 Murdock, A B,‡ 27, D, Feb 8, dia.
321 Murley D, 9, D, April 2, dia.
7862 Murphy, C, 17, D, Sept 5, ana.
5488 Murphy, F, 17, D, Aug 13, scs.
1680 Murphy, Michael, 12, K, June 6, des.
12783 Murphy, P, 27, H, March 15 scs.
5041 Murray, Thomas, 19, A, Aug 8, scs.

9241 Needham, J A, 1 art, B, Sept 19, scs.
9278 Nelson, J, 2 art, Sept 19, scs.
7006 Newcomb, John E, 2 art, G, Aug 27, scs.
9694 Nitchman, A, 19, B, Sept 24, scs.
1282 Noble, David, 17, D, May 22, dia.
12439 Norman, E, 1 art, E, Jan 12, pls.
350 Norton, F F, 39, H, April 14, dia.
10058 Nottage, I L, 2, F, Sept 30, scs.

7193 O'Brien, James, 2 art, G, Aug 29, dys.
2509 O'Brien, John, 36, K, June 26, dia.
5117 O'Connell, J, 9, C, Aug 9, scs.
12189 O'Connell, J, 15, H, Nov 28, wds.
9789 O'Connell, M, 2, H, Sept 26, dia.
11080 O'Conner, Wm, 29, K, Oct 17, dia.
11493 O'Donnell, J, 11, G, Oct 26, scs.
10592 Oliver, J, 39, E, Oct '10, scs.
4640 Oliver, S E, 27, B, Aug 3, dia.
7161 O'Neil, Charles, 25, B, Aug 29, dia.
4884 O'Neil, D, 25, E, Aug 6, dia.
4975 Osborn, W, 19, K, Aug 7, scs.

5340 Packard, N M, 27, C, Aug 11, scs.
6629 Page, Wm, 16, D, Aug 23, dia.
598 Paisley Wm, 17, D, April 17, dia.
10695 Palmer, T, 59, E, Oct 11, dia.
4714 Panier, J M, 17, K, Aug 4, dys.
11059 Pantins, A J, 15, H, Oct 17, scs.
6899 Pandes, L, 3 art, G, Aug 26, dia.
7811 Parrish, Charles, 1 cav, C, Sept 4, dys.
5380 Pains, F, 2 art, E, Aug 12, scs.
1074 Parker, H, 36, C, May 13, dia.
2327 Parsons, W D, 23, E, June 22, dia.
6860 Pasco, J M, 58, D, Aug 26, scs.
1231 Patterson, H W, 33, G, May 20, dia.
8888 Payne, G A, 57, H, Sept 16, scs.
4967 Payne, Wm A, 1, art, M, Aug 7, dys.
7556 Peabody, W F, 37, Sept 2, dia.
6471 Peckham, A P, 15, B, Aug 21, dia.
5441 Peeto, A, 36, A, Aug 12, td. f.
4003 Pennington, R A, 1 art, July 26, dys.
9603 Perry, N, 1 art, F, Sept 23, dia.
274 Perry, Samuel K, 39, D, March 31, e. f.
4986 Pettie, C, 2 art H, Aug 7, dia.
7671 Phillbrook, J E, 56, F, Sept 3, des.
7708 Phillips, A, 50, B, Sept 3, scs.
10383 Phillips, L M,§ 17, D, Oct 5, scs.
9006 Phipps, H B,‡ 1 art, B, Aug 20, dys.

4763 Phipps, M M, 27, C, Aug 4, dia.
11079 Pierson, R,§ 2 art, H, Oct 17, dia.
20 Pilhuton, John, 11, E, April 14, s. i.
5128 Piper, Charles, 28, G, Aug 9, dia.
6740 Piper, F 25, E, Aug 24, dia.
7080 Polshon, F B, 17, D, Aug 28, scs.
703 Poole, Charles,‡ G, April 23, dys.
6583 Pratt, Daniel, 27, I, Aug 27, dys.
12135 Pratt, D W, 2 art, G, Nov, 23, scs.
5742 Pratt, Henry, 23, C, Aug 15, scs.
2008 Price, Edward, 2 art, M, June 15, dia.
12473 Prichard, J,‡‡, G, June 18, scs.
5404 Prior, Michael, 56, I, Aug 12, ana.
11975 Puffer, E D, 34, A, Nov 12, scs.

4218 Quinn, James, 15, M, July 29, ana.
12804 Quirk, M J, 1, D, March 20, dia.

12094 Ragan, C,‡ 27, H, Nov 19, scs.
10156 Ramstell, H, 37, H, Oct 1, dia.
5500 Rand, M, 2 art, G, Aug 13, scs.
3358 Randall, J, 2, F, July 15, dia. c.
54 Raymond, C, 20, I, June 12, s. p.
8072 Reed, Charles, 2 art, H, Sept 7, dia.
1725 Rensseller, C N, 54, C, June 8, dia.
6122 Rapp, James, 28, A, Aug 19, dys.
2970 Reynolds, N A, 36, C, July 7, dia.
3272 Rice, C A, J 2 art, G, July 13, dia.
1285 Rich, C, 2, D, May 22, dia.
4233 Rich, Samuel, 27, B, July 29, dia.
4918 Richards, G, 16, I, Aug 6, brs.
3156 Richards, James, 27, C, July 11, dia.
11553 Richardson, L, 1 art, G, Oct 27, scs.
4167 Richardson, S R, 1 art, M, July 28, dia.
7546 Richard, Thomas, 20, B, Sept 2, dia.
7199 Ridiam, James, 19, C, Aug 29, dia.
10638 Riley, H J, 2 art, G, Oct 10, dia.
8642 Riley, M, 56, K, Sept 13, ana.
7200 Ripley, M A, 32, F, Aug 29, dia.
6650 Rippon, Wm, 58, G, Aug 23, scs.
6166 Roach, J, 35, F, Aug 19, mas.
11552 Roberts, J H, 18, I, Oct 27, scs.
9448 Roberts, Joseph, 1 cav, K, Sept 21, dia.
12505 Roberts, L, 13, F, Jan 22, pls.
11699 Robinson, J, 19, H, Oct 31, scs.
3833 Robinson, R, 27, F, July 23, dys.
5659 Roe, Wm, 2 art, H, Aug 14, scs.
4875 Roferty, John, 2, K, Aug 6, dia.
12393 Rome, R, 1, I, Jan 4, scs.
4219 Rover F, 4, E, July 29, dia.
6654 Rope, A R, 11, I, Aug 23, dys.
5336 Rowe, Asa, 1 art, K, Aug 11, i. f.
11521 Rowley, Charles, 19, K, Oct 26, scs.
3455 Russell, —, 27, C, July 17, td. f.
9349 Rustar, R, 27, A, Sept 19, dys.
5987 Ruth, F, 36, C, Aug 17, dys.
6036 Ryes, J C, 2 art, G, Aug 18, scs.

5276 Sabines, Edward, 19, K, Aug 11, dia.
9465 Samlett, P V, 1, A, Sept 21, scs.
8074 Sanborn, G B, 2 cav, B, Sept 7, dia.
392 Sanborn, T, 17, D, April 6, dia.
8281 Sanders, F, 2 art, G, Sept 9, dys.
10637 Sandwich, I, 19, G, Oct 10, dia.
3405 Sanford J D, 40, A, July 16, dia.
10406 Savin, J H, 34, C, Oct 6, scs.
11888 Sawer, John, 33, F, Nov 7, scs.
4180 Sawyer, S F, 1 art, B, July 28, dia.
11203 Sayer, G D, 11, I, Oct 20, dys.
5834 Schalster, S, 25, G, Aug 16, mas.
5623 Seeley, Charles H, 2 art, G, Aug 14, dia.
11731 Sergeant, J C, 19, E, Nov 2, scs.
11338 Shamrock, I, 19, H, Oct 23, scs.
6782 Shaw, Andrew, 25, K, Aug 25, dia.
12303 Shaw, C L,‡ 15, E, Dec 18, scs.
7827 Shea, J, 2 art, H, Sept 4, dia.
7481 Shehan, James, 2 art, G, Sept 1, scs.
2324 Sherman, P H, 37, E, June 23, i. f.
8822 Sherwood, F, 76, B, Sept 15, dia.
4950 Shindler, John, 1 art, I, Aug 7, dia.
6602 Shore, J J, 1, F, Aug 23, dia.
10946 Short, J, 2, B, Oct 14, scs.

7735 Shultes, A M, 23, B, Sept 3, scs.
10415 Shults, George, 28, H, Oct 6, scs.
1458 Simmonds, E, 17, D, May 29, dia.
6957 Simons, A, 2 art, M, Aug 26, scs.
4186 Simpson, D O, 34, D, July 28, dia.
9842 Simpson, W, 2 art, H, Sept 27, scs.
6141 Sinclair, A, 1, G, Aug 19, dia.
11189 Sloan, S, 20, K, Oct 19, i. f.
8375 Small, Z, 1 art, G, Sept 11, scs.
10404 Sma?ey, J H, 2, G, Oct 6, scs.
9 Smith, Warren, 12, F, March 5, phs.
10256 Smith, C, 27, D, Oct 3, scs.
8002 Smith, C A, 1 art, C, Sept 6, td. f.
4952 Smith, D H, 1, I, Aug 7, scs.
12499 Smith, E, 27, G, Jan 21, dia.
11804 Smith, E M, 1, D, Nov 4, dys.
7158 Smith, H, 57, D, Aug 29, dia.
7443 Smith, J,‡ 20, E, Sept 1, dia.
967 Smith, John, 17, K, May 8, dia.
7538 Smith, J P, 1 art, A, Sept 2, dia.
5780 Smith, J H, 19, G, Aug 15, des.
8184 Smith, W, 23, B, Sept 8, scs.
154 Smith, W H, 12, I, March 25, phs.
2304 Smith, Wm, 54, June 22, dys.
12748 Smith, V, 57, K, March 6, pls.
3745 Snow, W, 16, E, July 21, scs.
12063 Somers, F, 19, G, Nov 17, dia.
5316 Switzer, L, 16, E, Aug 11, dia.
8280 Southworth, J, 18, G, Sept 9, dys.
2469 Southworth, John, 18, E, June 25, dys.
2188 Spalding, J, 2, E, June 19, dia.
12160 Spar, H, 19, H, Nov 25, scs.
10342 Spellman, B F, 2 art, Oct 4, scs.
6179 Spence, David, 19, D, Aug 19, ces.
4153 Spooner, C L, 27, H, July 28, ana.
5600 Spooner, E O, 27, A, Aug 14, scs.
4652 Spooner, F, 18, A, Aug 5, dys.
3397 Stalder, E P,§ 17, H, July 16, pna.
9873 Stauf, J, 20, D, Sept 27, scs.
6501 Steadson, W, 16, G, Aug 22, dia.
5028 Stelle, F, 1 art, I, Aug 8, scs.
7991 Stevens, Henry, 28, F, Sept 6, scs.
9183 Stevens, N, 1, E, Sept 18, ana.
2881 Stevens, Thomas, 2, M, July 4, ts. f.
1758 Steward, J, 11, H, June 9, des.
11291 Stewart, E, 52, D, Oct 22, dia.
12420 Stone, F P, 27, A, Jan 9, des.
10181 Stone, A, 2 art, H, Oct 1, dia.
5957 Sullivan, John, 16, A, Aug 17, scs.
7401 Sullivan, John, 2, K, Aug 31, scs.
10890 Sullivan, M, 2, D, Oct 4, scs.
8203 Sullivan, P, 9, Sept 8, dia.
10792 Sullivan P, 15, I, Oct 12, rhm.
11671 Sullivan, F, 59, B, Oct 30, scs.
12788 Sylvester, D, 1, B, March 17, dia.
8325 Sylvester, E, 2 art, H, Sept 10, dia.
12053 Sylvester, J, 4, A, Nov 16, scs.

11957 Tabor, B, 35, C, Nov 11, scs.
10697 Tabor, F,§ 16, E, Oct 11, scs.
2067 Taggerd, John, 17, E, June 19, dia.
3368 Taylor, N, 37, D, July 15, scs.
2515 Taylor, Thomas, 2 cav, G, June 26, dys.
8805 Temerts, T J,§ 110, D, Sept 15, scs.
4386 Tenney, William, 3, G, July 31, td. f.
3812 Thayer, J, 27, A, July 23, dys.
8612 Thomas, J, 2 art, H, Sept 13, dia.
11123 Thomas, J A, 32, G, Oct 18, scs.
2421 Thomas, J W, 56, I, June 24, dia.
12527 Thompson, C, 1 art, B, Jan 26, scs.
1890 Thompson, George, 16, June 13, pna.
4536 Thompson, George, 58, F, Aug 2, scs.

3908 Thompson, J M, 27, H, July 24, dys.
3596 Thompson, W W, 58, G, July 19, scs.
4634 Tibbett, A, 23, F, Aug 3, scs.
7468 Tiffany, J, 4, F, Sept 1, dia.
6549 Tilden, A, 27, B, Aug 23, dia.
3898 Tillson, Chas E, 29, E, July 24, dia.
3549 Tooma, John, 28, E, July 18, dia.
407 Torey, L, 12, H, April 7, dys.
6019 Torrey, C L, 7, G, Aug 17, dia.
10131 Townley, J J, 1, F, Oct 1, scs.
9108 Travern, W, 2 art, G, Sept 18, dia.
7860 Travis, H C,‡ 59, C, Sept 5, dia
7996 Trescutt, W M, 15, I, Sept 6, dia.
8132 Turner, H, 34, F, Sept 8, c. f.
12161 Tuith, F, 20, F, Nov 25, scs.
5428 Twichell, J, 17, K, Aug 12, dia.
6332 Twichell, —, 36, C, Aug 21, des.

9517 Usher, Samuel, 17, I, Sept 22, dia.

8466 Wade, A D L, 2 art, G, Sept 11, scs.
5959 Waldon, William, 36, B, Aug 17, dia.
12444 Walker, A, 19, F, Jan 12, scs.
3377 Wallace, P, 57, B, July 16, scs.
11494 Walsh, M, 4, C, Oct 26, dys.
5191 Walton, E A, 57, H, Aug 10, dys.
8724 Walton, Nathaniel, 59, E, Sept 14, scs.
8304 Wanderfelt, —, 6, C, Sept 10, dia.
1733 Wardin, H, 17, I, June 8, ana.
5217 Ware, Samuel, 1, H, Aug 10, dia.
8864 Warffender, J W, 27, C, Sept 15, dia.
12131 Warner, A F,‡ 19, D, Nov 22, scs.
6454 Washburne, W E, 27, I, Aug 21, dia.
4721 Weidan, H, 17, H, Aug 4, ana.
1066 Welch, Frank, 17, B, May 13, dia.
6224 Weldon, Charles, 1 art, D, Aug 20, dys.
11796 Wells, S, 1, A, Nov 14, scs.
5214 Wellington, G W, 2, G, Aug 10, scs.
3547 Welwarth, C W, 18, D, July 18, dia.
3247 Werdier, W, 58, G, July 13, dia.
1334 West, E, 24, A, May 24, rhm.
7002 West, J G, 1 art, E, Aug 27, dys.
4577 White, F, 15, K, Aug 2, dia.
6807 White, Joseph, 2 art, G, Aug 25, dys.
7188 White, Joseph, 2, G, Aug 29, dia.
7902 Whiting, A, 27, H, Sept 5, dia.
6867 Whitney, F P, 1, G, Aug 2, dia.
635 Whittaker, S, 17, D, April 20, dia.
1115 Wiggard, George, 22, A, May 15, dia.
6715 Wilber, E, 27, G, Aug 24, ana.
4539 Wilcox, Allen, 14 art, C, Aug 2, dia.
5519 Wilder, L E, 2, G, Aug 13, dia.
7318 Wilkins, S O, 1, G, Aug 30, dia.
6661 Williams, Chas, 27, G, Aug 24, dia.
8668 Williams, J, 58, G, Sept 13, dia.
3469 Willis, C, 17, K, July 17, dys.
7549 Wilson, J, 2 art, H, Sept 2, dia.
6769 Wilson, Robert, 34, A, Aug 25, scs.
6742 Wilson, S, 2 art, G, Aug 24, r. f.
10545 Wilson, W, 18, B, Oct 9, dia.
6213 Witherill, O, 47, C, Aug 20, dia.
6483 Woodbury, B, 17, A, Aug 21, des.
6564 Woodward, W A, 27, B, Aug 23, i. s.
6368 Wright, C E, 27, B, Aug 21, scs.
6288 Wright, M E, 27, C, Aug 20, dia.
4923 Wyman, H C, 2 art, H, Aug 6, dia. c.
3562 Wright, W M, 3 art, G, July 18, dia.

8882 Young, E, 2, Sept 16, dia.
6922 Young, G W, 2 art, H, Aug 26, dia.
7152 Young, N C, 1, I, Aug 29, dia.

MICHIGAN.

2198 Ayres, J B,§ 22, C, June 17, dys.
2247 Acker, J 22, K, June 20, dia.
2461 Atkinson, P, 22, C, June 22, dia. c.
2546 Anderson, George, 23, E, June 27, des.
8257 Abbott, C M, 5, E, July 13, dys.

4947 Ammerman, H H, 23, A, Aug 7, scs.
5472 Aulger, Geo, 10, F, Aug 13, scs.
5601 Ackler, W, 3 cav, C, Aug 14, ana.
6119 Austin, D, 8, C, Aug 19, scs.
6713 Allen, A A, 14, I, Aug 24, des.

1240 El is, E, 2 cav, B, May 20, dia. c.
2788 Ensign, J, 11, A, July 2, dia.
7901 Edwards, S, 6, E, Sept 5, dia.
8255 Edmonds, B, 1, H, Sept 9, dia.
11065 English, James, 17, B, Oct 17, scs.
5817 Everett, J, 77, K, Aug 16, dia.

890 Force, F, 27, D, May 5, dia. c.
1064 Fitzpatrick, M, 1 cav, B, May 13, brs.
1367 Folk, C, 14, E, May 25, des.
2197 Fitse, T, 1 cav, C, June 19, dia. c.
2252 Fairbanks, J, 15 cav, G, June 20, dia. c.
2343 Face, W H, 6, June 23, dia.
4194 Fisher, F, 22, G, June 29, dip.
5081 Farmer, M, 22, D, Aug 8, dia. c.
5861 Flanigan, John, 5, D, Aug 16, mas.
6135 Farnham, A, 5, A, Aug 19, dia.
6363 Fox, James, 3, H, Aug 21, dia.
6680 Fritchei, M, 22, G, Aug 24, scs.
6983 Fitzpatrick, M, 8, E, Aug 27, dia.
7027 Fox, Charles, 1, B, Aug 27, dia.
7060 Forsythe, H, 5, F, Aug 28, phs.
7171 Forbs, C, 1 cav, B, Aug 29, scs.
8586 Fethton, F, 1 cav, G, Sept 12, scs.
10275 Fliflin, H, 27, F, Oct 3, scs.
11500 Freeman, B, 1 s s, Oct 26, scs.
11709 Fredenburg, F, 7, Nov 1, dia. c.
12688 Findlater, H, 7 cav, C, Feb 22, dia.
12845 Frederick, G, 9, G, April 23, dia.
8250 Face, C, 1 s s, B, Sept 9, scs.
11509 Fox, W, 22, E, Oct 26, scs.

145 Goodenough, G M, 23, K, Mar 25, dia. c.
566 Grover, James, 20, H, April 15, des.
784 Grippman, J, 5 cav, M, April 28, ts. f.
956 Graham, Geo W, 5, C, May 8, dys.
1049 Goodbold, Wm, 2 cav, L, May 12, dia.
1131 German, E,‡ 13, H, May 16, asc.
1234 Garrett, S H, 2 cav, G, May 20, dia. c.
1927 Grimley, James, 22, D, June 14, dys.
2192 Ganigan, J, 9 cav, L, June 19, dia. c.
2614 Gorden, Jas, 1, D, June 28, dia.
2862 Gilbert, F, 3, K, July 3, scs.
2928 Gibbons, M, 6, C, July 5, dia. c.
3863 Goodman, W, 5, I, July 24, ana.
4092 Griffin, G, 11, H, July 27, scs.
4225 Green, E, 11, H, July 29, dys. c.
5716 Galrin, M, 23, I, Aug 15, scs.
6482 Greek, C H, 1 cav, K, Aug 22, dia. c.
6866 Gillis, Jno, 4 cav, F, Aug 26, dia. c.
7476 Gaines, A, 22, F, Sept 1, scs.
7518 Guilz, H, 1, A, Sept 1, scs.
7624 Griens, G D, 8, I, Sept 2, dia. c.
7659 Graff, Jacob, 17, H, Sept 3, dia.
7741 Gibson, J, 1, K, Sept 3, scs.
7968 Grant, A H, 7, D, Sept 6, scs.
8628 Gray, George, 1 cav, E, Sept 13, scs.
10671 Gallett, L, 22, F, Oct 9, scs.
10726 Gibbs, J, 7, B, Oct 11, scs.
11207 Gask, I, 8 cav, C, Oct 20, wds.
11302 Gray, James, 6 cav, A, Oct 22, scs.
11352 Groucher, J, 6 cav, B, Oct 23, scs.
11647 Grabaugh, J, 5, G, Oct 30, scs.
12164 Gifford, L, 6, I, Nov 26, scs.
12443 Gowell, N, 19, F, Jan 12, scs.
12573 Goodel, M, 5, C, Feb 2, dia.
5818 Gurmane, B S,§ 77, K, Aug 16, dia.
4511 Grasman, E, 23, I, Aug 1, dia.
12207 Gabulison, J, 5 cav, F, Dec 1, dia. c.

6 Hall, William, 2 cav, M, Feb 5, pna.
339 Holton, S M, 1, B, April 20, dys.
367 Henry, James, 8, A, April 5, pna.
409 Hartsell, Geo, 7 cav, B, April 6, dia. c.
818 Hutton, S, 9 cav, G, April 30, dia. c.
860 Hood, Jas D, 22, H, May 3, dia.
947 Hart, J R,‡ 6, E, May 7, ana.
1452 Hannah, Jno, 22, C, May 29, ana.
1519 Hunter, F A, 22, F, May 31, ana.
1656 Herriman, D, 22, D, June 6, dia.
1788 Huntley, W, 5 cav, E, June 8, dia. c.
1813 Haines, R, 9 cav, G, June 10, dia. c.

1904 Hough, M, 22, June 13, dia. c.
1910 Harty, J S, 16, F, June 13, dia. c.
2660 Hays, C, 6, H, June 29, dia.
3015 Hardy, Jno, 4, H, July 7, dia.
3040 Hughey, James, 17, B, July 8, dia. c.
3206 Hopkins, N, 6 cav, E, July 12, dia. c.
4 Halson, David, 8 cav, A, March 27, s. p.
3343 Heil, H,§ 9, G, July 15, scs.
3483 Honsigner, W L,‡ 7, C, July 17, dia. c.
3889 Hance, C, bugler, 7, D, July 24, dia. c.
3927 Hawkins, George, 12, H, July 25, dia.
4166 Hunter, M W,‡ 22, D, July 28, dys.
4286 Heron, Juo,‡ 5, F, July 30, dia.
4426 Heath, M, 21, C, July 31, dia.
4674 Hale, S B, 7 cav, D, Aug 4, dys.
5332 Hollen, Geo, 1 cav, L, Aug 11, dia.
5370 Haynes, P, 1 cav, H, Aug 11, dys.
5376 Husted, J, 10, C, Aug 10, dia.
5556 Henrich, J, 3, C, Aug 13, scs.
5931 Hall, W, 26, 1, Aug 17, dia. c.
6110 Holmes, J F, 42, H, Aug 18, scs.
6276 Hibler, A,‡ 9 cav, D, Aug 20, mas.
6992 Henry, A, 27, B, Aug 27, dia.
6998 Hungerford, C,§ 20, E, Aug 27, dia.
6999 Hunt, L, 2, C, Aug 27, dia. c.
8100 Holcomb, J, 6 cav, K, Sept 7, dys.
8624 Harrington, G, 6 cav, D, Sept 13, dia. a.
9233 Hawley, C, 4, F, Sept 19, dia.
9686 Hartman, H, 29, A, Sept 24, dia.
9968 Hinkley, G C, 20, F, Sept 28, dia.
10348 Hoag, J M, 20, H, Oct 5, scs.
11027 Hankins, E, 5, E, Oct 16, scs.
11057 Hayes, James, 1, E, Oct 17, scs.
11070 Haywood, J B, 1 cav, H, Oct 17, scs.
11260 Hamlin, J H, 1 s s, K, Oct 20, scs.
11336 Hoag, J M, 20, H, Oct 23, scs.
11412 Hill, W, 1 s s, Oct 24, scs.
11480 Howard, F S,§ 8, E, Oct 26, scs.
11593 Hawk, H L,‡ 24, 1, Oct 28, scs.
11757 Hodges, M,§ 22, 1, Nov 3, scs.
11835 Hilmer, C, 6 cav, M, Nov 5, scs.
12067 Howe, J, 7 cav, F, Nov 17, scs.
12612 Hicks, C, 8, B, Feb 8, dia. c.
9718 Harper, D, 3, E, Sept 25, dia.

5141 Ingraham, W L, 5 cav, B, Aug 9, scs.

1817 Jackson, James, 7, I, June 7, dia. c.
2576 Jones, A, 6, E, June 27, scs.
3564 Jagnet, E B, 7 cav, C, July 19, dia. c.
3621 Jackson, Geo G, 22, F, July 20, scs.
4736 Johnson, J H, 7, G, Aug 4, scs.
6578 Johnson, J, 24, 1, Aug 23, dia. c.
7520 Jump, D O, 1, A, Sept 1, dys.
7753 Johnson, H, 9 cav, L, Sept 2, dia. c.
9746 Jackland, C, 8 cav, E, Sept 25, dia. c.
12010 Jamieson, H, 5 cav, H, Nov 14, scs.
12396 Jondro, M, 1, K, Jan 5, dia.
12463 Johnson, A, 5, C, Jan 16, dia.

368 King, Leander, 8, G, April 5, dia. a.
488 Keintzler, R, 5 cav, F, April 12, dys.
706 Karl, Wm, 2, A, April 24, dys.
4140 Klunder, Charless, 5 cav, F, July 28, dia.
4397 Kennedey, H, 27, H, July 31, scs.
4424 Kinney, Jno, 17, H, July 31, dia.
4728 Kendall, W, 6, D, Aug 4, dia.
8289 Kessler, J, 11, G, Sept 9, dys.
10789 Kinsell, George, 5 cav, B, Oct 12, scs.
10908 Kenkham, H C, 5 cav, E, Oct 14, scs.
12431 Kenney, C, 5 cav, H, Jan 11, scs.

1882 Lewis, F L, 9 cav, June 12, dia. c.
223 Lossing, Jno, 8 cav, B, March 29, scs.
960 Loring, Jno, 27, F, May 8, hep.
1187 Lewis, P, 5, D, May 18, dys.
1301 Lanereed, M, 14, B, May 23, dia. c.
37 Lumer, Jno, 17, F, March 28, s. p.
3303 Lanning, H B, 22, H, July 14, dia.
3700 Lyon, A D,‡ 5 cav, G, July 21, ana.
4243 Lonsey, L, 1 cav, L, July 29, dia. c.
4913 Luce, F, 1 art, A, Aug 6, scs.

4992 Lu Duk, Jas, 17, G, Aug 7, dia.
5142 Larke, J A, 23, F, Aug 9, scs.
5216 Lowell, Jas, 7 cav, E, Aug 10, dia. c.
5776 Laribee, L, 8, H, Aug 15, brs.
5923 Lofler, E E, 11, H, Aug, 17, dia.
6667 Lord, M,§ 3, M, Aug 24, dys.
8085 Leamon, G, 8 cav, H, Sept 7, scs.
9685 Lard, H O, 22, D, Sept 24, dia.
9760 Lund, Jas, 6 cav, H, Sept 25, scs.
10877 Laidham, G, 1, D, Oct 13, dia.
11969 Lutz, Wm, 6 cav, F, Nov 11, scs.

218 McCartney, H, 6 cav, K, March 29, dia. c.
268 McGuire, Jno, 20, A, March 31, ts. f.
542 Markham, D, 5 cav, B, April 14, pna.
612 McCarter, Jas, 22, H, April 18, dia.
1059 Mum, A F, 27, F, May 13, dia.
1062 Miller, Charles, 5 cav, D, May 13, dia.
1710 Miller, J, 3, C, June 7, dia, c.
2255 Maby, Ed, 8 cav, K, June 20, des.
2586 McDowell, J, 8 cav, F, June 28, scs.
2759 McSpoulding, W, 22, E, July 2, dia. c.
2828 Manwaring, Wm, 22, D, July 3, dia. c.
2976 Man, Thos G, 5, A, July 7, dia.
3090 Marshall, H E, 27, B, July 9, ana.
3150 Morris, A T, 14, K, July 9, dia.
3537 Marvey, Andrew, 17, G, July 18, dys.
3697 Miller W E, 2, K, July 21, ts. f.
3936 McCabe, F, 22, H, July 25, dys.
3954 Morgan, M, 2, E, July 26, scs.
4078 McFall, H, 17, E, July 27, dia. c.
4144 Miller, G, 5, I, July 28, dia.
4304 Mouny, Jno, 5 cav, L, July 30, dia.
4783 Monroe, D, 6 cav, A, Aug 4, dia.
4942 Morgan, E C, 23, G, Aug 7, scs.
5153 Miller, L, 7, F, Aug 9, scs.
5630 Mench, C,§ 20, I, Aug 14, dia.
6249 McCarty, Charles, 26, I, Aug 20, dys.
6229 Meyers, J, 6, H, Aug 21, dia.
6820 Myer, J, 4, I, Aug 25, scs.
7114 Moore, J, 27, B, Aug 28, j. f.
7269 Merrill, S B, 5, G, Aug 30, scs.
7279 McLaine, Thos, 1, I, Aug 30, dia.
7473 McCloud, A, 21, I, Sept 1, scs.
7513 Mason, F, 7 cav, L, Sept 1, scs.
7918 Martin, Peter, 17, H, Sept 5, dys.
7936 Musket, J, 4 cav, K, Sept 5, dia.
7962 Miller, F, 22, G, Sept 6, dia.
8025 Mundy, E, 17, G, Sept 6, ts. f.
8387 McClure, R, 7, D, Sept 9, dia.
8518 Miles, C S,‡ 1 cav, F, Sept 12, scs.
8590 McGinis, P,§ 16, Sept 12, scs.
8050 McKay, K, 10, Sept 6, dia.
8876 Munson, H C, 30, E, Sept 16, scs.
8897 Morrison, J, 21, F, Sept 16, scs.
8994 Maher, S L, 7 cav, I, Sept 17, dia.
9185 Marine, Wm, 22, E, Sept 18, ana.
9750 McArthur, W,§ 7 cav, D, Sept 25, scs.
9791 Moore, John, 6 cav, G, Sept 26, scs.
10011 Moses, C, 5 cav, I, Sept 29, scs.
10134 Moses, A, 6 cav, M, Oct 1, dia.
10423 Migele, J, 9, A, Oct 6, scs.
10575 Mays, Thos, 6 cav, M, Oct 9, dia.
10958 McMillen, Alex, 5 cav, M, Sept 14, scs.
11126 Miller, Jno A, 10, F, Oct 18, dia. c.
11536 Molosh, F, 3, D, Oct 27, scs.
11548 McMann, W, 17, A, Oct 27, scs.
11582 Mongby, D, 22, C, Oct 28, scs.
11798 Merrill, C, 4, K, Nov 4, scs.
12085 Miller, H, 9, A, Nov 18, scs.
12093 Magram, J, 1 s s, Nov 19, dia.
12252 McCame, W, 7, B, Dec 9, scs.
12458 Morton, J, 1, I, Jan 15, dia.
11511 Mackswarer, W, 1 s s, K, Oct 26, scs.
12674 Marshall, G, 4, M, Feb 19, dia. c.
12733 McNiell, C, 8 cav, M, March 5, dia. c.
3790 Major, Wm, 22, D, July 22, scs.
7916 Monroe, Jno, 7, I, Sept 5, dys.
9791 Moor, Jno, 6 cav, G, Sept 26, scs.
9965 McClary, W, 7 Cav, H, Sept 28, dia.

513 Nicholson, E 6 cav G, April 12, dia. c.

1209 Newbury, Jas cav, A, May 19, td. f.
2077 Nash, Charles 22, H, June 17, dia. c.
3343 Nail, H,§ 9, F, June 15, pna.
4102 Neck, H, 4, K, July 27, dia.
5092 Nirthhammer, J, 20, D, Aug 8, scs.
5400 Nagle, C, 11, G, Aug 11, scs.
5493 Narrane, A, 17, E, Aug 13, scs.
11011 Noyes, Jas E, 1, Oct 16, dia. c.
11911 Niland, H, 8, D, Nov 9, dia.
1005 Nurse, H W, 5 cav, L, May 10, dia.
9812 Northam, O H, 6, M, Sept 26, dia.

285 O'Brien, Austin, 9 cav, H, April 1, pna.
499 Oliver, Alex, 8 cav, G, April ?, dia. c.
1189 Orrison, George, 9 cav, M, May 18, dys
2267 Olney, G W, 4, A, June 20, dia. c.
4384 Osborn, S, 27, B, July 31, scs.
4874 Overmeyer, J F, 6 cav, E, Aug 6, scs.
5574 O'Neil, J, 22, K, Aug 14, dys.
5846 Orcutt, C, 3, F, Aug 16, ens.
8141 Ornig, S W, 20, C, Sept 8, dia.
8511 O'Brian, W H,§ 7 cav, A, Sept 12, dia.
9041 Ogden, E S, 5 cav, M, Sept 17, scs.
11940 O'Leary, J,‡ 1 s s, H, Nov 9, dia.
11999 Osborn, J L, 6, E, Nov 13, scs.
12500 Oathart, D, 18, C, Jan, 17, dia. c.

443 Parsons, G, 7, I, April 9, dia.
515 Pullman, Geo, 5, I, April 12, dia. c.
1038 Parker, B C,§ 8 cav, C, May 12, dia.
1276 Perigo, John, 2 cav, D, May 22, pls.
1374 Parish, Thos, 6, I, May 26, dys.
1892 Paisley, A G,§ 22, June 13, dia.
1997 Payne, R H, 6, I, June 15, dia. c.
2533 Piffer, J, 6 cav, l, June 26, dia.
3546 Pierson, Daniel, 3 cav, C, July 18, dia.
3594 Palmerly, J, 7 cav, C, July 19, dia. c.
4100 Post, R L, 10, H, July 27, dia.
4253 Pratt, M, 22, E, July 29, scs,
4486 Pelton, A,‡ 21, A, Aug 1, pna.
4662 Philbrook, F, 1 art, Aug 3, phs.
5056 Podroff, D, 13, D, Aug 8, ana.
5546 Peck, J H,‡ 1 cav, D, Aug 13, ana.
5612 Pond, C, 1, I, Aug 14, dia.
5745 Pettibone, E E, 7, D, Aug 15, dys.
4564 Porter, L, 1 s s, C, Aug 2, phs.
5760 Pentecost, W G, 18, Aug 15, scs.
5852 Palmer, D, 5, D, Aug 16, mas.
7389 Parks, V, 7, C, Aug 31, scs.
7354 Perrin, M, 8 cav, B, Aug 31, c. f.
7960 Parks, F, 5 cav, E, Sept 6, wds.
8195 Pearmell, J,‡ 23, B, Sept 8, scs.
8636 Pike, B H,‡ 2 cav, C, Sept 13, dia.
8986 Plant, Wm, 16, G, Sept 16, dia. c.
9331 Pharrett, Wm, 22, D, Sept 20, scs.
11046 Platt, R, 22, A, Oct 17, scs.
11177 Palmer, P, 5, H, Oct 19, scs.
11986 Preston, B, 7, K, Nov 13, scs.
12273 Plins, Wm, 5 cav, C, Dec 12, scs.
12409 Preston, J, 6, C, Jan 7, scs.
12578 Pratt, L, 8 cav, C, Feb 3, dia. c.
12762 Parmalee, C,‡ 8 cav, M, Feb 12, pls.

77 Roloff, Jno, 5 cav, E, March 20, ts. f.
324 Russell, Peter, 23, G, April 2, dia.
623 Rowland, B, 6, M, April 19, dia.
922 Robinson, Wm, 2, H, May 6, dia.
1804 Rhinehart, D, 5 cav, C, June 10, dia.
2291 Rolland, J, 6, G, June 21, dia. c.
2402 Ruggles, O, 32, H, June 24, dia. a.
3296 Rassan, A, 28, I, July 14, dys.
3732 Riley, Charles, 6, I, July 21, dia.
3740 Riggs, J, 22, I, July 21, dia.
3876 Russ, W J,‡ 22, C, July 24, dia.
5176 Rood, C, 22, C, Aug 9, dia.
5885 Roman, John, 5, C, Aug 16, dia. c.
6154 Relu, A, 17, G, Aug 19, scs.
5707 Ryan, W, 1, E, Sept 1, dia.
7750 Robinson, H, 5 cav, L, Sept 2, dia.
7955 Rich, A 11, B, Sept 6, dia.
8617 Riley, Miles,‡ 7 cav, F, Sept 13, scs.
9254 Rimer, J C, 1 cav, C, Sept 19, scs.

9914 Ryan, T, 22, I, Sept 28, scs.
10136 Robinson, T, 27, F, Oct 1, scs.
10380 Randall, H D, 6, D, Oct 5, dia.
11151 Riley, R,§ 24, H, Oct 19, dys.
11457 Ramsey, J,§ 5, H, Oct 25, scs.
11675 Raley, H, 24 cav, L, Oct 30, scs.
11705 Ricott, S, 1 s s, K, Nov 1, scs.
12553 Richardson, M B, 1, L, Jan 29, scs.
12589 Rodgers, W, 26, G, Feb 5, des.
12740 Robbins, A, 4 cav, H, March 6, pls.
12745 Reaves, M, 15, G, March 8, dia. c.

134 Snyder, E, 17, F, March 24, brs.
172 Smith, Wm, 7 cav, L, March 26, pna.
236 Soper, Calvin, 27, H, March 29, ts. f.
330 Sheldon, H S, 1, A, April 2, dia.
520 Shannon, Jno, 20, H, April 13, dia. c.
842 Smith, W W,‡ 5 cav, D, May 2, dia.
854 Stillman, L D, 6, M, May 3, dys.
1082 Stuck, L H, 2 cav, B, May 14, dia. c.
1328 Schemerhorn, J, 7 cav, C, May 24, dia.
1406 Samborn, H, 22, K, May 27, dia.
1446 Snow, Levi, 20, H, May 28, ana.
1626 Smith, A, 1 cav, L, June 4, ana.
1801 Smith, S, 17, C, June 10, dia. c.
1741 Stevens, S,‡ 22, K, June 8, dia.
1948 Shafer, W, 22, G, June 14, dia.
1966 Strickland, Thos, 10, E, June 14, dia.
2239 Sanburn, H, 22, K, June 20, dia.
2507 Smith, C, 1 art, E, June 26, dia.
2651 Sarmyes, C, 24, C, June 29, dia. c.
2664 Stevens, L, 6 cav, M, June 29, dia.
2685 Stewart, C A, 7, F, June 30, dia.
2807 Sprague, W B, 11, I, July 3, dys.
2986 Shaw, F N, 2, K, July 7, ana.
3001 Steele, E,§ 2 cav, C, July 7, dia. c.
3085 Sibley, J E, 1, G, July 9, dia.
3353 Stubbs, J, 9 cav, L, July 15, pna.
3518 Simpson, E T, 6 art, G, July 18, dia.
3524 Shultz, C, 5, B, July 18, dia. c.
3544 Shummay, Wm, 8 cav, L, July 18, scs.
3942 Shaw, F F, 7, D, July 25, scs.
3951 Sharp, Jas, 6, July 25, scs.
4103 Stines, H, 4, K, July 27, dia.
4311 Sprague, B, 7 cav, E, July 30, dia.
4433 Sale, Thos, 17, G, July 31, ana.
4859 Smith, Wm, 17, H, Aug 6, dys.
5193 Swain, D, 6 cav, H, Aug 10, dys.
5972 Stow, George, 10, C, Aug 17, ens.
6323 Simpson, T, 8, I, Aug 21, dia.
6506 Simons, A, 17, B, Aug 22, dia. c.
6686 Smoke, H B, 6, H, Aug 24, dia.
7014 Sullivan, Jno, 27, E, Aug 27, sys.
7303 Sherman, Fred, 22, G, Aug 30, dia.
7350 Sayrrer, J M, 1, G, Aug 31, dia.
7528 Schofield, C, 27, G, Sept 1, dys.
7676 Satterley, H J, 6 cav, E, Sept 2, dia. c.
8000 Sutherand, J, J, I, Sept 6, scs.
8580 Stanning, G W,‡ 5 art, G, Sept 12, dia. c.
9100 Suthphar, H W, 15, F, Sept 18, dia.
9469 Stewart, F, 6 cav, E, Sept 21, dia.
9481 Steward, W V, 5, E, Sept 21, ana.
9629 Snyder, J, 5 cav, M, Sept 24, dia.
10080 Straut, C A, 5 cav, F, Sept 30, dia.
10117 Spencer, George, 21, H, Oct 1, scs.
10254 Sammonds, A,§ 7, E, Oct 3, scs.
10285 Spencer, Jno, 2, I, Oct 3, scs.
10417 Skull, Wm, 7, B, Oct 6, dia.
10444 Simpson, J P, 22, A, Oct 7, scs.
11138 Swart, M M, 3, F, Oct 19, scs.
11148 Swesler, C,§ 5, K, Oct 19, scs.
11234 Sutton, H, 22, I, Oct 21, wds.
11265 Strander, A, 6, G, Oct 21, dia.
11354 Stoddard, S, 5 cav, F, Oct 23, scs.
11701 Steadman, S, 10, H, Oct 30, scs.
11717 Smith, S, 7, H, Nov 1, scs.
11773 Sickles, M, 14, I, Nov 3, dia. c.
12020 Seeley, H, 6 cav, B, Nov 15, scs.
1225 Spondle, C, 1 cav, C, Dec 5, dys.
2229 Sumner, H, 27, B, Dec 6, scs.
12261 Stedman, S D, 10, H, Dec 11, scs.

12310 South, Peter, 1 s s, K, Dec 19, dia.
12678 Smith, C B, 8 cav, L, Feb 19, dia. c.
12803 Smith, Geo, 8, B, March 20, dia.
12254 Stickner, J, 16, D, Dec 10, scs.
11508 Sockem, A, 1 s s, K, Oct 26, scs.
11510 Springer, J, 7 cav, K, Oct 26, scs.

1304 Turrell, Henry, 22, H, May 23, dia. c.
2945 Tubbs, P, 7, K, July 6, dia.
48 Tilt, George, 2 cav, D, May 24, s. p.
3498 Thatcher, E H, 6 cav, F, July 18, dia.
6703 Tompkins, N R, 1, B, Aug 24, dia.
7009 Tift, H, 5 cav, M, Aug 27, dia.
7544 Thompson, W, 8, F, Sept 2, dia. c.
7599 Tracy, D, 7 cav, K, Sept 2, dia.
7797 Thompson, M C, 5 cav, I, Sept 4, dys.
9103 Taylor, H, 32, F, Sept 18, dys.
11118 Taylor, J M, 11, A, Oct 18, scs.
11148 Twesler, C,§ 5, K, Oct 19, scs.

3945 Udell, W O, 2, D, July 25, dia.

731 Vanderhoof, Jas, 6 cav, G, April 25, dys.
1126 Vangieson, L,§ 5 cav, D, May 15, nes.
1467 Vogle, Jacob, 27, D, May 29, dia.
2270 Van Dyke, Jno, 6 cav, D, June 20, pna.
2994 Van Brant, W H, 9 cav, E, July 7, dia. c.
3278 Vanlin, C,§ 6, F, July 14, dia.
6864 Vanshoten, T, 6 cav, K, Aug 26, dia. c.
7595 Vansickle, L,§ 5 cav, G, Sept 2, dys.
8958 Vanmaker, F, 16, G, Sept 15, dia. c
9536 Vork, C, 5, K, Sept 22, dia.
9936 Vleight, A, 22, D, Sept 28, scs.
12166 Vanallen, C, 27, K, Nov 26, dys.
12690 Vincient, J, 8, K, Feb 22, dia. c.

340 Whittaker, J, 7, B, April 2, dia.
733 Whipple, G, 4, A, April 25, dia.
741 Wilson, Byron, 5 cav, D, April 26, dia.
749 Wright, Wm A, 7, K, April 26, dys. c.
957 Wilson, I, 22, K, May 8, dys.
2102 Wilson, W, 11, I, June 17, dia. c.
4961 Winegardner, A S, 1 cav, K, Aug 7, dys.
12723 White, C, 5, F, March 3, dia. c.
12796 Whitmore, C, 8 cav, M, March 18, scs.
6781 Wiley, E T,‡ 1, E, Aug 25, dys.
749 Wright, Wm A, 7, K, April 26, dys. c.
1089 Woolsey, R, 22, E, May 14, dia. c.
1701 Walker, J, 22, C, June 7, dia.
1920 Wolf, F, 13, E, June 14, dia.
3301 Wentdarbly, —, 5, G, July 14, dia. c.
2899 Whitlock, M, 2, B, July 5, scs.
3180 Willet, S,§ 22, K, July 11, dys.
3269 Wright, W, 5 cav, K, July 13, dia.
3437 Wolverton, C, 6, B, July 17, dys.
3992 Woodruff, H, 1 cav, E, July 26, dia.
4419 Warren, H, 4, B, July 31, dia.
4860 Walker, Geo, 22, G, Aug 6, scs.
5051 Williams, M, 1, A, Aug 8, dia.
5786 Williams, T, 2 cav, L, Aug 15, dia.
11323 Wolfinger, J M, 20, H, Oct 23, scs.
12307 Windlass, S, 8 cav, K, Dec 18, scs.
5559 Warner, C, 5, F, Aug 13, scs.
11096 Warner, J, 5 cav, K, Oct 18, des.
12723 White, C, 5 cav, F, March 3, dia. c.
9844 Wheeler, E, 24, A, Sept 27, scs.
5930 Wisner, Jno,‡ 6 cav, I, Aug 17, dia.
8331 Wood, A O,§ 8 cav, M, Sept 10, scs.
8076 Wilder, H S, 23, K, Sept 7, scs.
6996 Wolverton, S, 5 cav, A, Aug 27, dia. c.
7362 Way, F, 7, C, Aug 31, dia.
7812 Whalen, H,§ 6, I, Sept 4, dys.
7882 Wells, F, 7, F, Sept 5, dia.
9022 Wing, A, 17, G, Sept 17, dia.
9525 Whitworth, W G, 6 cav, A, Sept 22, dia.
12796 Whitmore, C, 8 cav, M, March 18, scs.

2910 Yacht, E,§ 22, E, July 5, dys.

2626 Zett, J, 22, D, June 28, scs.

MINNESOTA.

5964 Atkinson Geo 9, F, March 17, scs.
6567 Adcock, as, 9 B, March 23, i. s.
11977 Abrian, G, 1, B, Nov 12, scs.

4224 Becker, G, 9, E, July 29, scs.
5715 Barnard, H A, 9, A, Aug 15, scs.
6630 Buzton, M, 9, H, Aug 23, dia.
7841 Brese, D, 9, E, Sept 4, dia.
7892 Brayton, J M, 9, B, Sept 5, scs.
8053 Buckley, J F, 9, G, Sept 7, scs.
8253 Burrows, H, 9, K, Sept 9, dia.
9474 Babcock, L A, 9, D, Sept 21, cah.
9800 Besgrove, Isaac, 9, E, Sept 26, dia.
12778 Baker, J G, 1, A, March 15, dia. c.

2747 Conner, P, 11, A, July 1, dia.
3575 Clabaugh, J, 9, D, July 19, r. f.
4111 Conklin, S, 9, I, July 27, dia. c.
6970 Conklin, E, 9, C, July 27, dia.
10724 Cassady, J, 9, F, Oct 6, dia.

7692 Dunham, R H, 9, K, Sept 3, dia. c.
10971 Davis, E J, 9, E, Oct 15, scs.

8517 Fitch, W F, 9, F, Sept 12, dia.
12656 Fuchs, H, 9, D, Feb 14, dia. c.
9905 Freeschelz, F, 9, F, Sept 27, dia. c.

3287 Geer, O, 9, F, July 14, scs.
10401 Goodfellow, E C, 9, D, Oct 6, dys.
10579 Goodwin, Geo, 9, A, Oct 9, dia. c.
4130 Gordon, W C, 17, I, July 28, dys.

6033 Higly, M F, 9, G, Aug 18, dia.
6064 Hill, C J, 9, K, Aug 18, dia.
6605 Handy, J, mus, 9, I, Aug 23, des.
9144 Hearvay, J E, 9, K, Sept 18, dia.
4176 Holts, A, 9, F, July 28, dia.

7809 Johnson, N, 9, H, July 4, dys.

1211 Kerrick, Samuel, 4, K, May 19, dia.
9127 Kloss, L, 9, H, Sept 18, dia.

5079 Lindley, C, 9, B, Aug 8, dia.
7795 Large, M, 9, G, Sept 4, dia.
12165 Lewis, L, 9, E, Nov 26, dys.
12510 Latimore, W H, 9, D, Jan 22, dys.
9312 Lenyer, M, 9, G, Aug 30, dia.

5460 Myers, J, 3, I, Aug 13, dia.
7288 Mander, J W, 9, A, Aug 30, dia.
8180 McDougal, J 9, A, Sept 8, dia.
9195 Montenary, J, 9, G, Sept 18, dia.

2829 Nichols, John, 15, A, July 3, dia. c.

7789 Ollman, Wm, 9, B, Sept 4, dia.
8384 Orcutt, J,‡ 2, C, Sept 10, dia.

2841 Pitcher, E, 5, B, July 3, dia.
4813 Packett, C, 9, K, Aug 5, dia.
5506 Pericle, Jacob, 9, H, Aug 13, dys.
5909 Pence, Geo, 9, H, Aug 16, dys.
8353 Poinder, T, 9, B, Sept 10, dys.
8823 Pettijohn, S W, 9, H, Sept 14, dia. c.

4277 Roberts, J G, 9, E, July 29, dia.
5588 Robvin, J, 1, H, Aug 14, scs.
10327 Robertson, John, 9, B, Oct 4, dia.
10715 Reese, Wm, 9, E, Oct 11, dia. c.

5941 Short, M, 9, K, Aug 17, scs.
6216 Sperce, C, 9, G, Aug 20, scs.
6276 Sontor, C, 9, H, Aug 20, mas.
7185 Scheffer, H, 9, G, Aug 20, dia.
12058 Shiver, F,‡ 9, E, Nov 17, scs.
12808 Sarf, Henry, 5, E, March 22, dia.

8408 Thompson, W, 9, A, Sept 11, dia.
10186 Tiltam, N M, 9, B, Oct 1, dia.
11603 Thomas, W R, 9, E, Oct 28, scs.

12106 Ulrin, A,‡ 9, E, Nov 20, scs.

11505 Vanhouse, B A,‡ 9, C, Oct 26, dia. c.
11568 Vittum, E W, 9, B, Oct 27, dys.

986 Wood, Ashley, 2, B, May 9, dia.
3867 Walrich, P, I, C, July 24, dia. c.
4498 Wheeler, A, 9, C, Aug 1, dia.
4588 Woodbury, Jas, 9, C, Aug 2, dia.
5637 Wilson, F C, 9, E, Aug 14, dia.
8233 Winter, G, 9, H, Sept 9, dys.
8416 Whipple, J, 9, F, Sept 11, dia.
8459 Westorer, J, 9, E, Sept 11, des.
8777 Warren, E F, mus, 9, A, Sept 14, dia. c.

5006 Young, D S, 9, I, Aug 8, dia.

MISSOURI.

28 Burns, John, 17, I, April 1, pna.
1251 Burk, J H, 2, H, May 2, ana.
1464 Buel, J, 4, C, May 29, des.
2217 Bishop P, 15, I, June 20, dia.
2306 Bloomker, Wm, 2, F, June 22, dia.
4269 Broyer, J, 2, E, July 29, dia. c.
5855 Birley, Peter, 29, I, Aug 16, mas.
8664 Berger, J, 2, I, Sept 13, dia.
8772 Bitter, H, 29, F, Sept 14, dys.
11223 Bullard, James, 19, D, Oct 20, scs.
12795 Bates, P, 44, F, March 18, dia. c.

2861 Cling, C, 2, I, July 4, cah.
4328 Clemants, Jas, 2 cav, A July 30, dia. c.
6533 Cornell, James, 9 cav, H, Aug 23, dia.
12351 Coon, F, 15, K, Dec 28, scs.
12776 Chapman, R, 24, B, March 14, pls.

5200 Dicksen, D, 18, Aug 10, scs.
1641 Daley, M, 10 cav, H, June 5, dia. C.

848 Eddington, G W, 29, A, April 2, dia. c.

3963 Engler, John, 15, B, July 25, dia.

6987 Fogg, B F,§ 1 cav, H, Aug 27, dia.
8633 Folk, L,‡ 18, C, Sept 13, dia.
11266 Fay, J W,‡ 2, K, Sept 21, dia.
12805 Fry, M,‡ 12 cav, L, March 21, scs.
6914 Frick, S,‡ 2, E, Aug 26, dia.

2770 Guffy, R, 18, E, July 2, dia.
3725 Gallegher, F, 2, G, July 21, dia.

226 Houston, W E, 18, E, March 29, pna.
4505 Hunter, W, 1 cav, H, Aug 1, scs.
4568 Hartman, V, 29, G, Aug 2, scs.
4727 Huntsley, A,§ 22, H, Aug 4, scs.
7064 Haginey, F, 2, K, Aug 28, scs.
226 Houston, W E, 18, E, March 29, pna.
1552 Head, B J, 26, B, June 2, ana.
2655 Heltgen, G, 12, E, June 29, dys.
8026 Hasse, John, 14 cav, L, Sept 6, td. f.
9042 Hamilton, W,‡ 31, A, Sept 17, dia. c.
11941 Hanahan, A, 29, B, Nov 9, scs.

4440 Isenhour, J, 9, I, July 31, dys.

5709 Keyan, M, 2, D, Aug 15, dia.
7414 Keiler, A, 29, H, Aug 31, dia.
8178 Kline, C S,§ 2, F, Sept 8, scs.
10546 Kaunst, H, 18, G, Oct 9, scs.
12821 Keller, I, 40, H, April 1, dia. c.
7713 Kuhn, Jacob, 15, E, Sept 3, des.

8249 Lowe, John, 18, E, July 13, dia.
4803 Lewilley, Wm, 29, K, Aug 5, scs.
7035 Lang, C, 10 cav, B, Aug 27, dia.
12232 Litch, J, 4, A, Dec 6, scs.
5401 Lindsay, J, 18, A, Aug 12, scs.

7438 Miller, W, 4 cav, E, Sept 1, dia.
8913 Morgan, E,‡ 12 cav, F, Sept 16, td. f.
11035 Manning, S H,§ 30, A, Oct 16, scs.
12459 Menzt, W, 15, G, Jan 15, scs.
12706 Martin, J, 44 H, Feb 27, des.
12754 McGuire, O, 2 cav, I, March 12, dia. c.
12760 McDowell, J, 2, F, March 12, dia. c.

3456 Newkirk, Charles, 15, F, July 17, dia. c.
3539 Neclout, W, 2, E, July 18, dia. a.
4169 Nelson, John, 29, A, July 28, dia.

12774 O'Dell, E, 44, B, March 14, des.

12823 Purcell, J R, 44, G, April 5, dia.
755 Phillips, Pat, 11, E, April 27, dys.
25 Payne, Joseph,‡ 29, A, April 16, s. p.
4978 Perkins, A H, 29, I, Aug 7, scs.
6732 Plasmine, A, 26, D, Aug 24, dia.
10539 Plumer, E D, 24, B, Oct 8, dia.

1348 Reilly, P, 29, B, May 25, rhm.
3540 Riddle, F, 8, D, July 18, dia.
5110 Ritteman, Jno, 15, F, Aug 9, scs.
6915 Remers, J, 4, G, Aug 26, dia.
2422 Robertson, J C, 10 cav, F, June 25, dia. c.

1424 Schenck, Philip, 15, B, May 26, dia.
1478 Seebel, A, 12, G, May 30, dia.
1623 Search, Henry, 15, D, June 4, dia.
2464 Stickle, D, 4, D, June 24, scs.
2480 Stofacke, F, 15, D, June 25, dia. c.
28 Stiner, Gotlieb, 29, A, April 17, s. p.
5239 Stormn, F, 58, E, Aug 9, dia.
5667 Schmas, G, 15, G, Aug 14, nes.
6856 Segin, C,§ 2, H, Aug 26, dia.
6930 Shuman, Joseph, 1, B, Aug 26, dia.
7535 Sherman, H, 15, G, Sept 1, scs.
9821 Schaat, D B, 18, E, Sept 26, dia. c.

536 Trask, Geo K, 29, A, April 14, dia.
770 Terrill, Christian, 27, E, April 27, dys. a.
1509 Terrell, J, 12, A, May 31, dia.
5672 Tresler, H W, 4, I, Aug 14, dys. c.
12730 Turman, D, 44, B, March 4, des.

2803 Vance, H J, 26, B, July 3, dys.

373 Walham, H,§ 4, C, April 5, dia.
678 Watson, J J, 18, A, April 22, dia.
3106 Wigan, M, 2, J, July 10, dia.
7494 Williams, J M, 31, H, Sept 1, scs.
10889 Weidam, J,‡ 2 B, Oct 14, dia.
12550 Ware, J B, 40, K, Jan 29, scs.
12739 West, J, 40, K, March 6, dia. c.

NEW HAMPSHIRE.

26 Ames, John G,§ 2, F, March 8 pna.
29 Allen, E S, 2, H, March 9, pna.
4656 Allen, S, 9, C, Aug 3, scs.
4746 Abbott, C, 7, K, Aug 5, dia.
7130 Arches, J L, 9, A, Aug 28, dia.
9518 Atmore, G W, 3, G, Sept 22, scs.
9832 Anderson, J N, 7, E, Sept 24, scs.
11765 Avery, J, 1 cav, M, Nov 3, dia.
5721 Austendalph, I, 3, D, Aug 15, ens.

833 Bushby, N, 7, C, May 1, dia.
8346 Bailey, A D, 7, C, July 15, dia.
3380 Bush, A, 4, H, July 16, dia.
4447 Bachelor, J R, 1, Aug 1, dia.
4965 Baker, Wm, 4, H, Aug 7, dys.
4988 Babb, Jas, 7, D, Aug 7, wds.
6871 Brown, W F, 2, B, Aug 26, nes.
6765 Breakman, A, 12, I, Aug 25, dia.
7857 Baker, D W, 3, G, Sept 5, dia.
8463 Bell, Geo, 5, C, Sept 11, scs.
10294 Bond, J, 12, F, Oct 4, scs.

2228 Clark, G M,‡ 7, C, May 20, ana.
3326 Combs, John, 7, B, July 14, dia. c.
4230 Coon, Charles, 7, G, July 29, scs.
5137 Colby, John N, 13, D, Aug 9, dia.
7072 Cooney, Thomas, 9, C, Aug 28, dia.
8551 Connelly, M, 4, C, Sept 12, scs.
2796 Chadwick, C E, 7, F, July 2, dia. c.
11192 Carr, P, 1, H, Oct 20, dys.

1370 Downs, E, 7, I May 25, r. f.
2086 Doer, S, 7, D, June 17, dia. c.,
8668 Doge, C F,§ 7, K, July 20, scs
5577 Drake, Charles C, 1 cav, B, Aug 14, scs.

3566 Eschoymer, H, 1 cav, B, July 19, dys.
5337 Estey, E E, 4, C, Aug 10, dia.
8426 Edwards, John, 9, F, Sept 11, scs.
12841 Elliott, A, 7, I, April 21, dia.

1396 Fuller, Geo, 7, B, May 26, dia.

5240 Faucett, J, 7, C, Aug 10, dia.
6678 Flanders, O, 9, F, Aug 24, dys.
6894 Ford, W, 7, K, Aug 26, dia.
9460 Faggerty, Jackson, 1 cav, A, Sept 21, scs.
12440 Fetch, G P, 7, H, Jan 12, pls.

2838 Guingoclett, H, 2, E, July 3, phs.
4413 Gill, N, 7, A, July 31, scs.
4687 Gooley, J,‡ 7, G Aug 4, dia. c.
11905 Goodwin, A, 1, I, Nov 7, dia.
9671 Gardiner, A, 4, C, Sept 24, dia.
6516 Gray, G H, 4, E, Aug 22, i. f.

6143 Hunter, C, 4, K, Aug 19, dia.
6875 Hurd, Wm, 6, I, Aug 26, dia.
7868 Hartford, H, 4, A, Sept 5, dia.
8537 Hally, H, 7, C, Sept 12, ers.
10269 Huse, W,‡ 11, H, Oct 3, dia.
11156 Hamlin, G W, 1 cav, I, Oct 19, scs.
11439 Holmes, J,‡ 7, Oct 24, dia.
11468 Holmes, J, 7, Oct 26, scs.

7733 Jones, J B, 9, K, Sept 3, scs.
9198 Johnson, Q O, 5, Sept 18, scs.
11216 Juntplute, F, 12, E, Oct 20, scs.
11758 Johnson, P, 9, E, Nov 3, scs.

4314 Keyes, C, 1 cav, K, July 30, dia.
5114 Kemp, C H, 7, A, Aug 9, dia.,
5151 Kingsbury, H R, 9, K, Aug 9, dia.
5444 Karson, H B,‡ 2, C, Aug 12, ana.
7397 Kreaser, M, 4, I, Aug 31, dia.
11877 Klinsimth, J,‡ 10, I, Nov 6, scs.
11994 Kingsbury, J H,§ 1 cav, A, Nov 13, scs.

6144 Lawrence, A, 1 cav, C, Aug 19, des.
6787 Lenert, D, 9, K Aug 25, dia.
8048 Libby, A G, 4, H, Sept 6, gae.
11415 Leport, J, 3 cav, L, Oct 24, scs.
11484 Lucht, P, 5, C, Oct 26, scs.

2687 Mumford, A, 12, A, June 30, brs.

20

3652 Mantove, J, 4, H, June 20, dys.
4284 Miller, F, 11, G, July 30, dia.
4629 Miller, R, 11, H, Aug 3, dia.
7203 Milliot, P, 5, I, Aug 29, des.
7423 Morrison, O P, 9, C, Aug 31, scs.
7948 Marten, J, 4, C, Sept 6, dia. c.
8573 McCann, M, 9, G, Sept 12, dia.
9921 Matheson, F, 7, B, Sept 28, scs.
11207 McCann, O, 13, E, Oct 20, scs.
12234 Montegan, P, 35, F, Dec 6, scs.

1658 O'Brien, Charles, 7, I, June 6, dia. c.
11698 Osmore, J, 1 cav, C, Oct 31, scs.

6185 Patch, John, 3, F, Aug 19, dys.
819 Poore, Samuel,‡ 2, H, April 30, dia. c.
3260 Puny, J, 3, G, July 13, dia.
4764 Place, J K, 7, F, Aug 5, dia.
7011 Patterson, N, 9, L, Aug 27, scs.
11121 Parsons, Samuel, 5, H, Oct 18, scs.
11828 Pewen, H A, 7, A, Nov 5, scs.
11837 Phelps, M F, 9, D, Nov 5, scs.
5383 Pascal, E, 7, E, Aug 12, dia.

1572 Reed, F K, 2, H, June 3, dia. c.
2771 Ramsay, Wm, 7, G, July 2, dia. c.
3406 Richards, W R, 7, C, July 16, dys.
11300 Ringer, J K, sergt major, 11, Oct 22, scs.

1336 Smith, John, 7, K, May 24, dys.
2330 Sanburn, W, 7, H, June 22, dia. c.
2505 Sanlay, E, 9, E, June 26, dia.
2708 Simms, S, 9, C, June 30, dia. c.
2925 Searle, J R, 7, E, July 5, dia. c.
3472 Smith, L F, 13, C, July 17, dia. c.
4779 Steward, Geo, 10, A, Aug 5, dia.
5140 Smith, J, 7, B, Aug 9, dia. c.
5198 Schean, W, 7, A, Aug 9, dia.
5405 Shorey, Ed, 1, C, Aug 12, dia.
5438 Salsbur, J, 4, K, Aug 12, ana.

5621 Stanley, Jno, 9, A, Aug 14, scs.
6547 Smith, J, 11, E, Aug 23, dys.
7040 Swain, C, 7, D, Aug 27, scs.
8629 Smith, C, 3, F, Sept 13, dia. c.
8652 Stark, S, 15, A, Sept 13, dia.
8980 Smith, John, 3, F, Sept 17, scs.
9412 Smith, L, 12, B, Sept 21, scs.
10503 Shantz, J, 11, G, Oct 8, scs.
11887 Spaulding, T C, 4, K, Nov 7, scs.

3396 Taylor, A B, 5, H, July 16, ana.
3431 Tobine, T, 6, A, July 17, dia. c.
4072 Tilton, D B, 7, G, July 26, dia.
8098 Thompson, A, 9, K, Sept 8, scs.
10734 Tilton, L G, 11, B, Oct 11, dia. c.

10493 Upkins, A, 1 cav, B, Oct 7, dia. c.

5491 Valley, John, 10, K, Aug 12, dia.

794 Woodard, L A, 7, K, April 29, dia. c.
1991 Williams, J, 7, I, June 15, dia. c.
2345 Woodbury A, 7, H, June 23, dia. c.
2545 Whipple, John,‡ 11, C, June 27, des.
4156 Webster, J, 6, I, July 28, dia.
2710 Welson, W, 4, F, July 1, dia. c.
4104 Whalen, M, 9, M, July 27, dys.
4749 Welch, James, 7, I, Aug 5, scs.
4750 Weston, W W, 8, A, Aug 5, dys.
5702 Wagner, John, 7, H, Aug 15, scs.
7559 Welsh, J, 7, C, Sept 2, ana.
7834 Wolf, John D, 3, F, Sept 4, dia.
8083 Weilztramsen, F, 9, L, Sept 7, dia. c.
11278 Williams, P, 3, H, Oct 22, scs.
11472 Wingerd, D, 3, G, Oct 26, dys.
11768 Wilson, J, H, I, Nov 3, scs.
11878 Warren, E, 1 cav, M, Nov 6, dia.
12734 Whitman, G E,§ 1 cav, B, March 6, scs.

8736 York, Charles, 1 cav, B, Sept 14, dia.

NEW JERSEY.

3347 Aaron, Thomas, 2, B, July 15, dia. c.
3354 Aney, G, 1, K, July 15, dia.
4098 Austin, D B, 2, I, July 27, dia.
7138 Anderson, T, 2, E, Aug 28, dys.
8513 Allbright,—‡ 3 cav, I, Sept 12, dia.
11389 Alexander, W L, 3, C, Oct 24, scs.
12646 Amps, C, 33, I, Feb 13, v. s.

909 Broderick, J S, 2, A, May 5, dia.
1548 Beach, J, H, E, June 1, scs.
2181 Brannan, Pat, 11, B, June 19, des.
2260 Bells, J H, 2, M, June 21, dia. c.
2577 Buckley, John, 1, G, June 27, i. f.
2980 Bloon, Adam, 2, I, July 4, dia.
3099 Buffman, A C,‡ 1 art, B, July 10, dia. c.
5761 Bailey, L, 7, A, Aug 9, scs.
5272 Brunn, Geo, 1 cav, B, Aug 10, dia. c.
5357 Burns, P, 3 cav, C, Aug 11, dia.
5379 Baker, Wm, 1 cav, K, Aug 12, scs.
5483 Blanchard, G, 7, K, Aug 13, ana.
5934 Bennett, C, 14, B, Aug 17, scs.
11682 Brant, Charles,§ 1, E, Oct 31, scs.
12288 Buyer, A, 6, I, Dec 7, scs.
12640 Brewer, W H, 10, D, Feb 12, scs.

715 Corley, Daniel, 11, A, April 24, dia.
1437 Creamer, E, 35, A, May 28, dia.
6929 Creamer, E, 10, B, Aug 26, dia.
3209 Chamberlain, R, 1 cav, D, July 12, dia. c.
5730 Clark, C H, 2, C, Aug 15, scs.
8240 Coonan, J, 2, C, Sept 9, scs.
10552 Collar, H, 2, D, Sept 9, r. f.
11990 Clayton, L, 10, B, Nov 13, scs.
3476 Curtis, W O,§ 1 cav, L, July 17, phs.
8041 Coykendall, D, 15, K, Sept 6, dia.

??5 Disbrow, J P, 14, K, April 2, dia.

2473 Davenport, J, 7, I, June 25, td.f.
3444 Davis, H, 12, F, July 17, dys.
4926 Dayton, C, 2, C, Aug 6, ana.
5148 Dorland, A H, 10, I, Aug 9, dys.
6306 Dewinger, J, 2, G, Aug 20, des.
7076 Dunhain, L, 35, H, Aug 28, dys.
7304 Dilan, Edward, 9, G, Aug 30, dia.
7469 Dermer, J, 9, G, Sept 1, scs.
7734 Doremus, C, 2 cav, A, Sept 3, scs.
7804 Duncan, H P, 2, G, Sept 4, scs.
8440 Doyle, H, 16, C, Sept 11, scs.
10533 Dunn, G, 1, F, Sept 8, dia.

1426 Ebner, Charles, 1 cav, K, May 28, dia. c.
1715 Egbert, James, 15, B, June 8, dia.
4303 Esligh, Jacob, 10, D, July 30, dia.

1522 Farrell, J H, 5, G, May 31, dia. c.
3938 Foliand, M,‡ 1 cav, K, July 25, scs.
4693 Fitch, F,§ 35, F, Aug 4, dia.
5327 Fry, John, 9, G, Aug 4, scs.
6737 Fisher, Wm, 9, C, Aug 24, dia.
7285 Farren, J, 3, Aug 30, dia.
9972 Fairbrother, H, 35, D, Sept 28, scs.
11584 Ford, A, 7, K, Oct 28, scs.
7338 Fisher, N O, 9, I, Aug 30, dys.

5900 Gale, B,‡ 9, D, Aug 16, dia.
7039 Galloway, F C, 12, K, Aug 27, scs.
11165 Glenn, C H, 4, I, Oct 19, scs.
11120 Guier, G, 7, D, Oct 20, scs.

1508 Hallman, H, 6, C, May 31, dia. c.
3072 Hemis, Daniel, 1 cav, B, July 9, dia. c.
3819 Hick, James, 9, G, July 23, dia.
4151 Hegamann, J, 14, K, July 28, dia.
4189 Hammle, A, 1 cav, July 28, dia.

4744 Huber, C, 9, G, Aug 5, dia.
4862 Herbert, J S, 2 cav, I, Aug 6, dia. c.
4911 Halmann, M, 1 cav, A Aug 6, r. f.
7821 Hull, Alexander, 7, C, Sept 4, dia.
7870 Howell, J, 1, K, Sept 5, dia.
7900 Hilgard, P F,‡ 10, A, Sept 5, dys.
10761 Hatter, W, 3, I, Oct 12, scs.
12302 Humes, E M, 2, M, Dec 17, scs.
12416 Hook, J M, 2 cav, D, Jan 8, scs.

5252 Jennings, G H, 2 cav, A, Aug 10, dia.
9519 Jone, A, 1 cav, A, Sept 22, dys.
11117 Jay, H,‡ 5, K, Oct 18, scs.
11399 Jomson, G W, 6, G, Oct 24, scs.
12344 Johnson, A F, 9, D, Dec 26, scs.

3762 Krouk, Peter, 2 cav, H, July 22, dys.
5085 Kuhm, R, 9, A, Aug 8, dia.
8649 Kitchell, S, 7, K, Sept 13, scs.
12023 King, C, 15, G, Nov 15, dia. c.

1985 Lyons, D, 1 cav, K, June 15, dia. c.
795 Layton, Stephen, 11, A, April 29, dia.
1769 Lindsley, Samuel, 10, H, June 9, td. f.
3622 Lewis, S, 3 cav, G, July 20, dia.
4095 Leadbeater, J H, 6, B, July 27, dia.
5944 Leighton, Wm, 5, H, Aug 17, scs.
6157 Luney, Ed, 8, G, Aug 19, dia.
12102 Larime, C, 15, C, Nov 20, dia.

2019 Mennu, Jacob, 11, H, June 15, des.
2852 Miller, J, 1 cav, K, July 4, dia.
3323 McIntire, R, 8, I, July 14, dia. c.
3548 Marks, Charles, 2 cav, G, July 18, dys.
4594 Mulrany, I, 4, B, Aug 3, dys.
4645 Miller, S S, 2 cav, G, Aug 3, dys.
5250 Morell, A, 5, K, Aug 10, scs.
5832 Mahler, John, 35, I, Aug 16, dys.
6986 Munn, Charles, 4, K, Aug 27, dia.
8019 McElroy, E, 10, I, Sept 6, scs.
8332 Meunt, C H, 9, D, Sept 10, scs.
8592 Miller, J, 7, K, Sept 13, scs.
10959 Mullan, A, 39, B, Oct 14, scs.
11252 Mills, F, 2, I, Oct 21, dia.
11564 Millington, J, 1 cav, H, Oct 27, scs.

6780 Noll, M, 9, A, Aug 25, dys.
4983 Nichols, J, 1 s s, C, Aug 7, dys.

7131 Osborne, E, 14, E, Aug 28, dia. c.
10463 Osborn, J M, 9, H, Oct 7, scs.

1071 Pratt, J F, 1, M, May 13, td. f.
1072 Purdee, Charles, 11, C, May 13, dia. c.
5206 Peterson, Henry, 3 cav, H, Aug 10, dia.
6298 Peer, T, 9, K, Aug 20, dia.
6962 Pelger, M, 10, G, Aug 27, dia.
7451 Peterson, G, 12, I, Sept 1, dia.

8017 Post, C J, 4, I, Sept 6, dia.
9990 Parker, W, 2, I, Sept 29, scs.
12221 Prink, J, 2, Dec 4, scs.

2145 Rooks, H, 5, H, June 18, dia. c.
2821 Riley, M, 1 cav, L, July 3, ana.
4066 Robinson, Jacob, 1 cav, B, July 27, td. f.
4858 Radford, Wm, 18, B, Aug 6, des.
8282 Reed, A, 9, D, Sept 9, scs.
10461 Ray, J, 10, A, Oct 7, dia.
10708 Regan, D O, 8, C, Oct 11, scs.
11292 Reevis, F, 2, I, Oct 21, dia.

2548 Starr, N, 5, H, June 27, dia.
5087 Simonds, J, 9, K, Aug 8, dys.
5807 Shanahan, W, 9, C, Aug 16, scs.
7364 Stout, L,§ 2, C, Aug 31, dys.
7565 Street, John J, 9, D, Sept 2, scs.
7577 Stiffin, H, 3, M, Sept 2, dia. c.
7729 Skell, C W, 3 cav, M, Sept 3, gae.
8687 Swetser, P, 9, G, Sept 13, scs.
8751 Stevenson, W, 2 cav, M, Sept 14, dia.
9328 Shay, H H, 7, I, Sept 19, scs.
10846 Smith, A, 5, G, Oct 13, dys.
11615 Sutton, T, 12, K, Oct 28, scs.
11653 Stimmell, I, 5, A, Oct 30, scs.
11793 Sullivan, I, 8, C, Nov 4, scs.
11882 Steele, Geo, 2, B, Nov 6, scs.
10882 Sweet, B F, 10, K, Oct 13, dys.

1853 Tindel, E,§ 1, B, June 11, dia. c.
5112 Taylor, Peter, 9, Aug 9, dia.
6131 Townsend, J, 35, I, Aug 19, dia.
7937 Turner, B, 4, G, Sept 5, gae.
9398 Townsend, F, 10, C, Sept 21, dys.
11364 Thompson, S, 4, I, Oct 21, scs.
12451 Thatcher, J, 8, H, Jan 14, scs.
12705 Toy, J, 7, G, Feb 27, des.
10212 Thomas, Henry,§ 10, B, Oct 2, scs.
6448 Traittman, Jas, 9, D, Aug 22, dia. c.

2634 Utter, Stephen, 1 art, B, June 29, scs.

12100 Vallett, W, 5 art, A, Nov 19, scs.

1955 Weed, Wm,‡ 15, I, June 14, dia. c.
2246 Wood, W J, 12, E, June 20, ana.
4643 Widder, W, 5, G, Aug 3, dys.
4998 Wainwright, 9, C, Aug 7, dia.
5031 Wolverton, 1, I, Aug 8, dia.
5099 Warner, A, 4, A, Aug 9, dia.
5333 Willey, J, 2 cav, M, Aug 10, ana.
6168 Wynard, Wm, 2, I, Aug 19, mas.
7560 Willis, A, 35, I, Sept 2, ana.
8142 Wright, S M, 7, K, Sept 8, dia.
8307 Ward, J, 1 cav, H, Sept 10, dia.
12157 Williams, W, 1, D, Nov 20, scs.
12658 Wells, G, 10, C, Feb 15, dia. c.

NEW YORK.

2038 Abbey, O,‡ 174, June 15, dia. a.
2141 Abbey, W H, 85, E, June 18, dia. c.
4719 Abel, C, 15 art, C, Aug 4, dia.
4612 Aber, J, 104, I, Aug 3, dys. c.
5629 Ackerman, Sam'l, 97, K, Aug 14, scs.
64 Ackheart, David, 20, A, March 19, pls.
8497 Adams, H, 98, G, Sept 11, scs.
4581 Adams, J A, 10, F, Aug 2, pna.
6467 Adams, O, 61, C, Aug 22, dia.
8559 Adams, S,§ 100, Sept 12, scs.
8226 Adams, T R, 85, H, July 12.
1700 Ades, Ed, 8 cav, C, June 7, des.
5047 Adeler, A, 8, D, Aug 8, dys.
6575 Adney, F, 85, K, Aug 23, dia.
4382 Ahearn, Daniel, 170, July 31, dia.
3349 Aiken, J W, 85, H, July 15, pna.
3001 Akerman, M, 7 art, L, Sept 6, dia.
7062 Albarson, J, 42, C, Aug 28, dia.
6698 Albert, William, 24 bat, Aug 24, dys.

7007 Alderman, F, 15 cav, F, Aug 27, dia.
1755 Alexander, J, 125, C, June 9, dia. c.
11212 Alford, B C, 152, F, Oct 20, scs.
3293 Allen, A W, 14 art, M, July 14, dia.
12452 Allen, J I, 82, A, Jan 14, scs.
5568 Allen, W, 1 cav, H, Aug 13, dys.
5844 Allenberger, J, 39, B, Aug 16, ts. f.
7478 Allenberens, E, 39, D, Sept 1, scs.
11479 Allinger, L, 48, I, Oct 26, wds.
7587 Allman, Charles, 7 art, C, Sept 2, scs.
6941 Almy, F, 111, K, Aug 26, scs.
5938 Alphord, J, 75, G, Aug 17, scs.
7739 Alsaver, S, 47, H, Sept 3, scs.
800 Ambler, Fred, 47, H, April 29, dia. c.
2344 Ambrose, Jacob, 9 cav, C, June 23, scs.
10642 Ames, Henry, 2 art, Oct 10, scs.
4654 Ames, J R,§ 14 art, I, Aug 3, dia.
7743 Amgere, G, 47, E, Sept 3, scs.
1954 Amigh, A, 162, K, June 14, ana.

11718 Bolby, O, 14 art, D, Nov 1, scs.
8267 Boles, J, 22 cav, D, Sept 9, dia. c.
3606 Bomsteel, S A, 20, G, July 19, scs.
5269 Borst, J, 5 cav, B, Aug 10, ana.
4401 Bodler, D, 7, D, July 31, dys.
  51 Boughton, H, 77, A, March 16, pna.
7627 Boulton, T, 43, G, Sept 2, dia. c.
11066 Bowden, P, 16 cav, M, Oct 17, scs.
6744 Bowen, J H, 65, D, Aug 24, dia.
4601 Bowin, J, 7 cav, K, Aug 3, dia.
11944 Bowman, H 84, K, Nov 10, scs.
12521 Bowman, I, 1 cav, D, Jan 25, scs.
3635 Bowman, S, 147, H, July 20, dia.
1275 Box, G, 111, D, May 22, dia. a.
9728 Boyce, A, 3 cav, I, Sept 25, des.
2673 Boyce, R, 6 cav, M, June 30, dia.
  10 Boyle, Pat, 63, A, March 5, pna.
3912 Boyle, Pat, 48, F, Sept 16, dia. c.
11974 Boyle, I, 16, D, Nov 12, scs.
4365 Bradford, D B, 7 art, B, July 31, dys.
5232 Bradley, John, 69, K, Aug 10, dia.
16685 Bradshaw, R,‡ 120, E, Aug 24, dia.
12219 Brady, J, 140, E, Dec 4, scs.
3979 Bragg, J C, 2 cav, E, July 26, dia.
12263 Brain, Wm, 5 art, B, Dec 12, dia.
7704 Brandon, O, 15 art, A, Sept 3, dia.
1800 Breny, James, 178, K, June 10, dia. c.
5134 Brewer, Fred, 39, C, Aug 9, dia.
11685 Brewer, Henry,§ 2 cav, G, Oct 31, dia. c.
10221 Brewer, J S, 6, B, Oct 2, scs.
1365 Brewer, S, 15, K, May 25, dia. c.,
 519 Brewer, Thos, 111, F, April 13, dia.
9690 Briant, L A, 146, B, Sept 24, dia. a.
8116 Bright, 104, C, Sept 8, scs.,
11627 Brightman, E, 7, D, Oct 28, scs.,
8415 Brill, C, 140, F, Sept 11, dia.
6953 Brink, C, 109, K, Aug 26, gae.
9787 Britansky, J, 52, E, Sept 26, dia. c.
2997 Brobst, J, 52, B, July 7, dia. a.
9148 Brock, W, 76, F, Sept 18, scs.
6882 Broder, H, 76, F, Aug 26, dia.
12002 Brogan, J M, 85, B, Nov 14, scs.
1324 Brooks, Wm,‡ 10 cav, E, May 24, dia.
1221 Brott, Anthony, 1 cav, K, May 19, ana.
9838 Broscang, C, 150, C, Sept 27, scs.
7517 Brought, Charles, 14 art, I, Sept 1, scs.
  51 Broughten, H, 77, H, March 16, pls.
10668 Brown, A, 140, K, Oct, 11, scs.
5538 Brown, B M, 85, I, Aug 13, scs.
4112 Brown, C, 103, C, July 27, brs.
9556 Brown, C, 66, K, Sept 23, scs.
11953 Brown, C, 39, H, Nov 10, scs.
11928 Brown, C, 1 cav, M, Nov 8, dia.
6623 Brown, Charles, 97, F, Aug 23, dia.
7501 Brown, D, 118, B, Sept 1, dia. c.
3659 Brown, E G, 7 art, L, July 20, pna.
9674 Brown, G H, 85, H, Sept 24, dia.
7985 Brown, G H, 63, C, Sept 6, dia.
2465 Brown, H, 72 C, June 25, dia.
1879 Brown, H, 12 cav, June 12, dys.
7266 Brown, H,‡ 39, F, Aug 30, scs.
1887 Brown, J, 125, June 13, dia.
7658 Brown, J, 16, 3, Sept 3, dia.
6655 Brown, James, 4 cav, E, Aug 24, dys.
6691 Brown, James, 170, K, Aug 24, des.
7526 Brown, John, 66, Sept 1, dia.
7615 Brown, Wm, 5, D, Sept 2, dys.
 552 Brown, Warren, 120, K, April 14, dia.
 428 Brown, Wm, 42, A, April 8, ana.
7390 Broxmire, Thomas, 15, E, Aug 31, scs.
1559 Brumaghin, T, 125, E, June 2, dip.
4475 Bryant, D, 179, B, Aug 1, dia.
 248 Bryant, H, 82, P, Aug 30, ana.
7668 Bryan, Wm, 1 cav, I, Sept 3, scs.
3814 Buck, 24, H, July 23, dia.
9975 Buckbier, J, 7 art, F, Sept 28, dia. c,
10585 Buckley, W, 122, D, Oct 10, dia.
5714 Buel, G W, 115, E, Aug 15, scs.
 331 Buel, S, 42, B, April 2, des.
12417 Buffman, L,§ 100, K, Jan 8, dys.
7567 Bulkley, E A, 97, E, Sept 2, dia. c.
12509 Burfield, C, citizen, Jan 22, pls.

5953 Bullier, Wm, 25 cav, B, Aug 17, mas.
9642 Bullock, E,‡ 85, E, Sept 24, scs.
4137 Bundy, Joseph, 7 art, B, July 28, dia. c.
 540 Bunn, W H, 132, F, April 14, pna.
9870 Bunnell, W, 59, C, Sept 27, scs.
6452 Burbanks, J, 85, D, Aug 22, dys.
10924 Burdick, A, 85, C, Oct 14, scs.
 978 Burdick, C, 47, F, May 9, dys
2134 Burdick, Samuel, 125, A, June 18, dia. c
7838 Burdock, L, 22 cav, L, Sept 4, dia. c.
10016 Burleigh, L, 6 art, F, Sept 29, scs.
12389 Burley, C, 3, B, Jan 4, dia.
 619 Burns, E J,§ 13 cav, D, April 19, asc.
 477 Burns, John, 40, I, April 9, dys.
 924 Burns, John, 99, H, May 6, i. f.
11881 Burns, J, 118, F, Nov 6, dia.
8745 Burns, W, 3 cav, C, Sept 14, ts. f.
5991 Burns, Daniel, 5 art, D, Aug 17, ces.
7247 Burr, H, 59, C, Aug 30, dia. c.
6171 Bursha, Thomas, 2 art, M, Aug 19, mas
3165 Burshen, F, 54, C, July 11, scs.
2875 Burt, J, 2 cav, A, July 4, des.
7214 Burton, G E, 85, K, Aug 29, dys.
 217 Burton, Henry, 140, March 29, dia.
5847 Buserman, E, 97, E, Aug 16, ens.
6457 Bush, E, 20, D, Aug 22, dia.
1415 Bushnell, A, 65, D, May 27, dia. c.
 487 Bushan, J R, 132, G, April 11, pna.
11366 Bushley, Wm,‡ 5 art, A, Oct 23, scs.
1360 Buskirk, A, 47, A, May 25, dia. c.
2047 Buskirt, O, 13, June 15, dia. a.
 721 Butler, Thomas, 132, G, April 25, dia.
4183 Butler, W, 43, D, July 28, dys.
12651 Butoff, R,§ 124, C, Feb 13, dia. c.
10848 Butler, James, 2 cav, D, Oct 13, scs.
9235 Butter, P, 126, D, Sept, 19, dia. c,
5805 Button, James, 24 art, B, Aug 16, dys.
3446 Butts, A, 111, C, July 17, dia.
9790 Byron, J,‡ 69, A, Sept 26, dia. c.
1224 Burke, W H, 120, I, May 19, dia. a.
5196 Burk, John, 69, K, Aug 10, dys.
1073 Brower, John A, 5 art, D, Oct 17, dia.

12190 Cademus, C, 48, A, June 19, ana.
0765 Cady, Geo, 06, G, Oct 12, scs.
12377 Cady, J, 77, E, June 23, dia.
0721 Cady, J J, 14, H, Oct 11, scs.
3062 Cain, M, 132, E, July 9, dia. a.
2136 Cale, J, 85, G, June 18, dia. a.
19040 Caldham, L C, 8 cav, L, Sept 17, scs.
11807 Caldwell, A, 42, A, Nov 4, scs.
1530 Caling, Ed, 7, H, Oct 26, scs.
9706 Calkins, S V, 120, D, Sept 25, scs.
8411 Callbrook, J, 147, B, Sept 11, ana.
2848 Cameron, John, 1 cav, H, July 4, dia.
1770 Camp, H, 2 cav, F, June 9, dia. c.
1238 Campbell, D, 8 cav, H, May 20, ana.
7236 Campbell, J, 99, I, Aug 29, scs.
 946 Campbell, L R, 104, B, May 7, dys.
8793 Campbell, M, 169, K, Sept 15, scs.
11294 Campbell, W, 2, C, Oct 22, scs.
7378 Campbell, Wm, 76, B, Aug 31, dia.
12178 Card, A, 152, C, Nov 27, scs.
5034 Card, G, 109, F, Aug 8, scs.
8136 Carboines, W,‡ 39, C, Sept 8, dia.
6433 Cardon, E, 115, A, Aug 22, dys.
7555 Carey, D, 57, A, Sept 2, dia. c.
11512 Carey, F, 65, E, Oct 26, scs.
 372 Carl, Joseph, 14, A, April 5, dia.
5545 Carl, L, 120, G, Aug 13, cah.
12339 Carle, —, 1 cav, D, Dec 26, scs.
12268 Carmac, F, 2, D, Dec 12, scs.
7655 Carmer, Andrew, 85 B, Sept 3, ana.
11640 Carney, M, 9 cav, L, Oct 30, scs.
8470 Carnehan, Charles, 24 bat'y, Sept 11 scs
5258 Carney, D J, 132, G, Aug 10, dvs. a.
9879 Carney, Francis, 2 art, C, Sept 27, dia.
3102 Carnes, P, 13 cav, B, July 10, dia.
10806 Carpenter, Frank, 7 art, C, Oct 12, scs.
8854 Carpenter, G, 7, D, Sept 15, dia. c.
4632 Carpenter, H A, 2 art, A, Aug 3, dia
3916 Carpenter, L, 2 art, B, July 25, dia. c.

8695 Cromwell, T, 6 art, Sept 14, scs.
3324 Crosby, M, 24 bat, July 14, ts. f.
2273 Crouse, George, 24 bat, June 21, dys.
11297 Crowley, S, 2, B, Oct 22, dia. c.
5993 Cuff, S, 14, E, Aug 17, mas.
7159 Culbert, Wm, 39, D, Aug 29, dia.
4119 Culver, N L, 24 bat, July 28, dia.
8966 Cummings, —, 22, D, Sept 16, dia. c.
11269 Cron, F, 115, D, Oct 21, scs.
5476 Cunningham, J, 170, E, Aug 13, dia.
6721 Cunningham, J, 42, I, Aug 24, des.
1447 Cunningham, Wm, 45, B, May 29, dia. c.
1204 Curley, P, 125, E, May 19, scs.
3627 Currey, John, 146, B, July 20, dia.
4458 Custerman, F, 47, G, Aug 1, dia.
9540 Cute, A, 8 cav, A, Sept 22, dia.
9611 Cutler, C F,‡ 2, G, Sept 23, dia.
12434 Cutler, J P, 99, B, Jan 11, dia.
4846 Cutler, Wm, 59, B, Aug 6, dia.

8193 Daher, G, 66, D, Sept 8, dia.
8650 Daley, T, 42, I, Sept 13, pna.
10741 Damon, J D, 7 art, K, Oct 11, scs.
3577 Dailey, Wm, 5 cav, I, July 19, scs.
11122 Daniels, W O, 76, K, Oct 18, scs.
5599 Daratt, Louis, 111, G, Aug 14, cah.
1480 Daly, John, 99, 8, May 30, ana.
6641 Dawson, J, 47, K, Aug 23, dia. a.
8095 Darley, J,§ 14 art, D, Sept 7, dia. c.
6726 Darling, G H, 18 cav, F, Aug 24, dys.
5083 Darling, J, 4 cav, C, Aug 8, dia.
7562 Dart, Charles W, 85, C, Sept 2, dys.
6404 Davidson, M, 15 cav, M, Aug 21, dia.
6391 Davis, D, 164, G, Aug 21, dia.
6037 Davis, G, 1, H, Aug 18, scs.
1383 Davis, H, 85, I, May 26, dia. c.
7670 Davis, H, 1 art, D, Sept 3, scs.
8089 Davis, H J, 85, C, Sept 7, scs.
961 Davis, H R,‡ 99, I, May 8, dia. c.
12652 Davis, H T, 5 cav, A, Feb 14, dia. c.
5129 Davis, J, 85, H, Aug 9, brs.
7894 Davis, J J,‡ 43, B, Sept 5, scs.
11817 Davis, John, 47, E, Nov 4, scs.
10241 Davis, P,‡ 94, I, Oct 3, scs.
10018 Davy, J J, 2 cav, A, Sept 29, scs.
5338 Day, J W, 32, D, Aug 11, pna.
3866 Dean, C, 43, E, July 24, dia.
9400 Dean, J, 3 cav, G, Sept 21, dia.
2305 Dean, John, 6 art, K, June 22, dia. c.
10523 Debras, J, 9, A, Oct 8, dia. c.
9958 Decker, A, 82, I, Sept 28, dia.
3660 Deckman, J G, 104, B, July 20, dys.
7505 Declercy, W E, 22 cav, E, Sept 1, dia. c.
10555 Dedrich, P, 9, K, Oct 9, scs.
12320 Deman, W, 66, E, Dec 22, scs.
7059 Dessotell, J, 98, D, Aug 28, scs.
7935 Deet, F, 90, D, Sept 5, dia.
4400 Deffer, Louis, 40, H, July 31, ana.
4914 Degammo, J, 48, E, Aug 6, scs.
6283 Degroff, C, 115, H, Aug 20, dia. c.
12074 Degrout, W, 7 art, I, Nov 18, scs.
12228 Devit, Charles, 7 art, G, Dec 5, scs.
7261 Delane, M, 111, C, Aug 30, des.
11206 Delany, C, 52, H, Oct 20, scs.
12271 Demara, John, 108, M, Dec 12, scs.
5689 Demerest, D, 5, A, Aug 15, scs.
10103 Demerest, H V, 2 cav, M, Sept 30, dia.
8761 Demhart, W, 111, F, Sept 14, scs.
9592 Demming, F M, 85, H, Sept 23, dia.
278 Dempsey, John, 85, B, Aug 30, dia.
1623 Demming, L,† 85, D, Sept 2, scs.
9930 Dennis, A A, 106, H, Sept 28, dia.
1489 Dennis, Thomas, 132, G, May 31, r. f.
4099 Dennison, J, 12 cav, A, July 27, dia.
12257 Dennison, J,§ 155, I, Dec 10, scs.
7461 Dennison, W, 14 art, M, Sept 1, dia.
13259 Denorf, F, 147, B, July 13, wds.
2320 Densamore, S F, 115, G, June 22, dia. c.
6324 Densmore, E,§ 85, K, Aug 21, ana.
12603 Desmond, D,‡ 82, C, Feb 6, scs.
1799 Deveny H, 99, I, June 10, dia. c.
7598 Devlin, A, 1 art, M, Sept 2, dia.

5502 Devlin, J, 12 cav, F, Aug 13, dia. c.
10077 Dewire, Dennis, 7, E, Sept 30, ana.
2839 De Witt, S C,§ 120, E, July 3, ts. f.
9334 Dewitt, J S,§ 48, H, Sept 20, scs.
9855 Dickinson, N, 152, K, Sept 27, dia. c.
10597 Dickerman, W B, 6 art, A, Oct 10, scs.
11854 Difendorf, R, 2 art, L, Nov 6, dia.
2234 Dykeman, F, 47, C, June 20, dia. c.
10089 Dingle, J,§ 122, G, Sept 30, scs.
1821 Dingley, C, 4 cav, A, June 10, dia. c.
8588 Dighard, F, 15 cav, A, Sept 12, scs.
8245 Doan, A, 85, C, Sept 9, dia.
3773 Dodson, E, 85, C, July 22, scs.
1959 Dolan, J, 48, E, June 14, dia. a.
11805 Dolan, M, 6 cav, F, Nov 4, scs.
5658 Dolan, P, 30, I, Aug 14, dia.
11884 Domick, E, 4 art, E, Nov 6, dia.
4886 Donaghen, J, 16, A, Aug 6, dia.
2809 Dond, Daniel, 155, I, July 3, dia. a.
6149 Dondall, B, 111, G, Aug 19, dia. a.
11357 Donely, M, 10, F, Oct 23, dia.
3081 Donovan, J, 14 art, July 9, dia.
229 Donely, E J, 2 M Rifles, K, Mar 29, dia. c.
12718 Donnell, W, 4 art, A, March 2, pls.
655 Donnelly, Jas C,§ 2 cav, D, April 21, des.
10102 Doolittle, W, 76, D, Sept 30, dia.
3533 Dorchester, H S, v s, 12 cav, July 18, at.a.
12715 Dormity, M, citizen, March 1, des.
10320 Dotsey, J, 139, E, Oct 4, scs.
9416 Dougherty, E S, 85, I, Sept 21, dia.
4650 Dougherty, J, 9, C, Aug 3, dys.
2052 Dougherty, O, 99, 1, June 16, dia. c.
10992 Doughty, E S, 48, A, Oct 16, dia.
9298 Downey, H, 11, I, Sept 19, uls.
5705 Downey, J A, 85, H, Aug 15, i. f.
7275 Douglass, M, 48, D, Aug 30, ts. f.
10356 Douglass, P, 147, C, Oct 5, dia.
6149 Dondall, B, 111, G, Aug 19, dia. a.
2561 Doyle, John, 5 cav, G, June 27, dys.
4827 Doyle, James, 120, H, Aug 5, scs.
9142 Doyle, W, 7 art, I, Sept 18, dys.
9308 Dow, M, 125, H, Sept 20, dia.
3929 Drake, D W, 2 art, H, July 25, dys.
2347 Drake, D B, 158, F, June 23, des.
699 Driscoll, —, 52, B, April 23, dia. c.
2826 Drum, A, 155, A, July 3, dia. c.
9357 Druse, I, 15 art, D, Sept 20, dia.
394 Durfee, James, 99, H, April 6, dia.
3063 Dumfrey, Dennis, 100, I, July 9, dia.
3490 Dudley, J C,§ 10 cav, H, July 17, dia. c.
3957 Duell, R, 6 art, F, July 25, dia.
5264 Dumond, A, 85, E, Aug 10, i. f.
5810 Dumond, C, 120, A, Aug 16, dia. c.
6773 Dumond, S, 5, B, Aug 25, dia.
10144 Dumond, F, 146, A, Oct 1, scs.
9116 Dunlap, C, 85, B, Sept 18, dia.
8669 Duane, T, 95, E, Sept 13, dia.
8453 Dritman, William, 42, C, Sept 11, dia. a.
6905 Duble, Henry, 61, F, Aug 26, dys.
6087 Dule, Levi, 5, B, Aug 18, dia.
10948 Duger, P, 67, A, Oct 14, scs.
11104 Dunham, R, 14 art, G, Oct 18, dys.
7621 Dunn, J, 40, G, Sept 2, dia. c.
8244 Dunn, L H, 50 Eng, E, Sept 9, dia.
5732 Dunn, James, 88, D, Aug 15, scs.
1695 Dunn, J H, 99, I, June 7, dia. c.
10948 Dwire, P, 67, A, Oct 14, scs.
123 Dunbar, Thomas, 2, F, March 23, ts. f.
3234 Dunn, M, 99, I, July 12.
919 Dunn, Owen, 126, H, May 6, dia.
1033 Dunn, Pat, 149, A, May 11, ana.
3584 Dunning, Wm, 132, G, July 9, dys.
2972 Dunsham, Abr, 120, C, July 7, dia. c.
7554 Durand, M, 82, K, Sept 2, scs.
4832 Durand, Jas E, 10 cav, E, Aug 6, dia. c.
9716 Dyer, S, 7 art, D, July 27, dia.
4086 Dyer, John S, 10 cav, M, Sept 25, scs.
3574 Dykeman, D, 22 cav, F, July 9, pna.
12271 Dunaram, John, 108, F, Dec 12, scs.

9033 Earl, C, 85, D, Sept 17, dia.
2443 Earl, H, 174, H, June 25, dia. c.

6150 Letch, John, 5 cav, C, Aug 19, ces.
8774 Levalley, C, 140, A, Sept 14, scs.
9045 Lewis, C, 85, F, Sept 17, dia. c.
3727 Lewis, C F, 52, E, July 21, dia. c.
1329 Lewis, F A, 9, G, May 24, ts. f.
11515 Lewis, G W, 146, G, Nov 8, scs.
8297 Lewis, J, 1 art, E, Sept 9, brs.
5115 Lewis, P W, 85, B, Aug 9, dia.
10365 Lickley, P, 1 cav, E, Oct 5, scs.
11551 Limbach, S, 7, D, Oct 27, scs.
8419 Linch, J H, 76, I, Sept 11, ts. f.
5845 Linchler, F, 1 cav, E, Aug 15, dia.
10559 Lindlay, D, 147, E, Oct 9, dia.
7815 Lineham, Thomas, 125, C, Sept 4, dia.
6759 Ling, John, 4 art, F, Aug 25, dia. a.
38 Link, Gotlieb, 54, K, March 12, dys. c.
10073 Little, C, 76, F, Sept 30, scs.
10933 Livingston, A, 1 cav, C, Oct 14, dia.
4543 Locher, Conrad, 15 art, Aug 2, dys.
5565 Lock, A, 98, B, Aug 13, dia. c.
2142 Lodge, T, 12, A, June 18, dia. a.
8246 Loftern, H, 12 cav, F, Sept 9, dia. c.
9722 Loftus, M, 11 cav, E, Sept 24, dia.
7010 Longs, R, 2 art, A, Aug 27, scs.
11591 Long, J, 75, A, Oct 28, scs.
7924 Long, L, 40, I, Sept 5, ana.
4514 Longle, William, 4 art, B, Aug 1, scs.
5434 Loomis, John, 14 art, M, Aug 12, scs.
9712 Loony, C, 40, A, Sept 25, dia.
9988 Lorzbran, J, 64, E, Sept 29, dia.
11906 Louis, C, 16 cav, C, Nov 7, scs.
12329 Love, J, 125, A, Dec 24, scs.
7146 Lovejoy, F, 1 cav, I, Aug 29, scs.
10248 Lovering, F, 14 art, I, Oct 3, scs.
12313 Lowery, G, 7, A, Dec 29, dia.
2568 Lowery, James F, 140, A, June 27, dys. a.
9663 Lows, H, 22 cav, E, Sept 24, dia.
8395 Loyd, S, 47, D, Sept 10, dys.
9354 Luce, V, 140, D, Sept 20, scs.
10311 Lucia, A, 95, H, Oct 4, scs.
7268 Lurcock, E, 14 art, M, Aug 30, scs.
9002 Lutton, O, 14 art, H, Sept 17, scs.
5772 Lynch, D, 164, A, Aug 15, dia.
6895 Lynch, F,‡ 43, K, Aug 26, ana.
931 Lynch, Pat, 99, H, May 7, dia. c.
12633 Lyons, Charles, 2 cav, M, Feb 10, des.
1427 Lyons, Michael, 99, E, May 28, dia. c.
8419 Luch, J H, 76, I, Sept 11, ts. f.
6151 Lucah, John, 5 cav, C, Sept 19, ces.
8342 Lyons, J H, 5 art, Sept 10, scs.
6156 Lyons, Thomas, 6 art, G, Aug 19, dia. a.
7913 Lyons, W,‡ 47, A, Sept 5, dia. c.

37 Mace, Jeff, 134, I, March 12, dia.
6665 Mace, L, 48, H, Aug 24, scs.
10850 Mack, J, 39, D, Oct 13, dia.
5016 Mackin, Wm, 85, F, Aug 8, dia. c.
3933 Madder, P, 155, E, July 25, dia. c.
10506 Madden, F,§ 122, E, Oct 8, dia. c.
4822 Madden, —, 1 cav, D, Aug 5, dys.
11257 Madezan, John, 125, B, Oct 21, scs.
9798 Madison, D, 75, D, Sept 26, scs.
11714 Magrath, G H, 61, D, Nov 1, dys.
4028 Mahon, E, 170, G, July 26, tonsilitis.
122 Mahon, James,§ 132, K, March 23, ts. f.
1422 Mahon, Thomas, 120, C, May 28, dia. c.
5842 Mailer, J R,§ 134, B, Aug 16, ers.
11679 Maine, F O, 85, A, Oct 31, scs.
11580 Mainhart, F, 39, B, Oct 28, scs.
12069 Makay, J, 5, E, Nov 17, scs.
7942 Malleck, M,‡ 6 cav, D, Sept 5, dia. c.
9427 Malley, S S, 16, K, Sept 21, dia.
9457 Malone, Pat, 123, F, Sept 21, scs.
3284 Maloney, C, 6, C, July 14, dia. c.
11447 Maloney, J, 73, G, Oct 25, scs.
7600 Mandeville, Wm, 85, F, Sept 2, scs.
2802 Mangin, M, 7 art, F, July 3, scs.
10621 Manning —, 33, Oct 9, scs.
7139 Manning M, 6 art, D, Aug 28, scs.
10540 Manning Thomas, 125, B, Oct 8, scs.
2952 Mannilly J, 74, C, July 6, dia a.
2856 March, J 22 cav, C, July 4, dia. c.

4000 Marley, John, mus, 53, E, July 28, dia.
1123 Marron, J, 99, H, May 15, dys.
11764 Martaugh, J, 6 cav, A, Sept 3, scs.
3824 Marsh, Ira, 6 art, M, July 23, scs.
5407 Marsh, J, 104, D, Aug 12, dia.
11997 Marston, A, 65, G, Nov 13, scs.
3441 Martin, A, 12 cav, F, July 17, dys.
435 Martin, C, 10 cav, A, April 8, ana.
6543 Martin, Charles, 42, G, Aug 23, dia.
11600 Martin, E A, 5 cav, C, Oct 28, scs.
12208 Martin, J, 39, G, Dec 2, dia.
4321 Martin, H, 76, H, July 30, dys.
5086 Martin, J C, 24 bat, Aug 8, dia. c.
9164 Martin, P, 99, H, Sept 18, scs.
6293 Martin, John, 16 cav, L, Aug 20, scs.
1256 Martin, Peter, 40, I, May 21, dia. a.
8003 Martin, W, 142, F, Sept 6, scs.
3939 Martin, W B, 12, I, July 25, scs.
8746 Martin, W H, 24 art, M, Sept 14, dia.
1073 Martin, Wm, 13 cav, D, May 13, dia. c.
676 Marvouey, James, 132, G, April 22, phs
10483 Mason, F,‡ 14 art, I, Oct 7, scs.
2315 Martin, Samuel, 85, I, June 22, dia. c.
11290 Masterson, E, 2, D, Oct 22, scs.
11296 Massen, H L, 86, C, Oct 22, scs.
10498 Maxwell, J, 85, D, Oct 8, scs.
1477 Maxwell, Robert, 48, D, May 30, wds.
11788 Matthews, W, 155, I, Nov 4, scs.
4472 Matthews, H, 12 cav, M, Aug 1, dia.
2100 Mattice, H C, 134, E, June 17, dia. c.
5651 Mattison, R, 85, D, Aug 14, scs.
4946 Maxum, S G, 12 cav, A, Aug 7, dia c.
10519 McAllister, J, 125, I, Oct 8, scs.
7995 McBride, —, 52, K, Sept 6, scs.
4508 McCabe, James, 88, D, Aug 1, dia.
2517 McCabe, P,§ 12 cav, F, June 26, dia. c.
732 McCabe, Peter,§ 2 cav, E, April 25, dys.
2196 McCabe, J, 44, C, June 19, dia. a.
8324 McCafferty, W, 100, D, Sept 10, dia. c.
10716 McCain, L, 18, C, Oct 11, scs.
9864 McCardell, W, 15 cav, H, Sept 27, scs.
7620 McCarten, L, 9 art, B, Sept 2, dia.
3413 McCarty, D, 155, G, July 16, dia. a.
4480 McCarty, Denis, 2 art, D, Aug 1, dia. c.
5122 McCarty, I, 99, H, Aug 9, dys. c.
9633 McCarty, I, 2, m r, K, Sept 24, dia.
4759 McCarty, John, 69, K, Aug 5, dia.
6136 McCarty, John, 104, E, Aug 19, ces.
1035 McCarty, P, 132, K, May H, dia.
2965 McCarty, S, 99, C, July 6, dia. a.
6227 McCarty, W, 9 cav, L, Aug 20, dys.
8242 McClusky, F, 173, E, Sept 9, dia.
1344 McColigan, Pat, 99, F, May 24, dia. a.
9266 McCauley, J H, 47, G, Sept 19, scs.
6440 McCloud, John, 97, A, Aug 22, scs.
4416 McConnell, E, 9 art, July 3, dia.
6012 McCord, H, 7 art, G, Aug 17, dia.
11110 McCormie, M, 93, K, Oct 18, dia. c.
6697 McCormick, H, 69, K, Aug 29, scs.
9018 McCormick, H, 178, F, Sept 17, scs.
3629 McCormick, J, 155, H, July 20, dys.
6203 McCormick, J, 24 bat, Aug 19, scs.
7441 McCormick, J, 43, F, Sept 1, dys.
10258 McCormick, P, 43, D, Oct 5, scs.
1433 McCormick, Peter, 39, I, May 28, dia. c.
5203 McCormick, W, 2, I, Aug 10, dia.
7730 McCracker, B, 7 art, B, Sept 3, scs.
8644 McCrass, J, 148, Sept 13, scs.
2279 McCrember, M, 85, I, June 21, dia. c.
8507 McCullen, D, 57, F, Sept 12, dia.
10778 McDavid, J, 5, D, Oct 12, scs.
6912 McDermott, P, 164, H, Aug 26, scs.
8969 McDonald, A, 24 bat, Sept 16, dia. c
7745 McDonald, A H, 85, E, Sept 3, dia.
7140 McDonald, B, 52, D, Aug 29, dia.
4013 McDonald, John, 164, E, July 26, dys.
12138 McDonald, F, 16 cav, L, Nov 23, scs.
10002 McDonald, F,‡ 95, A, Sept 29, dia.
7259 McDonnell, Wm, 14 art, D, Aug 30, scs
8126 McDurie, C, 71, Sept 8, scs.
4089 McElray, John, 43, I, July 27, dia.
9581 McErmany, P, 7 art, G, Sept 23, dia.

9937 Puff, I, 15 art, Sept 28, dia.
2321 Puley, Daniel, 115, I, June 22, ts. f.
729 Pullers, U H, 132, E, April 25, dia. c.
2395 Putnam, L, 14 art, L, June 24, las.
1515 Purkey, Jacob, 84, B, May 31, dia. c.
4063 Purstle, S, 49, A, July 27, dys.
1432 Prunan, L,‡ 147, H, Oct 24, dia.

9046 Quackenbuss, P, H, K, Sept 17, dia. c.
8227 Quigley, J, 99, I, Sept 9, dys.
8064 Quinn, Edser, 10 cav, B, Sept 7, dia.

4305 Randolph,—, 9, E, July 30, des.
11648 Raforun, W, 59, C, Oct 30, scs.
512 Rafferty, M, 132, G, April 12, dys.
2534 Rafferty, P, 5 cav, M, June 26, dys. a.
11330 Rafferty, T, 5 art, B, Oct 23, scs.
4593 Raker, L, 1 cav, E, Aug 3, dia.
8751 Ranch, J, 100, D, July 22, dia.
0875 Randall, John, 99, A, Oct 13, dia.
6503 Ralinger, J, 47, D, Aug 22, scs.
6794 Rangheart, John, 100, A, Aug 25, dia.
7778 Rastifer, John, 100, A, Sept 4, dys.
4216 Rattery, John, 104, I, July 29, dys.
10987 Ray, C, 3 cav, B, Oct 14, dia. c.
10246 Ray, R S, 154, A, Oct 3, dia.
4336 Raynard, F, 125, F, July 30, dia. c.
3435 Rattersboom, J, 3 art, K, July 17, scs.
2880 Ramsay, Isaac, 86, I, July 4, dia.
1265 Ramsay, Hiram, 31, K, May 21, dia.
2186 Reamer, W C, 111 B, June 19, dia. c.
2820 Redman, J, 3 art, k, July 3, dia. c.
11695 Reddo, D V, 8 cav, M, Oct 31, dia. c.
7232 Reed, F A, 64, E, Aug 30, scs.
8574 Reed, J, 140, H, Sept 12, dia.
406 Reed, S G, 13, D, April 6, dia. c.
6041 Reed, W D, 146, H, Aug 18, scs.
10232 Reed, W J, 41, I, Oct 2, dia.
8492 Reed, William, 14 art, I, Sept 11, scs.
7369 Reetz, John, 52, A, Aug 31, dia.
5694 Reeve, G, 152, C, Aug 15, scs.
1680 Reeves, John, 57, H, June 6, scs.
10467 Redmond, J, 43, C, Oct 7, scs.
10911 Regler, W H, 22 cav, M, Oct 14, dia. c.
9122 Reiley, P O, 164, B, Sept 18, dia.
7195 Renback, C, 29, Aug 29, dia.
12455 Rebman, J, 59, C, Jan 15, dia. c.
8431 Rencermane, J R, 5 cav, B, Sept 11, scs.
9320 Randall, A B, 76, F, Sept 20, dia. c.
3352 Remsen, C, 2 cav, M, July 15, scs.
8209 Reynolds, O, 155, E, Sept 8, scs.
6799 Reynolds, O S, 85, E, Aug 25, dia.
0265 Reynolds, Samuel, 92, H, Oct 3, dia.
6350 Reynolds, William, 140, I, Aug 21, dys.
6546 Reidy, J D, 65, I, Aug 23, dys.
4318 Rice, F,‡ 39, I, July 30, dia. c.
3077 Rich, T D, 24 bat, July 9, dia.
12289 Rich, J, 82, C, Dec 15, scs.
3561 Richey, R, 66, C, July 18, dia.
2427 Rider, E, 178, E, June 24, dia. c.
8005 Rhenevault, R H, 21, B, Sept 6, dia.
11904 Rehm, W, 7 art, C, Nov 7, scs.
3891 Richistine, C,‡ 132, D, July 24, dia. c.
5317 Richards, A, 52, D, Aug 11, dia.
3674 Richards, A, 41, E, Aug 14, gae.
12243 Richards, A, 9, C, Dec 7, scs.
3682 Richards, H, 47, E, July 21, dys.
7578 Richards, N J,§ 146, C, Sept 2, dia. c.
4240 Richardson, H M, 20 cav, M, J'ly 29, dia. c.
12193 Ricker, M, 2 art, M, Nov 29, scs.
8155 Rickhor, J, 85, E, Sept 8, dys.
415 Rikel, Robert, 125, G, April 7, dia. c.
12382 Riley, I, 73, E, Jan 2, dys.
2885 Riley, J, 99, C, July 4, dys.
5021 Riley, John, 176, C, Aug 8, scs.
6347 Riley John, 39, D, Aug 21, dia.
11163 Ripley, F A, 152, C, Oct 19, scs.
11760 Ripp, W, 42, B, Nov 3, scs.
3514 Rising, C, 75, B, July 18, dia.
10310 Risley, Geo W, 46, G, Oct 4, dia.
2558 Ritcher, F,§ 132, D, June 27, dys.
7245 Ritson, S, 18 cav, E, Aug 29, dys.

9224 Ritzmillin, John, 115, Sept [?], scs.
1775 Roach, F, 99, F, June 9, ana.
1842 Roach, Chas, 85, E, June 11, dia, c.
2354 Robberger, P H, 46, B, June 23, dia. c.
11195 Roberson, C A, 122, B, Oct 20, dys.
2346 Robertson, W H, 134, B, June 23, dia. c.
8554 Robertson, W M, 96, B, Sept 12, scs.
9970 Robinson, H, 39, K, Sept 28, dia.
7607 Robinson, A, 111, I, Sept 2, dia.
3680 Robinson, H C, 95, I, July 21, scs.
6419 Robinson, John, 115, A, Aug 22, dia.
27 Robins, L [?] 154, K, March 8, pna.
7663 Roberts, A, 173, C, Sept 3, dys.
7585 Rockwell, N C, 14 art, D, Sept 2, scs.
3813 Rockfellar, R E, 85, D, July 23, dia.
11342 Rockfellar, H, 15 art, M, Oct 23, scs.
3959 Rock, F, 6 art, F, July 25, dys.
4350 Rogers, A, 7 art, 1, July 31, scs.
6059 Rogers, A, 125, H, Aug 18, scs.
5791 Rogers, G, mas, 85, F, Aug 15, rhm.
3011 Rogers, James, 132, H, July 7, dia.
4287 Rogers, H C, 85, C, July 30, dia.
8369 Rogers, H J, 2 art, E, Sept 10, scs.
4912 Rogers, M, 43, D, Aug 6, ana.
7208 Rogers, O S,§ 85, C, Aug 29, scs.
6824 Rogers, Thomas, 12, F, Aug 25, dia.
11772 Romer, F, 9, A, Nov 3, dia. c.
8468 Rook, G, 6 art, E, Sept 11, scs.
9963 Rooney, John, 152, G, Sept 28, dia.
9102 Rooney, M, 132, F, Sept 18, scs.
8922 Rooney, P, 2 art, C, Sept 16, dys.
5569 Root, A N, 85, C, Aug 14, ana.
2998 Roots, W T, 120, H, July 7, dia.
1735 Root, Legrand, 24 bat, June 8, pna.
10278 Rose, A, 16, L, Oct 2, scs.
9550 Rosecrans, J E, 125, H, Sept 23, dys.
8171 Ross, C, 23 cav, A, Sept 8, dys.
8874 Ross, E F, 111, I, July 24, ts, f.
5591 Ross, David, 27, D, Aug 14, scs.
6741 Ross, G, 76, K, Aug 24, dia.
9751 Ross, A, 1 cav, M, Sept 25, scs.
11963 Ross, J H, 121, G, Nov 11, scs.
5929 Rosenberger, John, 4, D, Aug 17, ena.
3616 Rosser, Lewis, 84, A, July 20, dys.
2924 Rosenburg, J, 30, A, July 5, dia. c.
8737 Rosson, Chas, 24 cav, E, Sept 14, dia.
12259 Roswell, J, 93, K, Dec 10, scs.
727 Ross, Jacob, 151, A, April 25, dia. c.
1940 Row, W J, 120, B, June 14, dia. c,
5097 Roth, Louis, 39, D, Aug 9, scs.
8504 Rothwell, M,‡ 20 cav, M, Sept 12, scs.
3722 Rouge, Wm, bug, 12 cav, F, July 21, dia.
7709 Rowbotham, R, H cav, L, Sept 3, scs.
5857 Rowell, J E, 70, G, Aug 16, mas.
3492 Rowell, L N, 99, H, July 17, dia.
59 Roberts, A B,§ 8 cav, B, March 18, pna.
2609 Ruddin, C, 120, H, June 28, dia.
867 Rudler, William, 120, May 3, dys.
40 Rue, Newton,§ 5 cav, A, March 13, dia. c.
8667 Runey, F, 69, H, Sept 13, dia.
12635 Russ, John, 2, K, Feb 10, dia.
8856 Russell, J,‡ 7 art, A, Sept 15, dia. c.
5094 Ryan, D, 106, D, Aug 8, dia.
8599 Ryan, J, 95, E, Sept 12, scs.
8741 Ryan, J, 22 cav, E, Sept 14, ts. f.
7258 Ryan, Owen, 12, A, Aug 30, dia.
4762 Ryonch, John, 66, I, Aug 5, scs.
6413 Ryson, John, 7 art, L, Aug 22, scs.
6206 Ryne, J M, 39, E, Aug 9, dia.
684 Rush, John, 111, E, April 23, dys. c.

7234 Sackett, R S, 85, G, Aug 29, dia. c.
1929 Sadley, M, 77, H, June 14, dia.
1880 Safford, B J, 24, bat, June 12, dys.
11870 Salsbury, H, 1 art, M, Nov 6, dia.
10652 Salisbury, E, 16, D, Oct 11, scs.
10923 Samlett,—, 13 cav, I, Oct 14, scs.
10880 Samet, W, 15, H, Oct 13, scs.
3769 Sampson, J, 106, K, July 22, dia.
346 Sanders, Charles,‡ 9 mil, A, April 2, [?]
3818 Sanders, J, 99, C, July 23, dia. c.
9857 Sanders, J, 12, cav, A, Sept 27, scs.

5169 So pers, John, 2, E, Aug 9, des.
2773 Sopher, Jas, 132, F, July 2, dys.
2403 Sopher, S, 102, K, June 24, des.
4352 Sotter, J M, 47, C, July 31, dia.
3534 Southard, H, 5 cav, C, July 18, des
10526 Southard, N, 2, H, Oct 8, scs.
11346 Southard, W A, 18, I, Oct 23, gae.
2877 Souther, Henry, 69, K, July 4, dys.
8124 Southworth, R, 22 cav, E, Sept 8, dia.
10488 Skall, S, 7 art, L, Oct 7, dia.
12029 Skeeley, T, 66, H, Nov 15, scs.
9954 Spark, G,§ 16 art, C, Sept 28, scs.
6975 Sparks, E, 10, B, Aug 27, dia.
5421 Spaulding, H, 1 cav, F, Aug 12, scs.
5567 Spellman, John, 66, B, Aug 13, scs.
10712 Spencer, A, 93, D, Feb 28, scs.
10989 Sperry, A, 51, F, Oct 16, scs.
3532 Span, Jas, 147, H, July 18, dia. c.
5982 Spanbury, S, 14 art, C, Aug 17, dia. c.
5821 Sprague, E H, 10 bat, Aug 16, scs.
3593 Sprague, J, 85, I, July 19, dia.
10730 Sprig, Jas A, 24 cav, E, Oct 11, scs.
4877 Sprink, A, 146, F, Aug 6, dys.
9035 Strats, John, 15, A, Sept 17, scs.
889 Stacey, John, 99, I, May 4, td. f.
4574 Stadler, J,§ 39, A, Aug 2, scs.
10078 Stancliff, A B, 106, H, Sept 30, scs.
2570 Stanton, H H, 22, E, June 27, dia. c.
5187 Stark, J D,‡ 100, A, Aug 9, dia.
11740 Starkweather, L, 146, E, Nov 2, dys.
12650 Star, C, 15, D, Feb 13, des.
7381 Stanton, L H, 7 art, K, Aug 31, dys.
2520 Stark, J H, 121, A, June 26, dia. a.
1698 Stanley, J C,‡ 85, C, June 7, pna.
10290 St Dennis, L, 16, F, Oct 4, scs.
9903 Stewart, Peter, 5, B, Sept 27, scs.
7636 Stevens, E, 120, C, Sept 2, dia. c.
95 Stevenson, Wm, 132, G, March 22, ts. f.
3782 Sternhoff, A, 15 art, C, July 22, ana.
4678 Stevens, John S, 100, F, Aug 4, dia. c.
5530 Steiner, C, 7 art, 1, M, Aug 13, cah.
7028 Stevens, Wm, 99, I, Aug 27, scs.
2543 Stead, J, 115, F, June 27, ts. f.
6531 Stebins, C, 85, C, Aug 23, ana.
3872 Stevenson, W, 10, F, July 24, dys.
6443 Stead, J, 15, D, Aug 22, scs.
2034 Stewart, John, 89, June 15, dys.
1863 Stebbins, H, 85, B, June 12, dys.
6049 Stelrocht, D, 22 cav, C, Aug 18, ces.
10149 Stickler, E, 169, A, Oct 1, scs.
11755 Stivers, R, 111, F, Nov 2, scs.
7075 Still, D, 132, D, Aug 28, dys.
6102 Stump, W, 6, K, Aug 18, dia.
4193 Still, James, 164, E, July 29, phs.
4385 Stillwell, S, 2 art, E, July 31, dys.
915 Stone, John, mus, 5 cav, C, May 6, dys.
11043 Stoddard, I, 111, F, Oct 17, dia. c.
6722 Stone, L, 24, E, Aug 24, dia.
2053 Stoup, J, 15, A, June 16, dia.
3415 Strue, G N, 1 art, B, July 16, dia. c.
3997 Storing, A, 54, B, July 26, dia. c.
8520 Strain, N W, 2 cav, I, Sept 12, dia.
3905 Streeter, F, 76, F, July 24, scs.
4665 Storms, A N, 7 art, I, Aug 4, dia. c.
4798 Strale, J, 178, B, Aug 5, scs.
5342 Strater, Geo, 85, K, Aug 11, scs.
6988 Stratten, J H, 140, H, Aug 27, dys.
11967 Strip, W,‡ 42, E, Nov 11, scs.
116 Streight, Lewis, 127, A, March 23, pna.
2401 Stratten, Chas, 125, K, June 24, dia. c.
7845 Sturdevant, G, 5 cav, I, Sept 4, dia.
5994 Stutzman, I, 39, D, Aug 17, mas.
6102 Stump, W, 60, K, Aug 18, dia.
1832 Styler, G W, 7 art, I, Nov 5, scs.
9953 Sughem, I, h a, B, Sept 28, scs.
640 Sullivan, Ed, 69, A, April 20, dia.
6048 Sullivan, M, 69, K, Aug 18, ces.
1492 Sullivan, Pat,‡ 99, H, May 31, des.
7728 Sullivan, P C,‡ 155, E, Sept 3, dia.
5440 Susear, Fred, 39, I, Aug 12, ts. f.
1051 Sutliff, E,‡ 15 cav, M, Oct 11, dia c.
1 Swarner, J H, 2 cav, H, Feb 27, p a.

4005 Swarner, J, bugler, 2 cav, H, July 26, ana.
6466 Swartz, M 2 cav, M, Aug 22, dia.
12267 Swager, G, 103, F, Dec 12, dys.
2322 Sweeney, James, 155, I, June 22, dia. a.
5835 Sweeney, M, 122, C, Aug 16, mas.
3527 Sweet, E, 93, F, July 18, scs.
2921 Sweet, L, 4 art, M, July 5, dia.
4960 Sylurs, S, 140, E, Aug 7, dia. c.
12765 Swancent, J, 2, A, March 13, dia. c.
10559 Stratton, E, 76, E, Oct 10, scs.

1934 Taylor, A, 2 cav, F, June 14, dia. c.
4867 Taylor, C, 115, F, Aug 6, dia.
551 Taylor, Charles B, 154, April 14, dia.
11321 Taylor, D, 149, D, Oct 22, scs.
2742 Taylor, R H, 125, F, July 1, dia. c.
493 Taylor, Thos B, 10 cav, E, April 11, rhm.
9993 Taylor, L R,‡ 147, K, Sept 29, scs.
12290 Taylor, W, 12 cav, A, Dec 15, scs.
12480 Taylor, W, 42, B, Jan 17, scs.
10370 Taylor, W H, 7 art, C, Oct 5, scs.
10738 Taylor, W H, 7 cav, C, Oct 11, dia. c.
10157 Taylor, Wm, 22 cav, C, Oct 1, dia.
8961 Taylor, W W,§ 2, I, Sept 16, scs.
8988 Tarvis, G W, 1 drag, K, Sept 17, dia.
9480 Tare, W, 115, D, Sept 21, dia.
3681 Tambrick, A, 16 cav, A, July 21, scs.
3976 Tanner, M, 1, E, July 25, dia.
4326 Tanschivit, Ed, 15 art, E, July 30, dys.
7019 Tell, William, 59, C, Aug 27, dys.
9143 Thompson, A, 9, D, Sept 18, dia.
133 Terry, Aaron,§ 12, K, March 24, brs.
9064 Teneych, M, 14 art, E, Sept 17, dia.
4909 Tewey, J, 99, H, Aug 6, scs.
6445 Terwilliger, D R, 85, D, Aug 22, i. f.
10352 Thomas, J, 2 cav, D, Oct 5, dys.
3598 Thomas, H,§ 88, D, July 19, dys.
3711 Thomas, W, 3, H, July 21, dia. c.
4619 Thomas, J, 85, G, Aug 3, ts. f.
10361 Thearer, J, 1 bat, Oct 5, scs.
8161 Thompson, C W, 85, K, Sept 8, dia.
4781 Thompson, J, 39, H, Aug 5, dia.
5510 Thompkins, Ira, 6 art, Aug 13, scs.
5524 Thompson, P, 10, E, Aug 13, scs.
6730 Thompson, N B, 146, A, Aug 24, scs.
5784 Thompson, J, 104, G, Aug 15, dia.
2613 Thompson, T, 12 cav, F, June 28, dia. c.
320 Thompson, Daniel, 142, E, April 2 dia.
3538 Thresh, G, 5 cav, K, July 18, dys.
5147 Thruston, N E, 85, C Aug 9, dia.
11235 Thornton, J, 14 art, L, Oct 21.
6309 Thorpe, W C, 82, I, Aug 20, dia.
4393 Thurston, G W, 85, E, July 31, dys.
12843 Thayer, G, 70, E, April 22, dia. c.
679 Thierbach, P M, 39, D, April 22, ts. f.
11230 Tilton, H, 24 art, Oct 20, scs.
8283 Tillitson, N P, 51, A, Sept 9, dia. c.
8849 Timerson, Wm, 2 art, I, Sept 15, dia.
2680 Timmish,—,85, C, June 30, dia. a.
659 Tiner, David, 79, E, April 21, des.
10422 Townsend, W, 111, B, Oct 6, scs.
8068 Townsend, L, 22 cav, G, Sept 7, dys.
3883 Townsend, John, 52, A, July 24, dia. c.
535 Townsend, Geo M, 111, F, April 14, dia.
9050 Johnson, E, 22, Sept 17, dia.
4774 Toney, L, 100, D, Aug 5, scs.
10727 Tolal, Pat, 164, K, Oct 11, scs.
5833 Tonner, L, 5 cav, G, Aug 16, ens.
6047 Tobias, A, 120, G, Aug 18, dys.
2112 Toomey, J F,‡ 85, I, June 17, dia. c.
12465 Tourney, P, 99, B, Jan 16, dia. c.
12636 Tocdt, H, 1, K, Feb 10, dia.
12708 Tomlinson, W F, 22, G, Feb 28, dia. c.
3193 Tripp, Ira,§ 77, B, July 12, dia.
10442 Tripp, O S, 3 art, K, Oct 7, scs.
9507 Truman, A M, 2 art, D, Sept 22, scs.
7629 Trueman, R, 7 art, G, Sept 2, dia. c.
8544 Tremor, M, 76, F, Sept 12, scs.
7317 Trumpp, E, 22 cav, F, Aug 30, scs.
3882 Trumbull, H, 115, I, July 24, dia. c.
7187 Travis, T, 8 cav, G, Aug 29, dia.
4052 Truesdale, W J, 85, H, July 27, dia.

21

3425 Trompter, F § 140, B, July 18, wds.
 100 Tracey, Pat, 39, I, March 22, ts. f.
 707 Turner, Wm,‡ 5 cav, G, April 24, dys. c.
7970 Turuer, John, 49, A, Sept 5, scs.
11376 Turner, J, 22 cav, M, Oct 24, scs.
1688 Turner, Thomas, 16 cav, B, June 6, dia.
2120 Turner, J B, 85, C, June 17, dia. c.
10535 Tuthill, C, 22 cav, G, Oct 8, scs.
 968ʸ Tuthill, S D, 2 art, M, Sept 24, dia.
.0604 Tuft, E, 29, C, Oct 10, dys.
7915 Turden, E S, 15 cav, D, Sept 5, dia.
7421 Turton, W F, 2 art, I, Aug 31, dia.
3796 Tubbs, W H, 85, D, July 22, dia. c.
3084 Tupple, H,§ 154, H, July 9, pna.
3129 Tucker, L, 120, D, July 10, dia.
2883 Tuttle, W, 48, K, July 4, ts. f.
10404 Tyrrell, I, 22 cav, A, Oct 8, dia.

4217 Uncer, James, 15, H, July 29, dia. c.
 416 Uber, Charles,§ 14, A, April 7, dia. c.
12401 Udell, J, 7 art, H, Jan 5, scs.
10837 Ulmer, H, 15 art, K, Oct 14, scs.
231ʸ Underburg, L W, 77, G, June 22, des.
 254 Underhill, H, 47, E, March 30, i. f.
1495 Underwriter, A, 62, F, May 21, pna.

1091 Van Clarke, Wm, 106, D, May 14, dia.
9087 Van Allen, C, 7, E, Sept 18, dys.
1025 Van Buren, J W, 3 art, K, May 11, dia. c.
 664 Van Buren, Henry, 3 art, K, April 21, dia.
10071 Van Bethysen, H, 7 art, I, Sept 30, scs.
12539 Van Bramin, T, 71, K, Jan 27, dia. c.
1577 Van Derbreck, A, 132, B, June 3, dys.
3463 Van Dugen, 24 cav, M, July 17, dys.
6560 Van Hosen, C, 95, A, Aug 23, dia.
10656 Van Housen, B, 12 bat, Oct 11, scs.
3371 Van Haughton, J, 124, C, July 15, dia.
1418 Vanderbrogart, W, 104, F, May 27, dia. c.
8957 Vanarsdale, P, 1, G, Sept 16, dia.
8782 Vanalstine, H, 152, A, Sept 14, scs.
8806 Vanclack, F, 5, D, Sept 15, scs.
7564 Vanvelzer, J M, 85, I, Sept 2, dys.
7635 Vanburen, J, 15 cav, B, Sept 2, dia.
11446 Vanscott, L, 59, C, Oct 25, scs.
11596 Vanarnum, J, 8 cav, E, Oct 28, scs.
7054 Vanwagner, C, 2 art, F, Aug 28, dia.
7244 Vanesse, M, 2 cav, K, Aug 29, dys.
7252 Vanzart, Wm, 7 art, E, Aug 30, dia.
6472 Varney, C, 169, E, Aug 22, dia.
6634 Vanalstine, C, 7 art, C, Aug 23, dys.
3333 Vanest, J H, 14 art, B, July 15, dia.
  83 Vanvelsen, J, 120, A, March 21, hrs.
2089 Vaughan, W H, 8 cav, K, June 17, dia. c.
 973 Vespers, Jas W, 85, D, May 9, dia. c.
7506 Van Osten, C, 52, H, Sept 1, dia.
5631 Vencot, L, 2 cav, H, Aug 14, scs.
4196 Veil, Wm, 6 art, F, July 29, dia. c.
1539 Vernon, S, 2 cav, M, June 1, scs.
7846 Vincent, R, 178, I, Sept 4, dia.
2782 Vincent, Richard, 1, K, July 2, dia. c.
2879 Vinsant, G M, 14 art, I, July 4, dia.
2715 Vish, O, 178, E, July 1, dia. c.
6525 Vibbard, Geo, 22 cav, E, Aug 22, dia.
10023 Voerling, H, 15 art, C, Sept 29, dia.
4623 Vogle, Anton, 10, C, Aug 3, dys.
5503 Voorhies, A H, 1 cav, H, Aug 13, dia. c.
11507 Voorhies, E R, 85, C, Oct 16, scs.
6682 Voorhies, Geo, 85, C, Aug 23, dia. c.

1184 Walls, Peter, 4 cav, D, May 18, dia. c.
5001 Wall, Jas,§ 15, G, Aug 7, scs.
1898 Wallace, John, 11 cav, B, May 26, dia.
10211 Watt, H, 12 cav, A, Oct 2, scs.
9977 Watts, C, 6, C, Sept 28, dia. c.
10313 Waters, A L, 8 cav, F, Oct 4, dys.
10477 Warner, Chas L, 2 cav, D, Oct 7, dia. c.
4026 Warrer, L, 95, I, July 26, dys.
7351 Warner, P P, 14 art, M, Aug 31, dia.
7444 Warner, A J, 76, F, Sept 1, dia. c.
12449 Warner, Luther, 12 cav, A, Jan 9, dia. c.
10543 Ward, Patrick, 88, C, Oct 8, dia.
5527 Ward, J, 99, G, Aug 9, asc.

10920 Ward, ₍ 40, H, Oct 14, sz a.
2238 Ward, ᵗ 95, I, June 2¹, des.
 400 Ward, W A, 99, B, April 6, dia.
12816 Warden, H B, 5, B, March 25, dia. e
9858 Walters, D, 125, E, Sept 27, scs.
1557 Walters, Nelson,§ 120, K, June 2, dia. s
3381 Walterhouse, Ed, 9, I, July 16, dys.
2827 Wallace, J, 2 cav, M, July 3, pna.
8932 Watson, G, 6 art, C, Sept 16, scs.
10965 Watson, Jas, 15 art, M, Oct 15, scs.
6947 Watson, T, 99, I, Aug 26, dys.
9856 Wade, M, 14 art, D, Sept 20, dia.
8146 Walker, J, 2 art, D, Sept 8, dia.
8198 Wall, J, 64, I, Sept 8, dia.
7276 Warhurst, Samuel, 7 art, I, Aug 30, dia
8731 Washington, I, 76, G, July 21, scs.
5679 Washburn, H, 5 cav, D, Aug 14, scs.
2023 Wagner, C, 39, E, June 15, dia. c.
10686 Wagner, C, 93, K, Oct 11, scs.
11001 Warren, P, 7 art, G, Oct 16, uls.
6537 Warren, E, 22 cav, L, Aug 23, scs.
4120 Warren, Geo R, 2, F, July 28, scs.
11082 Warrell, E C,§ 57, I, Oct 17, scs.
11945 Waterman, S, 169, K, Nov 10, scs.
6978 Waldron, N, 146, A, Aug 27, dys.
7249 Walz, M, 14 art, I, Aug 30, dia.
6425 Walling, Geo, 76, B, Aug 22, scs.
6046 Watchler, J,§ 119, G, Aug 18, scs.
4000 Wails, C H, 108, K, July 27, dia.
3336 Walser, John, 15 art, D, July 15, dia.
1564 Walcott, G P, 67, D, June 2, des.
2294 Wales, J,§ 85, D, June 22, dia. c.
1637 West, James, 3 art, H, June 1, dia.
9572 West, T, 13 cav, F, Sept 23, dia.
3064 West, Wm, 152, E, July 25 scs.
 739 West, Jas.§ 2 cav, E, April 25, dys.
10556 Webster, L, 115, F, Oct 4, dia.
9731 Webster, G, 29, C, Sept 25, dia.
5593 Webster, E, 76, E, Aug 14, scs.
1598 Webster, Jas, 137, C, June 4, dia. c.
9889 Wendle, John, 7 art, E, Sept 27, scs.
9041 Wellstruff, C, 100, D, Sept 28, scs.
10013 Welch, W, 76, G, Sept 29, scs.
5030 Welch, C, 3 cav, B, Aug 8, dia.
8555 Welch, E G, 120, K, Sept 15, dia.
8208 Weil, E C, 164, B, Sept 8, dys.
7561 Welson, James H, 74, K, Sept 2, dys.
8177 Welch, C, 30, H, Sept 8, dia.
5181 Welch, E, 24 bat, Aug 9, dys.
6692 Welch, J, 5 cav, K, Aug 24, scs.
2310 Welsh, L, 146, B, June 22, dia. c.
8855 Welber, E G, 120, K, Sept 15, dia. e.
9428 Weaver, J, 1 cav, E, Sept 21, dia.
7078 Weaver, B S, 95, I, Aug 28, dia.
9448 Webber, C H, 85, C, Sept 21, dia.
9506 Westerfield, P S, 7 art, B, Sept 22, scs.
8731 Werting, John, 52, D, Sept 14, scs.
7987 Wellington, G R,§ 12 cav, A, Sept 6, dia
8204 Weeks, J, 7, G, Sept 8, dia.
7472 Wells, Jeff, 9, H, Sept 1, dia.
12036 Wells, E, 69, K, Nov 16, scs.
7647 Weismere, H, 82, I, Sept 3, ts. f.
4915 Wedder, N C, 184, E, Aug 6, dys.
11061 Wellder, C M, 22 cav, G, Oct 17, dys.
11397 Westbrook, D, 155, H, Oct 24, des.
6927 Weafer, Chas, 115, A, Aug 26, dia.
7256 Wertz, Jas, 12 cav, I, Aug 30, des.
6370 Webb, M E, 14 art, F, Aug 21, scs.
11127 Welch, J, 5 cav, D, Oct 18, dia. c.
6002 Weiber, J, 6 art, E, Aug 17, dia.
4272 Weller, W H, 85, E, July 29, dia.
3235 Westfall, John, 151, H, July 12.
 285 Weldon, Edson, 20 cav, M, M'ch 31, dys. e
 507 Westhrop, H, 125, B, April 12, dia. e.
6755 Webster H, 22 cav, A, Aug 24, scs.
10308 Weston, L, 115, F, Oct 4, scs.
7543 Whitmore, D, 140, I, Sept 2, dys.
10423 Wharton, J R, 5 cav, L, Oct 6, scs.
9743 Whittle, J C, 85, E, Sept 25, dys.
9578 Whertmour, M, 15 art, M, Sept 13, dia.
8611 Whipple, M, 22 cav, D, Sept 13, dia. c.
8680 White, Jas, 1 drag, D, Sept 13, scs.

11879 White, L, 8 art, G, Nov 6, dia.
3034 White, E, 10 cav, D, July 8, dys.
8792 Whiting, M, 85, D, Sept 15, scs.
7417 Whitney, John,§ 39, K, Aug 31, dia.
5207 Whitney, J, 104, E, Aug 10, dia. c.
10972 Whitman, J, 16, H Oct 15, scs.
12049 Whitmans, P, 66, E, Nov 16, scs.
11724 Whifbeck, J,‡20, D. Nov 1, dia. c.
6611 Wheeler, D, 147, H, Aug 23, dia. c.
5770 Whitmore, O B, 40, A, Aug 15, dys.
4155 Whitlock, Wm, 14 art, I, July 28, dia.
1133 Wilson, Jas, 132, K, May 16, pna.
8757 Wilson, John, 95, A, July 22, dia.
6832 Wilson, M, 2 art, H, Aug 25, scs.
11983 Wilson, W, 153, H, Nov 13, dys.
5870 Wilson, A J, 57, A, Aug 16, dia. c.
1645 Wilson, D, 46, H, June 5, dys.
6233 Windness, A, 15 art, C, Aug 20, wds.
4030 Williams, F, 125, A, July 27, dia.
4522 Williams, Ed, 42, A, Aug 2, dia.
11130 Williams, H, 2 cav, M, Oct 18, scs.
12697 Williams, S, 94, I, Feb 23, scs.
9516 Williams, L D, 85, G, Sept 22, dia.
8478 Wilcox. T E, 85, B, Sept 11, scs.
7945 Williams, Jas, 63, G, Sept 5, dia.
4603 Williams, Geo,‡ I cav, K, Aug 3, scs.
4701 Williams, John, 52, K, Aug 4, scs.
3947 Williams, O,§ 24 bat, July 25, dia.
1567 Williams, H, 9 s m, A, June 2, pna.
6861 Williams, L, 16, A, Aug 26, scs.
7112 Williams, J B, 24 cav, C, Aug 28, dys.
6219 Williams. C R, 85, E, Aug 20, ana.
3069 Winn, F, 20 cav, M, July 9, dia.
3273 Wicks, D, 63, D, July 13, dia. c.
1938 Wilcox, Geo, 12 cav, F, June 14, r. f.
2044 Wilcox, R, 14, June 15, dia.
9496 Wilcox. W, 43, G, Sept 21, dia. c.
3576 Wilcox, J, 85, D, July 19, scs.
11111 Wilcox. H R, 55, C, Oct 18, scs.
11428 Wilcox, C,§ 5 cav, G, Oct 24, dia. c.
12607 Wiley, I, 59, B, Feb 7, dia. c.
10122 Willis, J, 121, G, Oct I, scs.
9057 Willsey, D, 7 art, Sept 17, scs.
8729 Wiggins, James, 52, D, Sept 14, scs.
7980 Winn, James, 7 art, I, Sept 6, scs.
8208 Will, E C, 164, B, Sept 8, dys.
7622 Wiley, W, 115, G, Sept 2, dia. c.
3728 Wilkey, S, 8, B, July 21, dys.

10977 Wilkinson, J N,‡ 42, A, Oct 15, scs.
5663 Wicks, Frank, 1 art, K, Aug 14, dia.
11474 Winney, G A, 100, D, Oct 25, dys.
11520 Winter, G, 10 cav, L, Oct 26, acs.
11689 Wilds, J, 154, B, Oct 31, dia. c.
7122 Winser, J, 117, I, Aug 28, dia.
7581 Wood, E G, 24 bat, Sept 2, dia.
3607 Wood, F, 5 cav, I, July 19, dia.
9874 Wood, H, 115, G, Sept 27, scs.
10063 Wood, H, 15, D, Sept 30, scs.
9715 Wood, J, 10 cav, M, Sept 25, scs.
7686 Wood, John, 97, D, Sept 3, dia.
3881 Wood, M, 111, H, July 24, dia. c.
5039 Wood, J S, 6 art, A, Aug 8, dia. c.
9132 Woodmancy, D M, 3 cav, M Sept 18, dia.
10141 Wood, W J, 95, H, Oct 1, scs.
8382 Woodworth, B, 56, D, Sept 10, dys.
7884 Woodand, H, 1, I, Sept 5, ana.
5696 Woodhull, D F, 8 cav, E, Aug 15, scs.
12356 Wooley, G C, 7 art, K, Dec 30, scs.
11821 Wolf, T, 88, D, Nov 5, scs.
11031 Wolfe, W, 2 art, M, Oct 16, scs.
6130 Wolfe, Fred,‡ 24 cav, E, Aug 19, des.
591 Wolfran, A, 52, C, April 16, dia. c.
4847 Wright Charles S, 118, E, Aug 6, dia. c.
10941 Wright D, 4? G, Oct 14, scs.
5126 Wright, J J, 148, I, Aug 9, scs.
4281 Wuag, C, 39, E, July 30, dia.
7784 Wulslager, John, 85, G, Sept 4, dia.
4589 Wyatt, James, 147, G, Aug 2, dia.
7334 Wyncoop, G,§ 12 cav, H, Aug 30, scs.
2104 Winegardner, L, 18, G, June 17, dia. c.

7433 Yales, W G, 71, H, Sept 1, dia.
4984 Yencer, J D, 24 bat, Aug 7, dys.
12501 Yeomand, G, 7, A, Jan 21, dia.
6539 Young, C, 41, D, Aug 23, scs.
5598 Young, Charles, 15, C, Aug 14, scs.
8224 Young, E, 2 art, L, Sept 8, dia. c.
1306 Young, Eugene, 111, G, May 23, dia.
8733 Young, George, 22, H, Sept 14, dia.
6946 Young, J,§1 cav, B, Aug 26, dia.
7411 Young, T B, 148, A, Aug 31, dia.
10481 Yonker, W, 10 art, B, Oct 7, dia.

7480 Zaphan, H P, 7 art, E, Sept 1, scs.
12204 Zolber, F W, 40, D, Dec 1, scs.
12617 Zeigler, S, 145, G, Frb 9, scs.

NORTH CAROLLNA.

1596 Barker, J, 2, F, June 3, dys.
849 Briggs, Wilson, 1, A, May 3, dys. c.

275 Collowill. B, 2, F, March 31, c. f.
475 Cox, William C,§ 2, F, April 9, i. f.
864 Check, W F,‡2, F, May 8, dia. c.

144 Dunbar, Alex, 2, F, March 25, dia. c.

1057 Milier, J, drum, 2, D, May 13, phs.
10705 Masey, Henry, 7, Oct 11, dia.
11844 Moss, Wm, I, F, Nov 5, scs.

8690 Norfield, Warren, 1, G, Sept 14, dia.

370 Stone, Jno A, 2, F, April 5, dia. a.
2636 Smith, Jas, 2, F, June 29, dia. c.
4899 Smith, Geo, 2, E, Aug 5, scs.

333 Turner, F, 2, I, April 2, dia. a.
798 Turner, H, 1 col'd, I, April 29, dia. c.

204 Weeks, Nathan, 2, F, March 28, dia. a.
712 Williams, Thos, 2, D, April 24, dia.

OHIO.

12846 Akers, J W, 4, B, April 24, dia.
251 Arther, George, 7, B, March 30, dia.
789 Arrowsmith, W R, 45, K, April 28, dia. c.
1118 Ames, George, 100, K, May 15, dys.
1550 Allen, W, 45, B, June 1, dia. c.
1569 Alinger, D, 51, C, June 2, dia. c.
1724 Anderson, D, 111, B, June 8, dia.
1779 Augustus, T, 89, K, June 9, pna.
1805 Akers, A A, 94, F, June 10, ana.
2040 Aldridge, C W, 33, June 15, pna.
2935 Adam, Miller, 103, I, July 5, des.
8046 Anderson, R, 93, C, July 8, dia.

3197 Aldbrook, C W, 60, July 12, dia.
3485 Arthur, J C,§ 89, A, July 17, dia.
3852 Armebrish, A, 21, A, July 24, scs.
3932 Almond, A, 72, A, July, 25, dia.
4529 Arnold, Charles, 9 cav, G, Aug 2, dia.
4990 Ailes, T G, 20, I, Aug 7, dia.
5048 Andrews, Samuel, G, Aug 8, dia. c.
6422 Adams, E, 2 cav, C, Aug 22, scs.
7429 Allen, A B,‡ 121, C, Aug 31, scs.
7482 Alward, A, 135, B, Sept 1, i. s.
7736 Arthur, J, 69, I, Sept 3, des.
7843 Arne, I, 64, D, Sept 4, dia.

9818 Alown, A, 34, D, Sept 26, dia.
10393 Andrews, J R, 63, K, Oct 6, dia. c.
10425 Adams, J, 122, I, Oct 6, dia.
10874 Allen, James C, 91, F, Oct 13, scs.
11198 Andermill, John, 24, K, Oct 20, scs.
12495 Allen, J W,‡ I, G, Jan 20, scs.

188 Baiel, W T,§ 45, F, March 27, dia.
207 Bodin, Thomas S,§ 44, March 28, dys. a.
691 Beaver, George E, III, B, April 23. ts. f.
829 Beeman, Richard, 125, E, May 1, dys.
861 Biddinger, M, mus, 94, K, May 3, dia, c.
952 Branigan, James, 82, F, May 8, dia.
1094 Blangy, S, 70, B, May 14, dia. c.
1212 Botkins, A S, 45, G, May 19, des.
1226 Black, G W, 99, F, May 20, dia.
1366 Bates, L B, 1 cav, A, May 25, dys.
1368 Bodkin, W, 45, K, May 25, ana.
1376 Baldwin, N, 9 cav, F, May 26, dys.
1385 Bowers, James, 89, A, May 26, mas.
1468 Boyd, H J, 7, H, May 30, dia.
1602 Boman, John, 2, C, June 4, dia. c.
1609 Bryan, R, 16, C, June 4, dia. c.
1781 Balcom, D, 19, F, June 9, pna.
1919 Brownles, John, 7, I, June 14, ana.
1937 Brooks, J, 135, I, 135, I, June 14, dia. a.
1970 Bothin, W J, 45, F, June 15, ana.
1993 Bartholomew, E W, 205, C, June 15, des.
2065 Belding, F, 105, D, June 16, dia.
2067 Brookheart, W, 45, I, June 16, dia. c.
2087 Benor, H, 100, E, June 17, scs.
2110 Bishop, S, 49, K, June 17, dia. c.
2170 Berry, J C, 90, E, June 19, dia. c.
2264 Beers, A, 45, A, June 20, dia.
2292 Burnham, W, 1, art, K, June 21, ana.
2415 Bird, J, 45, A, June 24, dia. c.
2492 Bratt, G,§ 21, G, June 26, r, f.
2599 Boughfman, J, 39, C, June 28, ana.
2696 Brandon, John, 15, F, June 30, pna.
3058 Barnes, V H, 92, II, July 9, dia.
3245 Brown, Charles, 23, D, July 13, dia.
3299 Burns, M G, III, B, July 13, dia.
3608 Brackneck, H, 7 cav, A, July 19, dia.
3656 Bogart, John, 9, G, July 20, scs.
3766 Bontrell, C, 6, G, July 21, dia.
3756 Batch, O, 45, I, July 22, dia.
3831 Bowman, S, 51, K, July 23, dys.
4073 Brockway, M, 2 art D, July 27, dys.
4279 Boyle, W H, 11, H, July 30, dia.
4684 Britton, B H, 125, H, Aug 4, rhm.
4968 Berdy, M J, 45, D, Aug 7, scs.
5138 Buckle, John J, 126, E, Aug 9, dia.
5219 Brabham, George, 9 cav, B, Aug 10, scs.
5498 Baldwin, George, 9 cav G, Aug 13, dia. a.
5653 Bonestine, W H,‡ 107, I, Aug 14, cah.
5656 Burna, J M, 121, K, Aug 14, dia.
5758 Balmet, J, 19, I, Aug 15, scs.
5771 Brutch, E, 10, cav, I, Aug 15, dys.
5819 Bond, S F, 123, B, Aug 16, mas
5825 Boyle, H, 130, B, Aug 16, mas.
5937 Bower, F, 61, I, Aug 17, dys.
5985 Birch, L F, 31, H, Aug 17, mas.
6008 Bowman, A, 104 E, Aug 17, dia.
6020 Bright, N, 6, E, July 17, dys.
6152 Brown, G S, 111, F, Aug 18, scs.
6839 Baren, T J,‡ 89, A, Aug 25, scs.
7280 Barrett, S C, 26, F, Aug 30, dia.
7283 Bell, A, 70, B, Aug 30, dia.
7484 Baxter, P D, 121, D, Sept 1, sec.
7490 Brenning, C, 14, G, Sept 1, dys.
7529 Brown, W, 26, G, Sept 1, scs.
7806 Bear, E, 33, A, Sept 4, dys.
7983 Bender, C, 54, C, Sept 6, dia.
7993 Brown, M,‡ 110, F, Sept 6, dys.
7994 Barnes, T S, 31, B, Sept 6, scs.
8365 Benear, W A, 135, F, Sept 10, scs.
8376 Barston, G H, 135, F, Sept 10, scs.
8476 Brenner, N 60, F, Sept 11, scs.
8496 Barnes, A, 36, G Sept 11, dia.
8508 Blythe, C, 1, I, Sept 12, ana.
9509 Brinhomer, J, 65, C, Sept 12, dia.
8676 Brown, H H, 41, A, Sept 13, scs.

8693 Bell, James, 135, B, Sept 14 scs.
8872 Buckly, J G, 126, A, Sept 1, dys.
8939 Blessing, C, 9, F, Sept 16, scs.
9287 Baker, W C, 94, Sept 19, dia.
9446 Brookover, Geo, 135, B, Sept 21, dia.
9473 Briace, J R, 122, C, Sept 21, dia.
9625 Bradley, A, 101, A, Sept 24, dia.
9679 Blackman, S, 72, G, Sept 24, scs.
9897 Burehfield, EH, 14, Sept 27, dia.
9949 Beant, H T. 34, m i. D Sept 28, dia.
10120 Brewer, D C, 43, K, Oct 1,wds.
10199 Brown, E N, 21, E, Oct 2, scs.
10281 Brum, W H,§ 20, B, Oct 4, dia.
10581 Briggs, F, 11, G, Oct 10, dia.
11072 Bavmher, L G, 153, A Oct 17, scs.
11307 Boles, G, 112, H, Oct 22, scs.
11308 Brunker, J, H, K, Oct 22, scs.
11313 Burns, M 12, K, Oct 22, scs.
11626 Bricker, J J,§ 126, H, Oct 28, dia.
11920 Bumgardner, Joel, 3 C, Nov 8, scs.
11939 Barber, B, 10 cav, D, Nov 9 dia. c
12296 Bissel, J, 2 cav, E, Dec 16, scs.
12383 Beckley, G, 102, F, Jan 3, dia. c.
12524 Barnes, E H, 2, D, Jan 26, scs.
12641 Bower. A, 37, F, Feb 12, dia, a.
517 Blackwood, J, 92, I, April 12, dia. c.
12772 Bowens, W H, 100, A, March 13, pls.

5 Carpenter, White,‡ 92, D, March 4, pna.
458 Copeland, C, I, A, April 9, wds.
561 Coats, Geo H, 7 cav, I, April 15, dia.
563 Campbell, James, 7 cav, H, April 15, dia.
723 Callaway, Wm, 7 cav F, April 25, dia. c.
763 Coleman, G, 101, A, April 27, dia.
911 Chapman, Geo, 75, A, May 1, phs.
928 Crosser, M, 111, B, May 7, dia.
965 Corley, W C, 111, B, May 8 dia.
1269 Cruct. Wm. 89, C, May 21, dia.
1291 Collins, Thomas,‡ 21, G, May 22, dia. c.
1521 Capeheart, H, 70, I, May 31, dia.
1587 Clark, H S, 62, E, June 3, dia. c.
1631 Conklin, W, 121, B, June 5, pna.
1679 Clark, D V, 111, B, June 6, dia.
1900 Childers, Wm, 89, B, June 13, dia.
1945 Crocker, Geo, 1 art, A, June 14, dia.
1992 Christy, W, 89, K, June 15, dia. c.
2017 Curtis, N, 45, D, June 15, ana.
2025 Careahan, G M, 65, F, June 15, dia. c.
2101 Caldwell, J,§ 15, D, June 17, dia. a.
2162 Corneclius, L C,‡ 89, C, June 19, cas.
2207 Cochrane, James,§ 22, G, June 20, dia c.
2468 Church, E, 2, G, June 25, dia.
2578 Combston, J, 7 cav, L, June 27, dia. c.
2963 Cameron, H, 69, B, July 6, dia. c.
3002 Callahan, H, 34, C, July 7, dys.
3241 Covner, Geo M, 89, D, July 13, dia.
3307 Canard, J Q A, 14, G, July 13, dia.
3356 Cruer, J W, 60, B, July 15, dia. c.
3541 Cole, B, 82, A July 18, dia.
3578 Collins, T, 15, I July 19, dia.
3604 Cook, L B, 2 cav, C, July 19, dia.
3617 Clark, J C,§ 31, H, July 20, scs.
3774 Clayton, D J, 9 cav, D, July 22, scs.
3937 Cover. L, 49, B, July 25, dia. c.
4128 Clayton, J, 89, G, July 28, dia.
4342 Conway, J, 103, A, July 30, dia.
4493 Cordray, J J, 89, G, Aug 1, scs.
4865 Cahill, J N, 90, C, Aug 6, dia.
5105 Charles, F, 100, A, Aug 9, dia. c.
5451 Collyer, J, 11, G, Aug 12, dia.
5548 Chandler, M, 124, E, Aug 13, dia.
5922 Clark, James, 89, A, Aug 17, des.
6022 Cline, K, 111, B, Aug 17, dia.
6108 Church, Geo E,§ 14, C, Aug 18, dia.
6188 Chambers, R S, 89, A, Aug 19, scs.
6258 Copir, S A,‡ 33, C, Aug 20, ana.
6281 Conklin, J R, 45, L, Aug 20, dia. c.
6562 Craig, D,§ 2, D, Aug 23, cah.
7483 Caswell, G, 21, C, Sept 1, dys.
7486 Coons, David, 57, C, Sept 1, scs.
7495 Crooks, J M. 92, K, Sept 1, dia.
7695 Chard, C W, 2, H, Sept 3, dia.

1465 Greer, R J, 6, cav, C, May 29, dia.
2542 Gilanni, J, 35, K, June 27, dys.
2926 Garner, C, 1 Cav, K, July 5, dia.
3130 Goffe, P E, 19, K, July 10, dia. c.
3251 Gaunt, Wm,‡ 14, I July 13, dia.
3327 Gibson, R, 40, B, July 15, dia. c.
3962 Gingeng, P S,‡ 21, E, July 25, dia.
4037 Gillette, G W, 6, G, July 26, scs.
4242 Gilbert, J, 19, B, July 29, dia. c.
4301 Grafton, D, 118, D, July 30, brs.
4383 Graham, J W, 31, C, July 31, dia.
4445 Goffy, P, 113, G, Aug 1, ana.
4655 Gragrer, H, 125, H, Aug 3, scs.
4802 Greer, G G, 49, D, Aug 5, cah.
4902 Granbaugh, 85, scs.
6023 Gordon, Wm, 45, B, Aug 17, dia.
6075 Gallagher, James, 30, F, Aug 18, scs.
6207 Green, E, 4 cav, D, Aug 19, ts. f.
6346 Gordon, W, 10, G, Aug 21, dia.
6408 Gruff, A J, 13, E, Aug 22, cah.
6486 Gates, H, 13, G, Aug 22, dia.
6821 Groovs, L, 12, C, Aug 25, scs.
7111 Gilland, A, 27, F, Aug 28, wds.
8330 Goodrich, J S, 9, A, Sept 10, dia.
8367 Ganold, L, 60, A, Sept 10, scs.
9566 Gould, J M, 124, A, Sept 23, dia. c.
9813 Graft, P, 20 bat, Sept 26, dia.
9927 Galbraith, J S,§ 6 cav, M, Sept 28, dia.
11215 Ginther, J, 60, B, Oct 20, scs.
11850 Gardner, G, 1, K, Nov 5, scs.
12033 Glissin, A,§ 2 cav, M, Nov 15, scs.
12064 Gillenback, J, 77, E, Nov 17, scs.
12109 Goodbrath, C, 28, G, Oct 21, scs.
12560 Griffith, J H, 58, C, Jan 31, dia. c.
12842 Gassler, P, 64, A, April 22, dia. c.

35 Hall, J W, 4, A, March 9, pna.
295 Hochenburg, N, 45, C, April 1, dia.
420 Hanney, W F, 45, A, April 7, dia. c.
424 Hill, J,§ 7 cav, L, April 7, dia. c.
437 Henry, James, 7 cav, L, April 8, dia. c.
464 Haner, Jacob, 45, B, April 9, dia. c.
527 Hickcox, M R, 2 cav, B, April 13, pls.
580 Holdman, F, 1 bat, D, April 16, pna.
748 Hanning, Mark, 7 cav, I, April 26, dia.
748 Harvey, Charles, 76, E, April 26, dys. c.
875 Henry, G W, 95, E, May 4, dia.
949 Hawkins, W W,‡ 103, G, May 8, ts. f.
1129 Hudsonpilfer, R L, 7 cav, L, May 15, dia. c.
1354 Hend, George, 103, H, May 25, dia.
1390 Holloway, G W, I, C, May 28, dia. c.
1524 Harrison, J, 21, I May 31, dys. c.
1666 Hazlett, Wm, 2, K, June 6, i. f.
1822 Hull, S,§ 21, E, June 10, dia. c.
1979 Harris, E D,§ 99, I, June 15, dia.
2029 Hugle, John, 1 cav, C, June 15, dys.
2185 Humphreys, Wm, 45, C, June 19, pls.
2263 Hanley, C, 15, F, June 20, dia.
2300 Henderson, S W,§ 40, June 22, dia. c.
2369 Howard, J mus, 70, D, June 23, dia. c.
2424 Hayford, A E, 125, C, June 24, dia.
2597 Harrington, S J, 103, I, June 28, brs.
2671 Hurles, I, 126, C, June 30, i. f.
2775 Hurlburt, O, 14, H, July 2, dia. c.
2842 Hudison, J,‡ 111, B, July 3, dia.
3185 Hall, T,§ 2, H, July 11, dia.
31 Heaton, Ames, 45, F, April 20, s. p.
3388 Hudson, Wm, 74, G, July 16, dia.
3420 Hunt, W H, 113, G, July 16, dys.
3736 Harman, L, 9, F, July 21, dia.
4030 Hansbury, E A, 6, G, July 26, scs.
4408 Hendershot, John, 45, D, July 31, scs.
4411 Harris, J, 1, E, July 31, scs.
4506 Hartman, H, 13, K, Aug 1, dia. c.
4599 Harrison, J M, 105, M, Aug 3, dia. c.
4993 Hendrickson, O, 19, F, Aug 7, scs.
5293 Holibaugh, J A, 23, E, Aug 11, dia.
5296 Hatfield, George W, 126, K, Aug 11, dys.
5396 Holman, A, 68, K, Aug 12, wds.
5554 Honnill, F R, 9, G, Aug 13, dia.
5636 Hany, B F, 89, C, Aug 14, scs.
5819 Hicks, F, 40, H, Aug 16, dia.

5853 Hibbet, Wm, 21, D, Aug 19, mas.
5858 Hoit, P, 116, B, Aug 16, mas.
6058 Hamm, E J,‡ K, Aug 18, ces.
6123 Higgins, J W,§ 14, C, Aug 18, dia.
6174 Honser, W R, 89, K, Aug 18, ces.
6522 Hicks, J, 11, D, Aug 22, dys.
6625 Hughes, Henry, 33, A, Aug 23, scs.
6639 Henricks, E, 34, H, Aug 23, scs.
6647 Hartman, J, 2, K, Aug 23, scs.
6793 Herrig, N, 7 cav, D, Aug 25, cah.
6802 Hine, T E, 2 cav, D, Aug 25, dia.
7022 Hull, O, 89, B, Aug 27, dia.
7388 Hubbell, W A, 23, A, Aug 31, scs.
7446 Hurdnell, O, 72, C, Sept 1, ts. f.
7825 Holley, V H,§ 100, B, Sept 4, scs.
7946 Hughes, J, 12, E, Sept 5, dia.
8060 Herbolt, Daniel, 115, F, Sept 7, dia.
8067 Harper, J H, 60, I, Sept 7, dia.
8284 Halshult, A, 12, C, Sept 9, dia.
8481 Hechler, John, 36, G, Sept 11, scs.
8696 Hitchkock, G, 34, G, Sept 14, scs.
8725 Hifner, G, 86, C, Sept 14, scs.
9189 Hoyt, R, 7, K, Sept 18, scs.
9210 Hart, E, 10, H, Sept 19, scs.
9538 Hall, S, 126, F, Sept 20, scs.
9415 Hood, F, 13, F, Sept 21, dia.
9510 Hamilton, J, 13, A, Sept 22, dia.
9582 Hoover, J, 18, K, Sept 23, dia.
9622 Hurley, John C, 124, C, Sept 23, dia.
10094 Holmes, Wesley, 135, F, Sept 30, dia.
10207 Harrison, J, 2 cav, A, Oct 2, scs.
10208 Holcomb, L, 7, L, Oct 2, dia.
10225 Harkins, M, 60, D, Oct 2, dia.
10390 Hinton, Wm, 72, A, Oct 5, dia.
10492 Hererlin, B, 32, Oct 7, dia.
10518 Herbert, Wm, 4, L, Oct 8, scs.
10524 Homich, C, 110, D, Oct 8, scs.
10647 Herman, R, 135, F, Oct 11, scs.
11029 Hilyard, J, 98, F, Oct 16, dia.
11032 Hubber, D, 5, A, Oct 16, scs.
11053 Heymers, B, 2, G, Oct 17, scs.
11209 Hanard, J B, 123, C, Oct 20, dys.
11228 Hoyt, W B, 29, A, Oct 20, scs.
11335 Henderson, D, 122, H, Oct 23, scs.
11588 Hintz, D, 1, B, Oct 28, scs.
11592 Hutchins, G W, 135, A, Oct 28, scs.
11696 Hutchins, J W, 153, A, Oct 31, dia.
11856 Hayner, B, 135, A, Nov 6, scs.
11938 Hatfield, A G, 114, E, Nov 9, des.
12353 Hume, J A,‡ 32, F, Dec 29, mas.
12371 Haines, N S,‡ 72, E, Jan 1, scs.
12404 Hill, W L, 54, A, Jan 6, scs.
12446 Hill, E P, 89, G, Jan 13, scs.
12512 Hagerman, R, 33, B, Jan 23, dia.
12569 Hart, II C, 2, C, Feb 1, scs.
12611 Hagerly, D G, 72, E, Feb 7, des.
12743 Holtz, W, 101, I, March 7, des.
1129 Hudson, R L,‡ 7 cav, L, May 15, dia. c.
1132 Hank, George B, 7 cav, L, May 16, pna.
2607 Handa, L C, 92, E, June 28, dia. c.

1280 Irving, Ester, 114, H, May 22, f.
1967 Ingler, Wm, 31, C, June 14, dia. c.
7489 Imboden, J, 44, E, Sept 1, dys.
8744 Irwin, A, 1, I, Sept 14, des.
10700 Idold, A,§ 7 cav, C, Oct 11, dia.
12579 Isham, D, 89, G, Feb 3, scs.

354 Justice, George W, 45, B, April 2, dia. c.
1637 Johnson, J H, 98, D, June 5, ts. f.
3590 Jacobs, P O, 45, E, July 19, scs.
3754 Jones, R, 45, C, July 22, scs.
3903 Jones, S, 111, B, July 24, i. f,
4381 Jewell, I, 99, F, July 31, dys.
5120 Johnston, John W, 89, H, Aug 9, dia.
5508 Johnson, M, 126, C, Aug 13, dys.
5583 Jones, H, 40, G, Aug 14, dys. c.
5624 Jewell, W A, 126, G, Aug 14, dia.
5839 Jolly, G, 21, K, Aug 16, scs.
6265 Jelfries, H, 36, I, Aug 20, i. s.
6810 Jones, John,‡ 40, G, Aug 25, scs.
7308 Johnson, E, 124, I, Aug 30, dia.

1861 Jones, R, W, 118, F, Sept 5, dia.
8647 Jenk?is, Wm, 3 bat, Sept 13, scs.
8757 Johnson, D, 43, B, Sept 14, dia.
8760 Johnson, I, 51, A, Sept 14, dia.
9306 Jordan, A, 103, G, Sept 20, scs.
9700 Jones, I B, 30, M, Sept 25, dia.
9744 Johnson, I B, 2, C, Sept 25, dia. c.
9850 Jones, Win,‡ 84, B, Sept 27, dia.
11014 Jones, S D, 135, F, Oct 16, dys.
11203 Jennings, John,‡ 24, K, Oct 20, scs.
11942 Jones, G L, 105, G, Nov 9, scs.
12126 Jarvitt, W, 15, A, Nov 22, scs.
12231 Johnson, A S,§ 45, I, Dec 6, dia. c.
12335 Jones, W H, 2, C, Dec 26, scs.
12428 Jackson, S, 72, E, Jan 10, pls.
7947 Jacobs, H,‡ 26, F, Sept 6, dia.

836 Kelley, Josiah, 45, C, May 1, pna.
4615 Kimble, S, 98, A, Aug 1, des.
4715 Knight, J, 21, E, Aug 4, ana.
5381 Kelfey, E, 21, D, Aug 12, dia.
5448 Knidler, J, W, 33, H, Aug 12, dys.
5576 Kelly, H, I, I, Aug 14, dys.
6195 Kelsey, John,‡ 3, I, Aug 19, des.
7177 Kenedy, S J B, 45, E, Aug 29, scs.
7424 Kelley, G, 15, E, Oct 31, ana.
9377 Kelly, Wm, 46, C, Sept 20, ana.
9436 Kerr, J H, 122, C, Sept 21, dia.
9680 Knapp, J, 54, E, Sept 24, dia.
10139 Killar, J, 15, D, Oct 1, scs.
10607 Kirby A, 4 cav, A, Oct 10, scs.
10853 Keanshoff, L, 28, I, Oct 13, dia.
11055 Kerr, A, 13, I, Oct 17, dia. c.
11732 Kingkade, S, 18, C, Nov 2, scs.
12661 Kennedy, J, 70, K, Nov 16, brs.
12746 Kaler, J, 72, B, March 8, dia. c.
12802 Karch, J, 183, B, March 20, pls.
765 Kinney, John,‡ 67, E, April 27, dia. c.
2406 Knowlton, E, 6 cav, B, June 24, dia. c.
13 Kiger, J H,‡ 45, E, April 9, s. p.

834 Lowry, Jsmes, 49, I, May 1, dia.
935 Lewis, Frank, 103, D, May 7, dia. c.
1286 Larme, Charles, 45, K, May 22, dia. c.
1364 Larkin, Joseph, 1 art, May 25, dia. c.
1470 Logan, Frank, 89, F, May 30, dia.
1615 Logan, H, 6 cav, E, June 4, dia. c.
1828 Leonard, John, 21, A, June 11, scs.
2173 Lever, H B, 2, C, June 19, dys.
2372 Lisure, Samuel, 7, A, June 23, ts. f.
2426 Lemons, M, 89, E, June 24, ts. f.
3495 Lutz, M,‡ 14, C, July 18, scs.
3497 Love, John, 96, E, July 18, dia.
3649 Linsay, J, 21, D, July 20, dia.
4097 Lyon, L L, 1 art, E, July 27, dia.
4354 Law, S S, 124, I, July 31, dia.
4262 Lawsen, J,‡ 2, E, July 29, ana.
4641 Lucas, J, 89, H, Aug 3, ana.
4628 Legrand, D, 111, B, Aug 3, scs.
4692 Long, John, 45, H, Aug 4, dia.
5195 Lightfoot, Wm,‡ 9 cav, G, Aug 10, scs.
5246 Latta, W H, 89, H, Aug 10, dia. c.
5449 Lehigh, W, 22, B, Aug 12, dys.
5665 Lamphare, G W, 125, K, Aug 14, dia.
5676 Larisen A, 63, D, Aug 14, wds.
6066 Lowe, G H, 72, C, Aug 18, ces.
6344 Leasure, Isaac, 122, K, Aug 21, wds
7123 Leasure, F, 45, K, Aug 28, scs.
7744 Linway, J, ?, H, Sept 3, scs.
8016 Lambert, James, 89, A, Sept 6, dia.
8739 Lickliter, Henry, 135, B, Sept 14, scs.
8874 Lindsley, A K, 99, K, Sept 16, dia.
9336 Leonard, T M, 12, II, Sept 20, scs.
9358 Lovely, John, 100, K, Sept 20, dia.
9361 Lawyer, J B, 89, L, Sept 20, dia.
9419 Lefarer, W E, cit, Gardner, Athens Co.
10039 Laley,—, 28, Sept 29, dia.
11161 Lepe, A, 7, K, Oct 19, scs.
11196 Lantz, A W, 45, A, Oct 20, scs.
11344 Lochner, M, 72, E, Oct 23, scs.
11440 Laughlin, M W, 1, I, Oct 2, scs.
11490 Lips, F,‡ 2, H, Oct 26, scs.

11816 Lane, D, 91, D, Nov 4, scs.
12007 Lay, John, 123, K, Nov 19, scs.
12201 Lohmeyer, H, 35, K, Nov 30, shot by g'rd
12297 Livingood, C B,‡ 35, G, Dec 16, scs.
12525 Longstreet, W F, 31, A, Jan 26, scs.
12698 Lewis, D, 7, A, Jan 23, dia. a.
12826 Little, Wm, 175, D, April 7, dia.

66 Metcalf, Milo R, 100, E, March 19, c. f.
96 Malsbray, Asa, 40 cav, A, March 22, ts.
113 Moore, T J,§ 2, D, March 23, pna.
141 McKeever, James, 8, G, March 24, scs.
165 Mickey, Samuel, 45, E, March 26, dis.
215 Murphey, John, 7 cav, B, March 28, dis.
412 Mitchell, J, 120, F, April 7, dia.
444 McKindry, M, 7, I, April 9, dia.
575 Malone, R J,? 40, H, April 16, dia.
880 McCormick, J W E, 33, B, May 4, c. f.
984 Musser, D, 43, B, May 9, dia.
998 Meek, David, III, K, May 10, dia.
1262 McKnight, H, 11, G, May 21, dia.
1283 McMunny, George,§ 21, G, May 22, dia.
1630 Moore, Charles, 19, H, June 5, dia. c.
1849 Masters, Samuel, 17, I, June 11, ana.
1930 Martin, G, 105, F, June 14, ana.
2075 McCling, B, 7 cav, I, June 17, dia.
2139 Maloney, A, 4, H, June 18, dys.
2150 Mitchell, W H, 31, D, June 18, dia. c.
2290 Massey, J C, 33, A, June 21, dia. c.
2471 Mullin, J, 65, K, June 25, ana.
2667 McCloud, A, 35, G, June 29, dia.
2682 Miller, T, 4 cav, A, June 30, dys.
2743 McFarland, L, 2, I, July 1, dia.
2806 McInness, A, 45, B, July 3, dia.
2873 Moriatt, Joseph, 5, K, July 4, scs.
2991 Mitchell, James, 17, D, July 7, ana.
3104 Matone, L B, 7 cav, L, July 10, dia.
3122 Mitchell, C, 1, K, July 10, dia.
3137 Minshall, R, 45, C, July 10, ana.
3290 Mahin, B, 51, I, July 13, dys.
3491 Master, J, 13, A, July 17, dia.
3718 Miller, E, 4, July 21, dia.
4040 Marshall, T,‡ 21, G, July 26, dys.
4199 Myer, C, 21,‡ I, July 29, dia.
4252 Meek, J, 19, E, July 29, dys.
4298 McKell, M J,§ 89, D, July 30, ana.
4361 Mooney, James, 50, D, July 31, dia.
4421 Morris, C E, 11, H, July 31, scs.
4591 McCann, A, 33, C, Aug 3, dys.
4657 Maher, P, 7, E, Aug 3, dia.
4789 Martin, D, 3 cav, L, Aug 5, scs.
5738 McCabe, H, 12, C, Aug 15, dia.
5777 Mansen, W, 9, G, Aug 15, brs.
5883 McIntosh, D, 50, D, Aug 16, dia.
6026 Manahan, Thos, 21, D, Aug 18, dia.
6040 McKee, James, 51, A, Aug 18, des.
6055 McHugh, W S, 2, D, Aug 18, ces.
6063 McClair, P M, 27, A, Aug 18, dys.
6478 McCabe, J, 66, C, Aug 22, scs.
6841 McCormick, W P, 2, G, Aug 25, dia.
6855 McSorley, D, 49, F, Aug 26, dia.
6862 McCoy, J B, 98, A, Aug 26, dia.
6920 McDell, Wm, 89, K, Aug 26, dys.
7108 McDonald, J, 99, H, Aug 28, dia.
7133 Mason, J, 45, D, Aug 28, scs.
7136 More, John H, 60, D, Aug 28, dys.
7515 Myers, L H, 135, B, Sept 1, scs.
7896 Morris, J, 105, A, Sept 5, dia.
8021 Meek, Robert, 111, K, Sept 6, scs.
8044 Myers, A, 51, I, Sept 6, wd?.
8385 Maymer, R, 68, D, Sept 10, ts. f.
8408 McCabe, J, 70, C, Sept 11, scs.
8482 Morens, H, 51, A, Sept 11, scs.
8688 Moore, T H, 59, C, Sept 13, scs.
8726 Miller, Samuel, 135, F, Sept 14, sca.
8838 Mackrill, R, 50, I, Sept 15, scs.
8885 Manlig, S, 60, A, Sept 16, dia.
9039 Miller, C, 28, I, Sept 17, scs.
9096 McMillan, J F, 123, A, Sept 18, dia.
9241 McComb, J S, 14, K, Sept 19, scs.
9348 Maxwell, P, 12, A, Sept 20, dia.
8236 Moor, D D, 2, A, Sept 9, dia.

1773 Simmons, John, 22 bat, June 9, dia.
2220 Shannon, E, 35, A, June 20, scs.
2230 Stanett, J, 45, C, June 20, dia. c.
2376 Stiver, J, 93, C, June 23, dia. c.
2524 Smith, G W, H, K, June 26, dia.
2575 Sampson, C, 89, D, June 27, scs.
2638 Stults, P, 45, F, June 29, dia.
2783 Shiver, L, 31, B, July 2, pna.
2792 Smith, N H, 1, H, July 2, dia. c.
3116 Smith, G,§ 21, I, July 10, dia.
  42 Sabine, Alonzo, 100, A, May 11, s. p.
3252 Short, James,§ 4 cav, A, July 13, dia.
3288 Smith, D, 7, H, July 13, scs.
3361 Saffle, J, 2, E, July 15, scs.
3536 Steward, C S, 33, K, July 18, dia.
3602 Stevenson, D, 111, B, July 19, scs.
3298 Squires, Thomas, 49, C, July 20, dia.
3744 Snyder, Thomas,§ 9, G, July 21, dia. c.
3770 Smith, D‡ 2, I, July 22, dia. c.
3794 Sever, H H, 2, C, July 22, dys.
4249 Shephard, J H,‡ 2, E, July 29, dia.
4275 Smith, J B,§ 1, B, July 29, dia. c.
4294 Steward, J,§ 2, K, July 30, dia. c.
4745 Steiner, M J, 72, F, Aug 5, dia.
5018 Smock, A, 93, D, Aug 8, dia.
5054 Smarz, A, 93, E, Aug 8, scs.
5066 Shipple, John, 6 cav, G, Aug 8, ana.
5133 Scott, S E, 4, I, Aug 9, scs.
5287 Stevenson, John, 111, B, Aug 11, scs.
5330 Spegle, F, 14, D, Aug 11, scs.
5373 Schem, J, 101, K, Aug 11, dys.
5455 Stevens, G W, 101, K, Aug 12, scs.
5896 Sullivan, W, 78, D, Aug 16, dia. c.
6010 Staley, G, 89, A, Aug 17, dia.
6032 Smith, Wm, 9 cav, G, Aug 18, dia.
6178 Simpson, W J, 32, F, Aug 19, wds.
6199 Sheddy, G, 2, K, Aug 19, dys.
6214 Shaw, George W, 105, A, Aug 20, dia.
6253 Shoulder, E, 24, F, Aug 20, scs.
6779 Soper, P, 72, G, Aug 25, dys.
6870 Scarberry, O, 89, D, Aug 26, dia.
7034 Sutton, J, 4, A, Aug 27, dia.
7065 Shoemaker, J,§ 47, E, Aug 28, dys.
7436 Stinchear, F E,§ 101, A, Sept 1, dia.
7475 Shafer, J, 9, G, Sept 1, scs.
7540 Sell, Adam, 125, E, Sept 2, dia.
7788 Stewart, John S, 19, B, Sept 4, dia.
7897 Smith, H H, 2 cav, A, Sept 5, dia.
7986 Selb, Jacob, 28, Sept 6, dia.
8014 Shriver, George, 45, K, Sept 6, dia.
8015 Snider, James, 4, C, Sept 6, ana.
8156 Sturdevant, W, 72, A, Sept 8, des.
8197 Shrouds, J, 6 bat, Sept 8, dia.
8200 Stroufe, A, 7, E, Sept 8, scs.
8229 Shaw, W, 15, I, Sept 9, dia.
8300 Smith, N, 121, H, Sept 9, scs.
8319 Sheldon, W, 49, E, Sept 10, dia.
8422 Sullivan, John, 135, F, Sept 11, scs
8728 Sisson, P B, 18, H, Sept 14, scs.
8752 Sickles, J, 51, I, Sept 14, dia.
8914 Simmonds, S P, A, Sept 16, uls.
8931 Stull, G, 15, G, Sept 16, scs.
9009 Sharp, F S, 63, K, Sept 17, dia.
9244 Scmall, J D, 12, E, Sept 19, dia.
9386 Smith, L, 153, H, Sept 20, scs.
9645 Scott, J H, 33, H, Sept 24, gae.
9649 Skiver, J, 114, H, Sept 24, dia.
10250 Sheets, W, 81, A, Oct 3, ana.
10312 Spencer, S M, ‡ 89, E, Oct 4, scs.
10434 Shingle, D, 2 cav, L, Oct 6, dia.
10437 Stanford, P W,§ 2 cav, A, Oct 6, dia.
10576 Stonehecks, J D, 51, F, Oct 9, scs.
10618 Schafer, P, 101, I, Oct 10, dia.
10703 Stouts, Samson, 2, F Oct 11, scs.
10833 Sheppard, John, 34, D, Oct 13, scs.
11139 Shork, H, 72, F, Oct 17, scs.
11146 Smith, G A,‡ 45, F, Oct 19, scs.
11249 Sullivan, F, 76, C, Oct 21, dia.
11433 Swaney, E, 124, A, Oct 24, scs.
11579 Smith, P, 69, I, Oct 28, scs.
11595 Sapp, W N,§ 20, E, Oct 28, dia.
11711 Spiker, J, 122, Nov 1, scs.

11797 Shaler, F,‡ 72, E, Nov 4, scs.
12105 Sly, F, 89, G, Nov 20, scs.
12281 Singer, J, 6, G, Dec 13, scs.
12305 Sweet, M,§ 49, F, Dec 18, scs.
12441 Shoemaker, C, 8, F, Jan 12, pls.
12538 Stewart, A F, 2, D, Jan 27, dia. c.
12562 Sponcerlar, George, 71, B, Jan 31, dia
12668 Shorter, W, 89, K, Feb 17, dia. c.
12769 Sloan, L, 123, D, March 13, dia. c.
12789 Stroup, S, 50, B, March 17, dia. c.
12793 Seeley, N, 132, D, March 18, dia.
12810 Scott, R, 75, G, March 24, dia.

  730 Tweede, R, 1 cav, A, April 25, dia.
  743 Trescott, Samuel, 2, C, April 26, dia.
  999 Trimmer, Wm, 40, H, May 10, dys.
1196 Turney, U S, 2 cav, G, May 18, dys.
1496 Thomas, Wm, 10 cav, M, May 30, r.
2860 Thomas, W B, 89, C, July 4, dia.
4784 Thompson, J, 2, E, Aug 5, dia.
4951 Toroman, W R, 13, E, Aug 7, scs.
5356 Tierney, W, 1 art, L, Aug 11, dia.
5552 Tensley, M, 90, B, Aug 13, scs.
5668 Terilliger, N, 12, C, Aug 14, scs.
6330 Taaner, A,§ 32, G, Aug 21, wds.
7224 Thompson, V B, 26, C, Aug 29, dia.
7246 Turner, S B, 45, B, Aug 30, cah.
7640 Thomas, James, 44, C, Sept 2, dia.
8850 Talbert, R, 135, F, Sept 15, ts. f.
9774 Thomas, N, 103, B, Sept 26, scs.
9945 Townsend, J, 26, C, Sept 28, dia.
10471 Tattman, B, 153, C, Oct 7, dia.
10800 Tinway, P, 93, Oct 12, dia.
11820 Townsley, E M,§ 89, B, Nov ?, ?s.
12577 Tensdale, T H, 2 cav, E, Feb ?, pls.

12251 Uchre, S, 12, E, Dec 9, scs.

2194 Vining, W H H, 45, G, June 1?, dia. c.
3902 Valentine, C, 123, H, July 24, scs.
4450 Vaugh, B, 125, F, Aug 1, dia.
4497 Vangrider, H, 103, H, Aug 1, dia.
5263 Vatier, J F, 6 cav, Aug 10, dia.
6170 Vail, John L,§ 17, C, Aug 19, ces.
6859 Vanaman, M, 21, E, Aug 26, scs.
6985 Vanderveer, A, 6, H, Aug 27, dia.
7756 Victor, H, 1 art, D, Sept 4, gae.
9576 Volis, J, 34, H, Sept 23, scs.
10252 Vail, N, 12, C, Oct 3, scs.
10389 Vail, G M, 7, D, Oct 5, scs.
10472 Van Fleet, H, 14, I, Oct 7, scs.
11095 Vankirk, G, 135, B, Oct 18, scs.
11097 Van Malley, J M, 89, G, Oct 18, des.
1255k Vanhorn, S, 9 cav, C, Jan 30, scs.

  77 Wiley, Samuel, 82, A, March 5, pna.
 185 Wickman, Wm, 111, B, March 27, ts.
 779 Wooley, John, 45, B, April 28, dia. c.
 807 Werts, Louis, 45, D, April 30, dip.
1085 Wood, William, 89, A, May 14, dia. c.
1449 Wentling, Joseph, 100, K, May 29, ana
1604 Wood, Joseph, 15, B, June 4, dys.
1836 Wilkinson, W,‡ 89, D, June 11, dys.
1913 Wilson, James, 93, I, June 13, dia. c.
2020 Way, John, 44, I, June 15, dia.
2041 Windgrove, S R, 15, June 15, dia. c.
2172 Webb, E, 45, A, June 19, dia.
2358 Walters, F, 9, E, June 23, dia. c.
2536 Wing, F, 2 cav, M, June 26, dia. c.
2815 Willis, A, 89, A, July 3, dia.
2840 Wroten, L, 89, H, July 3, dys. c.
3188 Williams, D, 90, A, July 12, ana.
  34 Wright, Wm, 7, H, April 24, s. p.
3310 White, H, 15, A, July 15, r. f.
3325 Whitton, G, 75, K, July 14, dia. c
4214 West, J B, 89, B, July 29, dia.
4681 Witt, John T, 93, G, Aug 4, dys.
4688 Wou, J,‡ 111, B, Aug 4, scs.
4695 Wile, A,‡ 33, D, Aug 4, dys.
5121 Winder, P, 70, D, Aug 9, scs.
5211 Wood, N L, 4 cav, L, Aug 10, dia.
5726 Winters, George, 145, K, Aug 15, scs.

6314 Wainwrignt, S G, 89, G, Aug 20, scs.
6318 Wisser, F J, 35, A, Aug 20, dia.
6362 Wistman, N, 9 cav, G, Aug 21, dia.
6397 Wilson, E, 4, A, Aug 21, des.
6700 Watson, G, 21, A, Aug 24, dys.
6761 Wood, S, 123, A, Aug 25, dia.
7056 Wood, W H, 59, E, Aug 28, dia.
7373 Wyatt, J, 90, B, Aug 31, dia.
7582 Wentworth, L 72, A, Sept 1, dia. c.
8298 Wright, J S, 89, E, Sept 9, dia. c.
8396 Warner, 7, 14, C, Sept 10, scs.
8907 Wyckman, D, 73, G, Sept 16, scs.
9384 Worte, J, 116, Sept 20, scs.
9527 Woodruff, J M, 135, F, Sept 22, dia.
9691 Wagner, J, 93, F, Sept 24, dia.
0007 Whitney, E, 21, K, Sept 29, ana.
0230 Williams, Orland, 7 cav, K, Oct 2, dia.
10309 Weaver, M, 72, H, Oct 4, gae.
10402 Ward, Francis, 21, H, Oct 6, dys.
10464 Whitehead, A B, 33, E, Oct 7, scs.
10528 Wiley, A, 26, I, Oct 8, scs.
10733 White, I, 73, E, Oct 11, scs.
10844 Westbrook, R L,‡ 135, F, Oct 13, dia.
11013 Walker, C, 65, I, Oct 16, scs.

11034 Waldron, H, 14, A, Oct 16, scs.
11418 Williams, S M, 60, F, Oct 24, dia. c.
11770 Worthen, D, 122, B, Nov 3, scs.
11874 Weason, J, 36, F, Nov 6, scs.
12042 Wickham, J, 14, H, Nov 16, scs.
12073 White, R M, 15, D, Nov 18, scs.
12158 Warner, B F, 35, E, Nov 25, scs.
12584 Whitaker, E, 72, A, Feb 4, rhm.
12722 Wella, E, 57, A, March 3, rhm.
12759 Winklet, T, McL's sq'n, March 12, scs.
12786 Warner, M, 102, G, March 16, dia. a.
4833 Webricks, Joseph H, 9, G, Aug 6, dys.

638 Yuterler, W A, 45, E, April 20, dia.
5477 Younker, S, 80, F, Aug 13, scs.
6068 Young, John, 7, E, Aug 18, dys.
7816 Yeager, John, 7 cav, B, Sept 4, dia.
7816 Young, J, 9, F, Sept 5, dia.
10583 Young, W, 6, G, Oct 10, dys.
12659 Young, W, 15, A, Feb 16, pls.

3225 Zubers, J M, 100, B, July 12.
11253 Zink, A J, 72, E, Oct 21, scs.

PENNSYLVANIA.

224 Attwood, Abr'm, 18 cav, I, March 29, dia.
250 Armidster, M, 4 cav, A, March 30, dia.
468 Ackerman, C, 8, B, April 9, dia. c.
758 Arb, Simon, 4 cav, C, April 27, dys.
846 Allbeck, G B,§ 52, F, May 3, wds.
975 Algert, H K, 54, F, May 9, brs.
1382 Arble, Thomas, 13 cav, A, May 26, dia. c.
1837 Ajt, M, 21, K, June 11, i. s.
2348 Akers, George, 90, H, June 23, dia. c.
2398 Allison, E, 55, K, June 24, dys.
2547 Anderson, D,§ 103, K, June 27, ts. f.
2648 Able, J, 54, F, June 29, dys.
2956 Amagart, Eli,‡ 103, F, July 6, dia. c.
3018 Ackley, G B, 3 art, B, July 7, dia.
3317 Alexander, M, 1 cav, F, July 14, dys.
3967 Ardray, J F,§ 13, F, July 25, dia.
4055 Anderson, J,‡ 79, I, July 27, dys.
4143 Aches, T J, 7, H, July 28, dia.
4149 Alcorn, George W, 145, F, July 28, dia.
4195 Archart, H, 51, C, July 29, dia. c.
4673 Allen, C, 8 cav, K, Aug 4, scs.
4973 Andertin, J, 4 cav, L, Aug 7, dia.
5286 Aler, B, 103, D, Aug 11, dia. c.
5511 Ault, J L, 101, C, Aug 13, scs.
5862 Armstrong, Chas,§ 4 cav, C, Aug 16, dia.
6029 Anersen, John, 91, C, Aug 18, mas.
7163 Arnold, Daniel, 184, C, Aug 29, dia.
7887 Angstedt, Geo W, 1, F, Sept 5, dys.
8185 Allen, J L, 101, I, Sept 8, scs.
8232 Ambler, C, 13 cav, D, Sept 9, dia. c.
8388 Alexander, W, 2 reserve, I, Sept 10, dia.
8653 Armstrong, A, 7, K, Sept 13, dia. c.
8655 Arnold, L, 73, A, Sept 13, scs.
8765 Altimus, Wm, 7, E, Sept 14, dia.
1743 Ainley, Wm, 3 cav, E, June 8, ana.
9150 Alcorn, J W, 18 cav, D, Sept 18, scs.
9896 Allison, D B, 55, K, Sept 27, dia.
10487 Andersen, A, 135, F, Oct 7, dia.
10570 Allen, D, 126, A, Oct 9, dia. c.
10823 Allin S, 7 cav, H, Oct 13 wds.
11419 Applebay, T M, 149, K, Oct 24, scs.
11607 Antill, J, 61, I, Oct 28, scs.
11710 Anger, W, 118, Nov 1, scs.
11852 Afflerk, J, 2, F, Nov 6, scs.
11860 Amandt, J, 184, D, Nov 6, scs.
12520 Atchinson, W P, 142, F, Jan 25, scs.

228 Bull, Frank, 4 cav, H, March 29, dia. c.
249 Burton, Lafayette, 18 cav, D, M'ch 30, dys.
332 Briggs, Andrew, 13 cav, H, April 2, dia. c.
427 Beagler, A, 27, C, April 8, dia. c.
543 Breel, Jacob, 27, H, April 14, pna.
569 Black, James A, 14 cav, D, April 15, pna

661 Bradley, Alex, 3 cav, F, April 21, dia.
671 Burns, Samuel, 73, K, April 22, ts. f.
673 Barra, J, 54, F, April 22, dia.
822 Bayne, Wm, 145, I, May 1, dys.
874 Bradley, M, 3 art, A, May 4, dys.
897 Brown, Henry, 90, H, May 5, dia. c.
938 Brown, D, 4, C, May 7, dia. c.
974 Batting, Isaac,‡ 8 cav, H, May 9, dia.
1046 Baker, J D, 57, F, May 12, dia. c.
1188 Butler, Wm, 90, B, May 18, scs.
1300 Boyd, Thomas, 9, D, May 23, dia. c.
1309 Bryson, J, 2 cav, D, May 23, dys.
1327 Brining, J, 13 cav, B, May 24, dys.
1375 Burney, J, 13 cav, G, May 26, dys.
1393 Brown, J B, 4 cav, K, May 26, dia. c.
1576 Boman, Samuel, 3 art, B, June 3, dia.
1601 Berfert, R, 103, B, June 4, ts. f.
1654 Brumley, Geo, 4 cav, I, June 6, dia.
1790 Butler, J D, 76, B, June 10, dia.
1859 Berkhawn, H, 73, G, June 12, scs.
1872 Brooks, D S, 79, June 12, dia.
1923 Brian, Charles, 183, F, June 14, dia. c.
1999 Bixter, R, 73, C, June 15, dia.
2026 Burns, Owen, 13 cav, C, June 15, dia.
2046 Bigler, M, 4 cav, June 15, dia.
2127 Brown, C, 3 cav, B, June 17, dia.
2134 Buckhannan, W, 3 art, B, June 18, des.
2180 Ball, L, 26, K, June 19, dia.
2236 Barr, J T, 4 cav, K, June 20, dia. c.
2323 Baker, Henry, 18 cav, I, June 22, dia.
2483 Bisel, John,§ 18 cav, K, June 25, dia. c.
2538 Balsley, Wm, 20 cav, F, June 26, dia. a
2610 Brown, M, 14 cav, C, June 28, dia.
2727 Brenn, J, 73, K, July 1, dys.
2733 Bolt, J H,§ 18 cav, E, July 1, dia. c.
2741 Beam, John, 76, E, July 1, scs.
2816 Burns, John, 13 cav, A, July 3, dia. c.
2913 Bish, J, 103, F, July 5, dys.
2918 Belford, John, 145, F, July 5, dia.
3005 Bryan, P, 3 art, A, July 7, dia.
3019 Barr, S, 103, G, July 7, dia.
3027 Braney, J, 48, E, July 7, dia.
3051 Barnes, W,‡ 101, H, July 8, scs.
3097 Butler, L J, 118, E, July 10, pna.
3109 Brunt, A, 119, G, July 10, ana.
3216 Beraine, A A, 101, B, July 12.
3294 Burns, James, 103, F, July 14, dia.
3442 Brinton, J, 157, D, July 17, dys.
3477 Baker, Wm, 103, F, July 17, dia.
3535 Burnside, J,§ 57, H, July 18, dia.
3600 Black, W O, 103, G, July 19, dia. c.
3693 Billig, J L, 3 cav, H, July 21, scs.
3716 Brenlinger, Wm R,§ 4 cav, D, July 21, scs.

7282 Day, S,‡ H, A, Aug 30, gae.
7360 Dively, J, 110, C, Aug 31, dys.
7488 Dilks, C, 1, K, Sept 1, dia.
7651 Dewell, Samuel, 50, G, Sept 3, dia.
7828 Dougherty, J, 184, D, Sept 4, dia.
8211 Dixon, J, 105, B, Sept 8, ts. f.
8334 Doherty, J,§ 73, F, Sept 10, scs.
8569 Duff, J,§ 4 cav, B, Sept 12, dia.
8579 Dougherty, F, 90, C, Sept 12, dia.
8718 Durharse, B, 11 cav, G, Sept 14, scs.
8828 Donnelly, J, 97, H, Sept 15, scs.
8887 Dean, R, 2 cav, M, Sept 15, scs.
9109 Davidson, C, 90, G, Sept 18, dia.
9146 Driscoll, N C, 26, I, Sept 18, scs.
9191 Duffie, J, 52, F, Sept 18, ts. f.
9289 Delaney, E, 7, G, Sept 19, scs.
10004 Davidson, G,‡ 12, K, Sept 29, scs.
10193 Dougherty, M, 3 cav, D, Oct 2, uls.
10436 Durkale, John, 1 cav, F, Oct 6, dia.
10917 Dalzell, J G, 139, I, Oct 14, scs.
11295 Derry, Frederick, 20, C, Oct 22, scs.
11350 Dichell, Espy, 55, D, Oct 23, scs.
11394 Dewitt, M, 1 cav, E, Oct 24, scs.
11628 Davidson, S, 184, A, Oct 28, scs.
11988 Dickens, Charles, 2 art, A, Oct 13, dia.
12136 Dalrysuffle, J E, 145, K, Oct 23, scs.
12399 Donley, P, 120, G, Jan 5, wds.
12575 Deeds, J, 13 cav, H, Feb 2, dia.
11181 Dixon, B, 145, K, Oct 19, scs.

972 Ellers, Henry, 13 cav, H, May 9, dia.
1081 Eisley, John, 18 cav, K, May 14, dia.
1436 Engle, Peter, 14 cav, K, May 28, dia.
2105 Elliott, John, 13 cav, F, June 17, dys.
2794 Elliott, J, 69, D, July 2, dia. c.
3038 Erwin, C, 78, D, July 8, des.
3052 Epsey, James,§ 145, H, July 9, r. f.
3295 Elliott, J P, 103, D, July 14, dia.
3823 Ebright, Benj, 9 cav, A, July 23, scs.
4278 Eaton, Nat, 1 rifle, E, July 30, dia.
4761 Elenberger, P, 145, D, Aug 5, dia.
5687 Eunies, Andrew, 145, K, Aug 15, scs.
6424 Ewetts, James, 103, G, Aug 22, scs.
6607 Ellis, F, 53, G, Aug 23, dia. c.
6872 Eckles, E, 77, E, Aug 26, dys.
6889 Ensley, C, 184, A, Aug 26, dys.
7300 Ellis, H H, 18 cav, I, Aug 30, dia.
7657 Egan, John, 55, C, Sept 3, des.
8066 Exline, Jacob, 55, K, Sept 7, dia.
8543 Eichnor, C, 143, F, Sept 12, scs.
8964 Earlman, J, 7, K, Sept 16, dia. c.
10009 Elfrey, B S, 7, K, Sept 29, dia. c.
10694 Elliott, John H, 83, D, Oct 11, dia.
10731 Erdibach, C,‡ 5 cav, B, Oct 11, dia.
10799 Ervingfelts, Jacob, 187, D, Oct 12, dia. c.
11834 Edgar, W H,§ 7, G, Nov 5, scs.
11838 Erebedier, J,§ 5, B, Nov 5, scs.
12001 Etters, D, 145, D, Nov 14, scs.
12673 Ebhart, J,‡ 87, E, Feb 18, dia. c.
9490 English, J C, 100, K, Sept 21, dia.

200 Fluhr, John, 73, D, March 28, dia.
511 Fich, John, 83, B, April 12, dia. c.
791 Fry, L,§ 4 cav, D, April 12, dia.
1010 Fuller, H, 13 cav, H, May 10, dia. c.
1098 Fifer, Charles, 27, I, May 14, ers.
1431 Fry, Alexander,‡ 4 cav, B, May 28, dia. c.
1728 Fink, Peter, 73, C, June 8, scs.
1957 Freeman, W M,§ 4 art, A, June 14, dys. a.
2078 Fulton, Thomas A, 103, H, June 17, dia.
2099 Friday, S D, 101, H, June 17, dia. c.
2147 Fish, Charles, W, 101, B, June 18, dia. c.
2155 Farley, James, 54, F, June 18, dia. c.
2261 Fox, George, 78, E, June 21, dia.
2477 Flay, L, 26, G, June 25, dia.
2530 Funkhanna, Jas, 101, C, June 26, ts.
2537 Fatleam, A, 50, D, June 26, dia. c.
2594 Fagartus, T, 90, K, June 28, scs.
2853 Fancy, George, 13 cav, F, July 4, scs.
3088 Ford, M, 53, K, July 9, scs.
3258 Fisher, B M,‡ 101, H, July 13, dia.
3582 French, A, 2 art, G, July 19, dys.

3742 Forsyth, J, 18 cav, H, July 21, dia. c.
3870 Fingley, John, 14 cav, D, July 24, dia.
4307 Flick, L, 184, G, July 30, dia.
4439 Filey, J H, 53, E, July 31, wds.
4452 Foreman, G S,‡ 1 cav, B, Aug 1, pna.
4521 Flasharge, B, 12 cav, A, Aug 2, dia.
4586 Flynn, M, 13 cav, B, Aug 2, dia.
4642 Fewer, E, 87, H, Aug 3, dys.
4668 File, C, 145, D, Aug 4, scs.
5062 Fish, J, 85, Aug 8, dys.
5172 Fleming, W‡, 97, E, Aug 9, scs.
5586 Flickinger, Jno, 50, B, Aug 14, scs.
5788 Ferry, W, 79, A, Aug 15, ana.
5873 Fee, George M, 103, G, Aug 16, scs.
6092 Faiss, A, 145, E, Aug 18, ces.
6134 Farman, E, 57, E, Aug 19, ces.
6135 Feltharsen, 145, G, Aug 19, scs.
6180 Fantlenger, F, 53, K, Aug 19, scs.
6365 Fanen, James, F, 7 reserve, G, Aug 21, dia.
6396 Finlaugh, S, 14 cav, G, Aug 21, dys.
6649 Fox, R, 155, H, Aug 23, scs.
6675 Fritzman, J W,§ 18, K, Aug 24, scs.
6694 Finlin, Thomas, 143, G, Aug 24, dia.
6881 Fuller, G, 2 cav, A, Aug 26, dia.
6884 Frederick, L, 148, B, Aug 26, scs.
6890 French, James, 101, H, Aug 26, dys.
6892 Ford, Thomas, 7, 1, Aug 26, dys.
7041 Fullerton, E, 99, E, Aug 27, scs.
7097 Fester, John, 103, B, Aug 28, des.
7169 Fisher, W 54, I, Aug 29, dia. c.
7198 Fry, S, 101, E, Aug 29, dia. c.
7575 Fitzgerald, M, 145, K, Sept 2, dia. c.
7588 Fahy, John, 13 cav, B, Sept 2, dys.
7776 Fritz, D,‡ 18 cav, K, Sept 4, dys.
8006 Felter, H M,§ 13 cav, K, Sept 6, dys.
8149 Fullerton, J, 118, I, Sept 8, ana.
8175 Fetterman, J, 48, H, Sept 8, dia.
8321 Francis, N, 69, G, Sept 10 dia.
8631 Fagan, R, 118, F, Sept 13, scs.
9062 Fisher, C, 4 cav, Sept 17, dia.
9099 Floyd, B, 67, K, Sept 18, dia.
9232 Farry, J C, 107, H, Sept 19, scs.
9869 Faith, Alexander, 183, C, Sept 27, scs.
10176 Fessenden, N E, 149, F, Oct 1, dia.
10408 Fingley, S, 14, B, Oct 6, dia.
10639 Fisher, W, 101, E, Oct 10, dys.
10667 Flynn, S,‡ 76, C, Oct 11, scs.
10688 Free, J, 145, H, Oct 11, dia.
11026 Flemming, J, 97, E, Oct 16, scs.
11112 Flanney, J, 106, K, Oct 18, scs.
11164 Ferguson, J R, 11 cav, D, Oct 19, scs.
11367 Fox, M, 8 cav, H, Oct 23, scs.
11378 Frill, D, 55, C, Oct 24, scs.
11601 Ferguson, John, 134, A, Oct 28, scs.
11811 Frishi, H, 115, E, Nov 4, scs.
11916 Freed, S, 53, B, Nov 8, scs.
11962 Fairbanks, E, 140, A, Nov 11, scs.
12000 Fagley, C,‡ 14 cav, I, Nov 14, scs.
12025 Foust, S L, 149, 1, Nov 15, scs.
12207 Foster, C W, 76, B, Dec 1, scs.
12244 Falkenstine, F, 148, C, Dec 8, scs.
12336 Fruce, J, 52, A, Dec 26, scs.
12445 Fisk, J, 67, H, Jan 13, scs.
12605 Faile, W, D, 20 cav, A, Feb 7, des.

71 Goodman, Robt, 13 cav, M, March 19, dia.
131 Gesse, Christian, 54, F, March 23, c. f.
314 Graffoll, Wm, 73, B, April 2, pna.
529 Guley, J, 145, G, April 12, dia.
573 Green, Wm, 3 cav, A, April 16, dia. c.
968 Garman, B, 18, cav, E, April 9, dys.
1001 Greer, J A,‡ 3 cav, E, May 10, dys.
1008 Graham, W J, 4, C, May 10, dia. c.
1063 Goodman, Henry, 27, I, May 13, pna.
1302 Gray, M, 7, B, May 23, dia. c.
1373 Gilbert, John, 29, G, May 25, dia. c.
1399 Gilroy, Berney, 73, F, May 26, scs.
1528 Getts, B, 84, G, May 31, ana.
1649 Griffil, G W, 13 cav, L, June 5, dia.
1761 Genst, J W, 57, I, June 9, dia.
1793 Gardner (negro), 8, F, June 10, dia
1911 Gensle, John, 19 cav, F, June 13, dia. c.

4685 McKeral, James, 14, K, Aug 3, dia.
4710 Mathews, C W,‡ 145, B, Aug 4, scs.
4734 Moore, M, 71, I, Aug 4, scs.
4796 McDevitt, J, 3 art, D, Aug 5, dia.
4824 Miller, H, 14 cav, I, Aug 5, dia.
4876 Mills, Wm, 150, G, Aug 6, scs.
4898 Muldany, M, 96, K, Aug 6, dia.
5068 Martain, John, 103, E, Aug 8, dys.
5069 Measler, James, 108, E, Aug 8, scs.
5139 McCaffrey, John, h s, 3 art, A, Aug 9, dia.
5159 Martin, C, 8 cav, A, Aug 9, scs.
5266 Marey, H F, 103, F, Aug 10, dys.
5291 Mohr, J R, 14, G, Aug 11, dia.
5415 McCarty, Dennis, 101, K, Aug 12, i. f.
5433 McGee, J, 14, H, Aug 12, ana.
5595 Mickelson, B, 16 cav, B, Aug 14, dys.
5642 McClough, L C, 18, C, Aug 14, ana.
5704 Miller, John, 101, G, Aug 15, dys.
6728 McCann, John, 3 art, A, Ang 15, scs.
5781 Miller, S, 143, B, Aug 15, dia.
5809 Montgomery, R, 62, A, Aug 16, ana.
5868 McQuillen, A, 6 art, L, Aug 16, dia.
5893 McCuller, S, 4 cav, B, Aug 16, dia.
5926 Mulchy, J A, 50, D, Aug 17, dia.
5988 Mann, James,‡ 119, G, Aug 17, dia. c.
6014 McPherson, D, 103, F, Aug 17, scs.
6088 Moore, C, 103, G, Aug 18, scs.
6148 McCracker, J, 53, K, Aug 19, r. f.
6294 McLaughlin, Jas, 4 cav, A, Aug 20, scs.
6441 McWilliams, H, 82, I, Aug 22, scs.
5480 Martin, John, 103, D, Aug 22, dia.
6532 McGan, J, 18 cav, Aug 23, dia.
6664 McKee, ——, 144, C, Aug 24, scs.
6689 Manner, M, 73, K, Aug 24, dia.
6910 McGlann, H, 143, B, Aug 26, dia.
6925 McGuigan, H C, 7, K, Aug 26, dia.
7026 Marks, P, 143, B, Aug 27, dys.
7061 Moore, M J, 107, Aug 28, dys.
7107 Moyer, Wm M, 55, H, Aug 28, dia.
7119 Miller, John L, 53, K, Aug 28, i. f.
7127 McAfee, Jas, 72, F, Aug 28, scs.
7175 Moore, Thomas, 69, D, Aug 29, scs.
7263 Martin, John, 77, C, Aug 30, dys.
7255 Musser, John, 77, D, Aug 30, scs.
7305 Moser, S, 103, E, Aug 30, dys.
7333 Morris, John, 183, G, Aug 30, dia.
7407 Marchin, Wm, 50, E, Aug 31, scs.
7512 Millinger, John H, 7, C, Sept 1, dys.
7602 Moorhead, J S, 103, D, Sept 2, dia.
7719 Myers, H, 9, A, Sept 3, scs.
7875 Mayer, W, 8, M, Sept 5, dia.
7925 Mays, N J, 103, H, Sept 5, dia.
8027 Murphy, A, 13 cav, I, Sept 6, ts. f.
8047 McKnight, J, 18 cav, I, Sept 6, dia. c.
8122 Miller, J,‡ 101, C, Sept 8, scs.
8123 Mullings, W, 145, G, Sept 8, scs.
8128 Munager, W, 13 cav, I, Sept 8, dia.
8134 Mehaffey, J M, 16 cav, B, Sept 8, scs
8153 McCantley, W, 2 art, A, Sept 8, dia.
8158 McLane, T, 12, E, Sept 8, scs.
8194 McKink, J,‡ 119, D, Sept 8, dia.
8216 Mansfield, J, 101, G, Sept 8, dia.
8322 Myers, A, 118, I, Sept 10, dia.
8462 Magill, H, 103, I, Sept 11, scs.
8506 Morrison, J, 146, E, Sept 12, scs.
8627 McKinney, D, 90, C, Sept 13, scs.
8691 Moritze, A, 118, D, Sept 14, dia. c.
8802 McCulloyt, ——, 101, E, Sept 15, scs.
9071 Maynard, A, 3 art, Sept 17, dia.
9060 McCall, Wm, 22 cav, B, Sept 18, dia.
9228 McCullough, G, 138, K, Sept 19, wds.
9270 Mayhan, F, 20 cav, Sept 19, scs.
9315 Marsh, W, 149, K, Sept 20, scs.
9339 Meyers, J A, 138, C, Sept 20, scs.
9526 McQuigley, John, 101, C, Sept 22, scs.
9583 Mead, H J, 184, B, Sept 23, scs.
9588 Martin, J, 17 cav, C, Sept 23, scs.
9644 Morris. J, 54, I, Sept 24, scs.
9646 Morgan, J E, 2, A, Sept 24, gae.
9651 McCook, B, 118, A, Sept 24, scs.
9761 McMurray, Wm, 1 cav, I, Sept 25, scs.
9871 Masen, John, 112, A, Sept 27, scs.

4678 McKern's, 8, 73, A, Aug 2, ana.
10050 Mesin, James,‡ 9, F, Sept 30, scs.
10060 Morgan, C, 45, A, Sept 30, scs.
10119 McClany, J, 101, C, Oct 1, scs.
10154 McElroy, Wm, 13 cav, L, Oct 1, dia.
10306 Meese, J, 48, A, Oct 4, dia.
10396 McGraw, John, 3 art, A, Oct 6, scs.
10407 Miller, H, 79, K, Oct 6, scs.
10486 Miller, Washington, 18 cav, C, Oct 7, dia
10610 McKearney, J W, 118, K, Oct 10, scs
10620 McClief, Wm, 7, A, Oct 10, scs
10641 Marker, W H, 118, D, Oct 10, dia.
10678 Martin, J P, 7, I, Oct 11, scs.
10684 Miller, James, 7, I, Oct 11, dia.
10803 Mattis, Aaron, 138, Oct 12, scs.
10825 Moore, C H, 13 cav, C, Oct 13, dys.
10929 Mortin, Geo H, 108, I, Oct 14, scs.
10981 Maxwell, S, 14 cav, B, Oct 15, scs.
10981 Moses, W, 16 cav, H, Oct 16, scs.
10993 McKuight, Jas, 118, K, Oct 16, scs.
11081 Mitchell, J O, 55, H, Oct 18, scs.
11142 Mansfield, George, 101, I, Oct 19, r. f.
11229 McClay, J, 11 cav, D, Oct 20, scs.
11305 McBride, J, 2 cav, H, Oct 22, scs.
11326 Marshall, L, 184, A, Oct 23, scs.
11387 Moore, S, 101, F, Oct 24, scs.
11459 Moore, J, 13 cav, B, Oct 25, scs.
11464 MeNelse, J H,‡ 100, E, Sept 26, scs.
11542 Miller, F, 54, K, Oct 27, scs.
11655 Midz, J, 20 cav, A, Oct 30, scs.
11658 Menk, W, 12 cav, F, Oct 30, scs.
11683 Morrow, J C, serg maj, 101, E, Oct 31, scs
11684 McCann, J, 11 cav, L, Oct 31, scs.
11686 Moore, W, 184, B, Oct 31, dia.
11692 Muligan, J, 7, H, Oct 31, pna.
11909 McCune, J, 67, E, Nov 8, scs.
11913 McClush, N, 9, E, Nov 8, scs.
11982 Manee, M, 53, H, Nov 13, scs.
12008 McCray, J, 145, A, Nov 14, scs.
12088 Maher, D, 118, E, Nov 18, scs.
12103 Miller, W, 31, I, Nov 22, gae.
12248 Murray, W, 14 cav, H, Dec 8, scs.
12326 McIntire, J, 55, C, Dec 24, scs.
12334 Myers, A D, 52, A, Dec 26, scs.
12554 Matthews, J, 6 cav, F, Jan 30, scs.
12595 Maloy, J M, 184, D, Feb 5, scs.
12625 McGenger, J, 20, C, Feb 9, dia. c.
12606 Myers, H, 87, E, Feb 23, dia. c.
12771 McDonald, ——, 9, G, March 13, des.
12806 McGarrett, R W, 103, F, Feb 21, dia. c.

1134 Nicholson, John, 3 cav, H, May 16, des.
1298 Nelson, Wm, 76, H, May 23, dia. c.
2832 Nolti, Wm, 6, F, July 3, dia. c.
3658 Newell, G S, 183, A, July 20, ana.
4246 Nicholson, W, 1 cav, H, July 20, dys.
4489 Nelson, George, 2, K, Aug 1, scs.
4936 Nayier, G W,§ 13 cav, L, Aug 7, dia.
5109 Nichols, D A, 125, D, Aug 9, scs.
6001 Neal, H G, 90, B, Aug 17, dia.
6011 Nickle, C, 37, G, Aug 17, dia.
6702 Nickem, James, 77, G, Aug 24, scs.
8154 Naylor, S, 20 cav, H, Sept 8, dia.
8907 Noble, J, 73, D, Sept 16, scs.
9424 Nice, Isaac, 11, L, Sept 21, dia.
9488 Neff, J, 4 cav, D, Sept 21, scs.
10146 Nelson, G, 55, A, Oct 1, dia.
10286 Nelson, J A, 145, G, Oct 4, dia.
10704 Newberry, John, 20 cav, A, Oct 5, gae.
11107 Nelson, A, 160, E, Oct 18, dia. c.
11264 Noble, Thomas, 19 cav, G, Oct 21, dia. a
11776 Nichols, G, 20, C, Nov 3, dia.

414 Osborne, S R, 4, K, April 7, dys.
622 Ogelsby, J, 4 cav, K, April 19, dia.
1318 O'Brien, P, 13, A, May 23, dia. c.
1409 Ottinger, J, 8 cav, I, May 27, dia.
1897 O'Nell, John,§ 69, June 12, dia. c.
2589 Oswald, Stephen, 55, G, June 28, dia. a
3161 O'Conor, ——, 83, July 11, scs.
3199 O'Neil, J, 63, I, July 12, ana.
3704 Olmar, H,§ 2 cav, H, July 21, dia

3861 O Connor, H, 49, E, July 24, dys.
4161 Owens, G H, 7, A, July 28, dia.
5119 Offleback, Z, 90, K, Aug 9, dia. c.
5184 Oliver, W, 103, D, Aug 9, dia.
5939 O'Hara, M, 101, E, Aug 17, scs.
6254 O'Connell, Wm, 183, G, Aug 20, scs.
6535 O'Hara, John, 150, E, Aug 23, scs.
6658 Oiler, Samuel, 103, G, Aug 24, dys.
6908 O'Rourke, Charles, 109, C, Aug 26, dys.
7105 Otto, John, 5 cav, B, Aug 28, dia.
7552 ——, J M,§ 101, I, Sept 2, scs.
—— ——, 184, A, Sept 18, scs.
—— ——, N V B, 149, K, Sept 20, dia.
9330 Owens, E, 50, D, Sept 20, scs.
10805 Osborn, E,‡ 11 cav, A, Oct 13, scs.

30 Peck, Albert, 57, K, March 9, pna.
62 Patterson, Robt, 2 res, E, March 18, ts. f.
125 Parker, Jas M,‡ 76, B, March 23, dys. c.
500 Petrisky, H, 54, F, April 12, dia.
1110 Patterson, Thos, 3 cav, A, May 15, dia. c.
1119 Patent, Thos, 73, G, May 15, dia.
1258 Powell, Wm, 14 cav, D, May 21, dia.
1556 Powers, John, 26, I, June 2, dia. c.
1780 Preso, Thomas, 26, E, June 9, pna.
1884 Powell, Frank, 18, June 12, dia. c.
2566 Page, J, 183, G, June 27, ts. f.
2590 Porter, David, 101, H, June 28, dia.
2903 Parsons, J T, 103, D, July 5, dia.
3197 Painter, J G, 26, F, July 11, dia.
3445 Painter, S, 63, A, July 17, scs.
4049 Patterson, R, 101, H, July 27, dia.
4157 Pickett, J C, 3 cav, A, July 28, dia.
4177 Pratt, F, 14 cav, I, July 28, dys.
4191 Plymeer, W, 20 cav, B, July 28, dia.
4415 Page, John, 112, A, July 31, dia.
4473 Powell, H, 102, H, Aug 1, scs.
5323 Prosser, J, 63, Aug 11, scs.
5579 Pyers, Isaac, 72, G, Aug 14, dia.
5610 Phillips, Jas B, 101, I, Aug 14, dia.
5947 Parish, J A, 184, Aug 17, scs.
6341 Preans, H, 149, K, Aug 21, scs.
6439 Palmer, H, 140, D, Aug 22, scs.
6527 Poole, G, 52, B, Aug 22, dia.
6536 Pifer, M, 13, G, Aug 23, scs.
6574 Phillips, J W, 1 cav, F, Aug 23, scs.
6843 Peterson, G, 103, D, Aug 25, scs.
6844 Penn, John, 5 cav, E, Aug 25, scs.
6885 Pattin, H W, 2 art, F, Aug 26, dia. c.
7118 Potts, Edward, 183, H, Aug 28, brs.
7232 Perkins, N, 103, D, Aug 29, dia. c.
8030 Powell, A T, 149, C, Sept 6, dia.
8160 Pricht, F, 87, H, Sept 8, scs.
8763 Peck, C W, 145, H, Sept 14, dia.
8877 Persil, Frederick, 101, Sept 15, scs.
9220 Palmer, A, 143, D, Sept 19, ts. f.
9684 Perego, W, 143, G, Sept 24, scs.
9754 Phipps, J H, 57, E, Sept 25, scs.
10074 Price, G, 106, H, Sept 30, dia.
10573 Penstock, A, 144, B, Oct 9, dia.
10858 Powell, I, 101, I, Oct 13, scs.
11168 Price, O, 109, C, Oct 19, scs.
11261 Phav, M, 69, C, Oct 21, scs.
11637 Phillips, F, 61, K, Oct 28, scs.
11737 Pees, M T, 145, H, Nov 2, dia.
11883 Penn, J, 18 cav, I, Nov 6, scs.
11918 Phelps, W, 4 cav, G, Nov 8, scs.
11328 Porterfield, J K, 5 cav, M, Oct 23, scs.
12075 Pemer, W, 18, C, Nov 18, scs.
12191 Pryor, Wm, H, C, Nov 28, scs.
12359 Poleman, H, 1 cav, F, Dec 30, scs.
12378 Perry, H, 121, C, Jan 2, dys.
12388 Pritchett, J, 72, C, Jan 3, des.
12479 Potter, B F, 148, I, Jan 17, scs.

5756 Quinby, L C, 76, E, Aug 24, scs.

47 Reed, Sam'l, 4 cav, D, March 15, pna.
126 Robertson, J, 119, K, March 23, dia.
132 Rosenburg, Henry, 49, K, March 24, dia.
171 Reign, John, 33, K, March 26, ana.
308 Richpeder, A, 13, B, April 2, dia.

610 Ray, Wm, 8 cav, F, April 18, dia.
847 Rhinehart, J, 3 cav, D, May 3, ana.
895 Russell, F, 4, D, May 5, dia.
907 Rhinebolt, J, 18 cav, I, May 5, dia. c.
940 Robinson, C W,§ 150, E, May 7, dia. c.
1152 Randall, H, 4 cav, H, May 16, dia. c.
1218 Rigney, Chas, 4 cav, G, May 19, dys.
1454 Raleigh, A, 51, G, May 29, dia. c.
1485 Rudolph, S,‡ 13 cav, K, May 30, dia. c.
1599 Rhine, George, 63, I, June 4, dia.
1624 Rosenburg, H, 13 cav, H, June 4, dia. c.
1719 Raymond, John,§ 18 cav, H, June 8, scs.
1803 Rheems, A,§ 73, I, June 10, des.
1833 Ramsay, J D, 103, F, June 11, scs.
1922 Rush, S, 18, G, June 14, dia.
1942 Robinson, Wm, 77, D, June 14, dia. c.
2225 Roush, Peter, 101, E, June 20, dia. c.
2528 Rupert, F, 2 cav, H, June 26, dia.
2602 Roat, J, 54, F, June 28, scs.
2735 Rhodes, F, 79, E, July 1, dia.
2911 Rock, J E, 5, M, July 5, brs.
2979 Regart, John, 13 cav, E, July 7, dia.
2103 Ray, A,§ 77, E, June 17, dia. c.
3024 Rugh, M J, 103, D, July 7, scs.
3270 Robins, R, 69, B, July 13, dia.
3468 Ransom, H, 148, I, July 17, dys.
3827 Rinner, L, 5 cav, A, July 23, dys.
4074 Ringwalk, F J, 79, H, July 27, dys.
4241 Roger, L, 115, L, July 29, ts. f.
4309 Rogers, C, 73, C, July 30, dia.
4476 Ray, James R, 184, B, Aug 1, dys.
4507 Riese, S, 103, D, Aug 1, dia. c.
4844 Riche, James, 103, B, Aug 6, dia.
4940 Ruthfer, J, 2 art, F, Aug 7, dia.
5319 Rice, Sam'l, 101, K, Aug 11, cah.
5389 Ross, David, 103, B, Aug 12, dia.
5430 Robinson, John, 99, D, Aug 12, dia.
5537 Rose, B, 13, I, Aug 13, dys.
5800 Robins, J, 2 cav, M, Aug 15, ts. f.
5879 Reider, H, 7 cav, L, Aug 16, dia.
5894 Richards, E, 143, E, Aug 16, dia.
5912 Rease, Jacob, 103, B, Aug 17, dia.
5940 Richards, John,‡ 1 cav, G, Aug 17, scs.
6321 Robbins, G, 106, G, Aug 21, pna.
6373 Roger, John L, 110, H, Aug 21, scs.
6520 Reynolds, J, 14, H, Aug 22, scs.
6725 Rowe, E,‡ 103, A, Aug 24, dia.
6777 Rangardener, J, 149, H, Aug 25, dia.
6789 Richards, G, 13 cav, A, Aug 25, dia.
6790 Runels, John, 6 cav, L, Aug 25, dys.
6822 Rum, A, 188, C, Aug 25, scs.
6838 Reese, D, 148, K, Aug 25, gae.
6896 Raiff, T, 1, A, Aug 26, scs.
6933 Richardson, ——, 61, Aug 26, dia.
7067 Reese, D, 143, F, Aug 28, dys.
7202 Rueff, J, 103, F, Aug 29, dia.
7292 Redmire, H, 98, B, Aug 30, dia.
7293 Robins, George, 62, A, Aug 30, dia.
7410 Richardson, H, 103, K, Aug 31, dia.
7467 Richard, D, 18 cav, D, Sept 1, scs.
7716 Rice, E, 7, B, Sept 3, dia.
7738 Roads, Frederick, 101, E, Sept 3, dys.
8139 Rathburn, K, 2, F, Sept 8, scs.
8540 Russell, S A,‡ 79, A, Sept 12, scs.
8545 Ray, A, 149, D, Sept 12, dys.
8602 Richards, J, 106, H, Sept 12, scs.
8635 Rhangmen, G,§ 138, D, Sept 13, scs.
8742 Root, D, 48, B, Sept 14, dia.
9019 Ret, George, 18, A, Sept 17, dia.
9272 Ramsay, J I, 149, Sept 19, dia.
9585 Richie, H, H, F, Sept 3, scs.
9590 Renamer, W H, 87, H, Sept 23, dia.
9612 Richards, John, 113, D, Sept 23, dia.
9653 Reed, R, 103, A, Sept 24, dia.
9766 Ramsay, R, 84, D, Sept 25, scs.
9882 Richards, J, 53, K, Sept 27, dia.
10174 Reed, J, 55, A, Oct 1, dia.
10863 Ramsay, Wm, 87, B, Oct 13, scs.
10622 Reedy, E T,§ 87, B, Oct 10, dia. c.
10935 Roundabush, H B, 55, A, Oct 14, dia.
10947 Rockwell, A, 2 cav, L, Oct 14, dia.
11071 Raeff, J B, 72, E, Oct 17, scs.

11115 Rinkle, John A, 20, A, Oct 18, scs.
11293 Rolston, J, 28, F, Oct 22, scs.
11147 Rudy, J, 13, F, Oct 19, scs.
11444 Riffle, S G,‡ 189, C, Oct 25, scs.
11566 Richardson, A, 144, E, Oct 27, scs.
11868 Rowland, N, 111, F, Nov 6, scs.
12008 Rapp, A E, 18 cav, I Nov 15, scs.
12048 Ruth, B S, 23, I, Nov 16, scs.
12206 Rothe, C, 101, A, Dec 1, scs.
12355 Reese, D, 7, A, Dec 29, dia.
12372 Reed, W S, 128, H, Jan 1, des.

377 Smith, M D, 18, B, April 5, dia. a.
788 Smith, Geo, 5 cav, H, April 28, dia. c.
881 Smith, Wm, 4, A, May 4, dia. c.
882 Smith, T, 19, G, May 4, dia.
921 Steffler, W J,§ 12 cav, G, May 6, dia.
1014 Serena, H, 4 cav, D, May 10, dys.
1030 Shebert, Gotheb, 73, C, May 11, dys.
1058 Spilyfiter, A, 54, F, May 13, ana.
1105 Sullivan, D, 101, K, May 15, dia. c.
1114 Shindle, S R,§ 140, K, May 15, dia.
1155 Stearnes, E K, 14 cav, A, May 16, dia. c.
1169 Sloat, D, 76, I, May 16, dia.
1175 Scott, Wm, 4, B, May 16, dia. c.
1216 Severn, C, 139, A, May 19, dia.
1256 Sammoris, B,§ 2 cav, B, May 21, dia.
1349 Smith, Charles, 26, A, May 24, ana.
1453 Schlenbough, C, 4 cav, G, May 29, dia. c.
1503 Smith, Martin, 18 cav, H, May 31, dia. c.
1535 Stone, Samuel, 26, F, June 1, des.
1543 Shoemaker, M,§ 13 cav, H, June 1, dia.
1605 Swearer, G, 13, H, June 4, dia. c.
1620 Schiefeit, Jacob, 54, F, June 4, dia.
1632 Schmar, R, 45, F, June 5, dia.
1963 Smith, D, 11 cav, H, June 14, dys.
2033 Slough, H, 53, June 15, ts. f.
2070 Stevens, A, 13 cav, M, June 16, dys.
2121 Sherwood, C H,§ 4 cav, M, June 17, dia. c.
2123 Stall, Samuel, 75, D, June 17, pna.
2126 Say, J R, 4 cav, K, June 17, dia. c.
2163 Steel, J S, 7 cav, F, June 19, dia.
2259 Scoles, M, 27, K, June 21, dia. c.
2331 Sims, B, 14 cav, G, June 22, dia. c.
2412 Shoop, Jacob, 2, M, June 24, ts. f.
2622 Springer, John, 101, E, June 28, ts. f.
2650 Stewart, J B, 103, A, June 29, dia. c.
2725 Scott, Allen, 150, H, July 1, dys.
2738 Schimgert, J, 73, G, July 1, scs.
2791 Shimer, J A, 13 cav, A, July 2, dia. c.
2864 Scott, Wm (negro), 8, D, July 4, dia.
2905 Stump, A, 11, I, July 5, dys.
2941 Smith, Jacob, 51, H, July 6, dia.
2982 Shaw, W, 140, B, July 7, dia. c.
2999 Smulley, Jno, 112, K, July 7, r. f.
3057 Sutton, R M, 103, I July 9, dia.
3113 Sweet, H, 57, K, July 10, dia.
3136 Shoemaker, M, 148, G, July 10, scs.
3154 Sillers, Wm, 77, D, July 11, scs.
3214 Stone, W F, 53, G, July 12, scs.
3480 Swelser, J, 103, D, July 17, dia. c.
3567 Smalley, L, 58, K, July 19, dia.
3568 Stevens, S G, 150, H, July 19, scs.
3586 Sickles, Daniel, 116, K, July 19, dys.
3632 Serders, J S, 142, K, July 20, dys.
3670 Stopper, Wm, 16, B, July 20, ana.
3763 Stillenberger, F, 172, F, July 22, dys.
3775 Strance D, 11, H, July 22, scs.
3855 Smith, J, 19, F, July 24, dia. c.
3906 Smith, O C,§ 77, G, July 24, dia. c.
3956 Seilk, A, 144, D, July 25, dys.
3960 Sullivan, T, 7, F, July 25, dia.
4006 Smith, F, 64, K, July 26, ana.
4009 Shater, J H, 84, E, July 26, dia. c.
4012 Shapley, Geo, 103, G, July 26, dys.
4043 Strichley, C, 53, H, July 27, dia.
4064 Shrively, E S, 19 cav, M, July 27, dys.
4113 Sheppard, E, 145, G, July 28, dia.
4164 Smith, S W, 101, B, July 28, dia. c.
4213 Shaffer, Peter, 52, F, July 29, dia.
4223 Shister, F, 3 cav, A, July 29, scs.
4228 Stein, J, 7, G, July 29, dia.

4274 Sloan, J, 11, E, July 29, ana.
4285 Shone, P, 4 cav, D, July 30, scs.
4345 Stobbs, W W,‡ 101, E, July, 30, dia.
4348 Scott, A, 22 cav, F, July 31, des.
4351 Seundler, J, 67, A, July 31, dia.
4372 Smith, P, 72, C, July 31, dia.
4566 Sale, Thomas, 15, M, Aug 2, scs.
4775 Shink, James, 81, F, Aug 5, scs.
4791 Sullivan, Ed, 67 H, Aug 5, scs.
4797 Sear, C, 14 cav, L, Aug 5, dia.
4845 Shember, Jno, 11 cav, D, Aug 6, dia.
4928 Slicker, J, 77, D, Aug 6, scs.
4931 Sheit, P, 61, G, Aug 7, dia.
4945 Swarts, P,‡ 27, I, Aug 7, dys.
5160 Stiner, John, 22 cav, G, Aug 9, scs.
5189 Striker, F, 14 cav, C, Aug 9, scs.
5215 Sworeland, Wm, 184, A, Aug 10, dia.
5232 Speck, A, 118, A, Aug 10, dys.
5411 Shaffer, Daniel, 13 cav, F, Aug 12, pna.
5529 Shangrost, A, 103, D, Aug 12, dia.
5437 Shears, J S, 149, K, Aug 12, dia.
5463 Stibbs, W, 56, H, Aug 13, dys.
5494 Shape, F, 18 cav, A, Aug 13, dia.
5603 Somerfield, W, 69, E, Aug 14, dia.
5700 Stineback, A, 150, C, Aug 15, dia.
5730 Spears, W M,§ 2 cav, K, Aug 15, pna.
5874 Sheppard, N, 79, F, Aug 16, scs.
5965 Shultz, F, 13 cav, K, Aug 17, dia.
6205 Shoop, G, 103, K, Aug 19, scs.
6289 Smith, H, 26, K, Aug 20, ts. f.
6337 Smith, W, 18 cav, B, Aug 21, des.
6382 Swager, M, 101, F, Aug 21, dia.
6436 Spain, Thos, 118, H, Aug 22, dia.
6523 Stover, J, 49, F, Aug 22, scs.
6526 Stahler, S, 149, G, Aug 22, ana.
6534 Snyder, John, 118, C, Aug 23, scs.
6584 Sloate, E, 50, D, Aug 23, dys.
6595 Shirley, Henry, 105, I, Aug 23, dia. c.
6669 Sherwood, P, 84, I, Aug 24, dys.
6776 Shellito, R, 150, C, Aug 25, dys.
6823 Spain, Richard, 118, H, Aug 25, ana.
6829 Sturgess, W A,‡ 79, G, Aug 25, scs.
6880 Stahler, D, 4 cav, A, Aug 26, ana.
7029 Strickler, J W, 11, F, Aug 27, dys.
7106 Smith, John F, 55, C, Aug 28, ics.
7137 Sloan, J M, 18 cav, D, Aug 28, dys.
7141 Springer, J, 103, F, Aug 29, dys.
7262 Shriver, B, 18 cav, K, Aug 30, dia.
7302 Singer, J, 2 art, A, Aug 30, dia.
7358 Scoleton, J, 53, F, Aug 31, scs.
7363 Sweeney, D, 14 cav, E, Aug 31, dia. c.
7379 Scott, W B, 4 cav, D, Aug 31, dia.
7631 Streetman, J, 7, E, Sept 2, dia.
7638 Steele, J, 62, M, Sept 2, dia.
7648 Speneer, Geo, 20, C, Sept 3, dia.
7662 Snyder, M S, 183, A, Sept 3, dys.
7705 Swartz, Geo, 5 cav, A, Sept 3, r. f.
7770 Stockhouse, D,‡ 18 cav, I, Sept 4, dia.
7905 Sellers, H, 149, G, Sept 5, dia.
7939 Shultz, John, 4 cav, I, Sept 5, ana.
7969 Smith, A C, 7, F, Sept 6, dia.
8038 Simpson, T, 53, K, Sept 6, dia.
8103 Stump, J, 105, I, Sept 7, dia.
8112 Slade, E,‡ 150, H, Sept 7, scs.
8444 Shirk, M B, 142, A, Sept 11, scs.
8567 Simons, Wm H, 76, K, Sept 12, scs.
8659 Spould, E, 90, E, Sept 13, scs.
8773 Smith, Wm, 2, K, Sept 14, gae.
8795 Stella, J F, 15, B, Sept 15, dia.
9296 Signall, —,‡ 79, H, Sept 19, scs.
9012 Steadman, W, 54, F, Sept 17, dia.
9123 Schably, J, 54, A, Sept 18, dia. c.
9138 Shoup, S, 16 cav, B, Sept 18, dia. c.
9310 Smith, Charles, 7, H, Sept 20, dia.
9365 Stebins, Z, 7, H, Sept 20, dia.
9411 Scott, D, 149, G, Sept 21, scs.
9567 Snyder, A, 148, I, Sept 23, dia.
9593 Sternholt, Wm, 38, Sept 23, dia.
9742 Supple, C M,‡ 63, B, Sept 25, dys.
9780 Surplus, W,§ 13 cav, L, Sept 26, dia.
9890 Siherk, Christian, 145, Sept 27, scs.
9698 Sweeny, W P, 13 cav, Sept 27, scs.

9912 Sanford, C, 69 H, Sept 28, ana.
9985 Sheppard, C,§ 118, E, Sept 29, scs.
10088 Sloan, P, 115, A, Aug 30, scs.
10132 Smith, J S, 22 cav, B, Oct 1, dia.
10299 Strong, H, 55, E, Oct 4, scs.
10323 Smith, E, 10, H, Oct 4, scs.
10516 Snyder, Wm, 54 H, Sept 8, dys.
10525 Stones, T, 121, K, Oct 8, dys.
10530 Smallwood, C, 7, F, Oct 8, scs.
10609 Small, H, 101, H, Oct 10, scs.
10720 Smallman, J W, 63, A, Oct 11, dia.
10808 Steele, F F, 20 cav, A, Oct 12, scs.
10837 Shank, A, 184, C, Oct 13, scs.
11044 Smith, Andrew, 22 cav, B, Oct 17, dia.
11069 Stevens, C P, 11, A, Oct 17, scs.
11233 Smith, H W, 53, B, Oct 21, scs.
11246 Smith, James, 57, E, Oct 21, ts. f.
11355 Silvy, David, 18 cav, I, Oct 23, scs.
11368 Seyoff, H, 81, C, Oct 23, scs.
11488 Sunderland, E, H, D, Oct 26, scs.
11529 Stevenson, John, 111, I, Oct 26, scs.
11661 Speck, Olive, 67, H, Oct 30, scs.
1174 Smith, H, 183, D, Nov 2, scs.
11785 Snodgrass, R J, 145, H, Nov 4, scs.
11792 Sellentine, M, 145, C, Nov 4, scs.
11825 Seltzer, D, 20, K, Nov 5, scs.
11885 Smith, W B, 14 cav, E, Nov 6, scs.
11890 Shure, J P, 184, F, Nov 7, scs.
11895 Snively, G W, 20 cav, F, Nov 7, scs.
11926 Scover, J H, 79, G, Nov 8, scs.
11951 Shefiley, W, 118, G, Nov 9, scs.
12057 Stitzer, G, 2, E, Nov 16, scs.
12081 Stensley, D,‡ 184, A, Nov 18, scs.
12217 Smith, J S, 118, F, Dec 3, dia.
12218 Skinner, S O,‡ 77, A, Dec 4, scs.
12282 Shafer, T, 184, E, Dec 13, scs.
12308 Stafford, W, 67, H, Dec 19, scs.
12384 Sourbeer, J E, 20, A, Jan 3, scs.
12590 Sipe, F, 87, C, Feb 5, dia. c.
12598 Stauffer, J, 1, K, Feb 6, dia. c.
12648 Stain, G W, 20 cav, K, Feb 13, des.
12669 Slough, E B,‡ 1 cav, D, Feb 17, pls.
12670 Scott, A J, 14, D, Feb 17, dia. c.
12676 Sheridan, M, 103, F, Feb 19, dia. c.
12817 Sharks, J N, 14, D, March 27, dia.
12824 Shultz, H H, 87, A, April 5, dia.

778 Thistlewood, J, 73, E, April 28, c. f.
785 Tolland, D, 13 cav, D, April 28, las.
1144 Taylor, J F, 13, E, May 16, ts. f.
1145 Tull, D,‡ 4, D, May 16, pna.
1153 Toner, Peter, 19, A, May 16, dia. c.
1814 Thompson, H, 57, C, June 10, dia. c.
2182 Thompson, A, mus, 4 cav, C, June 19, dia.
2302 Townsend, D, 18 cav, D, June 22, dia. c.
2635 Tyser, L, 145, D, June 29, dia. c.
2897 Terwilliger, E,§ 103, H, July 5, dys.
3003 Thompson, R, 103, F, July 7, dia.
47 Taylor, C W, 84, D, May 24, s. p.
8329 Titus, W, 171, D, July 14, des.
3473 Todd, Wm, 103, K, July 17, scs.
3571 Thompson, J S, 183, H, July 19, dys.
3768 Terrell, A, 12 cav, B, July 22, dia.
3968 Trumbull, H, 3, E, July 25, scs.
4116 Thompson, Jas,§ 18 cav, G, July 28, dia.
4160 Tinsdule, —, 149, E, July 28, dia.
4713 Thompson, J, 3 art, A, Aug 4, scs.
5179 Thompson, W W, 101, E, Aug 9, scs.
5345 Thomas, F, 7, F, Aug 11, scs.
5966 Thompson, J B, 100, H, Aug 17, scs.
6146 Thompson, F A B, 69, I, Aug 19, ces.
6447 Tubbs, E, 143, I, Aug 23, scs.
6476 Toll, Wm, 11 res, I, Aug 22, scs.
6790 Turner, John, 118, H, Aug 25, dia.
7250 Thomas, E, 23, F, Aug 30, dia. c.
7409 Thorpe, L, 61, E, Aug 31, dia.
7904 Trash, Seth, 81, A, Sept 6, dia.
8231 Truman, E W, 9, G, Sept 9, scs.
8531 Tilt, W, 115, A, Sept 12, dia.
8619 Tutor, C, 184, A, Sept 13, scs.
9027 Tits, P, —, C, Sept 17, scs.
9212 Thorpe, D, 18, D, Sept 19, dia.

9302 Thompson, H, 18 cav, I, Sept 20, dia.
9726 Tonson, J, 99, B, Sept 25, dia.
9775 Thuck, I, 7, C, Sept 26, scs.
9981 Tones, E, 145, F, Sept 26, dia.
10008 Thompson, J, 90, H, Sept 29, scs.
10725 Tibbels, Geo,‡ 69, K, Oct 11, scs.
11002 Thatcher, R, 14, C, Oct 16, dia. c.
11407 Thompson, J, 12 cav, E, Oct 24, dia.
11754 Trespan, P, 67, H, Nov 2, scs.
12080 Townsend, C,‡ 103, E, Nov 18, scs.

971 Ulrick, John, 17, E, May 9, ts. f.
4184 Urndragh, W, 4, B, July 28, dia.
12133 Utler, Wm, 45, H, Nov 23, dia.

1369 Ventler, Chas,§ 75, G, May 25, rhm.
7739 Vogel, L,‡ 150, A, June 8, dia. c.
2428 Vernon, S, 7, K, June 24, des.
4265 Vanholt, T, 13, A, July 29, dia.
5392 Vandeby, B,§ 7, A, Aug 12, dia.
6877 Vanderpool, F, 57, B, Aug 26, dia.
7716 Vancampments, George, 52, I, Sept 4, dia.
8270 Vail, G B, 77, G, Sept 9, dia.
8791 Vaughan, J, 108, A, Sept 15, dia.
8948 Varndale, J, 112, A, Sept 16, dia.
9688 Vandier, Wm, Phila, Sept 24, scs.

57 Wilkins, A, 12 cav, L, March 17, c. f.
128 Waterman, John, 88, B, March 23, dys.
193 Wise, Isaac, 18, G, March 27, pls.
496 Wheeler, J, 150, I, April 12, dia.
516 Warren, J, 76, A, April 12, dia.
587 Weed, A B, 4, K, April 17, dys.
657 Wentworth, Jas, 83, G, April 21, ts. f.
665 Watson, F F, 2, B, April 22, dys.
686 Wahl, John, 73, C, April 23, rhm.
764 Wilson, John, 14 cav, H, April 27, dia.
852 Williams, S, 18, cav, I, May 3, dia. c.
941 Wolf, J H, 13 cav, H, May 7, dia. c.
1021 Wright, J, 12 cav, B, May 11, dia. c.
1067 Whitton, Robt, 145, C, May 13, dia. c.
1093 Wright, Wm, 16 cav, A, May 14, dia. c.
1386 Wymans, Jas,‡ 150, C, May 26, dia. c.
1387 Wilson, James, 13 cav, D, May 26, dia. c.
1443 Williams, F, 3 cav, B, May 28, dia. c.
1494 Williams, Fred, 101, K, May 30, dia.
1525 Wallace, H, 13 cav, H, May 31, pna.
1563 Waltermeyer, H, 76, H, June 2, dia. c.
1721 Whitney, W, 83, A, June 8, dia.
1749 Woodsides, W I, 18, E, June 9, dia. c.
1791 Wolf, Samuel, 77, A, June 10, dia.
1903 Woodward, G W, 3 cav, June 13, dia.
1977 Wyant, H, 103, G, June 15, dia. c.
2338 Walters, C, 73, B, June 22, dia. c.
2616 Williams, J, 83, F, June 28, dys.
2699 Wike, A, 96, B, June 30, dia.
2790 Whitaker, — (negro), 8, July 2, dia.
2937 Winsinger, S, 96, E, July 6, dia.
3023 Weider, L, 50, H, July 7, dia. c.
3135 Wallace, A, 116, I, July 10, dia. c.
3277 Wright, W A, 20 cav, G, July 14, dia.
3384 Woodruff, W D, 103, B, July 16, dia.
3392 Wait, Geo, 1 cav, G, July 16, dia. c.
3605 Walker, E, 7, A, July 19, dys.
3694 White, E D,§ 2 cav, H, July 21, dia.
4181 Wisel, M, 18 cav, K, July 28, dip.
4338 Ward, Daniel, 138, E, July 30, dia.
3880 White, M, 7, C, July 24, dia.
3822 Wilson, Andrew, 103, H, July 23, dia.
4069 Wolf, A, 146, D, July 27, dia.
4046 Winegardner, A, 73, G, July 27, dia.
3921 Wilson, Wm, 43, July 25, dia.
4428 Williams, George, 54, H, July 31, dia.
4702 Willebough, E, 148, I, Aug 4, scs.
4828 Ward, P, 103, B, Aug 6, dia.
4966 Wetherholt, C, 54, F, Aug 7, des.
4981 Waserun, G, 4 cav, I, Aug 7, dia.
4996 White, S, H cav, B, Aug 7, dia.
5106 Weaver, James, 90, K, Aug 9, scs.
5353 Wilks, S, 77, G, Aug 11, pls.
5458 Wilson, Wm, 7, K, Aug 12, dys.
5677 Weeks, D, 53, G, Aug 14, dys. c.

6050 Williams, J, 7, A, Aug 18, dia.
6052 Waterhouse, W, 3 cav, L, Aug 18, ces.
6133 Workman, A, 118, D, Aug 19, dia.
6305 Whipple, H,‡ 18, B, Aug 20, des.
6427 Wart, C, 143, E, Aug 22, scs.
6530 Winerman, Jas, 77, A, Aug 23, scs.
6563 Wible, Paul, 57, A, Aug 23, i. s.
6626 Walker, S A, 103, I, Aug 23, scs.
6808 Wick, R C, 103, E, Aug 25, dys.
6980 Woolsluer, W H,† 77, C, Aug 27, scs.
6981 White, Jas P, 149, D, Aug 27, des.
7023 Woodford, J A, 101, E, Aug 27, dia.
7277 White, Ed, 103, K, Aug 30, dia.
7382 Webb, J S, 69, K, Aug 31, dys.
7386 Walton, A,§ 4 cav, A, Aug 31, scs.
7680 Wallwork, T, 118, D, Sept 3, dia.
7714 Warner, L, 5 cav, C, Sept 3, dia. c.
7799 Wynn, H, 101, F, Sept 4, dia.
7809 Wiggins, D, 2 art, D, Sept 5 dia. c.
7914 Weekland, F, 101, K, Sept 5, dia.
7933 Wade, Geo W, 118, E, Sept 5, dia.
8081 Weber, W, 116, F, Sept 7, dia.
8360 White, D, 2 art, F, Sept 10, dia. c.
8879 Wheeler, J, 7, C, Sept 15, scs.
9091 Wheeler, C C, 14 cav, M, Sept 18, dia.
9343 Williams, W, 20 cav, Sept 20, scs.
9434 Wilson, W H, 3, I, Sept 21, dia.
9534 Woolman, H, 18 cav, A, Sept 22, scs.
9573 Wingert, C, 111, I, Sept 23, wds.
9634 Wismer, J, 100, A, Sept 24, dia.
9657 Wilson, G M, 7 cav, M, Sept 24, dia.
9825 Walke, G, 4 cav, K, Sept 27, dia.
9909 Wentley, J, 155, G, Sept 28, dia.
10092 Watson, Wm, 99, I, Sept 30, dia.
10217 Weeks, C, 76, F, Oct 2, dia.
10229 Waltz, J, 7, H, Oct 2, dia.
10236 Weekley, John, 14, A, Oct 2, dia.
10253 Weeks, C, 76, F, Oct 3, scs.
10315 Wolfhope, J, 184, A, Oct 4, dys.
10400 Wilson, G, 55, C, Oct 6, dia.
10426 Wilson, J, 118, D, Oct 6, dia.
10521 Williams, W, 46, K, Oct 8, dys.
10568 Walk, W, 87, E, Oct 9, dia. c.
10632 Welry, John M,‡ 116, E, Oct 10, dia. c.
10659 Watts, A J, 12 cav, I, Oct 11, scs.

10729 White, J M, 21, G, Oct 11, scs.
10797 Walker, Wm, 148, B, Oct 12, scs.
9464 Warner, Cyrus W, 184, B, Oct 21, scs.
10840 Wright, Wm, 16, I, Oct 13, scs.
10902 Wofford, D, 54, K, Oct 14, scs.
10974 Watson, C, 184, E, Oct 15, scs.
11048 Wilderman, E, 14, D, Oct 17, scs.
11108 Walker, A, 45, D, Oct 18, dia.
11129 Wilson, G, 140, F, Oct 18, scs.
11498 Warrington, J H, 106, H, Oct 26, dia.
11503 Waiter, W, 184, F, Oct 26, scs.
11557 Wood, J,§ 19, C, Oct 27, scs.
11722 Woodburn, D J, 7, G, Nov 1, scs.
11750 Wyncoop, F P, 7, I, Nov 2, scs.
11899 Webster, J,§ 20 cav, L, Nov 7, dia. c.
11978 Wilkinson, C,§ 104, I, Nov 12, scs.
11987 Weaver, J, 53, K, Nov 13, dia.
12095 Walder, John, 5 cav, L, Nov 19, scs.
12098 Wider, N H, 184, F, Nov 19, scs.
12123 Weatherald, H W, 7, H, Nov 22, scs.
12129 Webb, C M,§ 101, H, Nov 23, scs.
12222 Williams, J, 145, A, Dec 4, scs.
12137 Wood, J M, 2, A, Nov 23, scs.
12380 Watson, H, 184, A, Jan 2, dia. c.
12485 Williams, B, 75, B, Jan 19, dia.
12493 Walker, N C, 87, B, Jan 20, des.

10158 Van Dyke, D L, 103, A, Oct 1, dia.
11810 Vanmarkes, D, 6, E, Nov 4, scs.
12154 Vanhatterman, I, 4, G, Nov 25, scs.
3958 Vogle, V, 78, D, July 25, scs.

3799 Yocumbs, W B, 93, B, July 22, dia. c.
4900 Yocum, D, 1 cav, M, Aug 6, dia. c.
6103 Yingling, E, 78, E, Aug 18, dia.
6545 Yeager, Samuel, 158, D, Aug 23, dia.
10204 Young, J B, 49, G, Oct 2, dys.
11040 Young, W H, 145, F, Oct 17, dia. c.
11872 Yeager, J, 49, C, Nov 6, dys.

1806 Zerphy, J, 79, E, June 10, dia. c.
4255 Zimmerman, B, 148, B, July 29, dia.
6573 Zane, Wm, 19, K, Aug 23, i. s.
6818 Zerl, S, 103, F, Aug 25, scs.
11327 Zane, M, 118, E, Oct 23, scs.

RHODE ISLAND.

3266 Austin, J A,§ 1 cav, H, July 13, dia.
6231 Allen, Chas, 1 cav, D, Aug 21, dia. c.

1744 Bonley, Wm, 1 cav, M, June 8, dia. c.
1958 Bidmead, Jas, 1 cav, G, June 14, dys.
2521 Blake, J F, 1 cav, M, June 26, dia.
3647 Burk, Jas, 1, C, July 20, dys.
4261 Bether, J, 2, C, July 29, scs.
4576 Baine, H, 5, A, Aug 2, dia. c.

1339 Carpenter, P, 1 cav, E, May 24, ana.
1413 Carson, B F, 1 cav, K, May 27, dys.
3810 Canahan, Jas, bat, July 23, dys.
7966 Colvin, E O,‡ 5 art, A, Sept 6, scs.
12832 Collins, J H, 1 cav, A, April 16, dia. c.

651 Delanah, E B,§ 1 cav, G, April 20, dia.
1217 Dix, Geo, 1 cav, M, May 19, pna.
1435 Dickinson, Jacob,§ 1 cav, K, May 28, dia.
3036 Dearborn, G, 1 cav, July 8, r. f.
4742 Durden, Robert, 1 cav, F, Aug 5, scs.
4927 Doolittle, G S, 2 art, B, Aug 6, dia.
6676 Doyle, Jas, 5 art, A, Aug 14, dia.

827 Eustace, Geo C, 1 cav M, May 1, dia.
10203 Eaton, A, 5 art, A, Oct 1, scs.

939 Freelove, H, 1 cav, H, May 7, dia.
4538 Furrell, Jas F, 1 art, A, Aug 2, dia.
4672 Fay, John, 2, G, Aug 4, ts. f.
1356 Fey, A, 5 art, A, Aug 31, scs.

1866 Goudy, John, 5 art, A, June 12, dia. c.
4866 Gallagher, C, 5, A, Aug 6, dys.
5561 Garvey, Wm, 5 art, A, Aug 13, ana.
8308 Green, R, 2, B, Sept 10, dia. c.
9978 Green, Daniel, 2, H, Sept 29, dia.

1075 Henry, T, 1 cav, F, May 13, dia.
2656 Healy, A, 1 cav, D, June 29, ts. f.
2746 Hunt, C W, 1 cav, A, July 1, dia.
3904 Hampstead, J, 5 art, F, July 24, scs.
7032 Hooker, A, 1 cav, G, Aug 27, dia.
11843 Hawkins, D F, 5, A, Nov 5, wds.
12016 Hanley, T, 5 art, A, Nov 14, scs.

1962 Ide, S R, 1 cav, H, June 14, dys.

3049 Johnson, A G, 5 art, A, July 8, dia.

2968 Kettell, Jas, 1 cav, B, July 6, dia.
3096 Kiney, J, 2, B, July 10, dys. c.

4215 Lewis, Edward, 5 art, A, July 29, dys.
5827 Littlebridge, W H,‡ 5 art, A, Aug 16, dia.
6798 Lee, Cornelius, 5 art, A, Aug 25, dia.
7849 Leach, L D, 1 cav, F, Sept 5, dia.
11688 Livingston, J'n, mus, 5 art, A, Oct 31, dia.

1750 Miner, S, 1 cav, D, June 9, dia. c.
7393 Mckay, Thos, 2, F, Aug 31, dia.
8306 Mckenna, J, 3 art, Sept 10, dia.

3192 Northorp, E, 1 cav, H, July 12, dia.
7904 Navoo, G, 5, K, Sept 5, dia.

607 Peterson, John, 1, D, April 18, dys.

7219 Rathburn, J, 1 cav, A, Aug 29, des.

2382 Sweet, M, 1 cav, D, June 23, dia.
2563 Spink, J, 1 cav, H, June 27, dia.
2859 Slocum, Geo T, 2d lt, 1 cav, A, July 4, ts. f.
4158 Smith, P, 1 cav, A, July 28, dia.
4949 Stalord, J, 1 bat, A, Aug 7, scs.
6186 Sisson, Charles T, 5 art, A, Aug 19, dys.
6187 Seymour, H, 5 art, A, Aug 19, dia.
8351 Sullivan, J, 5 art, A, Aug 21, dia. c.
7129 Sander, Charles, 5 art, A, Aug 28, ana.

7425 Slocum, C A,‡ 5 art, A, Aug 31, ana.

3075 Turner, Charles, 7, E, July 9, dia.
8522 Thomas, J, 5, Sept 12, scs.

19 Wright, Moses, 2 cav, A, March 7, r. f.
1788 West, H, 1, A, June 10, dia. c.
3173 Wallace, Wm, 5 art, A, July 11, dia. c.
5908 Wood, J B, 5, A, Aug 16, dia. c.
6222 West, J, 2 cav, A, Aug 21, dia. c.
6766 Wayne, S, 1 cav, A, Aug 25, dia.
7831 Wilson, J, 5, A, Sept 4, ana.
9273 Witham, B, 1 light art, Sept 19, ana.

TENNESSEE.

883 Allen, James W, 11, B, May 4, dia. c.
987 Amos, F G, 2, C, May 10, dia.
2313 Allison, B F, 13 cav, D, June 22, dia. c.
2631 Andrewson, Joseph, 2, C, June 29, dia.
8167 Anderson, S, 8 cav, B, July 11, dia.
3194 Aber, A, 7 cav, A, July 12, dia.
3334 Anglon, Wm, 7 cav, A, July 15, dia.
4004 Athens, J H, 2 east, C, July 26, ana.
6411 Aikin, George W,‡ 7, K, Aug 22, scs.
6474 Ashby, J F, 7 cav, B, Aug 22, ts. f.
6541 Antoine, P, 13 cav, H, Aug 23, dys. c.
7572 Aspray Wm,§ 13, B, Sept 2, dia.
7907 Anderson, C S,§ 10, D, Sept 5, dys.
9151 Achley, A, 3, A, Sept 18, scs.
9910 Atkins, L, 2, D, Sept 28, scs.
1895 Arrowood, James, 8 cav, June 13, dja.
8493 Alexander, P S, 13 cav, D, Sept 11, dia.
12710 Allen, G W, 7, I, Feb 28, pls.

539 Boling, Wm, 11, E, April 14, dia.
585 Beason, Benjamin, 2, E, April 17, pna.
663 Bond, Jas J T, 2, F, April 21, dia.
695 Baker, T K, 5 cav, April 23, dys. c.
705 Batey, W H, 2, B, April 24, dys. c.
772 Burton, Wm, 1, art, A, April 28, dia. c.
808 Brannin, Ellis, 2, F, April 30, dia. c.
845 Browden, H V, 2, K, May 1, dia.
859 Byerly, W H, 1, A, May 3, dia.
920 Brewer, M, 2, E, May 6, dia.
1053 Boyden, A L, 2, B, May 13, dia.
1137 Beatty, Thomas, 2, B, May 16, dia.
1242 Bryant, James A, 8, I, May 20, pna.
1244 Barnard, W H, 2, A, May 20, dia.
1248 Boyd, A D,‡ 2, F, May 20, dia. c.
1527 Butler, J J,§ 7, B, May 31, dys.
1538 Bradshaw, A G, 2, B, June 1, dia.
1610 Browning, J, 2, F, June 4, dia. c.
1635 Brown, J, 13 cav, E, June 5, dia.
1847 Branon, Wm, 2, F, June 11, ana.
1876 Birket, W D,‡ 7, June 12, dia.
1883 Burchfield, W R, 2, June 12, dia. c.
1976 Berger, W, 2, B, June 15, dia. c.
2037 Berger, W M, 2, June 15, dia.
2555 Boutwright, A,§ 7, June 27, dia.
2744 Brewer, W T, 7 cav, D, July 1, dia.
2939 Bibbs, Alexander, 7 cav, D, July 6, dia. a.
2983 Bright, John, 8, G, July 7, dys.
3176 Blalock, H, 2, D, July 11, abs.
3198 Brown, J B,§ 2, F, July 12, ana.
6 Brandon, C, 4, D, April 4, s. p.
16 Burke, John, 2, D, April 12, s. p.
52 Brummell, A D, 2, H, June 3, s. p.
57 Broits, S, 4, F, June 20, s. p.
58 Beeler, Daniel, 5, D, June 25, s. p.
3328 Barton, F F, 13 cav, A, July 14, dia. c.
3330 Bynom, J W, 13 cav, C, July 14, dia. c.
3414 Brennan, James, 2, I, July 16, dia.
3636 Burris, D B, 13, B, July 20, ana.
3643 Brannan, J, 2, A, July 20, dia. c.
3726 Billings, W, 6, I, July 21, dia.
3786 Bowman, J, 7 cav, C, July 22, dia. c.
3934 Boles, H, 13, C, July 25, dia.
4108 Boyd, W H, 9 cav, C, July 27, dia.
4221 Barnes, A C, 15, H, July 29, wds.

4770 Bryant, Wm, 2, D, Aug 5, dia.
5017 Butler, W W, 7 cav, B, Aug 8, ana.
4371 Bradfield, E L, 7 cav, C, July 31, ana.
5049 Brummetti, B, 11, cav, C, Aug 8, scs.
5277 Barnhart, D F, 7 cav, B, Aug 11, dia.
5294 Baker, Isaac, 13, B, Aug 11, dys.
5313 Blackwood, G W, 11, B, Aug 11, pls.
5533 Boles, G W, 13 cav, B, Aug 13, scs.
5617 Baker, M A, 13 cav, E, Aug 14, dys. c.
6003 Boles, W G, 13 cav, B, Aug 17, ana.
6142 Bayles, K, 2, C, Aug 19, dys.
6194 Burnett, S H, 6, H, Aug 19, ana.
6287 Butler, W J, 7, B, Aug 20, dia. c.
6569 Barnes, Wm, 7 cav, M, Aug 23, i. s.
6672 Bishop, W, 7, cav, H, Aug 23, ts. f.
7430 Brewer, J, 2, D, Aug 31, gae.
7664 Bales, Henry, 2, K, Sept 2, dia.
7943 Boyer, D, 15, D, Sept 5, scs.
8222 Bird, S H, 13 cav, D, Sept 8, ana.
8998 Blackner, Thomas, 7 cav, L, Sept 17, ana.
9023 Bill, F, 5, I, Sept 17, dia.
9079 Boyle, R C, 7 cav, I, Sept 17, scs.
9149 Bean, C S, 3 cav, E, Sept 18, scs.
9478 Bowlen, C F, 13, B, Sept 21, scs.
9543 Bromley, H,§ 7, Sept 23, scs.
4888 Brannoh, L, 2, A, Aug 6, scs.
10098 Byerly, James, 1, e c, A, Sept 30, scs.
10452 Bible, W, 8, D, Oct 7, dia.
10617 Blackney, B, 7, E, Oct 10, dia. c.
10826 Bartholomew, John, 7 cav, H, Oct 13, scs.
11015 Bosworth, W H, 7 cav, E, Oct 16, scs.
11298 Brogan, John,‡ 2, C, Oct 22, dia.
11372 Brown, J B,‡ 2, K, Oct 23, scs.
12171 Bradford, H A, 7, E, Oct 26, scs.
12565 Brown, J W, 13, B, Jan 31, scs.
12613 Barnhart, G, 7, C, Feb 8, dia. c.
12662 Barnes, F B, 7 cav, D, Feb 16, dia. c.
462 Bell, E S, 4, C, April 9, dia. c.
4782 Barnes, G, 10, D, Aug 5, con.

189 Cardwell, W C, 6, C, March 27, dia.
216 Conaster, Philip, 2, D, March 28, dys. c.
230 Chimney, Jesse,§ 2, A, March 29, dia. a.
375 Colwell, J H, 2, C, April 5, dia.
436 Croswell, Samuel, 2, K, April 8, dia. c.
459 Childers, J M, 2, D, April 9, dia.
482 Clark, Lewis, 2 cav, B, April 9, dia. a.
615 Covington, A, 2, K, April 18, dia.
717 Chitwood, J H, 2, G, April 24, dia.
811 Carden, Robert, 2, C, April 30, dia. c.
840 Cardwell, W C, 6, G, May 2, dia.
1050 Cooper, C, 2, B, May 12, dia.
1213 Clark, Alexander, 2, C, May 19, ana.
1425 Cross, M C, 2, F, May 28, dia.
1574 Childers, J, 13, A, June 3, rua.
1636 Clemens, J D, 7 cav, D, June 5, dia. c.
1751 Campbell, W, 2, A, June 9, dys. a.
1839 Carden, A K, 7 cav, E, June 11, dia. c.
2931 Covington, J B, 2, K, June 15, dia.
2062 Carwin, James, 1, June 16, dia.
2071 Crow, J,§ 2, F, June 16, scs.
2289 Crawford, A, 13 cav, B, June 21, dia.
2466 Childers, Thos L, 2, G, June 25, con.
2632 Cooper, E, 1, A, June 20, ana.

39 Sandusky, G, 2 B, April 29, s. p.
56 Stout, D D, 2, F, June 18, s. p.
3035 Scarbrough, S N, 13, E, July 8, dys.
3276 Shrop, J B, 2 east, E, July 14, dia.
3298 Sells, W, 2 east cav, D, July 14, dys.
3332 Swappola, O B, 4, A, July 15, dia.
3520 Slaver, A, 11 cav, C, July 18, dia.
3865 Smith, John M, 12, M, July 24, dia. c.
4038 Sapper, S, 8, H, July 26, dia.
4170 Snow, W, 7 cav, M, July 28, dia.
5462 Smith, L, 13, L, Aug 13, scs.
5625 Sutton, Andrew, 13 cav, E, Aug 14, dia.
5859 Swan, John, 2, D, Aug 16, mas.
5962 Scott, John, 13, B, Aug 17, dia. c.
6643 Sutton, D, 1 cav, H, Aug 23, scs.
7056 Smith, J, 6, M, Aug 28, gae.
7296 Stewart, J W, 13 cav, B, Aug 30, dys.
7314 Smidney, E, 1 cav, E, Aug 30, dia. c.
7787 Scobey, L A H, 13 cav, B, Sept 2, dys.
7923 Sarret, Jas D, Tenn State Gd, Sept 5, dys.
8637 Smith, J, 3 cav, E, Sept 13, dia.
9192 Smith, T A, 13, C, Sept 18, dia.
9381 Southerland, J, 13 cav, C, Sept 20, scs.
9395 Stewart, E, 13 cav, D, Sept 20, scs.
9555 Smith, W H, 7, B, Sept 23, dia. c.
9719 Swatzell, W L, 8 cav, E, Sept 25, scs.
9803 Stratten, J L, 7 cav, M, Sept 25, scs.
10409 Stafford, S, 13, A, Oct 6, ana.
10454 Shonall, John, 13, C, Oct 7, scs.
11594 Shay, D, 11, E, Oct 28, dia.
12558 Smith, H, 2, E, Jan 30, scs.
12749 Stevens, J F, 2 cav, E, March 8, scs.
12756 Smith, J D, 4, C, March 12, dia. c.
12784 Stewart, R H, 7, C, March 15, pls.
12800 Shook, N A, 7, B, March 19, rhm.
12836 Smith, George, 2, B, April 18, dia. c.
36 Stiner, W H, 2, E, April 28, s. p.
3995 Slover, A W, 2, C, July 26, dia.

211 Tompkins, T B, 2, F, March 28, dys. c.
258 Thompson, W D, 2, F, March 31, dia. c.
793 Thompson, Charles, 2, April 29, dia. c.
932 Thomas, W H, 2, K, May 7, ana.
1657 Tomlin, A, 7 cav, M, June 6, dia. c.
1704 Thauton, S A, 1 art, H, June 7, dia.
2229 Tice, S J, 7, B, June 20, dia. c.
2718 Tipton, W H, 2, I, July 1, dys. c.
3460 Taylor, J, 13, D, July 17, scs.
4122 Tyffle, John, 1 cav, A, June 28, dys.
4778 Templeton, G W, 2, C, Aug 5, dia.
5646 Tite, W S, 13, C, Aug 14, dia.
7052 Thomas, W H, 7 cav, A, Aug 28, des.
9203 Tolley, D, 8, H, Sept 19, scs.
9375 Terry, D, 9 cav, D, Sept 20, scs.
10780 Thinu, R A, 7 cav, B, Oct 12, dia. c.
12694 Tidwell, T, 13, D, Feb 22, pls.
4825 Tidwell, J W, 13, C, Aug 5, r. f.

2592 Usley, T R, 2, A, June 28, brs.
4518 Undergrate, A, 2, I, Aug 2, scs.

885 Vaugh, I, 8, H, May 5, des.
1203 Vanhorn, J, 2, H, May 19, dia. c.
2915 Varner, T W, 11 cav, E, July 5, scs.
7217 Vanhook, J M,‡ 11 cav, H, July 29, ana.
4530 Vaughry, Frederick, 2, D, Aug 1, rhm.

60 Wolfe, John, 11, E, March 18, dia.
259 Woolen, I, 2, A, March 31, dia. c.
339 Webb, Robert, 2, B, April 2, ts. f.

359 Wuas, M, 2, I, April 2, pns.
501 Watts, C C, 2, A, April 12, dys.
570 Ward, Jordan, 2, A, April 15, scs.
810 White, John, 2, B, April 30, dia. c.
902 William, C, 7, B, May 5, phs.
1052 Ward, A, 3, I, May 12, des.
1756 Watts, J W, 7, M, June 9, ts. f.
1794 White, I, 2, D, June 10, dys.
1865 Wallace, L, 2 east, C, June 12, ana.
2057 Ward, C, 2, H, June 16, dia. c.
2066 Watts, T,‡ 2, I, June 16, dia. c.
2132 Wray, Samuel, 13, C, June 18, scs.
2496 Wilson, A, 8 cav, June 26, dys. a.
2764 Winningham, J, 2, B, July 2, dia. c.
2810 Wells, E, 8, H, July 3, scs.
3021 Watkins, J M, 4, I, July 7, scs.
3031 Woodsend, T, 7, K, July 8, scs.
3189 Webb, D, 8 cav, G, July 12, scs.
21 Winchester, J D, 1 cav, E, April 15, s. p.
19 Weaver, P, 2, D, April 13, s. p.
4554 West, W F, 2, H, Aug 2, ana.
4869 Ward, John, citizen, Aug 6, dia.
22 Whitby, R B, 2, C, April 15, s. p.
33 Weese, W, 2, I, April 23, s. p.
3297 Weir, I, 1 cav, B, July 14, dia. c.
3304 Wilson, H, 2, B, July 14, scs.
3319 Wolf, A, 10, C, July 14, pna.
3458 Williams, A, 3 cav, E, July 17, scs.
3615 Willis, James, Tenn St Gd, July 20, dys
3714 Webbe, J, 2, B, July 21, des.
3737 Wilson, J, 12, F, July 21, dia.
3982 Wilson, S L, 2, D, July 26, scs.
4033 Walford, W, 7, A, July 26, dia. c.
4704 Wallace, L, 2, C, Aug 4, ana.
5267 Wright, J W, 7 cav, B, Aug 10, con.
5572 Withyde, S, 1, A, Aug 14, scs.
6108 Wood, P D, 3, B, Aug 19, dia.
6580 Webb, Robert, 2, B, Aug 23, dia.
6608 Wortell, H H, 7 cav, I, Aug 23, dia. c.
7618 White, R O M, 13, B, Sept 2, dia. c.
8740 Whicks, N, 7, H, Sept 14, dia.
7231 Wood, J, 7, C, Aug 29, ana.
9193 Woolsey, J, 2, F, Sept 18, des.
9479 Walker, John, 13 cav, C, Sept 21, dia.
9658 Williams, C S, 9 cav, B, Sept 24, dia.
9670 Whittle, H W, 7 cav, C, Sept 24, dia.
9730 Webb, T, 6, G, Sept 25, dia.
9929 White, L S, 11 cav, D, Sept 28, dia.
10337 Wiggins, O M, 11 cav, C, Oct 4, dia.
10338 White, H,§ 7 cav, A, Oct 4, scs.
10739 Warrell, J W,‡ 7 cav, C, Oct 11, dia.
10605 Webb, W, 3, A, Oct 10, scs.
11386 Worden, J W,§ 7, E, Oct 24, uls.
12107 Winelug, J, 7, M, Nov 21, scs.
12125 White, Wm, M, H, Nov 22, scs.
12139 Watson, I C, 7 cav, C, Nov 23, scs.
12576 Walker, C, 6, H, Feb 3, scs.
12699 Woodruff, J, 4 cav, B, Feb 24, des.
12779 Woods, Thomas, 13, B, March 15, scs.
8190 White, J,§ 7 cav, A, Sept 8, dia.
5669 Wilson, Wm A, 6, A, Aug 14, dia.
4717 Westbrook, J H, 6 cav, A, Aug 4, dia.
4793 Wilson, J M, 13 cav, D, Aug 5, scs.

383 Yarbor, Wiley, 5, I, April 5, dia. c.
878 Young, James, 2, D, May 4, dia. c.
1142 Young, James, 2, F, May 16, ana.
14 Yeront, Samuel, 3, E, April 10, s. p.
5682 Yarnell, J E, S E, Aug 14, scs.

VERMONT.

3975 Averill, T E, 9, I, July 25, dia.
4579 Adams, Daniel, 1 cav, L, Aug 2, i. f.
8301 Albee, S,§ 11, G, Sept 9, dia. c.
9960 Atwood, A, 1, C, Sept 28, dia.
10664 Aldrich, L E,§ 11, A, Oct 11, dia.
11259 Aldrich, H B, 1 art, A, Oct 21, scs.
12092 Aiken, M A, 1, A, Nov 19, dia.

12766 Avery, B F, 3, C, March 13, dia. c.

2035 Bloomer, J, 2 bat, June 15, dia. c.
3166 Bailey, James, 2, A, July 11, dia. c.
4036 Brown, George, 16, B, July 20, scs.
4173 Bailey, S P, 1 cav, H, July 28, dia. c.
4200 Beadle, H H, 9, G, July 29, dys

5605 Poppins, Frank, 3, I, Aug 14, dia.
6586 Parmor, E, 4, C, Aug 23, dia.
7290 Park, Jas, 7 cav, E, Aug 30, des.
10040 Pillsbury, F, 4 cav, C, Sept 29, dia.
10237 Paul, John C, 4 cav, G, Oct 2, scs.
11041 Page, E, 4, I, Oct 17, scs.
11307 Powers, A, 4, H, Oct 22, scs.
11992 Packard, M G,‡ 1 art, A, Nov 13, dia.
12198 Pike, N N, 4, I, Nov 30, dia. c.
12721 Perry, A B, 4, H, March 3, dia. c.

1888 Reed, D W, 1 cav, June 13, dia.
6699 Ransom, Geo W, 1 art, L, Aug 24, dys.
7697 Rascoe, C, 11, H, Sept 3, dia.
8138 Roberts, J M, 11, K, Sept 8, dia.
8173 Richards, J, 1 cav, L, Sept 8, dia.
9462 Raynor, Louis, 4 cav, C, Sept 21, scs.
9894 Ross, H E, 11 bat, K, Sept 27, dia.
11009 Raynolds, F, 11, F, Oct 16, scs.
11426 Rancy, A, 4, A, Oct 24, scs.
11691 Rice, F W, 14, F, Oct 31, dys.
12519 Rouncervee, E T, 9, D, Jan 25, scs.

648 Spoore, W O, 1 cav, B, April 20, dia.
2943 Smith, J C, 1, H, July 6, pna.
3382 St John, A, 11, A, July 16, dys.
4580 Seward, O, 5, C, Aug 2, dia.
5707 Skinner, F A, 4, H, Aug 15, scs.
5963 Stone, Jas A, 1 art, H, Aug 17, dia.
6640 Simons, L, 1, G, Aug 23, dia.
7509 Seaton, T B, 4, F, Sept 1, dia.
7810 Sweeney, Henry, H, C, Sept 4, dys.
7813 Sprout, A, 17, F, Sept 4, dia.
8444 Stockwell, A, 11, H, Sept 11, scs.
10696 Sanburn, H, 4, G, Sept 11, dia.
10811 Styles, A B,‡ 4, K, Sept 12, dia. c.
10897 Sheldon, H, 1 cav, M, Sept 14, scs.
11282 Sarlett, L, 1, M, Oct 22, scs.
11476 Swaddle, W, 4, G, Oct 26, scs.
11966 Sanborn, M L, 1 art, A, Nov 11, dia.
12266 Scott, R O, 4, F, Dec 12, dys.

12514 Shay, J, 1 cav, K, Jan 23, dia. c.
12552 Sheldon, G, 1, K, Jan 29, scs.
12567 Stewart, E W, 11, A, Feb 1, scs.
5911 Scott, Geo W, 1 cav, C, Aug 17, dia.
8436 Suppes, T E, 1 cav, K, Sept 11, scs.

3784 Tuttle, C S, 1 cav, F, July 22, dia. c.
5833 Tatro, Alfred, 9, F, Aug 16, mas.
6587 Taylor, H C, 1 art, L, Aug 23, dia.
6659 Trow, H, 17, D, Aug 24, des.
9374 Tanner, H,‡ 11, I, Sept 20, scs.
9574 Talman, W C,§ 11, F, Sept 23, dys.
11171 Taylor, J W, 1 art, A, Oct 19, scs.
11220 Thompson, W A, 1 art, I, Oct 20, scs.

5693 Varnum, E G J, 11, F, Aug 15, scs.

3177 Weller, D, 9, B, July 11, ts. f.
4376 Whitehall, Geo, 6, B, July 31, dia.
4435 Wilson, A, 6, B, July 31, dia. c.
4585 Wilder, L F, 11, H, Aug 2, wds.
5075 Whitney, A, 9, D, Aug 8, dia.
5307 Warner, Geo O, 10, E, Aug 11, scs.
5751 Woodard, S P, 1 art, H, Aug 15, ens.
7063 Wells, Geo A, 4, F, Aug 28, dia.
7322 Wright, E S, 11 art, A, Aug 30, des.
7689 Witt, T, 1 cav, F, Sept 3, scs.
7920 Ward, Alfred, 11, A, Sept 5, dia.
8239 Watkins, G C, 1, C, Sept 9, dys.
9264 Woodmance, G, 11, F, Sept 9, scs.
9178 Welles, C, 11, H, Sept 18, dia.
10510 White, A, 11, A, Oct 8, scs.
10711 Webster, W A,§ 4, A, Oct 11, dia. c.
11289 Wakefield, J W, 4, H, Oct 22, scs.
11398 Woods, J M, 1, F, Oct 24, scs.
11783 Wheeler, B, 11, K, Nov 3, dia. c.
11840 Warden, G, 3, B, Nov 5, dia.
11865 Worthers, S T, 1 cav, D, Nov 6, dys.
12156 Willey, J S, 1 art, A, Nov 25, scs.
4533 Washburn, Tru, 1 cav, D, Aug 2, dys.

VIRGINIA.

824 Anderson, A, 2, H, May 1, dys.
876 Armstrong, —,§ 8 mil, C, May 4, dia.
942 Ayers, S V, 11, C, May 7, dia. c.
1968 Armstrong, G B, 8, C, June 14, ana.
2769 Armhult, W H,‡ 10, I, July 1, dia. c.
5011 Armstrong, J, 3, C, Aug 8, scs.
5341 Arbogast, C W, 1 art, C, Aug 11, scs.
8865 Abercrombie, W H, 12, C, Sept 15, scs.
11525 Allison, G, 1, F, Oct 26, dys.

221 Burns, S A,§ 8, C, March 29, dia. c.
255 Brooks, Samuel F, 10, I, March 30, i. f.
448 Boone, Jas, 1 cav, L, April 9, dia. c.
756 Bennett, L J, 11, C, April 27, dys. c.
943 Brake, J,§ 6, C, May 7, pna.
980 Blackburn, Geo, 10, I, May 9, dia.
1705 Bares, T E, 11, F, June 7, dia.
2518 Brown, M, 14, E, June 26, dia c.
2627 Bowermaster, S R, bu, 3 cav, D, Jn 28, scs.
3407 Bateman, D P, 8, July 16, dys.
4427 Barber, Jas, 1 cav, F, July 31, dia. c.
5495 Bishop, J C, 3, C, Aug 12, dia.
6706 Bearer, P, 10, I, Aug 24, scs.
10297 Boutnell, O, 4, F, Oct 3, dia.
7126 Beasley, P, 9, G, Aug 28, scs.
7909 Bogard, Jno R,‡ 14, A, Sept 5, scs.
8539 Baft, M, 18, E, Sept 12, ana.
9796 Butcher, Peter, 14, F, Sept 26, dia.
10198 Broom, J, 1 cav, B, Oct 2, r. f.
11090 Blessing, P, 15, K, Oct 18, scs.
11337 Bush, H H, 14, B, Oct 23, scs.
11411 Burton, W B, 6 cav, A, Oct 24, dia.
11669 Barnett, J F, 14, K, Oct 30, scs.
11924 Beach, J H, 14, K, Nov 8, scs.
12045 Boggs, H C,‡ 6 cav, E, Nov 16, scs.
12414 Burton, N, 3 cav, B, Jan 8, rhm.

110 Corbett, L B, W Va mil, C, Mar 23, dia.
403 Carr, Wm, 8, B, April 6, ts. f.
835 Clendeman, C L, 4 cav, D, May 1, dia.
1032 Caste, Jesse, 8, E, May 11, dia.
1100 Coon, Nathan, 14, K, May 14, dia. c.
2013 Carrington, Jas, 2, A, June 15, ana.
2235 Coffman, F, 3 cav, A, June 20, phs.
2569 Cunderson, —, 8, D, June 27, dys.
2661 Carnes, H, 10, E, June 29, dia.
2817 Conrad, H, 3, F, July 3, dia. c.
2930 Cunningham, J, 8, E, July 5, dys.
3315 Cox, T A,§ 3 cav, A, July 14, dia.
4363 Cool, J B,‡ 3 cav, H, July 31, dia.
4741 Crook, E H,§ 7, I, Aug 5, ana.
5174 Cuppett, J, 3, H, Aug 9, dys.
5384 Covll, Wm, 3, I, Aug 12, des.
6674 Clements, L, 3 cav, A, Aug 24, dys.
6809 Curtin, B, 4 cav, B, Aug 25, dia. c.
7091 Clark, —, 7, E, Aug 28, dia.
7179 Cremones, D, 9, D, Aug 29, scs.
8990 Cook, J, 7 cav, I, Sept 17, dia.
9406 Campbell, O H, 14, F, Sept 21, dia.
9755 Christain, J, 15, C, Sept 25, scs.
9762 Catnill, L, 9, B, Sept 25, scs.
9967 Cobin, J M, 14, B, Sept 28, dia.
10598 Childs, S P, 1 cav, C, Oct 10, dia.
11561 Castle, C H, 1, A, Oct 27, scs.
11830 Cooper, A H,‡ 7 cav, I, Nov 5, dia.
12174 Campbell, B, 12, I, Nov 26, scs.

24 Deboard, H A, 5, G, March 8, ts. f.
202 Douglas, Geo, 8, C, March 28, dia. c.
347 Dean, Samuel, 5, H, April 2, dys.
632 Defibaugh, W R,‡ 1 art, G, April 19, dia.
647 Davis, S, 3, D, April 20, pna.
843 Duncan, J M, 5, D, May 2, dys.

2081 Daly, Jas, 3 cav, A, June 17, dys.
8105 Duckworth, W B, 14, A, July 10, dia.
8246 Dyer, James, 10, I, July 13, pna.
5507 Drake, Samuel, 9, B, Aug 13, scs.
6588 Dorsey, A L, 15, K, Aug 23, dia.
6745 Daner, J, 10, I, Aug 24, ts. f.
6936 Darsey, M, 9, L, Aug 26, scs.
6949 Dodd, S,§ 9, F, Aug 26, scs.
7092 Dunberger, Geo, 9, C, Aug 28, dia.
8248 Divers, G, 15, D, Sept 9, scs.
8467 Dant, Jno M, 7 cav, H, Sept 10, scs.
8582 Dason, N, 8 cav, L, Sept 12, dys.
9159 Dunn, I, 2, K, Sept 18, dia.
12235 Duncan, W M, 6 cav, C, Dec 6, scs.
12807 Donohue, S, 9, C, March 21, pls.
12508 Doty, John, 6 cav, A, Jan 23, dia.

10975 Estuff, Jno, 1 cav, L, Oct 12, dia. c.

117 Fuller, Irwin, militia, March 23, pna.
613 Foster, Charles K, 9, H, April 18, dys.
355 Fox, H C, 1‡ D, May 8, dia. c.
5765 Fawkes, Wm, 14, D, Aug 15, wds.
7203 Foster, S, 8, A, Aug 29, dys.
7941 Feather, J B, 14, B, Sept 5, dia. c.
8698 Feasley, Len, 1 art, Sept 14, scs.
8723 Fusner, J E, 6 cav, D, Sept 14, dia.
10206 Freeborn, R L,§ 14, B, Oct 2, r. f.
10709 Furr, E, 10, K, Oct 11, dia.
11022 Fleming, W W, 6 cav, A, Oct 16, scs.
10314 Forth, R, 8, D, Sept 3, scs.

2485 Grey, P, 3, Va, A, June 25, dia.
2649 Greslioe, M, 11, C, June 29, brs.
2712 Golden, J, 2 cav, G, July 1, dia.
4738 Gorden, S, 2, G, Aug 4, scs.
6348 Guenant, A, 2, I, Aug 21, dia.
10581 Garton, Wm,‡ 2, I, Oct 10, scs.
11574 Gluck, A, E, 10, D, Oct 28, scs.
11864 Gibson, A, 1, A, Now 6, scs.

84 Hollingshead, S, 1, G, March 8, ts. f.
294 Harrison, D, 10, I, April 1, dia. c.
365 Henry, Robt O, 8, C, April 2, dia. c.
398 Hunter, G W, 8, A, April 6, brs.
568 Heller, Wm,‡ 3, D, April 15, dia.
839 Halpin, Jno, 2, D, May 2, dys.
997 Hottinun, G W, 8, E, May 10, dia.
1013 Hess, J, 11, C, May 10, dia.
1421 Hatfield, J, 1, B, May 28, dia. c.
1854 Harkins, H, 2, F, June 11, scs.
2702 Hoover, W H, 3, A, June 30, des.
2902 Howell, A, 14, E, July 5, dia. c.
2957 Howe, S, 2, I, July 5, dia c.
3930 Horant, E A, 3, C, July 25, dia. c.
4739 Hine, Wm, 2, A, Aug 5, dia. c.
5061 Hammer, S, 3 cav, G, Aug 8, dys.
5412 Hartly, Isaac, 3, I, Aug 12, dys.
5649 Hall, Henry, 10, F, Aug 14, scs.
6538 Harper, W, 8, H, Aug 23, ana.
8061 Hushman, W, 10, I, Sept 7, dia.
8268 Hardway, D B, 9, G, Sept 9, dia.
8341 Harden, G W, 6 cav, A, Sept 10, scs.
8344 Hutson, J, 14, A, Sept 10, scs.
9166 Hauslan, B, 6, cav, Sept 18, scs.
5537 Hudgins, J, 14, B, Sept 22, ana.
9794 Handland, H, 1, H, Sept 26, dia.
10990 Hollinbeck, W H,‡ 1 cav, B, Oct 14, dia.
11316 Hubert, W C, 12, G, Oct 22, scs.
11396 Hendershot, F F, 7, E, Oct 24, scs.
11739 Hurn, R, 8, E, Nov 2, scs.
12014 Hartzel, S, 1, D, Nov 15, dys.
12153 Hickman, E, 11, B, Nov 24, scs.

312 Johns, E K, 8 mil, C, April 2, dia. c.
3045 Jake, A R, 8, I, July 8, ana.
3969 Jackson, S E, 2, E, July 25, scs.
6098 Jones, G, 2 cav, D, Aug 18, dia.
7681 Johnston, I A, 1 cav, D, Sept 3, dys.
5371 Jenkins, W, 1 art, D, Sept 10, dia.

323 Kane, J, 4 cav, L, April 2, pna.

5822 Kimball, Jno, 14, K, Aug 16, ens.

589 Ludihing, W, 2, A, April 17, dia.
1565 Langstan, N H, 1 cav, A, June 2, dia a.
1592 Lanham, Henry, 8, C, June 3, des
1949 Logger, J, 3 cav, B, June 14, dia. c.
2734 Lyshon, Wm, 2, I, July 1, ana.
2739 Loud, Geo, 9, D, July 1, dia. c.
6924 Lansbury, W,§ 15, E, Aug 26, dia.
7237 Lough, H, 1 cav, L, Aug 29, scs.
10564 Liston, David, 6 cav, C, Oct 9, dia.
10569 Lowe, J, 9, C, Oct 9, dia.
11021 Lowe, W G, 13, G, Oct 16, scs.
11325 Laymon, W F, 14, C, Oct 23, scs.
11624 Laughlin, D,‡9, E, Oct 28, wds.
11989 Lucas, J, 9, D, Nov 13, scs.
12262 Lowring, J, 1 art, D, Dec 12, dis.

41 Maddons, W L, 4 cav, K, May 3, s. p
280 Mason, Peter, 10, G, April 1, dia. c.
387 Magalier, J, 3 cav, A, April 5, dys.
422 McNeily, Jas, 3 cav, A, April 7, ana.
582 McCormick, R, 2, F, April 16, asc.
786 McConnaughy, D, H, F, April 28, dia. c.
820 McGitton, J, 6, G, May 1, dys.
1068 Morris, J M, 3 cav, E, May 13, dia. c.
1419 Murphy, J, 8, D, May 28, dys.
1675 Moore, M, 14, K, June 6, ana.
2932 Milum, Jas, 8, I, Juky 5, dia.
3955 Mokie, R, 7 cav, July 20, scs.
6960 Miller, C W, 2, C, Aug 27, dia.
7018 Meiner, H, 12, I, Aug 27, dia.
9699 Menear, L B, 14, B, Sept 24, scs.
9767 Morris, G, 14, A, Sept 25, scs.
9955 Miller, D, H, C, Sept 28, scs.
10567 Moody, R W, 6 cav, E, Oct 9, scs.
10578 McKinney, Wm, 1 cav, L, Oct 9, scs.
10934 McConkey, A L,‡ 6 cav, B, Oct 14, dia.
10970 McLoughlin, R, 1 art, D, Oct 15, dia.
11546 Monsen, J F, 14, C, Oct 27, scs.
12099 Matt, Henry, 12, E, Nov 19, scs.
12272 McCausland, R, 1, G, Dec 12, scs.
9488 McGregor, P, 1, E, Sept 21, dia.
12068 McWilson, J, 14, F, Nov 17, scs.

2857 Norman, H, 2, I, July 4, dia.
3395 Newman, A, 1 cav, B, July 16, ana.
6442 Nichols, L D, 9, F, Aug 22, scs.
12472 Nicholson, J, 3 cav, B, Jan 17, scs.

241 Oxley, Robert, 14, C, March 30, dia. c.
1767 Osborne, Thos, 5, H, June 9, dys.

39 Packard, Myron, C, 2 cav, I, Mar 13, pls
1707 Porterfield, Jno, 4, F, June 7, dia. c.
2433 Porrellson, C D, 10, I, June 24, dys.
2645 Patny, J, 8, G, June 29, dia.
2737 Painter, C,§ 9, F, July 1, ana.
3055 Petit, J,‡ 1 cav, L, July 9, dia.
4707 Paine, M,‡ 8, F, Aug 3, des.
5004 Pugh, L, 3, I, Aug 8, dia.
5213 Polland, Jno, 10, I, Aug 10, scs.
6004 Polley, J, 8, C, Aug 17, ana.
6196 Perkins, James A, I2, K, Aug 19, dia. a.
11267 Palmer, Jno,§ 1 cav, L, Oct 21, scs.

349 Reakes, Wm, 8m, C, April 2, dia.
521 Rice, A, 4 cav, G, April 13, dys.
560 Randall, Jas A, 9, K, April 15, dys. c
959 Rinker, F A, 3 cav, A, May 8, dys.
1040 Robb, M, 4 cav, A, May 12, ts. f.
1916 Richards, G L, 14, D, June 14, dia. c.
3459 Rummer, L, 5, A, July 17, scs.
3465 Read, J, 12, B, July 17, scs.
3641 Redden, J, 9, F, July 26, dia.
4163 Ronsey, Wm, 9, C, July 29, dia.
7257 Rutroff, Jacob, 7, H, July 30, dia.
8082 Reush, Jas, 7, B, Sept 7, dia.
10527 Reed, J M,‡ 12, B, Oct 7, scs.
11518 Rock, J H, 12, C, Oct 26, scs.
11794 Raleigh, S, 1 cav, I, Nov 4, scs.
7005 Richardson, W, 14, K, Aug 27, dia.

273 Sayre, Michael, 14, I, Marh 31, dia.
680 Sprague, Geo, H, F, April 23, dia.
927 Stackleford, S, 3 cav, A, May 7, dys.
1510 Scott, Z,§ 8, D, May 31, dia.
2226 Steward, C, 2 cav, I, June 20, dia.
2359 Stagg, Wm, 10, I, June 23, scs.
2437 Stutfer, J N, 3 cav, B, June 25, dia. a.
2931 Skillington, G, 4 cav, D, July 5, dia.
8321 Stephenson, A, 1 cav, B, July 16, ana.
8588 Shilber, C A, 3, A, July 19, dia.
8747 Shaub, F, 2, E, July 22, dia.
8895 Simons, C E, 8, C, July 24, dia. c.
8865 Stewart, Wm A, 14, I, July 25, ics.
4463 Steele, A, 2 cav, C, Aug 1, scs.
4812 Snider, S, 3, K, Aug 5, scs.
4935 Sturn, E E, 12, F, Aug 7, wds.
5130 Smith, —, 2, F, Aug 8, scs.
5237 Simmons, E, 8, C, Aug 10, scs.
5727 Sprouse, A, 11, F, Aug 15, scs.
5975 Smith, J W, 8, G, Aug 17, ts. f.
6473 Sprouse, W, 11, F, Aug 22, dia.
6610 Squares, Samuel, 6 cav, D, Aug 23, dia.
7091 Stratton, B B, 1 art, F, Aug 28, dia.
7944 Stoker, S, 3 cav, C, Sept 5, dia. c.
8011 Sands, Wm, 10, F, Sept 6, scs.
8164 Scritchfield, W, 16, F, Sept 8, dia.
8390 Struck, H M, 14, B, Sept 10, dia.
8516 Smith, B, 9, H, Sept 12, dia.
8646 Sturgiss, W T, drum, 14, B, Sept 12, scs.
9217 Smith, G H, 7 cav, G, Sept 19, scs.
9714 Sullivan, E, 2, A, Sept 25, scs.
9786 Snyder, J V,§ 3, D, Sept 26, dia.
9872 Semeir, G S, 4 cav, Sept 27, scs.
9906 Sands, G W, 1, Sept 28, dia. c.
10151 Smith, J, 14, B, Oct 1, scs.

11276 Smith, J A, 9, B, Oct 22, scs.
11625 Slee, R,§ 1 cav, D, Oct 25, dia. c.
11824 Spaulding, F, 1 cav, A, Nov 5, scs.
11836 Stockwell, C H, B, Nov 5, scs.
7291 Saylor, C M, 9, B, Aug 30, dia.

1108 Thatcher, J P, 2, A, April 15, dys.
3404 Trobridge, S, 6, B, July 16, dys.
5136 Tyrm, T, 8, H, Aug 8, scs.
6379 Thurston, C C, 1, I, Aug 21, scs.
8663 Taylor, J, 8, G, Sept 13, dia.
12332 Thorpe, S S, 3, I, Dec 26, scs.
3846 Tomlinson, S,§ 3, I, July 24, dys.
8119 Tatro, L, 11, B, Sept 8, dia.

244 Vincent, Jas, 8, C, March 30, dys.
814 Very, W, 1 cav, C, April 30, dys.
1149 Vauscoy, A,‡ 3 cav, E, May 16, dia. c.
1322 Virts, R, 3 cav, A, May 23, dia. c.

945 Wilson, Walter, 11, F, May 7, dia. c.
1757 Weaver, M, 1 cav, C, June 7, dia. c.
2854 Worp, J, 3, F, July 6, dia. c.
3723 Wich, J, 1 cav, L, July 21, des.
3925 Whitney, W A, 8, F, July 25, dys.
3996 Whit, A, 5, F, July 25, dia.
7542 Wilson, J, 3, B, Sept 2, dys.
7832 Warwicke, E, 2, D, Sept 4, dia.
8598 Wells, E, 7, F, Sept 12, scs.
9626 Wolfe, C, 14, B, Sept 24, gae.
10854 White, J N, 6 cav, C, Oct 13, dys.

148 Young, A, 8, C, March 25, dia.
456 Young, A B, 8, C, April 9, dia.
694 Young, Ed, 8 cav, C, April 23, dia.

WISCONSIN.

2113 Allwise, J R, 24, E, June 17, dia. c.
4477 Austin, Issac, 25, G, Aug 1, dia.
5241 Abbott, A,§ 21, D, Aug 10, scs.
5453 Allen, C P, 2, G, Aug 12, wds.
8692 Adams, A F, 36, F, Sept 14, scs.
10830 Adams, P, 10, A, Oct 13, scs.
11492 Aultin, E V,‡ 13, E, Oct 26, scs.
12728 Antone, C, 31, D, March 4, dia. c.

1341 Bower, H, 1, A, May 24, dys.
1838 Burk, O, 15, B, June 11, dia.
2009 Bawgarder, B, 2, K, June 15, dia.
2055 Bail, H, 7, A, June 16, dia.
2128 Bowhan, H A,§ 10, F, June 18, ts. f.
2334 Brooks, E, 1 cav, 11, June 22, dia. c.
2451 Broomer, B F,‡ 10, I, June 25, dys. a.
2681 Brown, O, 15, G, June 30, dia. c.
3253 Brown, J, 4, H, July 13, dia.
3673 Bruce, H, 24, H, July 20, dia.
4870 Brumsted, G,§ 15, A, Aug 6, dia.
5026 Briggs, H, 1 cav, L, Aug 8, dys.
5100 Budson, John, 1 cav, L, Aug 9, scs.
5164 Bemis, H, 10, C, Aug 9, scs.
5322 Briggs, E, 1 cav, Aug 11, scs.
5564 Bailey, W,‡ 25, E, Aug 13, wds.
6204 Banick, S, 17, I, Aug 19, scs.
7295 Bailey, J, 36, I, Aug 30, dys.
7323 Burk, J, 10 cav, E, Aug 30, gae.
7755 Borden, E,‡ 21, K, Sept 3, dia.
7759 Boyle, P, 25, D, Sept 4, dia.
8576 Batchelder, J, 1, I, Sept 12, dia.
8641 Bushell, C C, 2, B, Sept 13, dys.
9607 Brinkman, J, 2, A, Sept 23, scs.
10686 Britton, H,§ 15, I, Oct 11, scs.
10919 Bohnsen, N, 15, I, Oct 14, scs.
11754 Butler, M, 10, K, Nov 2, scs.
12032 Blakeley, R, 7, F, Nov 15, scs.
11610 Batterson, L, 10, K, Oct 28, dia.

2369 Church, A, 7, H, June 23, ana.
2668 Chapman, J, 2, G, June 29, dys.
2969 Cowles, D, 10, B, July 6, dia. c.

3292 Cummings, S, 21, A, July 14, dia.
3828 Crane, R, drummer, 7, D, July 23, dys.
4390 Chapel, C, 1, E, July 31, dys.
5102 Cavanaugh, John, 1 cav, H, Aug 9, scs.
8105 Chase, F M,‡ 1, A, Sept 7, dia.
9418 Currier, C C, 21, F, Aug 22, wds.
9169 Carlintyre, G, 23, Sept 18, scs.
10752 Castle, C, 1, cav, C, Oct 12, scs.
11020 Cofam, W, 10, A, Oct 16, scs.
11088 Chusterson, F, 15, E, Oct 18, hes.
11535 Chamberlain, J, 21, I, Oct 27, scs.
11744 Clark, W C, 10, E, Nov 2, scs.
10346 Crommings, H, 7, C, Oct 5, scs.

1591 Duffey, E, 1, L, June 3, dia. c.
2522 Damhocker, E, 26, I, June 26, wds.
3244 Daggo, John, 1 cav, L, July 13, scs.
5830 Destler, Fred, 26, G, July 16, dia.
6967 Dick, Benjamin, 36, G, Aug 27, scs.
7455 Davis, J, 36, B, Sept 1, scs.
8530 Decker, G,§ F battery, Sept 12, scs.
8587 Depas, A, 21, A, Sept 12, scs.
8900 Daryson, W, 7, C, Sept 15, scs.
9739 Dacy, G, 12, I, Sept 25, dia.
10771 Davis, John, 1, B, Oct 12, dia. c.
12750 David, D P, 25, B, March 8, dia. a.

2419 Enger, J, 15, K, June 24, dys. c.
5247 Egan, John, 7, A, Aug 10, scs.
6160 Erickson, C, 15, B, Aug 19, dys.
8601 Ellwood, S,§ 10, C, Aug 13, scs.
9337 Erricson, S, 50, D, Sept 20, dys.
11687 Ellenger, P, 21, K, Oct 31, dia.
12286 Enkhart, H, 36, G, Dec 14, scs.

36 Fordrury, G W, 7, C, March 12, dys.
1260 Fuller, C W,‡ 7, E, May 21, dia. c.
2283 Fountain, W F, 10, A, June 20, dia. a.
5007 Forslay, W K, 8, K, Aug 8, scs.
5759 Fleins, Oscar, 1 cav, H, Aug 15, scs.
5811 Fisk, J B,§ 1 cav, H, Aug 16, dia.
6097 Fischnor, D,§ 36, H, Aug 18, ics.

6236 Fanon, Wm, 1, A, Aug 20, dys.
8460 Farnham, M B, 4, K, Sept 11, scs.
9664 Ferguson, 1,§ 15, G, Sept 24, dia.
10234 Fagan, M, 15, G, Oct 2, dia.
12618 Frost, A, 7, B, Feb 8, scs.
12653 Ferguson, W R, 24, D, Feb 14, rhm.

1529 Gilbert, O,§ 16, K May 31, dia.
2392 Grush, Fred, 15, I, June 24, dia.
3164 Guth, H, 1, D, July 11, dia.
3390 Greenman, D,§ 21, K, July 16, dys.
5557 Greenwall, M, 1 cav, C, Aug 13, dys.
7355 Grunds, L, 15, I, Aug 31, dia. c.
8326 Groupe, D, 4, F, Sept 10, dia.
10691 Gunduson, H,§ 15, I, Oct 11, scs.
6614 Goon, John E, 36, Aug 23, dia.

303 Helt, Carl, 26, E, April 1, dys.
710 Hale, A C, 21, I, April 24, ts. f.
1002 Haskins, J, 1, E, May 10, dys.
1655 Hoffland, — 1 sgt, 15, K, June 5, ana.
1673 Harvey, D M, 1, I, June 6, ts. f.
2384 Hanson, J, 15, K, June 23, dia. c.,
2556 Hough, B J,‡ 10, K, June 27, dia. c.
3720 Henderson, O, 15, F, July 24, i. f.
4542 Hewick, Nelson, 10, B, Aug 2, brs.
4570 Halts, S, 26, C, Aug 2, scs.
5312 Howard, F B, 10, K, Aug 11, pls.
5628 Holenback, A, 25, D, Aug 14, wds.
6468 Hall, A W, 21, I, Aug 22, dia.
7081 Hanley, T, 3 art, D, Aug 28, scs.
7149 Hutchings, B, 1 cav, E, Aug 29, dia. c.
7649 Hanson, L, 15, B, Sept 3, scs.
7791 Harding, W F,§ 21, C, Sept 4, scs.
8584 High, M, 25, E, Sept 12, wds.
9333 Halter, D, 22, D, Sept 20, scs.
9427 Hans, P, 10, D, Oct 6, scs.
11443 Holenbeck, C, 13, A, Oct 25, scs.
11927 Hanson, —, 1, B, Nov 8, scs.
12167 Harris, N, 12, D, Nov 26, wds.
12586 Hardy, E L, 6, E, Jan 4, scs.
12848 Hanson R, 1, F, April 28, dia.
12468 Hand, G, 10, D, Jan 16, scs.

8614 Ingham, J, 10, K, Sept 13, scs.
9808 Irwin, A, 25, C, Sept 26, scs.

2003 Jacobson O,‡ 15, D, June 15, dia.
3281 Jackson, T, 4, H, July 13, dia.
3478 Jillett, J, 7, H, July 17, dia.
6938 Jennings, J R,‡ 45, G, Aug 56, dia.
11284 Johnson, W H, 6, H, Oct 22, scs.

1165 Kemmett, J, 1, H, May 17, scs.
2498 Kundson, J, 15, E, June 26, dys. c.
4133 Kellett, John B,‡ 21, B, July 27, i. f.
4405 Kull, L, 24, C, July 31, dia.
4614 Klepps, C H, 1 cav, E, Aug 3, scs.
8592 Kendall,W, 32, Sept 12, scs.
9063 Keerroger, Wm, 36, G, Sept 17, dia.
10539 Kane, F, 26, E, Oct 8, dia.
10692 Knowles, H, 21, D, Oct 11, dia.
8299 Kinds, M O, 21, A, Sept 9, scs.

8009 Lack, Peter, 7, A, July 7, dia. c.
6397 Livingston, J H, 3 art, E, Aug 12, ana.
6642 Lansing, G, 10, A, Aug 23, scs.
7235 Lowe, F, 16, G, Aug 29, scs.
7522 Lawson, M, 15, B, Sept 1, dys.
8944 Laich, F, 26, K, Sept 16, scs.
9997 Latgen, E, 15, A, Sept 29, scs.
8977 Laich, F, 26, K, Sept 17, dia.

1752 Mauger, James,‡ 24, H, June 9, ana.
1896 Mulligan, J, 1, June 13, dia.
2732 McMann, W, 3 bat, July 1, dys.
2951 McCormick, E, 1 cav, L, July 6, dia.
2981 McKenzie, J, 1, F, July 7, dia.
8625 McLaulin, C, 36, I, July 20, dia.
4925 Mathison, E N, 2, E, Aug 6, dia.
5043 Many, J, 24, D, Aug 8, dia.
5163 McFadden, H, 1 cav, F, Aug 9, dia.

5683 Mortes, B, 10, D, Aug 15, scs.
5739 Main, Henry, 30, F, Aug 15, dia.
6231 McClury, A, 10, I, Aug 20, dia.
6377 Messer, F, 5, B, Aug 21, dia.
10289 Myers, S, 15, G, Oct 4, scs.
11936 Mulasky, E, 21, B, Nov 9, scs.

4289 Nelson, R, 15, R, July 30, scs.
4980 Northam, S R,§ 10, C, Aug 7, scs.
6090 Nichols, Wm, 10, I, Aug 18, dys.
10369 Neff, Wm, 33, I, Oct 6, scs.

3162 Olson, O, 15, B, July 11, dia.
11545 Ochle, F, 26, E, Oct 27, wds.
11931 Olston, M, 15, B, Nov 7, dia.

604 Palmer, John,‡ 7, C, April 18, dia.
2535 Plum, A, 4 cav, K, June 26, dia. c.
2847 Peterson, A,‡ 15, K, July 4, dia.
3511 Picket, T B,‡ 1, F, July 18, dia.
4340 Purdy, M, 10, E, July 30, dia.
6406 Piriris, J, 17, F, Aug 22, wds.
7630 Purdee, J, 10, I, Sept 1, scs.
7893 Peterson, S, 15, K, Sept 5, dia. c.
8515 Pillsbury, A J, 1 cav, H, Sept 12, gac.
8654 Patterson, J, 21, A, Sept 13, scs.
9014 Painter, H,§ 10, F, Sept 17, dia.
9902 Patterson, S,‡ 15, I, Sept 27, scs.
9461 Peterson, C, 15, I, Sept 21, scs.

2028 Roach, A, 21, F, June 15, dia.
3624 Renseler, H, 2, G, July 20, dia.
3665 Reynolers, F S, 10, K, July 20, dys.
4997 Reed, G, 1, K, Aug 7, dys.
5792 Rasmusson, A, 1 cav, L, Aug 15, dys.
6088 Robinson, W M,‡ 10, C, Aug 18, scs.
9860 Rice, J, 7, C, Sept 27, dia.
11812 Randles, J, 25, D, Nov 4, scs.
12233 Richmond, B,§ 1 cav, L, Dec 6, scs.
12242 Randell, P D, 1 cav, K, Dec 7, scs.

68 Schleassen, J J, 7, F, March 19, dys.
440 Shrigley, H, 10, G, April 8, dia.
2814 Stiffus, R, 15, F, July 3, dia. c.
3078 Sirbirth, F, 24, E, July 9, ana.
3503 Shoop, W, 1, G, July 18, dia.
3583 Sutton, J, 10, B, July 19, dia.
4343 Sharp, J W, 2, G, July 30, dia.
4378 Smith, W F, 10, B, July 31, dia.
4436 Shun, J, 24, H, July 31, dia.
4788 Scott, E G,§ 21, D, Aug 5, scs.
4882 Slingerland, John, 1 cav, B, Aug 6, i. f.
6943 Starr, E, 16, F, Aug 26, wds.
7614 Seaman, M,§ 21, D, Sept 2, dys.
8168 Smith, L, 4 cav, K, Sept 8, dia.
9693 Snyder, M, 26, E, Sept 24, scs.
11037 Smith, S,M,‡ 21, F, Oct 17, scs.
11047 Sales, A D, 4, K, Oct 17, ana.

2148 Tung, S W, 21, D, June 18, scs.
2385 Tav, S, 1, K, June 24, dia. a.
2588 Tomlinson, Robt, 6, B, June 28, dia. a.
3120 Thompson, D D, 36, B, June 10, dia.
3375 Tyler, J,‡ 10, A, July 16, dia.
3661 Tucker, C P, 1, I, July 20, dia.
4467 Taylor, A L, 25, E, Aug 1, dia.
6858 Taylor, I, 6, E, Aug 26, dys.
7160 Thorn, P C, 1 cav, L, Aug 29, dia.
8500 Troutman, A, 2, Sept 12, scs.
11236 Thurber, D,‡ 36, G, Oct 21, scs.
11420 Tyler, E P, 10, F, Oct 24, scs.
11475 Thorson, P, 24, G, Oct 26, scs.
12374 Thompson, O, 15, K, Jan 1, scs.

2309 Updell, J S, 15, B, June 22, dia. c.

2954 Vohoss, O H, 1, L, July 6, brs.
3076 Vilter, J, 6, F, July 9, dia.
8359 Vancoster, H, 1 cav, C, Sept 10, gae.
8427 Vanderbilt, J, 36, D, Sept 11, scs.
11390 Voclee, F,‡ 10, E, Oct 24, scs.

929 Webster, A C,§ 7, E, May 7, brs.
884 Winleis, P, 1, M, May 5, dia.
1007 Wilder, John, 1 cav, F, May 10, dia. c.
1520 Welcome, E D, 1 cav, L, May 31, dia.
1693 Walter, S P, 21, G, June 7, dia.
1909 Welton, M S, 1 cav, L, June 13, dia. c.
2591 Winchester, Geo, 21, I, June 28, scs.
2894 Weaver, H, 10, F, July 4, dia.
8378 Wens, Charles, 7, B, July 16, dia. c.

4706 Wakefield, D, 25, K, Aug 4, dia.
9484 Woodward, W B, 1, Sept 21, scs.
9938 Wick, J, 1 cav, H, Sept 28, scs.
10213 Willis, E, 7, E, Oct 2, scs.
10395 Winchell, S, 1, D, Oct 6, scs.
12111 Whalen, M, 12, B, Oct 21, scs.
12363 Ward, A, 1 cav, C, Dec 31, scs.

12626 Yessen, A, 24, A, Feb 10, scs.

UNITED STATES ARMY.

1798 Anderson, A, 16, C, June 10, dia. c.
8666 Atwell, Thos,§ 6 cav, M, July 20, phs.
4349 Allen, Chas, 18, H, July 31, scs.
4537 Ashley, D B, 16, C, Aug 2, i. f.
6077 Arnold, H, 18, H, Aug 18, ces.
6089 Adams, G, 14, C, Aug 18, dys.
8069 Austin, Jas,§ 4 cav, K, Sept 7, dys.
11523 Annis, Chas, 8 (colored), I, Oct 26, scs.
9250 Alfka, A H, 2 cav, D, Sept 19, dia.

102 Blossom, Chas, 6 cav, E, March 22, dys.
1122 Boughten, M, 15, E, May 15, ana.
1158 Bailey, Andrew, 16, K, May 16, dia.
1199 Britner, A, 16, K, May 18, ana.
1201 Banks, E E, 17, C, May 19, dia.
1266 Burton, George, 8 (col'd), 1, May 21, dia.
1397 Barden, Chas S, 15, E, May 26, scs.
1442 Beal, H, 15, C, May 28, dia. c.
1461 Becker, L, 2, B, May 29, dia.
1762 Brown, C, 16, D, June 9, ana.
2122 Bates, E L, 5 cav, E, June 17, dia.
2434 Brannagan, J, 18, D, June 24, des.
2436 Bigler, N M, 2 cav, B, June 25, dia. c.
2749 Bradshaw, H, marine corps, July 1, dia.
3370 Bush, W, 15, E, July 15, dia. c.
4861 Baldwin, G, 19, A, Aug 6, dys.
4969 Baker, F, signal corps, Aug 7, dia. c.
5657 Boyd, S,‡ 4, C, Aug 14, dia.
5774 Breen, A, 2, F, Aug 15, dys.
6126 Boyd, John B, 4, K, Aug 19, dia.
6628 Bradman, A M,§ 6 cav, M, Aug 23, dia. c.
6652 Burd, W H, 6, E, Aug 23, ana.
6937 Bowers, J, 4, K, Aug 26, ana.
7717 Burk, James, 1, K, Sept 3, dia.
7921 Brossessault, M, 2 art, M, Sept 5, dia.
8909 Banvall, J, 4, F, Sept 16, scs.
9477 Bartlett, E K, 2 s s, D, Sept 21, scs.
9631 Barstow, J, 18, D, Sept 24, dia. c.
9848 Barrett, J, 18, D, Sept 27, scs.
10621 Britzer, L B,‡ 15, C, Sept 10, dia.
11577 Brown, J, 12, H, Oct 28, scs.
11706 Brickley, H, 1, K, Nov 1, scs.
12077 Ball, W, 12, C, Nov 18, scs.
12112 Boyer, J, 1 cav, K, Nov 21, scs.
12564 Bromley, J, 18, G, Jan 31, scs.

760 Chisholm, J M,§ m. corps, Apr 27, dia. c.
1947 Clemens, D, 6, L, June 14, dia. c.
2174 Clemburg, J, 16, D, June 19, dia.
2216 Cassman, A, marine corps, June 20, dia.
2726 Carter, Thos, 15, H, July 1, dia. c.
3126 Cavanaugh, P, 16, A, July 10, dia.
3500 Conden, M, 12, A, July 18, dys.
3911 Crookey, S,‡ 15, H, July 24, dia.
4346 Chase, V, 16, G, July 30, dia.
4930 Campbell, S L, 15, C, Aug 7, ana.
5107 Croy, J, 18, B, Aug 9, dia.
5156 Cussey, Jas, 15, A, Aug 9, dia.
5234 Casey, J, 15, A, Aug 10, ana.
5436 Champney, P A, sig. corps, Aug 12, dys.
6420 Cammell, J, 12, H, Aug 22, dys.
7532 Coolidge, M, 17, B, Sept 1, dia. c.
7722 Connor, H, 15, H, Sept 3, dia.
7906 Corst, James, 14, D, Sept 5, dia. c.
8161 Connell, J, 14, D, Sept 8, scs.
8243 Chamberlain, C, 17, B, Sept 9, dia.
8570 Collins, M, 4 cav, H, Sept 12, scs.
8767 Carter, C A, 1, B, Sept 14, scs.

9034 Clifford, J, 6 cav, B, Sept 17, scs.
9113 Chase, L, 10, C, Sept 18, dia. c.
9186 Carroll, L, 2 cav, G, Sept 18, dia. c.
9295 Congreve, E, 5, A, Sept 19, dia.
9482 Cuyler, W, 16, B, Sept 21, ana.
9814 Crocker, Chas, 2, A, Sept 26, dia.
10210 Cargill, C, 12, F, Oct 2, scs.
10557 Clark, R W, 2 s s, Oct 9, dia.
11176 Casey, Jno, 19, A, Oct 19, scs.
11201 Childs, G, 16, B, Oct 20, dys.
11633 Cramer, A,§ 19, C, Oct 28, scs.

914 Dunn, John, 6, A, May 6, dys.
910 Dangler, W G, 5, M, May 5, dia. c.
1255 Doney, J W, 6 cav, D, May 21, dia.
1653 Dunn, Wm, 19, F, June 5, dys.
2274 Dunn, John, 18, H, June 20, dia. c.
2495 Donalan, M, 2 cav, L, June 26, dys.
3025 Deyer, H,§ 18, D, July 7, dys.
4377 Darvin, W W, 2 s s, B, July 31, dia.
4490 Dinslow, B F, 12, G, Aug 1, scs.
4626 Delaney, Jacob, 5 art, F, Aug 3, scs.
5348 Doll, R, 14, C, Aug 11, dia.
5459 Dolan, P, 19, F, Aug 12, phs.
5756 Davis, G,‡ 19, A, Aug 15, scs.
6025 Decker, James, 10, Aug 18, dys.
6210 Davis, J W,‡ 15, E, Aug 19, dia. c.
6297 Doran, J M, 19, E, Aug 20, dia. c.
6770 Doughty, D B, 3 art, C, Aug 25, scs.
6805 Davidson, J H, 15, C, Aug 25, ana.
6955 Delaney, E, 19, F, Aug 26, ana.
7049 Davis, G, 15, F, Aug 27, dia.
7241 Delaney, J, 2, F, Aug 29, dys.
7792 Dean, Samuel, 4 cav, B, Sept 3, scs.
8214 Downing, M, 10, D, Sept 8, dia.
8832 Doule, J, 10, D, Sept 15, scs.
10235 Davis, Clarke, 1 bat, K, Oct 2, dia.
10883 Draper, L, 14, F, Oct 14, scs.
11554 Davy, H, 18, G, Oct 27, scs.
11613 Diller, O M, 5 cav, I, Oct 28, scs.
12140 Drummond, J, 18, F, Nov 23, scs.
12591 Dunn, C, 15, C, Feb 4, scs.

5648 Evans, T, 14, F, Aug 14, dys.
6813 Edwards, Wm (negro), 8, A, Aug 25, dia.
7576 Erick, J, 2, K, Sept 2, dys.
7616 Ellerton, N, 16, D, Sept 2, scs.
12689 Emmict, S S, 5, C, Feb 22, scs.

42 Ferguson, J, 6 cav, E, March 15, cah.
1243 Fitzgibbons, Thos, 2, C, May 20, dia.
1509 Ferrell, J, 12, A, May 31, dia. c.
2355 Fifley, H, 18, E, May 23, dia. a.
2888 French, George, 1st lieut, 37, July 3, r. f.
3007 Feed, G, 6 cav, D, July 7, dia.
3256 Frenchy, D, 2, F, July 13, dys.
3543 Fielding, A, 13, E, July 18, dia. c.
5487 Eliestine, S, 16, C, Aug 13, ana.
6804 Felps, Daniel (negro), 8, H, Aug 25, dia.
7167 Flanigan, M, 2, I, Aug 29, des.
8536 Fannton, H, 14, F, Sept 12, scs.
9154 Flanery, M, 1 cav, H, Sept 18, dia.
9725 Frum, E, 3 cav, C, Sept 25, dia.
9983 Flarety, O, 16, Sept 29, scs.
10655 Fenall, J, 14, G, Oct 11, dia.
10839 Flanagan, P, 4 cav, D, Oct 13, scs.
11402 Fritz, A,§ 19, A, Oct 24, scs.
12312 Foster, J, 4, H, Dec 19, scs.

272 Gilligan, Mat,‡ 1, I, March 31, dys.
1639 Gardener, C, signal corps, June 5, dia. a.
2801 Gulterman, S,§ 16, D, July 2, dia.
4977 Gray,Wm, 18, C, Aug 7, dia.
6182 Gale, Walter, H, F, Aug 19, dia. c.
7220 Gulvere, David, 4, C, Aug 29, scs.
8057 Griffith, S, H, F, Sept 7, scs.
8671 Gunter, John, 4 cav, Sept 13, dia.
8857 Grace, Thos, 1, B, Sept 15, wds.
9851 Gilbert, A, 5, K, Sept 27, scs.
2066 Getts, F, 19, E, Nov 16, dys.
7335 Golton, R, 16, B, Aug 30, dia.

397 Hatch, T C, 11, A, April 6, pna.
533 Halbert, F, 2, H, April 13, dys.
1547 Halpin, P, 5 art, H, June 1, dia. c.
1585 Haney, H, 16, D, June 3, dia. c.
1608 Hurman, J H, 4 cav, E, June 4, dia. c.
2096 Hendricks, J, 16 D, June 17, ana.
2209 Hogan, M, 16, A, June 20, dia, a.
2706 Henry, Wm, 2, B, June 30, dia. a.
2730 Hurley, D, marine corps, July 1, dys.
2987 Hulit, Wm, 16, D, July 7, dia. c.
3753 Hill, Geo, 17, H, July 22, dia. c.
8893 Hopkins, W (negro), 17, C, July 24, ana.
4429 Hill, D S (negro), 16, C, July 31, dia.
7238 Heddington, W, 15, F, Aug 29, dys.
7405 Harshain, J R, 15, G, Aug 31, ana.
8004 Halley, J, 13, B, Sept 6, dia.
9104 Hook, H, 19, F, Sept 18, dia. c.
9155 Heir, H, 14, A, Sept 18, scs.
9665 Hildreth, Jas, 12, Sept 24, dia.
9918 Haney, J, 12, C, Sept 28, scs.
10054 Hasler, C, 13, M, Sept 30, gae.
10439 Hirshfield, G, marine corps, Oct 7, scs.
10857 Harman, J, 15, E, Oct 14, dia.
?11136 Hamilton, S, 2 s s, D, Oct 19, dia. c.
12369 Hill, M A, 2, G, Jan 1, pms.
12601 Hoit, E (negro), 35, H, Feb 6, dia. c.
10322 Hamman, W H, 15, F, Oct 3, scs.

5532 Imhoff, I, 15, E, Aug 13, pls.
7647 Ireland, Geo, 14, E, Sept 3, dia.
10742 Ireson, I, 4 cav, A, Oct 11, scs.

1111 Johnson, P, 6, C, May 15, dia. c.
8125 Johnson, P, 2 bat, Sept 8, scs.
8366 Jones, W, 1 art, K, Sept 10, scs.
10319 Jones, C B, 1 cav, H, Oct 3, scs.
11923 Jerald, W H,§ 18, F, Nov 8, scs.

495 Kingeny, J, 1, K, April 12, dia.
912 Kelly, John, 16, C, May 5, dia. c.
1662 Kain, P F,§ 15, A, June 6, dys.
8256 Kenley, D, 2, F, July 13, dys.
3341 Kerkney, F, 18, F, July 15, dia.
3685 Kilbride, J, 15, F, July 21, dia.
4245 Kane, Wm, 18, H, July 29, dys.
4266 Kalkrath, C, 3, I, July 29, dia.
4271 Kelly, D, 4, H, July 29, dia.
4694 Kester, J, 15, F, Aug 4, dia.
5640 Kay, Robt, 4, F, Aug 14, scs.
5643 Kelly, J, marine corps, Aug 14, scs.
6271 Kochel, J,‡ 19, G, Aug 20, mas.
6577 Kelly, Wm, 9, I, Aug 23, dys.
6764 King, I, 7, K, Aug 25, dia.
7465 Kinney, G W, 1 bat, D, Sept 1, scs.
8261 Klinty, H, 1 art, K, Sept 9, scs.
8490 Kricks, F, 14, C, Sept 11, scs.
8527 Kripp, J, 16, D, Sept 12, scs.
9082 Knapp, C, 11, A, Sept 18, gae.
11268 Kain, Pat, 15, A, Oct 21, scs.
11767 Kelly, J S, 2, D, Nov 3, cah.
11949 Kennedy, J, 12, A, Nov 10, scs.
12205 Kahl, Chas, 2 art, M, Dec 1, scs.
12532 Kemp, J W, 2, K, Jan 27, dia.

55 Love, Wm,§ 6, F, March 17, pna.
2282 Larreby, G, 16, D, June 20, dia.
2774 Little, J, 19, E, July 21, dys.
3999 Lackey, J, 16, B, July 26, dia. c.
4453 Langstaff, R, 10, F, Aug 1, dia.

5711 Lake, Horace, 4 cav, K, Aug 15, dia.
5891 Lynch, B 18, E, Aug 16, dia.
6116 Lattin, E, 12, A, Aug 19, ces.
6300 Lawrence, C, H, E, Aug 20, dia.
6352 Lyons, E, signal corps, Aug 21, dia. c.
6561 Little, R, 19, F, Aug 23, scs.
9732 Larqdell, Wm,§ 14, A, Sept 25, dia.
10317 Louby, O, 4 cav, H, Oct 3, scs.
10379 Lockewood, H (negro), 8, D, Oct 5, dia.
11038 Lyons, R, 1 cav, E, Oct 17, scs.,
11543 Lyman, O S, 18, A, Oct 27, scs.
11973 Lewis, Wm P, 8, B, Nov 12, scs.

180 McCoy, Augustus, 6, M, March 26, dia.
267 McClellan, J, 6 cav, D, March 31, ts. f.
828 Mason, C H, 12, I, May 1, dys
948 Murphy, D, 12, B, May 8, dys.
1012 McEvers, T L, 13, C, May 10, dia.
1043 McGuire, J, 3, C, May 12, dia.
1332 Murray, Thos, 1 art, I, May 24, dia.
1471 Mulhall, Peter,§ mar corps, May 30, dia.
1823 Marze, Jas, 12, D, June 10, dia.
1946 McLaughlin, J, 2, H, June 14, dia. c.
1965 McConaghy, P, mar corps, June 14, scs.
2444 Meadow, John, 6 cav, E, June 25, scs.
3054 Muller, J, mar corps, June 30, dys.
2920 Miller, C H, 6 cav, E, July 5, scs.
3054 McKinney, J, mar corps, July 9, dia. c.
3083 Maloney, B, 19, B, July 9, dia. c.
3950 Merkill, Peter, 14, H, July 25, dia.
4712 Murch, Wm, C, 14, A, dia.
4823 McClintock, J S, 18, H, Aug 5, dia. c.
4863 Martin, M, mar corps, Aug 6, dia.
5303 Martin, J, 1 cav, K, Aug 11, dia. c.
5364 McCann, B, 12, B, Aug 11, dia.
5456 Michols, R, 1 cav, K, Aug 12, scs.
5581 McLean, P, 17, C, Aug 14, scs.
5769 McCoslin, Robt, 1 art, B, Aug 15, ens.
6073 McDonald, 4 cav, E, Aug 18, dys.
6081 McClair, R, 11, G, Aug 18, scs.
6313 Munson, C, 12, D, Aug 20, scs.
6407 Mulhern, C, 4 cav, C, Aug 22, scs.
6315 Mantle, J M,‡ 15, F, Aug 22, ts. f.
6851 Marston, B, 51, s s, G, Aug 25, dia.
6973 McKinley, E W, mar corps, Aug 27, dia.
7341 McGuire, J, 12, D, Aug 30, scs.
8293 Mun, W, 18, H, Sept 9, scs.
8473 McGinness, A, 4 art, E, Sept 11, scs.
9110 Montgomery, C, 13, G, Sept 18, dia.
9231 McCoy, J M,§ mar brigade, Sept 19, dia.
9368 Miller, H, 2 art, Sept 20, dia.
9472 Morris, G J, 18, I, Sept 21, dia.
9830 McDermott, H, 18, E, Sept 26, scs.
10135 Manning, J, 15, A, Oct 1, scs.
10321 McCoy, J, 4, F, Oct 3, scs.
10457 Mills, A, 15, G, Oct 7, scs.
10554 McCord, G, 14, E, Oct 9, scs.
10855 McGee, P,‡ 2, Oct 13, scs.
11008 Murray, Jas, 17, G, Oct 16 scs.
12148 Murray, W, 1st sig corps, K, Nov 24, scs.
12151 Moran, J, 4 cav, F, Nov 24, scs.
7341 McGuire, J, 12, D, Aug 30, scs.
12364 McGorren, J, 17, C, Dec 31, scs.

2876 Northrup, H E, 4, H, July 3, dia.
6803 Newcombe, John, 18, G, Aug 20, ana.
6954 Nichols, H,‡ 12, A, Aug 26, dia.
10240 North, Jacob, 15, A, Oct 3, scs.
12386 Neise, J, 6, F, Jan 2, des.
12833 Naff, V, bugler, 1 art, B, April 16, dia.
12790 Newel, J, 18, G, March 17, dia. c.

2368 O'Reilly, Theodore,§ 3, K, June 23, scs.
7036 Ott, John, 10, A, Aug 27, scs.
11846 Osrans, J, 4 cav, I, Nov 5, scs.

492 Partridge, J W, signal corps, April 12, dia.
1607 Pace, J F, 18, C, June 4, dia.
1893 Pulliam, Wm, 1 cav, June 13, dia. c.
3219 Pigot, J, marine corps, July 12, dia.
3669 Ponter, —, 1 art, I, July 18, dia.
4631 Pearson, S C, 40, C, Aug 3, dia.

5309 Pratt, C E, 1 art, M, Aug 11, scs.
5729 Pike, Wm,‡ 5 cav, G, Aug 15, scs.
5731 Poulton, Henry, 19, A, Aug 15, scs.
6392 Page, J E, 18, B, Aug 21, dys.
7008 Phillips, C, 14, D, Aug 27, scs.
7267 Pruet, Jas M, 19, A, Aug 30, scs.
7311 Plummer, G, 2 s s, D, Aug 30, dia.
2611 Preston, John, marine crops, June 28, dia.
7752 Pratt, J, 3, B, Sept 3, dia.
9571 Post, A, 1 art, F, Sept 23, dia.
10951 Palmer, Wm E,§ 15, F, Oct 14, scs.
11170 Pattit, J S, 11, F, Oct 19, scs.
12142 Puck, C, 15, G, Nov 24, scs.

4022 Quinback, J, 18, G, July 26, scs.

1 1 Ross,—, 19, A, March 5, phs.
194 Rooney, Mark, 14, F, March 27, pna.
404 Reardon, D, 13, G, April 6, dys.
702 Reynolds, Edwd, in crops, April 23, dys. c.
3355 Roney, F J, 18, E, July 15, dia. c.
3820 Ritzer, Geo A, 5 cav, H, July 23, dia.
4276 Robinson, W R, 6 cav, H, July 30, dia.
4957 Rhodes, A, 18, B, Aug 7, scs.
5210 Rinkle, George, 2 cav, G, Aug 10, dia.
5984 Rouke, J, 10, D, Aug 17, dia.
7151 Richards, Theod, 2 cav, D, Aug 29, dia.
8438 Rogers, Wm, 18, G, Sept 14, scs.
9268 Reynolds, D, 4 cav, C, Sept 19, ana.
10792 Reilly, J, 3, B, Oct 2, scs.
2701 Rawson, J, 16, K, June 30, dia. c.

363 Striff, John, 2, F, April 2, dia.
1236 Shelton, C, 8, F, May 20, dia.
1253 Spalding, Wm, 3 cav, B, May 21, dia.
1295 Scripter, C E, 5 cav, D, May 23, dia.
1647 Sweitzer, M, 19, H, June, 5, scs.
1714 Smith, H, W, 15, C, June 7, dia.
2073 Stoltz,—, § 16, C, June 17, scs.
2082 Smith, James, 16, D, June 17, ana.
2298 Styles, J N, 13, A, June 22, dia.
2550 Sumser, J, 19, G, June 27, dia.
3110 Spaulding, James, 13, B, July 10, dia.
3114 Skinner, L, 13, C, July 10, dia.
3838 Smartkash, C,‡ 15, C, July 23, dia. c.
3978 Somers, P, 4 cav, C, July 26, dia.
4238 Scybert, J S,‡ 1 s s, H, July 29, dia.
4310 Smith, Allen, 4, H, July, 30, ana.
4666 Striper, M, 18, D, Aug, 4, scs.
5022 Sutgen, F, 16, C, Aug 8, dia. c.
5305 Sorg, A, 1 art, M, Aug 11, scs.
5393 Swagger, H, 4 cav, D, Aug, 12, dia.
5801 Sisson, J, 4, D, Aug 15, scs.
6620 Slaughterback, B, 15, H, Aug, 23, ana.
6833 Sutgen, F, 16, C, Aug 25, scs.
7377 Smith, F, 14, E, Aug, 31, scs.
7606 Starr, Darius,§ 2 s s, F, Sept 2, dys.
7874 Snider, J, H, B, Sept 5, dia. c.
8839 Scott, Jas H, 2 cav, B, Sept 15, scs.
9215 Stansbury, E, marine corps, Sept 19, dia.
9514 Souls, J, H, 15, F, Sept 22, ana.
10214 Sullivan, T, H, C, Oct 2, scs.

11144 Schroder, F, 15, C, Oct 19, scs.
11301 Smith, J, 8, D, Oct 22, scs.
11333 Stanton, R, 14, K, Oct 23, scs.
11664 Spencer, J H, 2, D, Oct 30, scs.
11690 Shortman, J, 14, E, Oct 31, dys.
12186 Streeter, J, 16, B, Nov 28, scs.
12211 Stanton, C, 2, I, Dec 2, dia.

92 Tooley, Michael, 13, G, March 21, dia. c.
489 Taylor, Amos, 17, H, April 12, dia. c
2603 Thompson, Wm, 18, G, June 28, scs.
2662 Truman, J, 5 cav, D, June 29, dys.
3466 Tyson E S, 14, D, July 17, pls.
4716 Tredridge, A, musician, 13, Aug 4, ana
7366 Taylor, M D, 18, E, Aug 31, dia.
7801 Turk, H, 18, H, Sept 4, dia.
8258 Thomas, J, 1 cav, D, Sept 9, dia. c.
8259 Trainer, M, 6, F, Sept 9, dia.
8279 Thomas, L (negro), 8, D, Sept 9, i. f.
9115 Taylor, E,‡ 18, I, Sept 18, dia. c.
11393 Topper, J, H, B, Oct 24, scs.

7829 Unmuch, C, 1 art, K, Sept 4, dys.

3657 Volmore, J, 3, K, July, 18, scs.
7042 Vancotten, Wm, 16, D, Aug 27, scs.
7135 Vickery, Wm, 1, H, Aug, 28, dia.
02041 Van Buren, W H, 16, B, Nov 16, scs.

1259 Walker, Wm, 6, D, May 21, dia.
1299 Worster, Chas B, 5 cav, H, May 23, dia. c.
2752 White, Thomas, 1, D, July 1, dia.
4023 Williams, D, 18, D, July 26, scs.
4248 Warner, S, 16, E, July, 29, dia. c.
4306 Williams, John, 4, D, July 30, dia.
5425 Walmor,— 10, D, Aug. 12, dia.
6125 Wickham, G H, 16, B, Aug 19, scs.
6637 Wills, S, 15, E, Aug, 23, dys.
7048 Wright, C S, 12, C, Aug 27, c. f.
7109 Wadsworth, B H, 12, C, Aug 28, dia.
7254 Warner, H, 2, D, Aug 30, dia.
9105 Whitney, J W,‡ 4 cav, K, Sept 18, scs.
9131 White, Samuel, 8, F, Sept, 18, dia.
9677 Walker, John (negro), 8, F, Sept 24, scs.
9834 Walter, I, 17, B, Sept 27, scs.
10355 Wigley, E, 17, C, Oct 5, dys.
10374 Waters,— § 8, C, Oct 5, dia.
10756 Waldo, J M, 1 art, K, Oct 12, scs.
11137 Williams, C, 1 art, K, Oct, 19, scs.
11395 Wizmaker, G, 2, M, Oct, 24, scs.
12009 Wilson, C W, K, Nov 14, scs.
12027 Wise, G B, 6, F, Nov 15, ana.

6496 Yarger, A, 18, Aug 22, scs.
7101 Young, Robert, 1 cav, K, Aug 28, dia.
10754 Young, F B, 2 art, M, Oct 12, scs.
11373 Young, J C, 19, A, Oct 28, scs.

7793 Zimmerman, J, 17, D, Sept 4, scs.
10428 Zing, P, § 10, C, Oct 6, scs.
10450 Zimmerman, M, 14, I, Oct 7, scs.

UNITED STATES NAVY.

2619 Akinson, A, Nepsia, June 27, dia.
4698 Anker, George, Norman, Aug 4, dia.
8071 Anderson, Chas, Saithfield, Sept 7, dia.

2919 Bradley, John, Southfield, July 3, dia.
3475 Broderick, W, July 17, dia.
5072 Bowers, W H, Water Witch, Aug 8, dia. c.
12047 Boucher, W, Shawsheen, Nov 16, scs.

1914 Carnes, Wm, June 13, dia. c.
2149 Conant, G S, Southfield, June 18, dia.
2580 Carter, W J. Montgomery, June 27, dia. c.
6201 Collins, Thomas, Southfield, Aug 19, dys.
7144 Corbet, E, Aug 29, des.
7508 Connor, J, Sept 1, scs.

9544 Culbert, J, Sept 23, dia.

164 Dillingham, J N, Housatonic, Mar 28, pha.
6437 Duffney, J, Aug 22, dia.

3086 Ellis, J H, Columbine, July 9, ts. f.
4134 Evans, John, Shawssheen, July 28, dia. c.
4462 Earl, Jas H, paym'r steward, Aug 1, scs.

5419 Foley, Daniel, Southfield, Aug 12, dia. c.

4605 Green, G C, Southfield, Aug 3, scs.
8871 Goundy, Thomas, Sept 15, dia.

1087 Heald, Wm, Canandaigua, Apr 14, dia. c.

469 Hunter, John, seaman, May 30, ana.
221 Hilton, John, Johana, June 20, dia.
8441 Hodges, L, Norman, July 17, brs.
3793 Hughes, Benj, Wabash, July 22, ts. f.
5875 Heald, H H, merch'tman, Aug 16, dia. c.
9284 Holas, Thos, Water Witch, Sept 19, dia.

1432 Jones, Wm, Underwriter, May 28, dia. c.
2178 Jones, Theo, Underwriter, June 19, dia. c.
2206 Journeay, John, fireman, June 19, dia. c.
6417 Jackson, J, Shawsheen, Aug 22, scs.
8291 Johnson, G P, Sept 9, dia.
8358 James, F A, Sept 15, dys.
9392 Johnson, M, Sept 20, dia.
10218 Joseph, F, Oct 2, dia.

602 Keefe, John, Housatonic, April 18, dys.
698 Kultz, A, T Ward, April 23, dys.
1546 Kelly, James, Underwriter, June 1, dia. c.
3850 Kinney, J, Water Witch, July 24, dia. c.

7375 Lodi, John, Aug 31, dia.
2843 Lindersmith, E, Montgomery, July 3, dia.
4291 Lawton, James, Ladona, July 30, dys.

235 Mays, A H, mate, Norman, Mar 29, dys.
2452 McDonald, John, June 25, dia.
2581 Moore, A, Anna, June 27, scs.
3128 Malaby, P, Montgomery, July 10, dys.
3348 Murphy, M J, July 15, dia.
3529 McDonald, John, July, 17, dia.
3804 Matthews, J, Underwriter, July 22, dia. c.
4208 McHenry, Daniel, Southford, July 29, dia.
4324 McCarty, T, Housatonic, July 30, dia. c.
4396 McVcy, K, July, 31, dys.
4679 McTier, J, Aug 4, dys.
4800 McLaughlin, E, Aug 5, dys.
5485 Meldon, J, Aug 13, pna.
6355 Marshall, N B, Leipsig, Aug 21, dia.
6571 McDermott, P, Montgomery, Aug 23, des.
6825 Mathews, W C, Aug 25, dia.
6917 McLaughlin, B, Aug 26, scs.
7251 McGowan, J, Powhattan, Aug 30, dia.
11863 Maston, J, Ratler, Nov 6, scs.

7824 Noe, M, Sept 4, I. f.

2227 O'Brien, Wm, June 20, dia.
3208 Ottinger, M, Water Witch, h y 12, scs.

3153 Page, Lyman, July 11, scs.
5325 Parkham, Jas C, Shawsheen, Aug 11, dia.
9024 Peterson, J, Sept, 17, dia.

2460 Quinlan, N, June 25, scs.
7867 Quade, M, Sept 5, scs.

2237 Ragan, John, T Ward, June 20, 1.f.
4661 Raymond, W, Ward, Aug 3, scs.
5108 Roland, John, Underwriter, Aug 9, scs.
7003 Reynolds, T J, Aug 27, dia.

169 Stark, John, March 26, dia. c.
2010 Sullivan, J, Underwriter, June 15, dia.
2883 Smith, John, W, Southfield, July 3, ts. f.
3261 Sampson, J R, nav battalion, July 13, dia
4611 Smith, B N, Mendota, Aug 3, scs.
6592 Stanley, Win, Sothfield, Aug 23, dia. c.
11299 Smith, Wm, Water Witch, Oct 22, scs.

1713 Thomas, Saml, Southfield, June 7, dia. c.
1851 Thomas, John, Southfield, June 11, dia. c.
3757 Turner, Wm, July 1, r. f.
4159 Trymer, James, Souhfield, July 28, dia.
7445 Tobin, Michael, Sept 1, dia.
8302 Ta, B F, Southfield, Sept 10, dia.

1646 Willis, J P, June 5, dia.
3004 Wilson, A, Southfield, July 7, dia. c.
3878 Williams, M W, July 24, dia.
4118 Willis, M, Southfield, July 28, scs.
4198 Williams, C, Aries, July 29, dia.c.
5820 Wordell, G K, Aug 16, mas.
5990 Warren, W H, Aug 17, dia.
6458 Wooley, M, Aug 22, scs.
7503 Walsh, Jas, Sept 1, dia.
8104 Weleh, V, Southfield, Sept 7, dia.
10565 West, John, Southfield, Oct 9, dia.

MISCELLANEOUS.

1460 Addley, A, citizen, Oct 25, scs.
887 Amos, J, Ringold bat, F, May 4, ts. f.
2977 Augar, A, July 7, dia.

282 Bane, S, Ringold bat, A, April 1, pna.
2972 Beatty, D,‡ Ring bat, F, June 17, dia. c.
4327 Baker, John, temnster, July 30, dia.c.
4904 Bennmar, L, Aug 6, dia.
5747 Butterfield, James, citizen, Aug 15, dys.
6190 Blair, H, citizen, Aug 18, ana.
6366 Bidwell, C, cit teamster, Aug 21, dys.
8102 Burkhead, W, Prunell's legion, Sept 7, dia.
9344 Blood, G P, Sept 20, scs.
9591 Brogdin, D C, Sept 23, dia.
10500 Burk, C, citizen, Oct 5, dia.
10602 Bishop, J, citizen teamster, Oct 10, dys.
10963 Brown,Geo,‡ Bridge's bat, Oct 15, scs.
12342 Boland, Jas, Prunell's cav, Dec 26, dia.c.

177 Cannon, Wm, teamster, March 26.
389 Campbell, D, Ring bat, E, April 6, dia.
431 Childers, C H, April 8, dia.c.
1195 Cobb, J, citizen teamster, May 18, pls.
1881 Clarls, M, citizen teamster, June 12, dia. a.
3399 Cable, C, citizen, July 16, des.
3972 Cregger, J F, musician, July 25, dia.
6315 Crowely, Pat, Aug 20, scs.
9245 Carroll, C, teamster, 19 ar corps, Sept 19, scs.
10485 Corbit, J, Oct 7, wds.
10872 Carey, Thos, Oct 13, scs.
11726 Collins, J, citizen teamster, Nov 1, scs.
12449 Carroll, J, ci zen teamster, Jan 13, scs.

752 Deems, P, Ringold bat, E, April 28, dia c.
2620 Delp, Geo, citizen teamster, June 28, dia.
4334 Davis, J, citizen, July 30, dia.
5866 Dantirth, Geo, A, Aug 16, dia.
8202 Delmore, W, citizen, Sept 8, dia.
11804 Dubin, M, citizen teamster, Oct 18, scs.
11248 Delhanta, Wm, citizen, Oct 21, dia.

182 England, E, March 27, pna.
3928 Evans, M, citizen, July 25, dia.
— Everett, T S, citizen, Md, Aug 30, dia.

157 Freeman, John, March 25, dys.
453 Fenley, R, citizen, April 9, dia c.
1116 Fannon, A, citizen, May 15, dys.
2332 Foster, W, tel operator, June 22, dia. c.
2435 Farrell, M, citizen, June 25, ana.
10478 Flickison, J, Oct, 7, dia.
4808 Fitzgerald,—, Aug 5, dia.
5078 Frank, F M, Wilder's bat, Aug 8, scs.
5609 Fox, Henry, cit teamster, Aug 14, scs.
7643 Ford, P, teamster, Sept 3, dia.
9084 Foncks, H C, Keye's ind't cav, Sept 18 ds
11315 Ferrall, M C, teamster, Oct 22, scs.

2729 Gildea, D, citizen, July 1, scs.
4115 Grogran, D, July 28, dia c.
4747 Gishart, J, Aug 5, ts. f.
6139 Graham, E, citizen, Aug 19, dia.
7854 Gorb, S, Sept 5, scs.
9747 Goodman, J O, Sept 25.
10672 Gillman, John, Oct 11, dia. c.

TESTIMONY OF THE U. S. HOUSE OF REPRESENTATIVES

TO THE ACCURACY AND VALUE OF

"The Soldier's Story."

By WARREN LEE GOSS.

Under Resolution of July 10, 1867, the House of Representatives of the 40th Congress appointed a committee to take testimony touching the treatment of prisoners of war by the rebel authorities.

The Committee consisted of the following eminent members of the house:

Hon. JOHN P. C. SHANKS, of Indiana.
Hon. WILLIAM A. PILE, of Maine.
Hon. ABNER C. HARDING, of Illinois.
Hon. AARON F. STEVENS, of New Hampshire.
Hon. WILLIAM MUNGER, of Ohio.

A long time was consumed in taking testimony. Returned prisoners were summoned from all parts of the Union. Testimony was also taken from rebel officers and privates. Among the witnesses was Mr. Goss, the author of the "Soldier's Story." In their report, which was accepted, the committee made voluminous extracts from this book, and prefaced their quotations with the following remarks complimentary to the author:

"He is the author of a book entitled, 'The Soldier's Story of his Captivity at Andersonville and other Rebel Prisons.' The statement of facts contained in his narrative is an interesting and well-sustained account of prison life at Andersonville; sanctioned, not only by the oath of the patriotic author, but fully corroborated by all concurrent testimony."

The value of this endorsement is seen when we consider the mass of testimony taken, and remember that there was no minority report, although the committee was composed of both republican and democratic members of the house.

www.ingramcontent.com/pod-product-compliance
Lightning Source LLC
Chambersburg PA
CBHW031230090426
42742CB00007B/144